# BARRON'S

# CANADIAN POLICE OFFICER EXAMS

**Earl L. Andersen, M.A.**

**BARRON'S**

**About the Author**

Earl Andersen, M.A.

Staff Sergeant, Vancouver Police Department

Instructor, Criminal Justice Program, Langara College, Vancouver

Note: Unless specifically indicated in a reprinted article, any resemblance to, or depictions of, people living or dead, or to incidents past or present, is coincidental.

**Photograph and Illustration Credits**

Page 10: POPAT Course illustration provided by Ryan Andersen.

Page 11: PREP Course illustration provided by Ryan Andersen.

Page 13: TAP-ENPQ Course provided by Ryan Andersen.

Page 108: Grocery Store Robbery photograph provided by the Vancouver Police Museum.

Page 121: Rooming House Murder photograph provided by the Vancouver Police Museum.

Page 215: Suspect Mug Shots illustrations provided by Ryan Andersen.

Page 324: Suspect Mug Shots illustrations provided by Ryan Andersen.

Page 325: Suspect Mug Shots illustrations provided by Ryan Andersen.

Page 326: Suspect Mug Shots illustrations provided by Ryan Andersen.

*All inquiries should be addressed to:*

Barron's Educational Series, Inc.

250 Wireless Boulevard

Hauppauge, New York 11788

**www.barronseduc.com**

*Library of Congress Catalog Card No. 2015937919*

ISBN: 978-1-4380-0473-0

PRINTED IN THE UNITED STATES OF AMERICA

9 8 7 6 5 4 3 2 1

**10% POST-CONSUMER WASTE**

Paper contains a minimum of 10% post-consumer waste (PCW). Paper used in this book was derived from certified, sustainable forestlands.

# CONTENTS

# Using This Guide

There are approximately 70,000 police officers in Canada and almost an equal number of individuals working in related fields such as federal and provincial corrections, sheriff services, private policing, and security services. Every day these law enforcement agencies are actively seeking select individuals who possess the personal qualities, skills, and attributes that are necessary to become a police officer. Do you possess these skills? Do you have what it takes to make yourself a competitive applicant? The current economic climate across Canada means that many law enforcement agencies are holding vacancies, downsizing through retirement and attrition, and only accepting a handful of applicants each year. This means that if you want into a policing career then you have to be among the best in terms of your aptitude, cognitive skills, physical fitness, and ability to interview and present yourself well. Simply meeting the minimum job requirements is no longer enough to get the job you want.

## STEP-BY-STEP GUIDANCE

Even though preparing to successfully pass a police entrance exam is an essential element in the application process, becoming a police officer involves much more than simply passing the entrance exam. There are many challenges and hurdles to overcome. The *Canadian Police Officer Exams* guides you through each step that you may face along the way. In addition to passing an entrance exam, many agency application processes involve submitting a résumé and cover letter, conducting simulation exercises, and being subject to a battery of psychological testing, polygraph examinations, and one or more interviews in front of a sergeant or an interview panel. Regardless of the number of stages that you'll have to pass during the application process, this guide provides sound advice and strategies to prepare you for all of these steps.

This *Canadian Police Officer Exams* preparation manual affords you the material necessary to give you a competitive edge. The information found within this guide will assist you in being successful in each step of the process. This manual follows the chronological order that many police application processes take and is divided into five main sections:

1. Introduction to Policing
2. The Application Process
3. The Entrance Exam
4. Next Steps
5. Practice Exams

The introductory section is designed to ensure that you are well versed in all aspects of police work in Canada. Police officers have a common law duty to preserve the peace, prevent crime, and protect life and property; however, police work involves much more than just arresting criminals—police officers work in an array of operational, investigative, and support services functions.

The second section of this guide lays out the basic and preferred recruit qualifications that many agencies seek. Basic qualifications refer to minimum standards that police agencies require before your application will be accepted. This includes minimum age requirements, level of education, driver's licence qualifications, and physical health and fitness. Preferred qualifications are unique skill sets and attributes that you may possess that give you a competitive edge. For example, police agencies across Canada are actively seeking out applicants that reflect the diversity of their communities. Therefore, speaking a second language or being a member of a visible minority in your community is often considered to be a preferred qualification. In addition, specific skills and qualifications, such as industrial first aid or computer skills, may also make you a more competitive applicant. Furthermore, many applicants are required to complete cover letters and submit résumés and background questionnaires. This section provides you with tips, techniques, and examples that you can use to ensure that your résumé gets read and that your application documents showcase your unique skills that make you a desirable candidate.

The third section of this manual is the Diagnostic Exam. This comprehensive assessment tool tests your knowledge and aptitude skills and provides feedback where you may need to make improvements and gives you the tools and strategies to increase your proficiency scores. The 135-question Diagnostic Exam is designed to specifically assess your aptitudes in six of the most frequently tested competency areas:

- Observation and memorization
- Vocabulary and mechanics
- Grammatical skills
- Reading comprehension
- Judgment and logic
- Problem solving

At the end of the exam, an answer key and detailed explanations are provided for each question. In addition, if you are finding that you need to improve your scores in any of these areas, you are directed to subsequent chapters that provide instructions and strategies that you can use to improve your scores in any of these subject fields. These chapters also include a quiz at the beginning and a "Have I Got It Right?" assessment at the end of each chapter so that you can be certain that you have acquired the knowledge and improved your skills in each competency. This section also provides you with a step-by-step planning guide for you to follow in the weeks prior to the exam and tactics that you can use to ensure that you are relaxed, confident, and well prepared to take the test on the day of the exam.

The fourth section of this book prepares you for everything that may follow during the recruiting process after you have successfully passed the entrance exam. For some police agencies, it means attending a day-long assessment centre where you will be required to complete role-playing and scenario simulation exercises. You may be required to complete paper-and-pencil psychological tests or even have a one-on-one interview with a psychologist. Other steps include medical and physical testing, driving competency evaluations, and many police agencies also require that you pass a polygraph examination prior to being hired. Finally, the last stage of the application process for most police organizations means being subject to an in-depth interview before a hiring panel or police manager. This section takes you through each of these processes, including the types of questions you may be asked, what evaluators are looking for during simulation exercises, and how to ensure that you showcase your skills and abilities and give yourself the best chance for success.

The final section of this book provides you with an opportunity to put your skills to the test by trying various examination formats that are used by six different police organizations across Canada. This includes the Ontario Provincial Police, the RCMP, and the Vancouver Police Department. The practice examinations replicate the type and number of questions that you will find when taking the actual tests and the amount of time that is allotted for each assessment. Included at the end of each practice exam is an answer key, complete with detailed explanations that you can put to use to help you achieve your goal of becoming a police officer.

# Police Work in Canada

1

→ **POLICING IN CANADA TODAY**
→ **POLICE OFFICER DUTIES**
→ **PATROL WORK**

## POLICING IN CANADA TODAY

Currently, there are nearly 70,000 police officers working across Canada. More than 18,000 are members of the RCMP, who either provide federal police duties or serve under contract to provide provincial or municipal police services across the country. There are 6,200 Ontario Provincial Police officers; 5,500 provincial police officers working for the Sûreté du Québec; and 400 members of the Royal Newfoundland Constabulary. The three largest municipal police services are: Toronto (5,500 officers), Montreal (4,600 officers), and Calgary (2,000 officers); however, there are also hundreds of small municipal police departments, some with fewer than 20 police members, spread across the country.

Over the past 50 years, a number of interconnected municipalities have merged to create regional police forces. Regional police forces offer the advantage of combining services, such as training, emergency response teams, forensics, and police service dogs so that they are able to provide a level of service similar to that of larger police agencies. Most regional police forces are located in Ontario, the largest being the Peel Regional Police (1,900 members) and the York Regional Police (1,500 members).

So what is it like to be a police officer in Canada? The most important thing to know about police work is that it is not universal. That is, the type of work that you'll be doing varies depending upon the region and city that you work in, as well as the district of the city that you are assigned to. For example, many of the types of calls that an officer attends to in the impoverished and high crime-rate district of Vancouver's Downtown Eastside are quite different from the service calls an officer would be dispatched to if he or she worked in the upscale Shaughnessy neighbourhood. Therefore, police work is never the same—no two shifts and no two calls are ever the same.

Nevertheless, a number of characteristics are common to police work in general. First, policing is demanding. This begins at the application stage, where you often must compete against many other qualified applicants for just one position, continues through the rigorous demands of recruit training, and follows you through most aspects of your career. Policing is certainly not a job for everyone, nor is it a career that everyone will do well. On occasion, police work can be very physically demanding when, for example, you have to wrestle with a violent drunk on the street as a bystander videotapes your actions with his smartphone for that two-minute clip on the six o'clock news. Throughout their careers officers are called upon to use various levels of force, up to and including deadly force, and they must be able to use that force appropriately and then be able to articulate and justify why they used that level of force.

Beyond physically challenging, police work is often mentally challenging. Police officers are required to deal with difficult people on a daily basis—and it is not always the verbally abusive drug addict that you arrested for robbing a convenience store. The teenager that you just stopped for excessive speeding—who tells you that he knows his rights and that his dad's a lawyer and will have your badge by the morning because you pulled him over because of the colour of his skin—can be even more taxing. Police officers also see people at their worst: they see their hopelessness and despair and witness the horrific aftermath of suicides, murder, and vehicle fatalities. Sadly, being a witness to deaths and serious injuries involving children or innocent victims can haunt police officers' memories for years.

The demands of police work also mean being potentially exposed to communicable diseases, viruses, and unsanitary conditions; dealing with personal injury and stress; working shift work and weekends; and missing family functions and important social events.

Although police work can be demanding and very exciting, it is not like what is portrayed in movies or even on reality television shows—a true "reality" police show would put most viewers to sleep. Even officers who work in large metropolitan police agencies with a large volume of crime find that most of their shifts are comprised of "paper work", following up on incident reports and investigations, responding to complaints, dealing with service calls that do not result in an arrest, taking statements, and tagging property. Police work is typified by long hours of mundane work interspersed with short periods of intense excitement.

Policing also requires sound knowledge of the Criminal Code and other federal statutes, provincial legislation, and a police department's policies and procedures. Officers must know how to apply the law as events unfold. Police officers need to evaluate situations based on their knowledge, experience, and information that is available to them when determining if a crime has occurred or not and make split-second decisions as to whether to arrest an individual or determine how much force is required in a situation. At crime scenes, officers must pay attention to details and make observations about suspect statements, body language, and demeanor. When an arrest occurs, officers must be able to accurately recall statements and describe events during court proceedings that often occur more than a year after the incident.

Policing is also about working with people from various ethnicities, cultures, socioeconomic backgrounds, and sexual orientations that may be quite different from your own. To ensure support for policing within the entire community, it is essential that police officers are able to build and maintain effective relationships with the cross-cultural diversity and various backgrounds present in any community.

Finally, and most importantly, police work can be very rewarding. Not only in terms of competitive salaries and benefits, but in terms of making a difference—helping to keep a community safe by locating and arresting violent and dangerous individuals, resolving disputes, assisting those less fortunate, and preventing crime.

## POLICE OFFICER DUTIES

Although the type of work that police officers do varies, there are a number of core functions that the police provide. Several of them are found in common law (i.e., case law that judges have previously established), while others are found in specific legislation. For example, the Supreme Court of Canada states that the common law duties of police officers are: "preservation of the peace, the prevention of crime, and the protection of life and property." However, Ontario's *Police Services Act* expands on these primary duties to include the following:

**(A)** preserving the peace;

**(B)** preventing crimes and other offences and providing assistance and encouragement to other persons in their prevention;

**(C)** assisting victims of crime;

**(D)** apprehending criminals and other offenders and others who may lawfully be taken into custody;

**(E)** laying charges and participating in prosecutions;

**(F)** executing warrants that are to be executed by police officers and performing related duties;

**(G)** performing the lawful duties that the chief of police assigns;

**(H)** in the case of a municipal police force,... enforcing municipal by-laws; and

**(I)** completing the prescribed training.

If you are going to pursue a career in policing, then these primary duties should be fairly well engrained in your mind by the time you take your entrance exam (especially if there's an essay component), and certainly before you are called for an interview.

Beyond the broad responsibilities listed above, policing generally falls within three categories of work: operations, investigations, and support services. Operations essentially cover all frontline patrol work—the first responders to incidents—and may also include other areas such as traffic enforcement duties. Investigative responsibilities relate to follow-up detective work and may be further divided into types of offences (e.g., major crime sections, robbery, arson, and sex crimes units). Support services are units or sections within a police organization that provide specialized functions that support operations (e.g., emergency response teams, surveillance teams, canine units, and forensic services), and other infrastructure support functions (e.g., human resource sections, training, and information and technology). However, as an applicant, the most important section that you should focus on, besides the recruiting unit, is patrol.

**Common Law Duties of a Police Officer:**

- **Preserve the peace**
- **Prevent crime**
- **Protect life and property**

## PATROL WORK

Upon completion of your police academy training, you will begin your career working in patrol. Patrol is the core function of policing, and you will often hear patrol referred to as the "backbone of our organization", meaning that all other functions are secondary and in place only to support the essential duties provided by patrol officers. Patrol provides a 24/7 police response to calls for service and in-progress incidents. Patrol officers primarily work in uniform, are assigned to specific areas or districts, and are deployed typically in patrol cars, but they also may work a beat on foot or a small geographic area on bicycle.

Some television shows occasionally portray young officers working in specialized forensic units, and you might think, "Hey, that's something that I would like to do right away!" Or perhaps you have excellent computer programming skills and believe that you can be hired to immediately assist with Internet fraud investigations. Although forensics may be an interest of yours, or you may one day add value to an organization with the specific computer skills that you possess, you should probably hold off on making those kinds of energetic statements to a recruiting officer at the outset. Recruiters are looking for men and women who want to start their careers working in patrol, who want to work evenings and weekends, and who are eager to be frontline first responders. Perhaps several years later, only after the officers have learned the craft of policing, will they be considered to work in specialized sections. Besides, patrol is where all the action is, and patrol work can be exciting and rewarding as a career in itself. Every year, there are many individuals who retire from policing having happily worked in patrol throughout their entire careers.

Patrol officers are responsible for the following duties:

### Responding to Reports of Crime

This includes a wide spectrum of calls from a serious crime in progress (e.g., armed robbery) to an incident that occurred more than a week ago (e.g., break-in to a detached garage).

### Following up on Investigations

For many police agencies, patrol officers not only take the original reports of crime but are also expected to carry those files with them, follow up on investigative leads, and attempt to identify and charge suspects. The exceptions to this would be that very serious crimes are almost always followed up by detective units, regardless of the size of the police force, and that some large police departments have specialized investigative sections for almost every category of serious offence that allow for patrol officers to forward many of their files to these units for follow-up.

### Arresting Suspects

This could mean arresting suspects who are wanted on warrants or locating and arresting someone who is committing, or has just committed, an offence.

### Responding to Civil Disputes and Disturbances

Many police calls for service require patrol officers to simply stand by and keep the peace or mediate disputes between parties where no criminal offence has occurred (e.g., neighbour dispute over dog droppings on an owner's lawn or a landlord-tenant dispute about the landlord turning off the tenant's heat). In these situations officers are required to assist in resolving the matter, if possible, direct the person to the appropriate agency to deal with their complaint, or, at the very least, ensure that the situation does not escalate to the point where a crime takes place (e.g., assault).

### Responding to Suspicious Circumstances

Officers are frequently called to investigate whether activity called in by a citizen is criminal in nature. These investigations include, for example, prowlers, alarm calls, loiterers, and apparent drug activity.

## Writing Reports

Patrol officers are required to complete an incident report for almost every call that they respond to. For serious crimes, this could mean many hours of "paper work".

## Pursuing Self-initiated Patrol

This includes driving/walking/cycling in and around high crime-rate areas looking for suspicious activity and criminal behaviour.

## Initiating Proactive Enforcement

This could include a wide range of activities from making bar checks for liquor offences, participating in undercover buy-and-bust stings, setting up drinking and driving road checks, and enforcing traffic laws.

## Developing Crime Prevention Strategies

Patrol officers are often responsible for developing community-based crime prevention initiatives with community partners in their geographic areas of responsibility. This could include anything from developing Block Watch sessions to working with the municipal officials to incorporate traffic calming measures in a neighbourhood to deter street-level prostitution in the area.

## Cultivating Sources/Informants

Patrol officers are the "eyes and ears" on the street. They have frequent contact with individuals involved in criminal activity and are responsible for recruiting individuals who will provide information about other criminals to the police.

## Acting as Agents of the Coroner

Probably the most unpleasant aspect of being a patrol officer is that in most jurisdictions police officers are required to attend all sudden deaths (suspicious or not) that occur outside of a hospital or care facility. You would likely be surprised to know just how many people die outside of hospitals every day and, worse, how many people are not discovered to have died until days later.

## Ensuring Traffic Safety

Patrol officers are expected not only to write violation tickets for observed motor vehicle infractions but also to investigate collisions and provide traffic control during demonstrations, parades, and serious collisions.

## Enforcing By-laws

This could include parking complaints, weekend construction noise, and unlicensed street vending.

# Police Officer Entrance Requirements

**2**

→ **BASIC QUALIFICATIONS**
→ **PREFERRED QUALIFICATIONS**

Across Canada, there are no standardized or universal entrance requirements for admission into the policing profession. For example, some police forces do not require any postsecondary education, others require a minimum of one year's equivalent of college or university credits, and a few require two or more years of specific postsecondary education. This chapter provides you with the minimum qualification standards that most police agencies require before an application will be accepted. In addition, preferred qualifications that many police services seek are also provided. You will be a very competitive applicant if you can present a strong balance of academic achievement, life experiences, work experience, and a demonstrated commitment towards community involvement and volunteering.

## BASIC QUALIFICATIONS

### Age

All police agencies in Canada require applicants to be either 18 or 19 years of age before an application will be accepted. In some instances, this is because under some provincial legislation a person is not considered an adult until he or she is 19 years old (e.g., British Columbia), whereas in other provinces a person is considered an adult at 18 years of age (e.g., you can legally purchase liquor when you are 18 years of age in Edmonton, Alberta). However, this is not a hard and fast rule because you can apply to the Saskatoon Police Service at 18 years of age, but the legal drinking age in Saskatchewan is 19 years. The RCMP will allow you to apply when you are 18 years old; however, you will not be hired before your 19th birthday. It makes sense that you must at least be the "age of majority" before being hired by any police service; otherwise, you would not be able to carry out all your mandated duties (e.g., conduct licenced premises checks).

## MINIMUM AGE REQUIREMENTS FOR POLICE IN CANADA

| POLICE AGENCY | MIN. AGE |
|---|---|
| Abbotsford PD | 19 |
| Calgary Police Service | 18 |
| Charlottetown Police Service | 19 |
| Edmonton | 18 |
| Halifax Regional Police | 19 |
| Manitoba | 18 |
| Montreal | 18 |
| Niagara Regional Police | 18 |
| Ontario Provincial Police | 18 |
| Peel Regional Police | 18 |
| Port Moody Police | 19 |
| RCMP | 18* |
| Saskatoon Police | 18 |
| Saanich Police | 19 |
| Sûreté du Quebec | 18 |
| Vancouver Police Department | 19 |
| Winnipeg Police Service | 18 |
| York Regional Police | 18 |

* 19 years at time of engagement.

Even though police departments specify minimum requirements in terms of chronological age, these agencies are actually more interested in your level of maturity. Some young men and women display levels of skill development and maturity well beyond their physical age, whereas others who are in their twenties might exhibit juvenile behaviour. Most police agencies tend to hire individuals who are between their mid twenties to early thirties, although there is always the occasional exception on both sides of the age spectrum. The reason for this is that these applicants have had an opportunity to complete a higher level of education and develop life skills and have had time to demonstrate years of consistent work performance.

## Citizenship

Almost all police agencies in Canada state that applicants must either be Canadian citizens or have already immigrated to Canada and have Permanent Residents Status. However, some police services (e.g., Calgary) state that if an applicant is a recent immigrant to Canada, he or she must have lived in either Canada or the United States for at least the past three years in order to have a proper security clearance conducted. Other agencies are less restrictive and simply indicate that the applicant must be legally entitled to work in Canada at the time of application.

## Health

All prospective police officers must demonstrate that they have been given a clean bill of health, either by way of a medical certificate or by undergoing a medical examination prior to being offered employment. Police services already have enough employees with significant medical issues (e.g., sleeping disorders, chronic back pain, high blood pressure, vertigo, and a host of other ailments) that prevent them from performing general policing duties. Police employers are looking for medically and physically fit men and women who are chomping at the bit to sit in a car for 12 hours straight; work through the night and then go straight to court in the morning; direct traffic for hours on end in the blowing snow or pouring rain; and relish the thought of doing it all again the next night.

## Physical Abilities

Regardless of the police agency, one of the first requirements for police applicants is to successfully pass a physical abilities test. These tests assess your ability to perform the physical demands of police work by having you run a timed circuit that requires you to perform tasks such as climbing, jumping, getting off the ground, and pushing, pulling, lifting, and carrying weights.

Prior to undergoing any physical abilities testing, most police agencies will require that you complete a health questionnaire (e.g., PAR-Q or PARmed-X) that will ask you questions about your health in relation to performing rigorous exercise. You might be asked questions such as "When you exercise, do you ever feel dizzy or lose your balance or consciousness?" "Do you ever feel chest pain, whether working out or at rest?" Perhaps you will also be asked questions about whether your doctor is currently prescribing you any medication for high blood pressure. Most agencies will also require that you sign a consent form, and they may also take your blood pressure immediately prior to physical testing. Some agencies require that if you are over a certain age, usually 40 years, then you will first be required to provide a note from your physician indicating that you are physically fit enough to undergo a police physical abilities test.

## PARE and POPAT

The Physical Abilities Requirement Evaluation (PARE) is used by the RCMP, Halifax Regional Police, the Royal Newfoundland Constabulary, and other police services in the Maritime Provinces. The Police Officers' Physical Abilities Test (POPAT) is almost identical to the PARE and is used primarily by police agencies in the provinces of British Columbia and Saskatchewan. The primary differences between the POPAT and the PARE are the weights used at the push/pull stations and the length of time given to complete the course.

The PARE and POPAT simulate a foot pursuit of a suspect over obstacles and require you to run, climb, and jump and then use levels of force similar to taking physical control of a suspect at the end of the foot chase. Both courses require you to run a six-lap obstacle course (350 m PARE, 400 m POPAT). On each lap, you will need to jump over a mat. The mat on the PARE is 1.5 m (5 ft); the POPAT mat is 1.8 m (6 ft). In both courses, you must ascend and descend six steps, and jump over two 0.5 m (1.5 ft) hurdles. In the PARE, you will be required

**Police Physical Abilities Tests**

- **PARE**
- **POPAT**
- **PREP**
- **TAP-ENPQ**

to vault a 0.9 m (3 ft) barrier and drop to the ground on each lap. In the POPAT, the vault is conducted later in the test, after the push/pull weight station, where you will be required to perform ten controlled falls, five on your chest and five on your back, on each side of the vault.

The next segment of the PARE and POPAT is the push/pull weight station. This requires you to push and then pull a weight of 32 kg (70 lb) for the PARE, and 36 kg (80 lb) for the POPAT, through six 180 degree arcs. The PARE requires you to conduct four falls, two to the front and two on your back, when changing between the push and the pull stage.

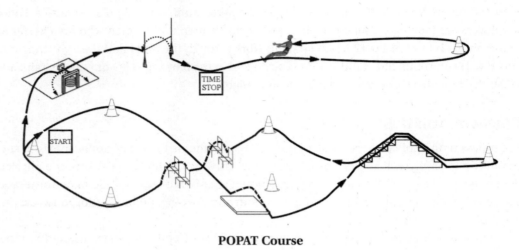

**POPAT Course**

The timed stage of the PARE ends at the completion of the push/pull station. The POPAT timing ends after the vault station. The PARE must be completed in 4:45 min. The maximum time for the POPAT is 4:15 min. If you are considering joining the RCMP, in order to graduate from Depot, you must complete the PARE time in 4:00 min and the weights for the push/pull and torso carry are equal to that of the POPAT.

After completing the timed portion, you must also carry a torso sack of 36 kg (80 lb) for the PARE, and 45 kg (100 lb) for the POPAT, for a distance of 15 m (50 ft) in either test. This is not timed, but you will not be permitted to drop the sack, put it down, drag it, or put it over your shoulders. Some agencies will put in additional requirements at the end of this stage. For example, the Vancouver Police Department also requires that you perform ten push-ups immediately after finishing the torso sack carry. On the POPAT day, you will also have to pass a Trigger Press and Hand Dynamometer Test of 35 kg (77 lb) of pressure for each hand.

## PREP

The Physical Readiness Evaluation for Police (PREP) is used by all police agencies in the provinces of Alberta and Ontario. There are four stages to the PREP. It begins with an obstacle course circuit just like the PARE and POPAT; however, there are only four laps, and the total distance is just 100 m. Another key difference is that in the PREP you must wear a 7 kg (16.5 lb) belt around your waist to simulate the weight of your duty belt—guns, ammo, radio, pepper spray, and handcuffs are heavy!

During each loop of the circuit, you have to run over four ascending and descending steps, and during the second and fourth rotations of the circuit, you must scale a 1.5 m (5 ft) fence.

The fence has a toe-hold 0.5 m (1.5 ft) off of the ground, and you have to use the toe hold to climb and roll over the fence.

Following the circuit, you move to the body control simulator, which is similar to the PARE and POPAT push/pull weight stations. This requires you to push and then pull a 35 kg (75 lb) weight through two 180 degree arcs. As you move from one side to the next, you are required to alternate between pushing and pulling the handle. This is immediately followed by the arm restraint simulator—a device that simulates taking physical control of a resistant person and using an arm bar lock on him. The device requires you to use 14.5 kg (32 lb) of force in order to depress the two handle grips and then, while maintaining the depressed grips, use an additional 14.5 kg (32 lb) of force to retract both arms of the device. You then return to the body control simulator and repeat two more arcs as before.

The last stage of the circuit is to drag a body weight of 68 kg (150 lb) for 15 m (50 ft). This dead-weight carry is significantly different from the POPAT and PARE in that the "body" is substantially heavier; however, you are allowed to drag the dummy by the wrists or ankles for the entire test. The combined circuit run, body control simulator, arm restraint simulator, and body drag must be completed in less than 2:10 min.

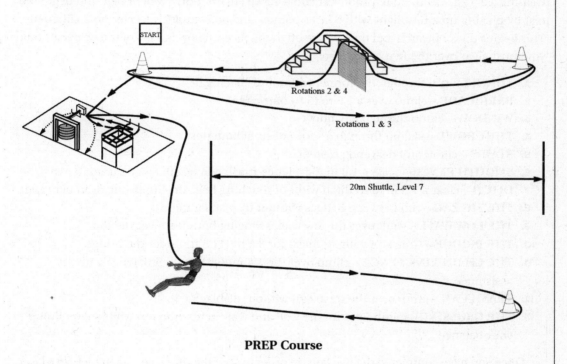

**PREP Course**

After the timed circuit run, you will be allowed to rest for 10 minutes before commencing the final stage—the Léger aerobic shuttle run. The shuttle run was designed by Dr. Luc Léger of the Kinesiology Department of the Université de Montréal, and the passing level was determined based on the minimum amount of aerobic power needed to meet the specific demands of patrol work. In this strictly aerobic endurance run, you will be required to run a 20 m (65 ft) shuttle and reach a warning line, placed 2 m (6.5 ft) ahead of the stop/start line, before a timed signal sounds. The timing of the signal shortens after each stage so that you begin with an easy paced jog between the lines and move to a progressively quicker pace. To pass the test, you must reach the 7.0 level without failing to cross the warning lines more than once before the signal sounds.

## TAP-ENPQ

Test d'Aptitudes Physiques—École Nationale de Police du Québec (TAP-ENPQ) is the physical abilities test used for all police applicants in the province of Québec. There are three parts to the test: Léger aerobic shuttle, the timed obstacle course, and individual stations.

The Léger aerobic shuttle is the same format as described in the PREP; however, in order to pass you must reach the 6.5 level without stopping or receiving more than three warnings. Warnings are issued if you fail to reach the warning line before the signal, if you leave the start/stop line early, or if you fail to come to a complete stop before returning to run to the other side.

The obstacle course is like that of no other police agencies in Canada—and is certainly the most challenging. In order to pass this stage of the TAP-ENPQ, you must run five laps of a 70 m (230 ft) circuit that has 13 different stations in less than 6.5 minutes. Each station assesses specific motor skills, and if you fail to perform the task correctly, you must start the station again and penalty time is added to your total time.

During the obstacle course you will be required to simulate the patrol environment by wearing a 2.5 kg (4.5 lb) bulletproof vest and a 4.5 kg (10 lb) "duty" weight belt. You begin the test by picking up a flashlight with a laser pointer and activating a receiver on a silhouette. This begins the stopwatch and then you're off to the races. Below is a list of the obstacles that you must clear over the five-lap course:

1. **TUNNEL**—run through the tunnel without displacing it
2. **BARRICADE**—climb over a 1.5 m (5 ft) barricade
3. **WINDOW**—climb through a window
4. **THE CROWD**—slalom through a series of six silhouettes
5. **STAIRS**—climb and descend six steps
6. **SMOOTH FENCE**—scale a 1.8 m (6 ft) fence (trash can or tub can be used to assist)
7. **DITCH**—clear a 1.5 m (5 ft) ditch without touching lines on either side or in between
8. **THE ZIG ZAG**—run between hedges without displacing them
9. **THE LOW WALL**—vault over the low wall, swinging both feet over the top.
10. **THE BRIDGE**—Crawl on your stomach for 3.5 m (11.5 ft) under the bridge
11. **THE CHAIN-LINK FENCE**—climb over the 1.8 m (6 ft) chain link fence without assistance
12. **TRASH CAN**—jump over the trash can without displacing it.
13. **THE CROSSING**—climb up onto the wall and walk across the top while maintaining your balance

Once you have completed the five laps, in order to stop the timer, you must pick up a laser pointer and successfully target a series of silhouettes until the timer stops. This completes the second stage.

The individual stations stage begins immediately after finishing the obstacle course, and you have 4 minutes to complete the required tasks in this segment. The first station is the push/pull device. You must complete four 180 degree arcs with the 32 kg (70 lb) weight pushed off the ground, followed by four more arcs with the weight pulled off the ground. The second station requires you to drag a 66 kg (145 lb) dummy for 20 m (65 ft). In this test, the dummy must have its head off the ground, and you cannot drag the dummy by the head—you are saving its life after all. The final stage of the TAP-ENPQ is to perform CPR on the dummy. You must do the following in the correct order:

- Verify the state of consciousness,
- Clear the airway,
- Check for breathing,
- Provide two breaths, and
- Perform 30 chest compressions.

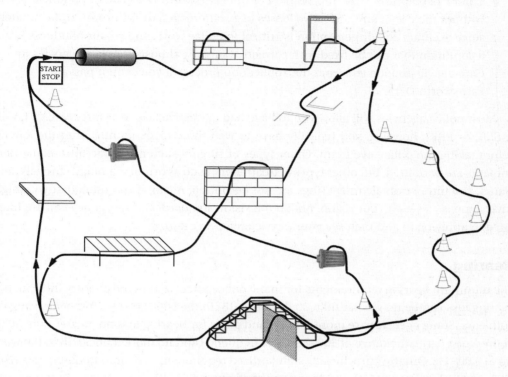

**TAP-ENPQ Course**

## Vision

The vision requirements by police agencies can be somewhat confusing, and you should schedule an eye exam with your physician before submitting an application so that you know whether you have any issues that need to be addressed. Essentially, employers want to ensure that you possess sufficient visual acuity to be able to read licence plates on vehicles that you are either attempting to pull over or the suspect vehicle that just passed you on a dimly lit street, provide street names and addresses that you are driving past, describe the colour of clothing that a suspect who just ran away from you is wearing; and be able to read the information on a driver's licence that a motorist handed you.

Minimum vision requirements vary from one police force to another. In addition, some agencies will require that you obtain a vision report that you will need to take to a qualified ophthalmologist or optometrist for completion. Other police agencies provide the basic vision testing in-house—typically through city hall or the city's dedicated service provider.

Typical minimum vision standards are

- **Uncorrected vision**—20/40 with both eyes open, with any one eye no worse than 20/100 (other agencies are 30/60 with both eyes open).
- **Corrected vision**—20/20 with both eyes open, with any one eye no worse than 20/40 (others are correctable to 20/30 with both eyes).

- **Eye disease**—Free from diseases that significantly impair visual performance or may produce unpredictable visual incapacitation.
- **Peripheral vision**—No blind spots (other than physiological blind spots).
- **Depth perception**—Typically, stereo acuity between 80 and 100 seconds of arc or better—ask your optometrist.
- **Colour perception**—Pass the Ishihara or the Farnsworth D-15 colour blindness tests without the use of any corrective lenses (e.g., chromagen or X-Chrom). Unfortunately, since accurate colour perception is critical to police work, and colour blindness is not a condition that can be fixed with corrective surgery, almost all police agencies in Canada will exclude you from the application process if you cannot pass the Farnsworth D-15.

**Colour Blind?**

Unfortunately, most police agencies will not accept an applicant who is significantly colour blind.

Most police agencies will allow you to have had corrective laser eye surgery (e.g., LASIK, LASEK, or PRK); however, you typically have to wait three to six months after the surgery before taking the police eye exam. Other types of surgery such as phakic Intra-ocular lens implants are permitted, but other types of treatments, such as orthokeratology, corneal transplants, and intra-stromalcorneal rings are not permitted. Again, if you think that you might have some issues with your vision, obtain the vision standards for the agency you are interested in applying to and then see your physician for an exam.

## Hearing

The minimum hearing requirements for many police forces across the country indicate that hearing loss can be no greater than 30 decibels (dB) in the 500–3,000 Hz frequency range in both ears. Some agencies are more relaxed and allow for hearing loss no greater than 30 dB in the worst ear in the range of 500–2,900 Hz frequency and no more than 50 dB in the worst ear at 3,000 Hz. Ontario's provincially standardized requirements test four frequency averages (500, 1,000, 2,000, 3,000 Hz) and that none shall exceed 35 dB and at 4,000 Hz the hearing loss shall not exceed 45 dB.

## Education

Every police agency requires that, at a minimum, you have completed Grade 12 or its equivalent (e.g., GED) before your application will be accepted. Grade 12, a GED, or four years of secondary school education is the minimum requirement of the RCMP, Edmonton Police Service, the OPP, the Toronto Police Service, and many others. If you have completed your secondary school education outside of Canada, you will need to produce an International Qualifications Assessment Certificate or be evaluated by the International Credential Evaluation Service or a similar program.

For many police forces, the minimum completion of Grade 12 is insufficient, and you must possess some form of postsecondary education in order to be accepted. For example, the New Westminster and Vancouver police departments both require a minimum of 30 credits of academic college or university courses from an accredited institution. Educational requirements are discussed in more detail under "Preferred Qualifications".

**Pre-employment Training**

Means you must graduate from a police college before being offered a career in policing.

## Pre-employment Training

Most police agencies train their recruits after they are hired by their police force, which is commonly referred to as postemployment training. For example, all non-RCMP municipal police agencies in BC send their newly hired recruits to the Justice Institute of BC for training. However, a number of police forces require specific pre-employment training before your application is accepted. For example, if you are applying to any police agency in the province of New Brunswick, you must first be a graduate of the Atlantic Police Academy Police Science Program (located in Summerside, Prince Edward Island) or have previously graduated from the Justice Institute of BC Police Academy; RCMP Training Academy; Canadian Armed Forces Military Police Training, Technical Qualification 3; École nationale de police du Québec (ENPQ); Canadian Police College; or the Ontario Police College. In other words, either you have completed the Atlantic Police Academy Course or you have already served as a police officer elsewhere in Canada.

## Driver's Licence

Having a clean driving record is an important quality that recruiters will scrutinize because it helps demonstrate responsibility, maturity, and a commitment to observance of the law. Most police agencies will allow for several minor infractions, but would probably defer you from the application process if you have received lengthy driving prohibitions or had alcohol-related driving charges. The maximum number of allowable cumulative penalty points varies from agency to agency. The table below provides a brief sample. You will also likely need to provide a driving abstract obtained from your local motor vehicle branch. This is usually required within 30 days of submission of your application.

| SAMPLE OF MAXIMUM POINTS ALLOWED | |
| --- | --- |
| POLICE SERVICE | MAXIMUM DEMERITS |
| Edmonton | 5 |
| Hamilton | 6 |
| Saskatoon | good driving record |
| Toronto | 6 |
| Vancouver | good driving record |
| Winnipeg | 4 |

Most police agencies require you to show that you have been driving responsibly for several years, and departments will generally not accept new drivers or drivers that are still under the restrictions of a graduated licensing programme. When I was a police trainer at the Justice Institute of British Columbia, there were several occasions where a recruit was sent to us for training who had almost no previous driving experience—especially in relation to a full-sized vehicle. This lead to challenges for both the training staff and the recruit in terms of building that person's confidence and competency to a point where he or she was fully capable of driving a police car in an emergency situation. Other police agencies that have dealt with similar situations have now incorporated a requirement that you pass a basic driving assessment using a police car on a closed track as part of the initial application process.

### First Aid/CPR

The RCMP, Toronto Police Service, and many other police forces require that you obtain a valid Standard First Aid certificate, including a certificate for cardiopulmonary resuscitation (CPR) for infant, child, and adults prior to an offer of employment. If CPR and first aid is not a requirement for employment by the agency that you are interested in applying to, you might want to take this extra training anyway as an example of your initiative and desire for continuous learning in a related field.

### Computer Skills

Many police forces now expect applicants to meet minimal typing standards (usually 25–30 WPM) and have a basic level of competency with word processing applications. If you are lacking in these skills, there are online classes and programs that you can download that will quickly enhance your typing speed and basic computer skills.

### Criminal Record Check

Obviously, all police services in Canada are interested in hiring only individuals who demonstrate a high level of integrity and moral values—no one wants to hire a red flag with a checkered past, who is a huge liability risk and has the potential of damaging the reputation of the police organization. As the saying goes, "Past performance is usually the best indicator of future behaviour." Nevertheless, recruiters realize that everyone makes mistakes, especially during their teenage and young adult years, and you will not be automatically excluded from consideration if you have had a past run-in with the law.

**Criminal Record?**

**Must obtain a pardon before application will be accepted.**

Most police agencies state that you must be clear of any detected or undetected criminal activity for at least three years, and that if you have a criminal record, you must first obtain a pardon before your application will be considered. Similarly, if you have been found guilty of an offence that has resulted in an absolute or conditional discharge, these records must first be sealed before your application will be considered. Also, your application will automatically be deferred if you have any current criminal charges awaiting prosecution.

The fact that you may have a criminal record will not be as much of a determining factor as to whether your application will be considered compared to what the record is for. For example, offences that call your integrity or morality into question (e.g., fraud charges or sexual offences) will likely be looked at much more negatively than what might be considered an error in judgment (e.g., a conviction under the Controlled Drug and Substances Act for possession of a marijuana joint). In addition, recruiters will evaluate how long ago these offences occurred, how old you were at the time, and what you have done with your life since the offense happened.

### Police Application Fees

It's worth mentioning here that many of the tests you will be required to perform or certificates you need to obtain have fees associated with them. Although some have argued that these expenses act as a deterrent, preventing individuals from lower socioeconomic backgrounds from applying to policing, others see this as a way of reducing policing administrative costs, while also acting as a screen and ensuring that only the serious applicants enter the process. The table below is not all-inclusive, but it provides you with some idea of the expenses you might face at the application stage. If your police agency requires pre-employment training from a specific police academy, you will have to pay for that first. However, even if your agency provides postemployment training, you may still have to pay separately for that as well. Most police academy training programs cost range from $7,000 to $10,000.

| TYPICAL EXAM AND TEST FEES | | | |
| --- | --- | --- | --- |
| **EXAM / TEST** | **EST. COST** | **EXAM / TEST** | **EST. COST** |
| Medical exam | $85.00 | Basic First Aid and CPR | $85.00 |
| Vision exam | $90.00 | POPAT | $60.00 |
| Chest X-ray | $65.00 | Language Proficiency Index | $100.00 |
| Hearing test | $35.00 | Ontario (PATI, WCT, PREP, BPAD) | $330.00 |
| Proof of typing speed | $20.00 | Academic Transcripts | $10.00 |

## PREFERRED QUALIFICATIONS

In today's competitive job market, you will likely need to offer more than the basic qualifications in order to be a successful applicant with any police agency. You need to demonstrate that you possess other skills that make you more marketable and desirable than other applicants. Some of these preferred qualifications are relatively easy to obtain, others are much more challenging, and some are simply beyond your control. The goal for you is to discover what additional qualifications you already possess, or can acquire, that give you a competitive edge.

### Language Skills

Every day police officers require assistance from fellow officers and interpretation services to explain to victims of crimes what happens next, take statements from witnesses, and advise suspects of their rights under the Charter and interview them in their spoken language. Even though contracted interpretation services can usually provide valuable assistance to frontline members, they are impersonal telephone conversations that often miss key information that can only be obtained through face-to-face contact. Therefore, being able to speak more than one language will put you at a great advantage over many other applicants, especially if it is a language spoken by one of the larger immigrant minority groups in your community. That is, being able to speak Mandarin in Vancouver would be considered a much more valuable asset than being fluent in Swahili. In addition, if you are able not only to carry on a conversation in another language but also to read and write it, then this will put you at an even greater advantage.

Some police departments have established specific requirements around language abilities. For example, in Montréal's SPVM you must possess a working knowledge of French and a knowledge of English. However, you must be able to pass an oral comprehension assessment where you will need to follow a conversation initiated by an administrator and participate actively.

**TIP**

**Speaking a second language puts you at an advantage over other applicants.**

## Cultural/Ethnic/Sexual Diversity

Every police agency in Canada is acutely aware that they must do more to reflect the cultural and ethnic composition of the communities that they serve. Across the country, with little exception, white males vastly overrepresent the makeup of police agencies. In order to address this deficiency, many organizations now specifically state that they are actively recruiting individuals that represent the diversity of their communities. For example, the Hamilton Regional Police Service states that one of its organizational goals is to specifically encourage applications from people who belong to one or more of the following groups:

- Aboriginal persons;
- Lesbian, gay, bisexual, transgendered, and questioning;
- Visible minorities reflective of the Community of Hamilton;
- Females; and
- Persons with a disability.

Across Canada, people of Aboriginal descent have been overrepresentative as victims of crime and offenders and underrepresentative as police officers. In order to promote the recruitment of Aboriginal individuals, some police forces have implemented Aboriginal-specific recruitment programs. For example, the Vancouver Police Department's (VPD) Aboriginal Cadet Program is a means of generating interest with young adult Aboriginal people to consider a career in policing. This is a paid mentorship program that allows qualified Aboriginal young people the opportunity to work at the VPD in a civilian capacity and also participate in ride-alongs with regular members. Similarly, the RCMP's Aboriginal Pre-Cadet Training Program offers First Nations, Metis, or Inuit individuals an opportunity to work at Depot over the summer and also to work near their home communities by riding along with patrol officers.

**TIP**

There are significant opportunities for female police applicants.

## Female

If you are a female interested in policing, there are significant opportunities for you. Even though considerable strides have been made in the last three decades to bring more women into policing, today females still account for only 20 percent of police officers in Canada. Although some females have experienced challenges associated with working in a historically male-dominated work environment, many women excel in their policing careers and enjoy healthy working relationships with their peers and supervisors. Female officers tend to do very well in many policing situations, including those involving deescalation of confrontations where the use of physical force can be avoided, crisis (e.g., hostage, suicidal person) negotiations, and interviewing female victims—especially victims of sexual abuse and domestic violence. Nevertheless, still far fewer women than men apply for policing careers; and since many police forces strive to ensure that half of their recruits are females, you have a competitive advantage as a female applicant.

## Work History

Without a robust work history that police recruiters can evaluate, you will likely not be considered for employment by most police agencies. You need to be able to demonstrate that you have been a diligent and hard-working employee and that you worked well with peers and your supervisor. Recruiters will prefer seeing a record of exemplary work performance that spans several years. Particular attention will be paid to whether you have been excessively sick, absent, or late and whether there were any negative incidents in which you were involved. If you have received any commendations, whether formal recognitions or perhaps a thankful email, you should keep them on file and make them available to recruiters during the application process.

The type of work that you have previously done is equally important. For example, policing involves effective communication skills, and employment that demonstrates those abilities is desired. Service industry jobs, such as retail store managers, often provide ample opportunity to hone these skills.

Owning and operating your own business, especially if it has been relatively successful, demonstrates another level of skills such as resource management, initiative, determination, and other desired qualities.

Previous employment in security and other peace-officer-related careers also provides a benefit. Security work, loss prevention officer, doorman at a nightclub, jail guard, auxiliary police or reserve officer, by-law enforcement officer, parks officer, correctional officer, and sheriff are often considered as excellent stepping stone careers to policing.

**Stepping Stone Careers**

- **Correctional Officer**
- **Sheriff**
- **Jail Guard**
- **Bylaw Officer**
- **Auxiliary / Reserve**
- **Loss Prevention Officer**

## Volunteering and Community Involvement

As Sir Robert Peel stated nearly 200 years ago, "The police are the public and the public are the police." Being a police officer means being part of the community that you serve. As an applicant, one of the best ways that you can demonstrate commitment to your community, and the concept of community-based policing, is to show active participation and volunteering in community events and services. Community volunteering is one of the easiest and potentially most beneficial preferred qualifications that you have the potential of demonstrating. Some community volunteering suggestions are provided below; however, you should only be limited by your imagination, as there are more than 150,000 nonprofit agencies and community services across Canada.

## Police-Related Volunteering

- **Victim Services**—Counseling and support services to victims of crime and tragic events.
- **Citizen's Crime Watch**—Acting as extra eyes and ears on the streets, observing and reporting crime and suspicious activity to patrol officers.
- **Speed Watch**—Monitoring speeds of vehicles, especially in schools, playgrounds, and high crash locations.
- **Block Watch**—Volunteering to help establish and maintain Block Watch programs in the community.
- **Community policing centres**—Operational support staff opportunities at neighbourhood and community policing offices. Participating in safety patrols and assisting citizens in making police reports.

## Community Volunteering

- **Crisis/Emergency Preparedness**—Volunteering with Red Cross and related agencies; volunteering at crisis telephone call centres.

- **Social assistance**—Volunteering at soup kitchens and other related facilities to help those less fortunate.
- **Health care support**—Assisting with meal preparation and delivery and providing emotional support to those confined to hospitals and other care facilities.
- **Recreational activities**—Working with children, seniors and people with disabilities as part of a team involved in fitness and exercise programs and in social events.

## Life Skills

When I was 19 years old, I had obtained a two-year diploma in Criminal Justice from a local college when I walked into the Vancouver Police Department Recruiting Section and confidently enquired about a job. I was fairly dismayed when they politely advised me that although I had obtained some academic skills, I wouldn't be considered until I had acquired more life skills.

Life skills can be a nebulous term and mean different things to different people. For some it means living on your own, experiencing life, and travelling the world; for others it means living on your own, paying your own bills, getting married, and having a family. You can also sign up for Life Skills courses or be a Life Skills coach. Various definitions and catch phrases have been used to characterize this term, but essentially it means having sufficient social skills, maturity, and personal experience to be able to handle the many daily challenges of an independent existence.

In my own experience, I further developed my life skills by working for three years as a provincial correctional officer in one of the toughest prisons in the country. When I began working at the prison, I had several co-worker friends who were about the same age as me. We all left the prison a few years later to move on to other careers. However, we often commented: "We entered the prison as boys, but left as men." Working at Oakalla Prison forced me to quickly acquire effective communication skills, learn to deal with conflict and violence, handle stressful situations, witness hardship and human misery, and learn to be compassionate to those less fortunate.

Although life skills can be difficult to define, it is critical that you are able to demonstrate that these skills are something that you possess. You need to show that you are mature, self-reliant, and able to handle whatever challenges life throws your way.

# Résumés and Background Questionnaires

# 3

→ **COVER LETTER DEVELOPMENT**
→ **COVER LETTER SECTIONS**
→ **SAMPLE COVER LETTER**
→ **RÉSUMÉ DEVELOPMENT**
→ **SAMPLE RÉSUMÉ**
→ **BACKGROUND QUESTIONNAIRES**

The formal commencement of your application to a police agency usually begins when you either attend a recruiting information session that is hosted by the specific police service that you are applying to or when you download a multidocument application package from the police agency's website. As a result, many police agencies no longer require you to submit cover letters and résumés or *curriculum vitae* (CV) since most of the information that you would provide (e.g., your tombstone data and employment, volunteer, and educational history) is now captured in their comprehensive application packages. Nevertheless, a number of police departments, such as Winnipeg, Hamilton, and Toronto police, require résumés as a component of the application process. If this requirement pertains to one of the agencies that you are interested in applying to, then it is imperative that you provide them with a professional and well-written résumé package. This chapter provides you with key tips and strategies that you can use to ensure that your cover letter and résumé get noticed and stand out in the pile of submissions that a police organization may receive each year.

## COVER LETTER DEVELOPMENT

A cover letter should add distinction to your résumé by highlighting specific abilities and qualifications that show you would add value to the organization and make an ideal police officer candidate. This step also provides you with one of your first opportunities to demonstrate your written communication skills. Therefore, this should not be taken lightly, and you should devote considerable time to planning and preparing your cover letter.

### Plan

Begin by discovering information about the police force that you are applying to and the jurisdiction that it serves. What are some of the unique qualities about this police organization? What are the most important policing challenges that it currently faces? What are the agency's mission statement, values, and goals?

Once you have done some research about the police service, list the most important qualities and skills that you possess. You do not want to simply regurgitate the information listed in your résumé; instead, you want to highlight your strongest attributes and align them with the values and objectives of the police agency. You can create a comparative list to help you elicit those character traits and qualifications that will have the greatest impact.

## ATTRIBUTE CHECKLIST

| Attributes Desired by the Police Agency | Attributes That I Possess |
| --- | --- |
| Values | Honesty, integrity, professionalism |
| Basic Qualifications | BA psychology, excellent physical condition |
| Preferred Qualifications | Diversity, second language, volunteering |
| Specialized Skills | Counsellor, IT, artist |
| Police-Related Experience | Reserve constable |
| Special Interests | Competitive hockey team member |
| Achievements/Awards | Award for CPR on child |

## First Impressions

Documents tend to fall into one of three categories: really good, average, and really bad. You want your application package to stand out and be memorable, but in a good way. You want to leave the reader with an impression of your personality and character by providing real-life examples of your accomplishments. Your accompanying résumé will provide a matter-of-fact account of your skills and achievements, but your cover letter should add substance, personal insight, and be a testament of your abilities.

## Length

Keep your cover letter short—a maximum of three to four brief paragraphs (250–300 words). The entire letter must not be longer than one page, and you should not even take up the entire page. At the initial application scanning stage, no recruiter will want to spend more than a minute reading about what an amazing person you are.

## Format

There should be plenty of white space on the sheet of paper. This is achieved by maintaining wide margins, using 1.5 to 2 spaces per line, and leaving spaces between paragraphs. Your document should be easy to read and not a strain on the eyes, so use a font between 10.5 and 12. Use a common typeface that is legible and does not contain fancy hooks and swirls. San serif fonts (e.g., Arial and Verdana) are typically easier to read and also electronically scan better than others. Whatever font and typeface you decide to use, be consistent and use the same for your résumé.

## Writing Style

Since your goal is to grab the reader's attention and keep him or her engaged in your letter, you need to write in an active voice (as opposed to a passive voice). For example, "I had four employees report to me..." is written in a passive voice, compared to: "I managed four employees...." You should also use action verbs to describe your skills and accomplishments. For example, if you've been involved in activities through previous employment or volunteer experiences that would demonstrate your leadership qualities, you should use action verbs to describe these desirable traits.

## COVER LETTER SECTIONS
### Your Information

Your cover letter should begin with your contact information, usually centred, at the top of the page. Your name should be in a larger font (14–16 pt) than the rest of the text and bolded so that it stands out. Below your name include the following:

- Current address,
- Telephone number (home or cellular only), and
- Email address—keep it professional.

### Date

Below your name, insert the date that you will be sending in the letter and résumé. You can either write out the date (e.g., September 1, 2014) or you use the YYYY-MM-DD format (e.g., 2014-09-01). All police officers in Canada are familiar with this format as it is the standardized method of entering (or running) a person's date-of-birth on CPIC—the national police databank.

## Recipient's Information

Next, enter the following contact information of the police agency you are applying to:

- Recipient's full name,
- His or her rank and/or title,
- Police agency's name, and
- Police agency's address.

## Reference Line

Below the recipient's information, include a reference line that provides a title or purpose for your cover letter, such as reference to a competition or posting number. (e.g., Re: Police Constable Application Posting #14-003).

## Salutation

Address your cover letter to the person that your application will be sent to—include his or her rank and title. Try to avoid addressing your letter: "To whom it may concern," as this might be interpreted that either you have not done your homework or you are sending out a boilerplate application to multiple police agencies.

## First Paragraph

The purpose of the first paragraph is to introduce yourself and advise the police agency that you are very interested in a career with that specific organization. You also want to start with a strong statement demonstrating that you possess the desired qualities the employer seeks. For example, you might want to state how your personal values align with the police organization's Mission Statement.

## Second (and Third) Paragraph

In the second paragraph you want to maintain the reader's interest. You might begin by relating a unique event or circumstance in your life that's drawn you to a policing career—especially with this particular organization. You may also describe several achievements or accomplishments that you have attained that directly relate to the policing profession. Be convincing—leave the reader with no doubt that you are fully prepared and are the right candidate to be considered for a career with this police agency. Attempt to be concise enough to provide this information within one paragraph. If you require another paragraph to capture your accomplishments, keep it brief.

## Final Paragraph

In the concluding paragraph state your willingness to move forward to the next stage of the application process. Advise the reader of your availability and the best way to contact you. Finally, thank the reader for his or her time and consideration.

## Closing

To close your cover letter it is okay to sign off with "Sincerely," "Regards," and so on. However, I would stay away from "Warmest wishes" (too soft and cuddly) or "Faithfully yours," (you are not the department's servant—yet). However, it would also be appropriate to acknowledge the rank of the recipient by concluding, "Respectfully submitted," for example.

Leave three spaces after your closing and type your first and last name. In the space between, write your signature. Use a black pen to ensure that your signature will photocopy and electronically scan well.

## Enclosure

Indicate whether you are submitting additional documents such as your résumé, letters of reference, and so forth by typing "Encl." on the line below your name.

## Cover Letter Checklist

Before sending off your cover letter, go through this checklist—especially the don'ts—to be certain that you have everything covered.

### DO

☐ Grab the reader's attention—make it interesting,

☐ Use action verbs,

☐ Use compelling illustrations of your achievements and experiences,

☐ Relate your personal attributes to the policing profession,

☐ Keep your cover letter concise (3–4 paragraphs maximum), and

☐ Have a trusted person proofread and critique your document.

### DO NOT

☐ Use clichés or flowery language,

☐ Come across as arrogant,

☐ Overstate your abilities

☐ Use fancy (or too large or too small) fonts,

☐ Use terms like "I believe that" or "I feel that,"

☐ Address cover letter "To Whom it May Concern," or

☐ Use tacky or unprofessional email addresses (e.g., zombieslayer@example.com).

# SAMPLE COVER LETTER

**Jane Sample**

3585 Graveley St, Vancouver, BC, V5K 5J5

(604) 555-1234—jane.sample@email.ca

2014-09-01

Corporal Garrett Danforth
Port Moody Police Department
3051 St. Johns Street
Port Moody, British Columbia
V3H 2C4

**Re: Police Constable Vacancy Posting #2014-001**

Dear Corporal Danforth:

I am pleased to formally apply to the Port Moody Police Department. Just as the mission of the department states that your officers serve the community with "excellence," I am also committed to delivering the highest level of service in everything that I do—whether it is my academic accomplishments, my exemplary work performance, or my achievements in sport.

In 2012, I graduated from Simon Fraser University with a Degree in Criminology (Honours), finishing with a GPA in the top 10 percent of my graduating class. While attending university I was also a member of the Varsity Rowing Team. As a member of the Quadruple Scull, I was responsible for steering the craft and played a pivotal role in our team winning a gold medal at the 2011 Canada Games. Since graduation, I have worked full-time at a local sports equipment retail store and have been recognized for my excellent communication, organizational, and leadership skills. I have recently been promoted to Assistant Manager and supervise a team of six employees.

I have a strong connection to the people of Port Moody as I lived and worked here during my undergraduate studies and I have also volunteered in the community for the past four years as a member of the Department's Citizen Crime Watch program.

I know that I possess the skills and desired qualities that will make me an asset to the Port Moody Police Department and I look forward to discussing this exciting opportunity with you. Should you require any additional information please call or email me directly. Thank you for your consideration.

Respectfully submitted,


Jane Sample
Encl.

# RÉSUMÉ DEVELOPMENT

Your résumé will provide your prospective employer with information about your educational background, work history, volunteer experience, accomplishments, and interests. As with the cover letter, your résumé needs to be more than an itemized list of previous duties and responsibilities and an indication of the level of education you've attained. Instead, your résumé needs to showcase the value that you have added to each category listed and demonstrate how these accomplishments will benefit the police organization that you are applying to.

## Résumé Sections

### OBJECTIVE STATEMENT

Stating an objective indicates to the recruiter that you know exactly what you are applying for and that you are prepared for this role. This is an optional field. Since there are so many steps in the application process, it will be clear to all that you know what your objective is.

> **EXAMPLE: OBJECTIVE STATEMENT**
>
> To obtain a constable's position with the Ontario Provincial Police that will enable me to use my strong communication skills, educational background, and ability to work well with people.

### HEADLINE/TITLE

A headline or title is a brief phrase that showcases your most significant attributes or achievements.

> **EXAMPLE: HEADLINE**
>
> Decorated Canadian Forces veteran awarded Medal of Valour for bravery.

### PROFILE

Most contemporary résumés begin with a brief (100 words or less) personal profile or summary of your qualifications. You can write this out as a brief paragraph, or use three or four bullets in point form.

> **EXAMPLE: PROFILE**
>
> - Award-winning Honours Graduate.
> - Excellent leadership, planning, and communication skills.
> - Fluent in English and French.
> - Energetic team player.
> - Project manager with six years' experience in developing high-calibre sales teams.
> - Accomplished financial analyst with cross-functional expertise in marketing, accounting, and business analysis.
> - Highly articulate manager with aptitude for establishing goals and engaging external and internal stakeholders in delivering exceptional customer service.

## PROFESSIONAL EXPERIENCE

This is also commonly labelled: "Work Experience," "Employment History," "Experience" or some variation thereof. This can be formatted in several ways, but the most visually appealing is as follows:

- Begin with your most recent work experience and then list others in reverse chronological order.
- Start with your title in bold font near the left margin, and then directly across the page, near the right margin, list the years that you were employed there, using a hyphen to separate the dates.
- Identify the name of the company you worked for, followed by city and province.
- Below the company name, use point form to list three or four of your most impressive accomplishments.
- Whenever practicable, use statistics to demonstrate and enhance the impact of your successes.
- Do not list your duties—unless you can make a specific connection with how these duties relate to police work.

---

**EXAMPLE: PROFESSIONAL EXPERIENCE**

Assistant Business Manager            2012–Present

*Kids Klothing Kompany*, Ottawa, Ont.

- Awarded Top Monthly Sales Associate on five occasions.
- Currently manage team of five sales associates.
- Responsible for 20 percent revenue increase from 2012–2013.

---

## QUALIFICATIONS/SPECIAL SKILLS

This is another optional field, and I would recommend using this as a separate category only if you possess a number of highly skilled qualifications. For example, stating that you are familiar with MS Excel and Wordperfect would not be overly inspiring to the reader. However, you might want to specifically highlight your IT skills if, for example, you are, highly skilled at C++, SQL Server, JavaScript, and Perl.

---

**EXAMPLE: SPECIAL SKILLS**

- First Aid CPR "C" Certificate—valid until September 2015
- Class 1 Driver's Licence with Air Brake Certification

---

## EDUCATION

Educational achievements should indicate the year that you graduated, the degree/certificate awarded, and any major or minor concentration. Specific courses that you took should not be listed, unless you think they are essential to showing a direct correlation to police work. You should only include postsecondary education and training that you have received;

however, since a number of police agencies only require a minimum of Grade 12 or equivalent, you can also include the secondary high school and year in which you graduated, or when and where you received your GED. You can also include any academic achievements that you have attained during this period.

---

**EXAMPLE: EDUCATION**

Bachelor of Commerce (Hons), Major in Information Systems, 2009

*McGill University*, Montréal, Qué.

- 4.0 GPA
- Selected to Dean's List for every semester

---

## VOLUNTEER EXPERIENCE

As an applicant to the policing profession, it is imperative that you not only possess some volunteer experience in your background, but that you specifically highlight this in your résumé. In contrast to your work and educational profiles, this will not be achievement focused, rather you can highlight the most important aspects of the volunteer work that you have done. Use the same format as your Professional Experience and Education to identify your volunteer work.

---

**EXAMPLE: VOLUNTEER EXPERIENCE**

Delivery Driver          2010–Present

*Lady of Mercy Soup Kitchen*

Moncton, NB.

- Providing meals to needy citizens unable to attend kitchen in person.
- Organizing community fund-raising drives.
- Facilitating referrals to other NGOs and support services.

---

## AWARDS/ACCOLADES/ACHIEVEMENTS

This is your last chance to boast, in point form, the incredible achievements that you have attained (and have not already mentioned elsewhere in your résumé). You can mention certificates of achievement, special awards, or recognition that you have received in sports, in your professional and academic endeavours, and in your personal life.

---

**EXAMPLE: AWARDS**

- Nominated—Community Spirit Award, 2014
- Awarded *Magnus Magna* Scholarship, 2013
- Southside Community Centre—Volunteer of the Year, 2009

---

## INTERESTS/HOBBIES

You may really enjoy going for moon-lit walks, making clay sculptures, or getting top scores on the Legion of the Deranged video game, but I would recommend leaving out all interests and hobbies that cannot be associated with policing in a meaningful way.

---

**EXAMPLE: INTERESTS/ACTIVITIES**

- SCUBA diving (PADI—Master Scuba Diver)
- Member of Brownsville Fish & Game Club—Competitive Pistol Team
- Student Representative to City University Academic Senate, 2012

---

## Résumé Checklist

Before sending off your résumé, go through this checklist and make certain that you have not missed anything.

### DO

☐ Use a profile or headline statement to capture the reader's attention.

☐ Maintain the same font size and style as your cover letter.

☐ Focus on work accomplishments and not work-related duties.

☐ Keep your résumé to under two pages in length.

☐ Be direct—avoid making lengthy statements.

### DO NOT

☐ Use too many heading types (e.g., change font size, **bold**, *italics*).

☐ State whether you are married, single, have children, and so on.

☐ List your date of birth, social insurance number, driver's licence number, or other personal information on the résumé unless specifically requested by the police agency to do so. They will ask for it elsewhere.

☐ Include names and contact information of employers, teachers, and so on.

☐ List references—indicate "available upon request"—unless requested at that time.

☐ Use terms like "I believe that" or "I feel that"—it comes across that you lack confidence.

☐ List related coursework and what grade you received in each class.

☐ Use the following archaic and meaningless terms:
- proven ability—according to whom?
- hard-worker/achievement-driven/results-oriented—are all assumed; just say what you did.
- utilized my skillset to…—again, get to the point and say what you did.
- transferable skillset—you might as well say that you are a Jack-of-all-trades, which translates to "I'm not proficient at anything, specifically."

# SAMPLE RÉSUMÉ

**Jane Sample**

3585 Graveley St, Vancouver, BC, V5K 5J5

(604) 555-1234—jane.sample@email.ca

| | |
|---|---|
| **Profile** | • Award-winning university graduate and championship athlete. |
| | • Business manager with excellent leadership, planning, and communication skills. |
| | • Fluent in English and French. |

**Professional Experience**

**Assistant Business Manager**      2012–Present

*Best Foot Forward Sports*, Burnaby, BC

• Awarded Top Monthly Sales Associate on three occasions.

• Currently manage team of five sales associates.

• Responsible for 20 percent revenue increase from 2012–2013.

**Loss Prevention Officer**      2010–2012

*Grape Foods*, Coquitlam, BC

Responsible for 36 shoplifting arrests.

Saved company in excess of $20,000 in losses.

Enhanced safety and security of business, employees, and customers.

**Sales Associate**      2009–2010

*Denver Meat Deli*, Port Moody, BC

Implemented web-based ordering system.

Developed enhanced marketing scheme.

Increased retail sales by 11 percent in 2009.

**Education**

**Bachelor of Arts—Criminology (Honours)**      2012

*Simon Fraser University*, Burnaby, BC

3.9 GPA—Top 10 percent GPA of Graduating Class.

Member, Undergraduate Student Council, 2011.

Recipient, Chamber of Commerce Athletic Scholarship.

Member, Varsity Rowing Team, 2010–2012.

**Volunteer Experience**

**Citizen's Crime Watch**      2010–2012

*Port Moody Police Department*

Responsible for reporting 4 crimes in progress.

Recovered 12 stolen vehicles.

**Awards**

**Gold Medal—Quadruple Scull, Canada Games**      2011

*Simon Fraser University Varsity Rowing Team*

# BACKGROUND QUESTIONNAIRES

Many police agencies will require you to complete a personal disclosure document or background questionnaire during the initial stages of the application process. The primary purpose of this step is for recruiters to gain as much of a comprehensive assessment of your background—especially your social and personal life—that has occurred prior to the submission of your police application.

It is important to be completely honest and thorough when providing answers to these questions. If you have done things that you are embarrassed or ashamed of, or perhaps are even criminal in nature (e.g., you once drove when you may have had too much to drink or you stole some office supplies from your previous employer), these events alone may not result in your rejection from the application process. However, if you are found to have intentionally omitted, concealed, or lied about anything in your background, you can be certain that your application will be terminated. It is essential that you fully disclose all pertinent background information at the outset because you do not want it to come up later (e.g., during interviews with friends, employers, family). Remember, any indication of deception is an automatic fail and will remain with your file for life.

This section lists many of the background categories that recruiting staff will explore and examples of the types of questions that you will be expected to answer.

## Education

You will be required to indicate where and when you graduated from high school or received your general equivalency diploma (GED). In addition, you will be required to provide details regarding all postsecondary education that you've acquired. Education-related questions that you may encounter are:

- Have you ever been officially reprimanded at school?
- Have you ever been suspended from school?
- Have you ever been accused of bullying or bullied another student?

## Employment

Ensure that you provide a complete list of your employment history, including temporary or casual work. You will be required to provide contact information of employers, supervisors, and letters of reference. If you have any significant gaps in your employment history (e.g., backpacked across Europe; laid off), you will be required to account for these periods. Below are some of the employment-related questions that you can expect to be asked:

- Have you ever called in sick for work (or said a family member was sick or dying, or claimed that you needed to attend a funeral) when this was not the case?
- Have you ever received income for any type of work, and you did not declare this income as required by law (e.g., for income tax purposes)?
- Have you ever been terminated or asked to resign (i.e., fired)?

## Financial

The agency you apply to will likely conduct a credit check and require you to list all loans, mortgages, credit cards, lines of credit, and financial institutions that you deal with. You will be required to provide a complete picture of your financial holdings and debts. Some of the types of questions that you can expect to be asked are:

- Have you ever declared bankruptcy?
- Have you ever had a problem with debt?

## Driving

Because a safe driving record demonstrates maturity, good decision making, and responsibility, most police agencies will require a five-year abstract of your driving record. In addition, you will often be asked to provide more detail about your driving record and habits. For example:

- Have you received any violation tickets or been stopped by the police for any driving offence since your abstract was submitted?
- Have you ever had your licence suspended, locally or in another jurisdiction?
- Have you ever been involved in reckless or careless driving that was dangerous, but never became known to the police?

## Drug and Alcohol Use

One of the biggest worries that potential applicants have relates to previous drug use—specifically marijuana. The reality is that many police agencies will probably not exclude you from the application process simply because you have at one time smoked marijuana. Rather, the decision of whether or not this is a fatal issue will typically relate to the frequency, duration, and how long it has been since you last used marijuana. For example, that you once tried a marijuana joint five years ago would be considered far less adversely than if you just quit the week before submitting your application. In addition, although all illicit drug use could potentially prevent you from becoming a police officer, soft drugs (e.g., marijuana and hashish) may be considered less damaging to your career eligibility than hard drugs (e.g., cocaine, heroin, crystal meth, GHB). In addition to questions pertaining to your possible experimentation with and use of various drugs, other related questions that you may be asked include:

- Have you ever illegally purchased pharmaceutical (e.g., Oxycodone, Percocet, steroids, and valium) or other drugs?
- Have you ever transported or stored illicit drugs for another person?

## Sexual Activity

Even though police agencies do not have the right to enquire about your sexual orientation and related lifestyle, they will want to know if you have engaged in prohibited sexual activity, or the type of activity that may embarrass the reputation of the police department (e.g., you recently worked as an exotic dancer at a local bar). Other questions about your sexual conduct may include:

- Have you ever obtained the services of a prostitute or an escort?
- Have you ever had sexual activity with a person who did not, or was unable to, give consent to the act?
- Have you ever had contact with an animal for a sexual purpose? (Yes, they will ask. What's more surprising are the answers!).

## Technological Offences

Unfortunately, the advent of the Internet Age and related technological advancements have not only produced an abundance of societal benefits but also led to myriad opportunities for those so inclined to engage in nefarious activities relating to fraud, harassment, and nuisance offences. You may be asked the following types of questions:

- Have you ever attempted or successfully gained unauthorized access to a computer system?
- Have you ever illegally downloaded or obtained pirated computer software, games, videos, or music?

If you are asked any of these types of questions and respond in the affirmative, then you will be required to provide specific details regarding when this occurred, on how many occasions, why this occurred, who was involved, whether there are any witnesses, and what the outcome or aftermath was.

No police department expects you to be perfect or have an unblemished background. However, police agencies deserve to know as much as possible about you—the good and the bad—and then be able to make an honest assessment of whether any issues that you may have had are outweighed by your positive attributes and skills.

# Preparing for the Entrance Exam

# 4

→ **PRIOR TO THE EXAM**
→ **EXAM DAY**
→ **TIME MANAGEMENT**
→ **MULTIPLE-CHOICE QUESTIONNAIRES**
→ **SHORT-ANSWER QUESTIONS**
→ **ESSAY-ANSWER QUESTIONS**

## PRIOR TO THE EXAM
### Research

Proper preparation for your police entrance exam begins with discovering the style and types of questions that you will be facing. For example, will you be taking a nationally standardized test (e.g., the RCMP RPAT) or a provincially standardized test (e.g., the Ontario Provincial Police PATI and WCT tests), or will the test be agency-specific (e.g., the VPD Intake Exam)? Although this guide provides you with sample test formats that are used by many police agencies across Canada, you should nevertheless still contact the police organization that you are interested in applying to and ascertain the format that they use. This will serve two functions: (1) you will discover whether the testing format has recently changed, and (2) understanding and being confident in the testing format will help reduce pretest anxiety. That is, you will be well-prepared for the types of questions you will face and not be blindsided by any stress-inducing surprises. You will know, for example, whether you will be required to write a short essay, complete a memorization exercise, complete a series of timed online tests, or all of the above.

If the police agency that you are interested in applying to does not provide any details regarding the layout or format of its entrance exam, do not worry because this preparation guide covers virtually every style and type of question, problem, and task included in police entrance exams anywhere across the country.

### Study

This study guide can assist you immensely in preparing for a police entrance exam; however, if this text sits on a shelf and you only thumb through the practice exams and do not utilize the strategies or try to memorize the tips until just a few days prior to your exam, you will likely find yourself ill-prepared to take the test. Instead, maximize the benefit that this guide provides by using the following study tips to prepare for the police entrance exam.

## SET ASIDE SHORT STUDY SESSIONS

Begin about six weeks prior to the examination date and set aside one to two hours, three times per week, where you can devote time specifically to preparing for the exam. Do not try to cram all the material into one weekend of studying—you will soon become fatigued and not retain very much information. In fact, retention of new material quickly fades after an hour of continuous studying. Therefore, one hour of intense studying will be more beneficial than two hours of moderate studying.

## STUDY DURING THE DAY

Although many postsecondary students seem to do most of their academic work while burning the midnight oil, this is usually because the assignment is due the following day and not because that is the best time of day (or night) to study. In fact, your memory retention is at its worst late at night. Instead, if possible, try to study during the morning or midday. You will likely grasp concepts and enhance your skills more effectively when both your body and your mind are not physically drained.

## PLAN FOR ALONE TIME

You will find that you retain information much more efficiently if you study while you are alone and free from distractions. That means turning off the television, muting your smartphone, and turning down the volume on your music device. Ideally, find a cool, well-ventilated location that is quiet and has good lighting.

## STICK TO YOUR PLAN

One of the most difficult challenges will be to consistently devote time to studying and practicing exam questions. Just as an effective physical fitness program requires a certain degree of regimen and commitment, so does your examination study plan. Think of it as a workout routine for your brain—no train, no gain.

## MAKE NOTES

Whether you make notes in the margins of this guide or on a separate piece of paper, using notes will help you recall specific pieces of information and strategies more effectively than just reading. For example, practicing to write out the correct spelling of challenging words is far more effective than simply reading the correct spelling of a frequently misspelled word.

## STUDY STRATEGICALLY

Begin with the diagnostic exam and discover your strengths and those areas that are a challenge for you. Spend two-thirds of your study time on the most challenging areas and the other third devoted to subject areas that you can master quickly. If, for example, you are having a difficult time correctly answering math word problems, then you should logically spend significantly more time practicing math problem-solving strategies and questions rather than other subject areas.

### REMEMBER THAT TIMING IS (ALMOST) EVERYTHING

When you take the Diagnostic Exam or any of the six Practice Exams, time yourself using a stopwatch or other device that has a countdown timer. Every entrance exam has a time limit that is used to create an additional stress-inducing element. You should simulate the timed component of an examination so that you can ensure that you are using effective time management strategies (see below).

### MEMORIZE HINTS AND TIPS

Throughout this text are information bubbles or memory triggers that contain various strategies and tips for mastering a specific challenge. For example, the mnemonic BEDMAS (Brackets, Exponents, Division, Multiplication, Addition, Subtraction) is used to recall the order of operations in mathematical equations. Write these tips down to help you memorize them.

### READ NEWSPAPERS

Reading a local newspaper every day as you prepare for the exam will assist you in several ways. First, you will stay in tune with current events (which you may be asked about once you make it to the interview stage). Second, reading a lengthy article and then mentally summarizing its key points will assist you in preparing for reading comprehension segments of the examination. Third, continuous reading will enhance your ability to identify proper spelling, word usage, and punctuation. Finally, most newspapers also contain word searches, crosswords, word jumbles, and other brain challenges that you can use to boost your cognitive effectiveness.

### REVIEW

If you follow a six-week study plan, you should have completed all of the tests and become proficient in all subject areas by the time you are in the final days leading up to your test date. During these last few days, you can shift your focus from practicing and understanding exam questions to reviewing your notes and the main tips and recommended strategies for each subject area. Therefore, once you have less than a week before the exam, you should be in a position to relax and be confident in knowing that you have acquired the skills necessary to be successful in taking any police entrance exam.

## EXAM DAY

There are a number of simple steps that you can take to ensure that your entrance exam date is successful.

## Be Physically Prepared

This guide provides you with numerous tips and strategies to assist you in being mentally prepared to take the entrance exam; however, you also need to be physically prepared. Ensure that you maintain a workout or fitness routine in the weeks leading up to the entrance exam. On the night before the exam, get a good night's sleep so that you are well-rested for the test. Eat a small meal no less than two hours beforehand; a large meal will make you feel sluggish. Also, do not forget to stay hydrated. You do not want to be physically fading by the time you take the test because you didn't get much sleep the night before and have been too nervous to eat or drink anything.

## Be Prompt

Plan in advance by clearing your schedule. You do not want to be burdened with other distractions on the day of your test and find yourself running late or worrying about other commitments. Give yourself sufficient travel time so that you arrive at the test location at least 15–20 minutes prior to the start of the exam. You definitely do not want to show up late and flustered.

## Dress Appropriately

You should dress professionally, yet comfortably—business casual is ideal. That is, you do not need to wear a suit and tie. Also, ensure that your clothes are not overly restrictive and that they breathe. If you are wearing a business jacket, it would be acceptable to remove it once the exam begins.

## Use the Washroom Facilities

Upon arrival, you should eliminate any potential bodily distractions. Some examinations may take up to three hours, and you may not be given the opportunity to leave the room once the exam begins.

## Bring Writing Material

Unless told otherwise, use a pencil, as you may want to change answers and edit your written responses. Bring extra pencils, a sharpener, and erasers. Do not rely on the examiners to supply this additional material. In addition, unless you are instructed otherwise, you may also wish to bring a small notepad to write out formulas, rough drafts of essay answers, and so forth.

## Understand Instructions

Listen to instructions and read them carefully. Do not think that you know what is expected and end up missing important directions. Attention to detail is a significant attribute that is expected of police officers. Careless mistakes are often a significant factor for those who do poorly on entrance exams.

## Check Exam Completeness

Flip through all the pages and check the number of questions. On rare occasions you may be handed an incomplete test. You do not want to have to retake the test or, worse, to have the examiners fail to notice that you never received all of the questions.

## Ask Questions

If you think that you've missed something, or you do not clearly understand the instructions, do not wait until the exam has started to ask questions. If possible, ask all clarifying questions before you start the test.

## Wear a Watch

Effective time management will be an important key to your success (see below).

## Relax

Use the relaxation breathing and visualization techniques if you are feeling anxious and overwhelmed. Just remember that it is a natural response to feel somewhat apprehensive and that although it may not be obvious, almost everyone in the room is feeling the same way that you do.

## Be Aware of First Impressions

Make a positive first impression, or at the very least, do not make a bad one. The entrance exam stage will likely be your first opportunity for a face-to-face encounter with the police agency's recruiting personnel. Depending on the size of the class taking the exam, the examiners might not remember you afterwards even if you were professional, presented well, and aced the test. However, they will certainly remember you, and report back explicit details to others, if you showed up late, looked disheveled, had an anxiety attack, had a coffee stain on your business clothes, or soiled yourself.

## TIME MANAGEMENT

All entrance exams are restricted by time constraints because your ability to manage time effectively is a critical component and a desired skill of a police officer. Therefore, aptitude tests are specifically designed to test your ability to effectively manage the time allocated. If you spend too much time on one section or question, you will likely run out of time before you have answered all of the questions.

Effective time management begins by ensuring that you build into your calculations a 10–15 percent buffer at the end of each section so that you will have sufficient time to review all your answers and return to any questions that you may have skipped. For example, if you have 30 minutes to answer 30 questions, do not give yourself just one minute for each question. Instead, allow 50 seconds per question, so you will have five minutes at the end to review all of your answers and complete any that you skipped.

A key to effective time management is to complete the exam strategically. You will likely have access to multiple sections so begin by quickly looking over the test and finding a section with which you are most familiar or comfortable. Answering the easy questions first will not only build confidence, but it will also allow you to quickly complete the section and move on to more difficult sections with considerable time to spare.

Do not spend too much time on questions that are very challenging and are only worth one or two points. If you find yourself struggling with a question or computation, put an asterisk beside the question and move on—you can always come back to it later. You do not want to risk running out of time and missing questions that you could have answered easily but never got to because you spent too much time on difficult ones that were worth the same points.

# MULTIPLE-CHOICE QUESTIONNAIRES

Most police entrance exams use multiple-choice formats extensively because answers are clearly defined, grader subjectivity is removed, and they can be electronically scanned and scored almost immediately. In fact, if you take the RCMP's new computer-based online entrance exam, you will have your personal score and know how well your score compares to a national profile before you leave the test site. Therefore, you are most likely to see significant components of many entrance exams in this format. The following suggestions will assist you in obtaining the highest scores in these areas.

## Read the Instructions Carefully

Multiple-choice exams are notorious for lost points resulting from failure to properly follow instructions. For example, there may be two multiple-choice answers that both appear to be correct; however, it is highly unlikely that you would be able to correctly indicate two choices. Instead, the instructions likely stated for you to select the best answer or the most appropriate answer.

## Answer the Questions Carefully

For many multiple-choice exams, you will be required to transpose your answers onto a Scantron-style answer sheet. These sheets use small bubbles (usually containing individual letters from A through E) that you shade in with a pencil to indicate your answer to each multiple-choice question. It is imperative that you make sure the numbers on your question booklet align with those on your answer sheet. The scanning sheets often have multiple sections—be certain that you are recording your answers in the correct section. It is very important to double check your work as you proceed through the test when using scanning answer sheets. You do not want to have to erase numerous answers because you have not properly transposed your responses onto the answer sheet.

## Clearly Indicate Response

Many answer sheets are electronically scanned and scored. Make sure that there are no extraneous markings and you completely erase any answers that you have changed. Far too often I have had to mark a multiple-choice answer wrong because there were so many circles, crossed out responses, and arrows from one letter to the next that I had no clue which choice the student was actually trying to indicate. If the answer sheet is electronically scanned and the scanner picks up markings in multiple bubbles, you will get the question wrong. In addition, for bubble answer sheet questionnaires you should:

- Use a No. 2 pencil that contains sufficient graphite to ensure your answer will be properly read by the scanner;
- Shade in each bubble completely. Do not put an X or check mark in the bubble. Do not lightly shade your response.
- Not fold, wrinkle, bend, tear, or otherwise manipulate bubble sheets. If the scanner cannot properly read your responses, they will be marked wrong.

## Do Not Panic

Do not get upset by a few challenging questions. If the test begins with several difficult questions, use your time management strategies to tackle the easier ones first. Remember, that you do not have to answer every question correctly to pass or to even get a good score. If you have sufficiently prepared, you will not fail, and there will be many questions that you will have no difficulty answering.

## Read All Options Before Answering

Do not stop reading your options when you come across an answer that you think is correct because you may find another answer that fits better. Sometimes you will encounter choices that indicate multiple correct responses. For example: "(E) Both A and D are correct." If you stopped at choice A, you would obviously get the answer wrong.

## Eliminate Wrong Choices

Even though the correct responses will sometimes leap off the page, you will have occasional difficulty choosing the correct response at other times. In these situations, begin by crossing off any obviously wrong answer on the question sheet. If you are not permitted to make any markings on the question sheet, simply list your choices (A, B, C, D, E) on a separate piece of paper and then go through a process of elimination. Usually, there will be one or two answers that are obviously wrong, and you can quickly cancel these options. Carefully reread the question, and the answer may become more obvious. Try using a true/false statement for each possible answer. If you are still uncertain, put an asterisk beside the question, move on, and come back to it later.

## Look for Key Words

Absolute words such as "always," "never," "all," or "none" are almost always incorrect because there is usually an exception to every rule.

## Avoid Highly Technical Language

Answers that contain highly technical and complicated language are usually a distraction and incorrect. Remember: flowery language is well-fertilized.

## Do Not Expect Tricks

Multiple-choice questionnaires are not made to trick you. Questions are not designed to be intentionally misleading; and although the entrance exam tests a variety of aptitudes, your ability to detect and avoid deception is not usually one of them.

## Do Not Look for Patterns

Questionnaires are not designed so that the answers are arranged in any particular pattern. That is, just because you answered C for the previous three questions, does not mean that the next answer cannot be C as well.

## Answer All Questions

If you are unsure of an answer, eliminate the obviously wrong responses and then select the answer that feels right. You may have previously learned why that particular answer is correct, even though you cannot put your finger on it now. Go with your gut feeling—your intuition. Remember: you get all of the answers wrong that you do not attempt.

## Do Not Change Answers

Unless you are absolutely confident of the correct response, do not start second guessing yourself and changing your answers. If you have followed the steps outlined above, you should have reached the correct choice.

## When All Else Fails

If you are really stuck, select B or C. It is probably an urban legend, but some people allege that B and C are statistically the most frequent correct responses on multiple-choice exams.

## SHORT-ANSWER QUESTIONS

Short-answer questions typically assess your reading comprehension, critical thinking, and summarization skills. In these situations, you will be required to read an article approximately one page in length and then respond to a question or series of questions that pertain to the document. Your responses should be limited to less than 125 words (approximately six sentences) and ought to be one paragraph in length only. The following guidelines provide tips for effective responses to short-answer questions.

## Manage Your Time

As with all aspects of any entrance exam, effective time management is essential. This requirement is further amplified when it comes to paragraph-style responses. You do not want to spend too much time thinking about what to say and how you are going to say it. Often there will be several short-answer questions in one section of the exam. Calculate the amount of time that is provided to answer the questions and then divide your time accordingly. For example, if you have 30 minutes for five questions, that leaves just six minutes to write each answer. However, you also need to build in a 10–15 percent time buffer to allow for review and editing of your responses. Therefore, in this example you should not spend more than five minutes on any short-answer question.

## Seek Out the Most Valuable Questions

Prioritize those questions that are most heavily weighted. That is, if one question is worth ten points and the others are only worth five, then you should address the question worth the most points first. For those questions that are weighted heavily, you should also allocate the amount of time to spend on that question accordingly.

## Complete Sentences

The answers that you provide will be evaluated on accuracy, content, and grammar. Therefore, write out your sentences fully and pay special attention to minor spelling or grammatical errors that can take away points from your answers. You should only write your answer in bullet point form if you have insufficient time to write complete sentences.

## Write Legibly

It would be a shame to lose valuable points simply because the assessor is unable to decipher your messy hieroglyphic handwriting. If need be, print your sentences, as it will usually increase legibility.

## Make Notes

If you are required to summarize a written report or document, write down the key words on a separate piece of paper while they are still fresh in your mind. These trigger words will help you flesh out and summarize the main concepts of the narrative.

## Summarize in Introductory Statement

Your first sentence should get directly to the point—state your position or finding. For example, in reviewing an article about the impact of the Charter on police procedures, you could state, "The article by Smith states that the Supreme Court's interpretation of various provisions of the *Canadian Charter of Rights and Freedoms* has hampered the ability of police officers to effectively investigate many crimes." This type of statement summarizes the essence of the article and indicates that you understand the point that the author was making.

## Use Supporting Statements

Following your introductory statement, the next few sentences should support your position. You should include two or three supporting arguments. In continuation of the previous example, you could state, "In her article Smith notes several instances where criminal charges fail because of technical burdens placed on police officers. For example, she claims that the inadvertent oversight of police officers to read suspects the Breath Demand at roadside often results in the Breathalyzer results being later excluded from the trial."

## Review

Reread the question and your answer to ensure that you have appropriately and completely answered the question. Some questions have more than one part—be sure you answer all parts. Finally, review your answer for any previously missed spelling and grammatical errors.

## ESSAY-ANSWER QUESTIONS

Many police entrance exams will require you to write an essay. Essay questions provide an opportunity to simultaneously assess an array of skills: reading comprehension, critical thinking skills, organizational skills, handwriting legibility, spelling, grammar, and time management.

Chapter 10 provides you with detailed essay composition instruction and skill development. Review the following essay writing tips just prior to writing a police entrance exam.

## Manage Your Time

Effective time management is most critical in essay composition. You need to be certain that you are not spending too much time planning or writing your essay, and then completely run out of time for other areas. The first step is to apportion your time: one-quarter planning, one-half writing the essay, and one-quarter revising and editing. The amount of time that you should spend actually writing depends on the amount of time permitted for the essay; however, a good rule of thumb is to allow from five to ten minutes maximum per paragraph. Therefore, if you have one hour to compose an essay answer and one-half of your time is spent actually writing out your response, this would mean you only have about 30 minutes to write an introduction, the body of your essay, and a concluding paragraph.

## Understand the Question

Are you being asked to take a stand on a particular issue, make a persuasive argument, explain something, or describe a situation? Identify the essay question's key action verbs and understand what they mean:

- *Explain*—Provide sufficient detail to demonstrate an understanding or to show the logical development of a concept.
- *Compare*—Examine the similarities and differences of two or more positions.
- *Evaluate*—Analyze the strengths and weakness of a position and provide an overall assessment.
- *Discuss*—Present in a detailed and methodical fashion the various attributes of a particular position.

## Be Grammatically Correct

In an essay, significant points will be given to spelling, punctuation, and word usage. Therefore, you should only use words that you know and can spell. It is better to write clearly, without spelling mistakes than to use elaborate words that are misspelled or used in the wrong context.

## Double Space

You are going to want to leave room for editing or making changes as you go. It is far easier to insert a word or two or make a minor correction in the extra space between lines than to cram it in a single-spaced paragraph.

## Do Not Use Bullet Point Form

You should not use point form responses in essay composition, even if you are running short on time. Your ability to write in complete sentences is being evaluated as much as your ability to demonstrate your understanding of a passage.

## Be Clear and Concise

Even though you should not write in bullet point form, you should get to the point. Do not write long run-on sentences that do not make your point right away. Remember the KISS principle: *Keep It Short and Simple*. Moreover, if you are spending considerable time crafting superlative clauses and phases, you are probably going to run out of time.

## Aim for 25-50-25 Distribution

There are three main parts to an essay. The introduction should account for 25 percent of the words (and time spent), the body of your essay should account for 50 percent, and the remaining 25 percent of your time and words should be used to write the conclusion.

## Think Cookie-Cutter Essays

All essay composition questions can be written effectively if you use the following timeless method:

- *Introduction*—Get right to the point. State what the topic is generally, what your position is specifically, and how you will support it.
- *Main Body*—Depending on the amount of time allotted, the main body of your essay should contain up to three paragraphs that support your position (thesis). Each paragraph relates to a specific theme or concept. Each sentence within that paragraph provides supporting details and examples relating to that specific theme. Back up your points with specific information, examples, or quotations from the reading.
- *Conclusion*—Your conclusion should, first, restate your position in a different way and then expand to generalizations about the issue.

## Review

Upon completion of your essay, spend up to a third of your allotted time editing your work. Correct any spelling mistakes and look for incomplete words or sentences. For instance, people often forget to write out words such as, "the", "as", and "to" when they are under time constraints. Confirm that these words are actually there, as our brains tend to insert missing words when we simply scan over essays that we have written. Ensure that you have a clearly stated theme and have transitions between sentences and paragraphs that support your theme and provide a logical and well laid-out connection between ideas.

# Diagnostic Exam

**5**

→ **PART 1: OBSERVATION AND MEMORIZATION**

→ **PART 2: VOCABULARY AND MECHANICS**

→ **PART 3: GRAMMAR**

→ **PART 4: READING COMPREHENSION**

→ **PART 5: JUDGMENT AND LOGIC**

→ **PART 6: PROBLEM SOLVING**

→ **ANSWER KEY**

→ **ANSWERS EXPLAINED**

This Diagnostic Exam contains 135 multiple-choice questions designed to evaluate your aptitude relating to the most common competencies assessed in Canadian police entrance exams. The Diagnostic Exam is comprised of six parts, with each section intended to measure a specific set of proficiencies (see Table below).

Each test has its own set of instructions and time allowances. You are not required to take the entire test in one sitting, although you may certainly wish to do so as some police agency exams take up to three hours to complete. You should, however, use a stop watch or other device to time each segment of the test so that you can simulate test conditions.

| DIAGNOSTIC EXAM COMPETENCIES | | | |
|---|---|---|---|
| **SECTION** | **COMPETENCY** | **QUESTIONS** | **TIME ALLOWED** |
| Part 1 | Observation and Memorization | 20 | 20 minutes |
| Part 2 | Vocabulary and Mechanics | 30 | 30 minutes |
| Part 3 | Grammar | 25 | 35 minutes |
| Part 4 | Reading Comprehension | 10 | 20 minutes |
| Part 5 | Judgment and Logic | 20 | 30 minutes |
| Part 6 | Problem Solving | 30 | 45 minutes |
| | Total | 135 | 3 hours |

Use the Answer Sheet on pages 49–50 to record your answers for each of the six tests. Ensure that the answer you provide on the sheet corresponds with the question number of the Diagnostic Exam. The purpose of the Diagnostic Exam is for you to identify your overall strengths and any areas where you need to improve. It will provide a baseline for you to assess how you may score on a police agency's entrance exam. Once you know where you stand, you can then use the information and strategies provided in the subsequent chapters and follow-up practice examinations to improve your overall competency in any of the specific subjects that you may need to target.

# ANSWER SHEET

## PART 1: Observation and Memorization

1. Ⓐ Ⓑ Ⓒ Ⓓ    6. Ⓐ Ⓑ Ⓒ Ⓓ     11. Ⓐ Ⓑ Ⓒ Ⓓ    16. Ⓐ Ⓑ Ⓒ Ⓓ
2. Ⓐ Ⓑ Ⓒ Ⓓ    7. Ⓐ Ⓑ Ⓒ Ⓓ     12. Ⓐ Ⓑ Ⓒ Ⓓ    17. Ⓐ Ⓑ Ⓒ Ⓓ
3. Ⓐ Ⓑ Ⓒ Ⓓ    8. Ⓐ Ⓑ Ⓒ Ⓓ     13. Ⓐ Ⓑ Ⓒ Ⓓ    18. Ⓐ Ⓑ Ⓒ Ⓓ
4. Ⓐ Ⓑ Ⓒ Ⓓ    9. Ⓐ Ⓑ Ⓒ Ⓓ     14. Ⓐ Ⓑ Ⓒ Ⓓ    19. Ⓐ Ⓑ Ⓒ Ⓓ
5. Ⓐ Ⓑ Ⓒ Ⓓ    10. Ⓐ Ⓑ Ⓒ Ⓓ    15. Ⓐ Ⓑ Ⓒ Ⓓ    20. Ⓐ Ⓑ Ⓒ Ⓓ

## PART 2: Vocabulary and Mechanics

21. Ⓐ Ⓑ Ⓒ Ⓓ    29. Ⓐ Ⓑ Ⓒ Ⓓ    37. Ⓐ Ⓑ Ⓒ Ⓓ    44. Ⓐ Ⓑ Ⓒ Ⓓ
22. Ⓐ Ⓑ Ⓒ Ⓓ    30. Ⓐ Ⓑ Ⓒ Ⓓ    38. Ⓐ Ⓑ Ⓒ Ⓓ    45. Ⓐ Ⓑ Ⓒ Ⓓ
23. Ⓐ Ⓑ Ⓒ Ⓓ    31. Ⓐ Ⓑ Ⓒ Ⓓ    39. Ⓐ Ⓑ Ⓒ Ⓓ    46. Ⓐ Ⓑ Ⓒ Ⓓ
24. Ⓐ Ⓑ Ⓒ Ⓓ    32. Ⓐ Ⓑ Ⓒ Ⓓ    40. Ⓐ Ⓑ Ⓒ Ⓓ    47. Ⓐ Ⓑ Ⓒ Ⓓ
25. Ⓐ Ⓑ Ⓒ Ⓓ    33. Ⓐ Ⓑ Ⓒ Ⓓ    41. Ⓐ Ⓑ Ⓒ Ⓓ    48. Ⓐ Ⓑ Ⓒ Ⓓ
26. Ⓐ Ⓑ Ⓒ Ⓓ    34. Ⓐ Ⓑ Ⓒ Ⓓ    42. Ⓐ Ⓑ Ⓒ Ⓓ    49. Ⓐ Ⓑ Ⓒ Ⓓ
27. Ⓐ Ⓑ Ⓒ Ⓓ    35. Ⓐ Ⓑ Ⓒ Ⓓ    43. Ⓐ Ⓑ Ⓒ Ⓓ    50. Ⓐ Ⓑ Ⓒ Ⓓ
28. Ⓐ Ⓑ Ⓒ Ⓓ    36. Ⓐ Ⓑ Ⓒ Ⓓ

## PART 3: Grammar

51. Ⓐ Ⓑ Ⓒ Ⓓ    58. Ⓐ Ⓑ Ⓒ Ⓓ    64. Ⓐ Ⓑ Ⓒ Ⓓ    70. Ⓐ Ⓑ Ⓒ Ⓓ
52. Ⓐ Ⓑ Ⓒ Ⓓ    59. Ⓐ Ⓑ Ⓒ Ⓓ    65. Ⓐ Ⓑ Ⓒ Ⓓ    71. Ⓐ Ⓑ Ⓒ Ⓓ
53. Ⓐ Ⓑ Ⓒ Ⓓ    60. Ⓐ Ⓑ Ⓒ Ⓓ    66. Ⓐ Ⓑ Ⓒ Ⓓ    72. Ⓐ Ⓑ Ⓒ Ⓓ
54. Ⓐ Ⓑ Ⓒ Ⓓ    61. Ⓐ Ⓑ Ⓒ Ⓓ    67. Ⓐ Ⓑ Ⓒ Ⓓ    73. Ⓐ Ⓑ Ⓒ Ⓓ
55. Ⓐ Ⓑ Ⓒ Ⓓ    62. Ⓐ Ⓑ Ⓒ Ⓓ    68. Ⓐ Ⓑ Ⓒ Ⓓ    74. Ⓐ Ⓑ Ⓒ Ⓓ
56. Ⓐ Ⓑ Ⓒ Ⓓ    63. Ⓐ Ⓑ Ⓒ Ⓓ    69. Ⓐ Ⓑ Ⓒ Ⓓ    75. Ⓐ Ⓑ Ⓒ Ⓓ
57. Ⓐ Ⓑ Ⓒ Ⓓ

## PART 4: Reading Comprehension

76. Ⓐ Ⓑ Ⓒ Ⓓ  79. Ⓐ Ⓑ Ⓒ Ⓓ  82. Ⓐ Ⓑ Ⓒ Ⓓ  85. Ⓐ Ⓑ Ⓒ Ⓓ
77. Ⓐ Ⓑ Ⓒ Ⓓ  80. Ⓐ Ⓑ Ⓒ Ⓓ  83. Ⓐ Ⓑ Ⓒ Ⓓ
78. Ⓐ Ⓑ Ⓒ Ⓓ  81. Ⓐ Ⓑ Ⓒ Ⓓ  84. Ⓐ Ⓑ Ⓒ Ⓓ

## PART 5: Judgment and Logic

86. Ⓐ Ⓑ Ⓒ Ⓓ  91. Ⓐ Ⓑ Ⓒ Ⓓ  96. Ⓐ Ⓑ Ⓒ Ⓓ  101. Ⓐ Ⓑ Ⓒ Ⓓ
87. Ⓐ Ⓑ Ⓒ Ⓓ  92. Ⓐ Ⓑ Ⓒ Ⓓ  97. Ⓐ Ⓑ Ⓒ Ⓓ  102. Ⓐ Ⓑ Ⓒ Ⓓ
88. Ⓐ Ⓑ Ⓒ Ⓓ  93. Ⓐ Ⓑ Ⓒ Ⓓ  98. Ⓐ Ⓑ Ⓒ Ⓓ  103. Ⓐ Ⓑ Ⓒ Ⓓ
89. Ⓐ Ⓑ Ⓒ Ⓓ  94. Ⓐ Ⓑ Ⓒ Ⓓ  99. Ⓐ Ⓑ Ⓒ Ⓓ  104. Ⓐ Ⓑ Ⓒ Ⓓ
90. Ⓐ Ⓑ Ⓒ Ⓓ  95. Ⓐ Ⓑ Ⓒ Ⓓ  100. Ⓐ Ⓑ Ⓒ Ⓓ  105. Ⓐ Ⓑ Ⓒ Ⓓ

## PART 6: Problem Solving

106. Ⓐ Ⓑ Ⓒ Ⓓ  114. Ⓐ Ⓑ Ⓒ Ⓓ  122. Ⓐ Ⓑ Ⓒ Ⓓ  130. Ⓐ Ⓑ Ⓒ Ⓓ
107. Ⓐ Ⓑ Ⓒ Ⓓ  115. Ⓐ Ⓑ Ⓒ Ⓓ  123. Ⓐ Ⓑ Ⓒ Ⓓ  131. Ⓐ Ⓑ Ⓒ Ⓓ
108. Ⓐ Ⓑ Ⓒ Ⓓ  116. Ⓐ Ⓑ Ⓒ Ⓓ  124. Ⓐ Ⓑ Ⓒ Ⓓ  132. Ⓐ Ⓑ Ⓒ Ⓓ
109. Ⓐ Ⓑ Ⓒ Ⓓ  117. Ⓐ Ⓑ Ⓒ Ⓓ  125. Ⓐ Ⓑ Ⓒ Ⓓ  133. Ⓐ Ⓑ Ⓒ Ⓓ
110. Ⓐ Ⓑ Ⓒ Ⓓ  118. Ⓐ Ⓑ Ⓒ Ⓓ  126. Ⓐ Ⓑ Ⓒ Ⓓ  134. Ⓐ Ⓑ Ⓒ Ⓓ
111. Ⓐ Ⓑ Ⓒ Ⓓ  119. Ⓐ Ⓑ Ⓒ Ⓓ  127. Ⓐ Ⓑ Ⓒ Ⓓ  135. Ⓐ Ⓑ Ⓒ Ⓓ
112. Ⓐ Ⓑ Ⓒ Ⓓ  120. Ⓐ Ⓑ Ⓒ Ⓓ  128. Ⓐ Ⓑ Ⓒ Ⓓ
113. Ⓐ Ⓑ Ⓒ Ⓓ  121. Ⓐ Ⓑ Ⓒ Ⓓ  129. Ⓐ Ⓑ Ⓒ Ⓓ

# PART 1: OBSERVATION AND MEMORIZATION

 **You have 20 minutes to complete Part 1 of the Diagnostic Exam.**

## Instructions

1. Study the photograph of a crime scene in Figure 1 below for a maximum of **two minutes** and memorize as much detail about the photograph as possible.

2. You are not permitted to make any written notes or refer back to the photograph when answering the subsequent questions.

3. After two minutes have passed, turn the page and read the Police Officer Safety bulletin (Figure 2). You are only permitted to study the bulletin for **three minutes**.

4. You are not permitted to make any written notes or refer back to the Police Officer Safety bulletin when answering the subsequent questions.

5. Answer the questions in sequential order.

Start your timer and begin Part 1 of the Diagnostic Exam now.

STUDY THE PHOTOGRAPH FOR A MAXIMUM OF TWO MINUTES.

**Figure 1.** Gambling Den Homicide

**OFFICER SAFETY BULLETIN**

| | |
|---|---|
| Caution: | Armed and Dangerous |
| | Mental Instability |
| Wanted: | Warrant of Arrest for assault causing bodily harm |
| Name: | McLean, Martin David |
| Aliases: | David Johnstone, Mick McLean, MC |
| Date of Birth: | September 12, 1963 |
| Description: | Caucasian male, 188 cm, 102 kg, stocky build, short salt and pepper hair, blue eyes |
| Scars/Marks: | Tattoo of eagle on left shoulder; tattoo "forever knights, knights forever" right forearm; 3 cm scar on left thumb |
| History: | Criminal record for armed robbery, drug trafficking, assault, assaulting a police officer, and driving offences |
| Occupation: | Motorcycle mechanic, scrap metal dealer |
| Address: | 17673 192A Ave. North Battleford, Saskatchewan |
| Associates: | Darrel Kingston, Martin Van Hoeven, Cynthia Cromwell |

McLean is the vice-president of the Dusty Knights outlaw motorcycle gang. He is becoming increasingly violent and showing signs of mental instability. On 2014-May-15, McLean was involved in an assault on two fellow Dusty Knights gang members. He attacked Jason Kingsly and his brother-in-law Angelo Cromwell with a ball-peen hammer, causing serious injuries to both of them. Kingsly will require facial reconstruction surgery and Cromwell has a broken left arm and right orbital fracture. He accused them of being police informants and threatened to kill anyone in the gang who was found to be an informant.

McLean is believed to have access to firearms. He is antipolice. Use extreme caution if located.

There is currently a warrant for his arrest for assault causing bodily harm. His current whereabouts are unknown.

**Figure 2.** Officer Safety Bulletin

QUESTIONS 1–10 RELATE TO INFORMATION PICTURED IN FIGURE 1.

1. How many bottles of beer were on the table in Figure 1?

   (A) 2
   (B) 3
   (C) 4
   (D) 5

2. What did the deceased person have in his left hand?

   (A) knife
   (B) playing card
   (C) gun
   (D) unknown

3. What is the approximate time that the photograph was taken?

   (A) 9:30
   (B) 2:45
   (C) 6:15
   (D) 12:50

4. The person that had been sitting on the left-hand side of the picture was likely drinking:

   (A) wine
   (B) beer
   (C) hard liquor
   (D) nothing

5. How many playing cards are visible "face up" on the table?

   (A) 13
   (B) 11
   (C) 9
   (D) 5

6. What weapon was used to kill the victim?

   (A) shotgun
   (B) butcher knife
   (C) unknown
   (D) pistol

7. How many individuals were apparently playing poker?

   (A) 2
   (B) 3
   (C) 4
   (D) 5

8. What was on the ledge beside the victim?

   (A) picture frame
   (B) vase of flowers
   (C) butcher knife
   (D) plant

9. The muzzle (front end) of the shotgun was facing

   (A) towards the left
   (B) towards the right
   (C) towards the top of the picture
   (D) towards the bottom of the picture

10. The victim was wearing a

   (A) long-sleeved dress shirt
   (B) sweater
   (C) striped shirt
   (D) checkered shirt

QUESTIONS 11–20 RELATE TO INFORMATION FOUND IN FIGURE 2.

11. Martin McLean has a warrant for his arrest for

   (A) assault
   (B) assault with a weapon
   (C) assault causing bodily harm
   (D) aggravated assault

12. McLean belongs to an outlaw motorcycle gang, where he currently is the

   (A) treasurer
   (B) secretary
   (C) president
   (D) vice-president

13. McLean's last known address in North Battleford, Saskatchewan was

   (A) 17673 192A Ave.
   (B) 16976 173A Ave.
   (C) 19263 169A Ave.
   (D) 13767 176A Ave.

14. McLean has a criminal history for

   (A) sexual assault, fraud, drug trafficking
   (B) assault, theft, driving offences
   (C) armed robbery, extortion, drug trafficking
   (D) assault, armed robbery, drug trafficking

15. Who did McLean allegedly assault?

    (A) Dusty Knight
    (B) Darrel Kingston
    (C) Angelo Van Hoeven
    (D) Jason Kingsly

16. One of the victims received the following injury

    (A) broken left leg
    (B) broken right arm
    (C) broken left arm
    (D) broken right leg

17. Which of the following is correct?

    (A) McLean has a tattoo of an eagle on his right shoulder.
    (B) McLean has "forever knights, knights forever" tattooed on his right forearm.
    (C) McLean has a 5-cm scar on his right thumb.
    (D) McLean has "Cynthia" tattooed on his left shoulder.

18. McLean is also known to use the following alias:

    (A) Marty
    (B) Double M
    (C) Big Mick
    (D) MC

19. McLean is known to previously work as a

    (A) roofer
    (B) general labourer
    (C) scrap metal dealer
    (D) heavy duty mechanic

20. Which month was McLean born in?

    (A) February
    (B) May
    (C) September
    (D) November

 **STOP** **END OF DIAGNOSTIC EXAM—PART 1**

# PART 2: VOCABULARY AND MECHANICS

 **You have 30 minutes to complete Part 2 of the Diagnostic Exam.**

## Instructions

This section is designed to assess your ability to use proper English vocabulary and the writing mechanics of spelling, punctuation, and capitalization. The first half of this section uses multiple-choice questions to measure your ability to identify proper word usage. These words are infrequently used words in common language; however, they frequently appear in entrance exams. The next segment asks you to identify one misspelled word out of four choices. There will be only one misspelled word per question.

Finally, the last part of this section provides questions that contain a written sentence that has various words and punctuation marks underlined. Identify which of the underlined parts of the sentence are grammatical errors. There is only one error in each question.

You have 30 minutes to answer the following 30 questions. Start your timer and begin Part 2 now.

21. The superintendent had a _____ voice that could be heard coming from his office at the opposite end of the building.

    (A) spurious
    (B) strident
    (C) mellifluous
    (D) ribald

22. The instructor's lecture was so _____ that nearly half of the police recruits were dozing off by the time he was finished.

    (A) idyllic
    (B) mundane
    (C) ribald
    (D) stringent

23. The drug addict was such a _____ user that he simply could not overcome his habit.

    (A) inveterate
    (B) frugal
    (C) pragmatic
    (D) gullible

24. The constables were bothered by the _____ presence of their supervisor; he seemed to show up at every call they went to.

    (A) vestigial

    (B) arcane

    (C) ubiquitous

    (D) morose

25. The forensic investigators went through the crime scene with _____ care.

    (A) iniquitous

    (B) irascible

    (C) litigious

    (D) meticulous

26. The traffic court judge was so self-absorbed; he would _____ at great length when explaining his reasons for judgment.

    (A) pontificate

    (B) ingratiate

    (C) commiserate

    (D) ornate

27. The stubborn sergeant was known for his _____ refusal to embrace community policing initiatives.

    (A) pragmatic

    (B) recalcitrant

    (C) toady

    (D) petulant

28. While searching the woods for a lost person, the police search team made a(n) _____ discovery of key evidence in an unrelated unsolved murder case.

    (A) obsequious

    (B) serendipitous

    (C) imperious

    (D) solicitous

29. The police spokesperson decided to ignore the reporter's _____ questions because they were all so ridiculous.

    (A) sycophantic

    (B) pragmatic

    (C) indomitable

    (D) inane

30. The new recruit respected her field trainer's opinions and work ethic and wanted to _____ her career after his.

    (A) instigate

    (B) exhort

    (C) emulate

    (D) ossify

31. Which of the following words is misspelled?

    (A) catalogue
    (B) vigilant
    (C) seperate
    (D) auxiliary

32. Which of the following words is misspelled?

    (A) camaraderie
    (B) deceive
    (C) corollary
    (D) handywork

33. Which of the following words is misspelled?

    (A) liason
    (B) foresee
    (C) accessory
    (D) susceptible

34. Which of the following words is misspelled?

    (A) silhouette
    (B) intersede
    (C) leisure
    (D) sacrilegious

35. Which of the following words is misspelled?

    (A) renowned
    (B) occurrence
    (C) maneouvre
    (D) harass

36. Indicate the error in the following sentence.

    RCMP Corporal Arnold said, he had to drive two hours east to Williams Lake to attend the motor vehicle collision.

    (A) Corporal
    (B) said,
    (C) east
    (D) Lake

37. Indicate the error in the following sentence.

    This winter, Constable Davis said she will enroll in Spanish classes on Tuesday evenings at McGill university.

    (A) winter
    (B) Spanish
    (C) Tuesday
    (D) university

38. Indicate the error in the following sentence.

I think Constable Trent has an attitude <u>problem,</u> I've heard him say to <u>motorists,</u> "I don't care if you fight the ticket,"<u> and</u> "Who cares if I lose the case in traffic <u>court."</u>

(A) problem,
(B) motorists,
(C) and
(D) court."

39. Indicate the error in the following sentence.

"You take out the <u>Police Wagon</u> <u>tonight,"</u> <u>said</u> Constable Smythe, <u>"and</u> I'll take it out tomorrow night."

(A) Police Wagon
(B) tonight,"
(C) said
(D) "and

40. Indicate the error in the following sentence.

Officer Johnson said to his <u>peers,</u> <u>"We</u> need to get a search warrant for the <u>premises</u> if we want the charges to <u>stick".</u>

(A) peers,
(B) "We
(C) premises
(D) stick".

41. Which of the following words means audacity?

(A) hateful
(B) violent
(C) disposable
(D) boldness

42. Which of the following words means absolve?

(A) fix
(B) understand
(C) forgive
(D) hinder

43. Which of the following words means reproach?

(A) blame
(B) deny
(C) retreat
(D) renew

44. Which of the following words means indigent?

    (A) angry
    (B) native
    (C) poor
    (D) harmless

45. Which of the following words means sublime?

    (A) robust
    (B) uplifting
    (C) severe
    (D) powerful

46. Indicate the error in the following sentence.

    Constable Greg had already loaned his ticket book to another officer, so he used Constable Bentleys' ticket book to write the violator a citation.

    (A) loaned
    (B) officer,
    (C) Bentleys'
    (D) violator

47. Indicate the error in the following sentence.

    The urban myth was that the criminal died from led poisoning four years after being shot.

    (A) urban
    (B) led
    (C) poisoning
    (D) years

48. Indicate the error in the following sentence.

    The Sergeant was upset that the constables' lunchroom was littered with discarded boxes and dirty dishes.

    (A) Sergeant
    (B) constables'
    (C) lunchroom
    (D) dishes

49. Indicate the error in the following sentence.

    Constable Farnsworth, the school's liaison officer, met with the principle to discuss the recent occurrences of graffiti around the school property.

    (A) liaison
    (B) principle
    (C) occurrences
    (D) graffiti

50. Indicate the error in the following sentence.

The new Real Time Intelligence <u>Centre</u> will <u>co-locate</u> law enforcement officers from various agencies, such as <u>provincial</u> corrections, <u>sherrifs</u>, and border guards.

(A) Centre
(B) co-locate
(C) provincial
(D) sherrifs

**STOP**   **END OF DIAGNOSTIC EXAM—PART 2**

# PART 3: GRAMMAR

 **You have 35 minutes to complete Part 3 of the Diagnostic Exam.**

## Directions

This section requires you to identify grammatical errors frequently found in sentence structure and word usage. For the many of these multiple-choice questions, you are required to identify in each question which one of the four sentences is most grammatically correct. That is, other choices may be complete sentences, but have poor structure, misplaced modifiers, poor subject-verb agreement, and so on. Therefore, these types of questions can be more challenging than the previous section.

Read over each question and corresponding answer choices carefully. Select the best answer.

You have 35 minutes to answer the following 25 questions. Start your timer and begin Part 3 now.

51. Which of the following statements is the most grammatically correct?
   (A) The superintendent said that the Robbery Squad position was between me and Constable Erickson.
   (B) The superintendent said that the Robbery Squad position was between Constable Erickson and me.
   (C) The superintendent said that the Robbery Squad position was between Constable Erickson and I.
   (D) The Robbery Squad position was between Constable Erickson and I, the superintendent said.

52. Which of the following statements is the most grammatically correct?
   (A) Tomorrow, it will be announced by the Chief, her new crime reduction strategy.
   (B) It is to be announced by the Chief tomorrow, her new crime reduction strategy.
   (C) Tomorrow, the Chief will be announcing her new crime reduction strategy.
   (D) The Chief is announcing tomorrow, her new crime reduction strategy.

53. Which of the following statements is the most grammatically correct?
   (A) The sergeant told the two officers that despite the fact the victim succumbed to her injuries, they tried real hard to save her life and done all they could.
   (B) Despite the fact that the victim had succumb to her injuries, the sergeant told the two officers they had tried really hard to save her and had done all they could.
   (C) The sergeant told the two officers that they had tried really hard and done all they could, despite the fact that the victim had succumb to her injuries.
   (D) The victim succumbed to her injuries, despite the fact that the two officers had tried real hard and done all they could, said the sergeant.

54. Which of the following statements is the most grammatically correct?

(A) The police academy instructor advised the recruits that among all the skills that each officer possess, common sense are the most important.

(B) The police academy instructor advise the recruits, that amongst all the skills that each officer possess, common sense will be the most important.

(C) Common sense are the most important skill, amongst all that each police officer possesses, advised the police academy instructor.

(D) The police academy instructor advised the recruits that among all the skills that each officer possesses, common sense is the most important.

55. Which of the following statements is the most grammatically correct?

(A) Its important to properly broadcast a suspects' approximate age, height, weight, hair colour, clothing and general marks (such as scars, tattoos, etc.).

(B) It's important to properly broadcast a suspect's approximate age, height, weight, hair colour, clothing, and general marks (such as, scars, tattoos, piercings, etc.).

(C) It's important to properly broadcast a suspects approximate age, height, weight, hair colour, clothing and general marks (such as scars, tattoos, piercings, etc.).

(D) It's important to properly broadcast a suspects: approximate age; height; weight; hair colour; clothing; and general marks (such as scars, tattoos, piercings, etc.).

56. Which of the following statements is the most grammatically correct?

(A) The duty officer wanted to be appraised immediately if the suspect breached the outer perimeter containment zone.

(B) The duty officer wanted to be apprised immediately if the suspect breeched the outer perimeter containment zone.

(C) The duty officer wanted to be apprised immediately if the suspect breached the outer perimeter containment zone.

(D) The duty officer wanted to be appraised immediately if the suspect breeched the outer perimeter containment zone.

57. Which of the following statements is the most grammatically correct?

(A) In order to insure the safety of the neighbourhood, the team heavily targeted all signs of illicit activity in the block.

(B) In order to ensure the safety of the neighbourhood, the team heavily targeted all signs of elicit activity in the block.

(C) In order to insure the safety of the neighbourhood, the team heavily targeted all signs of elicit activity in the block.

(D) In order to ensure the safety of the neighbourhood, the team heavily targeted all signs of illicit activity in the block.

58. Which of the following statements is the most grammatically correct?

(A) The staff was upset that their paycheques were over a week late.

(B) The staff was upset that their paycheques was over a week late.

(C) The staff were upset that their paycheques were over a week late

(D) The staff were upset that there paycheques were over a week late.

59. Which of the following statements is the most grammatically correct?

(A) Constable Franklin likes pistol shooting, is a good marksman and has enjoyed deer hunts.

(B) Constable Franklin likes: pistol shooting; is a good marksman; and, has deer hunted.

(C) Constable Franklin likes pistol shooting and deer hunting and is a good marksman.

(D) Constable Franklin, is a good marksman, and likes pistol shooting and has enjoyed deer hunts.

60. Which of the following statements is the most grammatically correct?

(A) Sergeant Conrad was one who liked to work with at-risk youth and also liked to work in the Drug Section, as a constable.

(B) As a constable, Sergeant Conrad was one whom liked to work with at-risk youth and also liked to work in the Drug Section.

(C) As a constable, Sergeant Conrad was one who liked to work with at-risk youth and also liked working in the Drug Section.

(D) As a constable, Sergeant Conrad liked to work in the Drug Section and liked to work with at-risk youth.

61. Which option best completes the following sentence?

The watch commander stated that with all the recent transfers, _____ going to take a while before the team returns to _____ authorized strength.

(A) it's / its

(B) its' / it's

(C) its / it's

(D) it's / its'

62. Which option best completes the following sentence?

Neither Constable Gunson _____ Constable Rudy could protect _____ from the knife-wielding attacker.

(A) or / themselves

(B) and / themself

(C) nor / himself

(D) nor / themselves

63. Which option best completes the following sentence?

The Chief wanted to know _____ arrested "Jimmy the Knife" last night, and _____ else assisted.

(A) whom / whomever

(B) who / whomever

(C) whom / whoever

(D) who / whoever

64. Which option best completes the following sentence?

Several personal attributes _____ for an effective police _____ strong communication skills is probably the most important.

(A) make / officer; however,
(B) makes / officer, however,
(C) make / officer—however,
(D) makes / officer. However

65. Which option best completes the following sentence?

Sergeant Jones stated, "Since _____ overdue to attend, either Constable Jack or Constable Sparks _____ assigned to the Block Watch meeting."

(A) where / is
(B) we're / are
(C) we're / is
(D) were / are

66. Which option best completes the following sentence?

The chief's executive assistant was asking _____ personal vehicle was parked in the chief's spot; it certainly _____ belong there.

(A) who's / doesn't
(B) whose / dosen't
(C) who's / don't
(D) whose / doesn't

67. Which option best completes the following sentence?

Constable Robertson and _____ searched the interior of the _____ for the suspect.

(A) me, premise
(B) I / premise
(C) I / premises
(D) me / premises

68. Which option best completes the following sentence?

Constable Bird always stated she would rather work an active night shift _____ have some _____ daytime office job.

(A) than / stationary
(B) then / stationery
(C) than / stationery
(D) then / stationary

69. Which option best completes the following sentence?

Detective Dillingsworth was an _____ investigator with an impressive arrest and was proud to _____ the Chief's Commendation.

(A) affective / accept

(B) effective / except

(C) effective / accept

(D) affective / except

70. Which of the following words means *demure*?

(A) modest

(B) insolent

(C) gloomy

(D) fragile

71. Indicate the error in the following sentence.

Constable Cory is a part-time <u>Criminology</u> instructor at the local <u>college</u>. Her students appear to enjoy the <u>courses</u> <u>immensely</u>.

(A) Criminology

(B) college

(C) courses

(D) immensely

72. Indicate the error in the following sentence.

Three provincial <u>attorneys-general</u> from across Canada assembled outside the <u>colisseum</u> before being introduced at the <u>national</u> police <u>memorial</u> service.

(A) attorneys-general

(B) colisseum

(C) national

(D) memorial

73. Indicate the error in the following sentence.

There must be some <u>instance</u> during <u>their</u> careers that all Canadian police officers ask <u>themselves</u>, "<u>have</u> I made a difference?"

(A) instance

(B) their

(C) themselves

(D) have

74. Which of the following statements is the most grammatically correct?

(A) Rocco, the legendary police service dog, having worked a long and successful career, was retired last year.

(B) Rocco, having worked a long and successful career, was a legendary police service dog and was retired last year.

(C) Having worked a long and successful career, Rocco the legendary police service dog, retired last year.

(D) Rocco the legendary police service dog, retired last year. Having worked a long and successful career.

75. Which of the following words is misspelled?

(A) Sergeant
(B) Inspector
(C) Superintendant
(D) Lieutenant

**STOP**    **END OF DIAGNOSTIC EXAM—PART 3**

# PART 4: READING COMPREHENSION

 **You have 20 minutes to complete Part 4 of the Diagnostic Exam.**

## Directions

This reading comprehension section requires that you read through two separate articles from law enforcement-related journals. The articles are approximately 700 words in length, and there are five multiple-choice questions for each article.

Answer each question based only on the information provided. You may refer to the reading material when answering the questions. The paragraphs for each of the articles are numbered so that you can refer to them when analysing your answers.

You have 20 minutes to read the two passages and answer a total of 10 questions. Start your timer and begin Part 4 now.

QUESTIONS 76–80 ARE BASED SOLELY ON THE INFORMATION CONTAINED IN THE FOLLOWING ARTICLE.

**ARTICLE ONE**

**Breaking the Cycle**

By Sigrid Forberg

1 A mark on their criminal record can limit a youth's options well into adulthood. Once they've entered the criminal justice system, it's hard to turn their lives around. But under the Youth Criminal Justice Act (YCJA), police can exercise extrajudicial measures when youth get involved in crime.

2 With that in mind, the RCMP in New Brunswick has set out to divert at-risk youth from the courts by linking them with community services. Research has suggested that if the risk factors that originally led youth to crime are dealt with, it has a long-term impact on reducing crime.

3 Insp. Rick Shaw, the officer in charge of the crime reduction unit in New Brunswick, says the RCMP is very good at catching bad guys and putting them in jail, but that the basic principles of policing speak to a responsibility to prevent crime as well.

4 "Canada is a safe country because parents and schools are doing a great job with most youth, but there is always that group who are starting to get involved in crime," says Shaw. "They aren't prolific offenders or career criminals, but they may be on that trajectory and we have an obligation to use the YCJA to assist them." That group of youth, the moderate to high-risk teens from ages 12 to 17, can often still turn things around with the help of the right services.

5 Shaw has overseen the implementation of the Youth Intervention Diversion program in New Brunswick. Community Programs Officers (CPOs) connect with various members of the community from school counsellors to mental health professionals and addiction services. The CPOs are civilian members of the RCMP. Until 2009, their jobs mostly consisted of doing school presentations and interacting with low-risk kids. Seema Poirier, a CPO in Campbellton, says the changes have been very positive for all involved.

6 "The whole point is to avoid youth getting a criminal record so they can get their lives back on track," says Poirier. "I think it's something we have to do for the kids. When we adjust their issues from the start, rather than 25 calls for service in the future, they might only need three."

7 But it's not only about reducing the burden for police officers. Poirier says the creation of the diversion committee and having those contacts makes it easier to share information and find more holistic solutions in a timely way.

8 On the other hand, it's not a get-out-of-jail-free card. If youth choose to continue committing crimes, they'll face charges the next time around. Véronique Essiembre, a social worker with addiction services in Campbellton, says keeping young people out of the criminal justice system can make a world of difference.

9 One youth that she dealt with recently was caught with a large amount of drugs. Just 15 years old, Essiembre says he didn't understand the implications of having a criminal record, which could stand in the way of finding work for the rest of his life. The unfortunate irony in limiting their ability to get a job is how helpful employment can be to getting youth back on the right track.

10 "When they have a job, my goodness, it makes such a positive difference in their lives, even with self-esteem or their drug use," says Essiembre. "But if they've been labelled as someone with a criminal record, they might continue that dangerous or risky behaviour."

11 Sometimes diversion can be a tough sell for members who already have a lot on their plates—it does take more time to intervene rather than press charges. But in the long run, it ends up taking files off their desks. "It just makes sense to put this on our plates," says Poirier. "Because a lot of us are already connected in the community, we're able to be here for consistency. I think just the fact that community partners and youth are willing to participate shows that it's successful." And they've seen success with many of the candidates. Essiembre says she thinks they got to the young man at the right time to turn things around. "This is about getting the right youth to the right services at the right time," says Shaw. "You can't do that until you know the circumstances behind their behaviour so you need to do those screenings and assessments. You have to diagnose before you prescribe."

*The above article is reprinted courtesy of the RCMP Gazette, as published in Vol. 75, No. 2, 2013.*

76. According to the article, the New Brunswick extrajudicial measures program

    (A) makes it difficult for youth to turn their lives around.

    (B) is implemented by a team of social workers and RCMP officers.

    (C) is designed to keep at-risk youth out of the court system.

    (D) is specifically tailored for drug addicted youth.

77. Why does Véronique Essiembre support the Youth Intervention Diversion program?

   (A) She does not believe that a young person should go to jail.
   (B) She's concerned about the lasting effects of labelling a youth as someone with a criminal record.
   (C) Because the program offers employment for youth.
   (D) Because these prolific offenders need treatment, not jail.

78. Why does Seema Poirier suggest that some police officers may not initially support the program?

   (A) Because police officers are already connected to their communities.
   (B) Because diversion programs create more work for officers than simply laying criminal charges.
   (C) Because the programs are like get-out-of-jail free cards.
   (D) Because many police officers do not like having to work with social workers.

79. In this specific article, what is a CPO?

   (A) social worker
   (B) Community Police Officer
   (C) RCMP constable
   (D) RCMP civilian employee

80. What does the article's title, "Breaking the Cycle" refer to?

   (A) The RCMP should stop simply arresting every youth that breaks the law.
   (B) At-risk youth need to be identified early and provided with holistic programs and treatment before they get criminal records.
   (C) The RCMP need to develop programs for youth that break the drug addiction cycle.
   (D) It's time to stop the circular belief that jailing offenders will prevent crime.

QUESTIONS 81–85 ARE BASED SOLELY ON THE INFORMATION CONTAINED IN THE FOLLOWING ARTICLE.

**ARTICLE TWO**

## Web-Based Tools Help Better Manage Major Events

By Ashley Bedard

1 As Canada's national police force, the RCMP often takes the lead on security for major events. When Vancouver won the bid for the 2010 Olympic and Paralympic Games, RCMP Protective Policing recognized a need for new technology to manage major events and the tremendous volume of security background checks required to grant individuals access to venues. With no suitable software or tools on the market, the RCMP developed its own.

2 To address major events management, the RCMP developed the web-based Event Management System (EMS), a user-friendly tool for managing the planning, mobilization, and situational awareness phases of an event.

3 The planning module allows coordinators to assign and manage tasks and upload shared documents. A collaborative tool, it can handle hundreds of users at once,

including partner agencies. For example, the Ontario Provincial Police shared information through the EMS planning module for the G8 and G20 Summits in Toronto, for which the RCMP was also the security lead.

4. The mobilization module facilitates human resource management for major events. A coordinator can set quotas for roles and shifts needed to secure venues or areas and assign specific qualifications to each position.

5. The EMS connects to the RCMP's Human Resource Management Information System, making it easy to search for people who match those requirements. Once people have been identified and accepted into the event, they can go online to view shift details, instructions, and travel and accommodation information.

6. Insp. John McCarthy, the RCMP officer in charge of mobilizing more than 6,000 people for the G8 and G20 Summits, and his team were the first to use the full EMS mobilization module. "We gave it a real workout," says McCarthy. "Having used the EMS, I can't imagine how people did this before."

7. The situational board module of the EMS is used to capture incidents such as protests and accidents at events. Occurrences are logged and viewed on a board or as icons on a mapping feature called the Common Operating Picture. Clicking on an icon provides security officials with incident details and applicable standard operating procedures, which helps track occurrences and reposition resources when necessary.

8. Although built for planned major events, the EMS has great potential for unplanned events, such as a potential bomb threat or a major accident. Hypothetical events can be created in the EMS to identify resources or crisis teams, standard operating procedures, and maps. "Should the event actually occur, this information would be ready," says Emmanuel Mazy, EMS team leader. "This kind of crisis planning can save time and lives."

9. To gain access to venues for major events, individuals such as staff, volunteers, and members of the media must seek accreditation through a security background check. To manage the high volume of requests, the RCMP developed the web-based Security Accreditation Management System (SAMS) to work alongside the EMS. Whereas security officials previously had to search several databases separately in a labour-intensive process, SAMS coordinates the process of checking various law-enforcement databases.

10. Depending on an event's requirements, this could include: the Canadian Police Information Centre, the Police Reporting and Occurrence System, and BC's Police Records Information Management Environment as well as those of partner agencies such as the Canada Border Services Agency, Citizenship and Immigration Canada, and the Canadian Security Intelligence Service. In May 2010, SAMS was expanded to connect to the Police Information Portal and Interpol. An individual's information is collected by the federal agency responsible for the event and entered into SAMS, where the RCMP and participating agencies can then access it. Each agency searches its own databases and marks the file as green or red in SAMS. When green marks are returned by all agencies, the RCMP informs the host agency that the person may be accredited. If a red mark is returned by one or more agencies, an RCMP risk assessor evaluates the information and makes a recommendation.

11. Using SAMS, the RCMP conducted more than 205,000 security background checks for the 2010 Olympic and Paralympic Games. The system was also used for United States

President Barack Obama's visit to Ottawa in 2009 and for the G8 and G20 Summits in 2010. "Without SAMS, this volume of background checks would have been a challenge," says Supt. Brendan Heffernan, the RCMP's director of major events. "SAMS has enhanced our capacity to secure major events."

12 Through their successful use at major international sporting events and meetings hosting world leaders, the EMS and SAMS are proving to be valuable technological advances that are helping the RCMP and its partners ensure safe and secure events, while saving both time and money.

*The above article is reprinted courtesy of the RCMP Gazette, as published in Vol. 73, No. 1, 2011.*

81. Why did the RCMP develop the EMS application?

(A) To manage resources and occurrences at major events
(B) To replace the outdated SAMS system
(C) To identify potential bomb threats during the 2010 Olympics
(D) To search multiple law enforcement databases simultaneously

82. Which of the following is not true of SAMS?

(A) It is an application used to assist in background checks.
(B) It is connected to the RCMP's Human Resource Management Information System.
(C) It coordinates searching multiple law enforcement databases.
(D) It can be used in conjunction with EMS at major events.

83. When did the RCMP first utilize the SAMS application?

(A) G8 Summit
(B) G20 Summit
(C) 2010 Olympic and Paralympic games
(D) President Barack Obama's visit to Ottawa

84. Why was RCMP Insp. John McCarthy so impressed with EMS?

(A) It streamlined the accreditation process for major events.
(B) It allowed the police to schedule and monitor the mobilization of thousands of RCMP officers.
(C) It could literally save lives during a major crisis.
(D) The situational board allows police to monitor and capture all occurrences during large-scale events.

85. Which of the following is not indicated as a function of the EMS application?

(A) Responding to unplanned major events, such as natural disasters
(B) Monitoring human resource deployment at major events
(C) Logging significant occurrences at major events
(D) Coordinating law enforcement database searches during major events

 **STOP** **END OF DIAGNOSTIC EXAM—PART 4**

# PART 5: JUDGMENT AND LOGIC

 **You have 30 minutes to complete Part 5 of the Diagnostic Exam.**

## Directions

This section is designed to assess your ability to use sound judgment and logical reasoning skills. Police entrance exams use a variety of tests to measure these competencies; however, the most common are decision-making scenarios, syllogisms, mapping, and pattern solving.

Decision-making scenarios provide a brief description of a typical policing event. You will be then provided with four options for what you believe should be your next step. You are to select the best option. You are not required to know police policy and procedures, the applicable law, or law enforcement tactics—just sound judgment. There are five decision-making questions.

Syllogisms are a form of deductive reasoning in which a logical conclusion is supported by two premise statements. For each question, you are provided with a major premise (first statement) and a minor premise (second statement). You must assume that each statement is true. Choose one of the four conclusion statements that is valid based on the first two statements.

Spatial orientation or mapping questions require you to study a street-view map or a diagram of a traffic intersection and make decisions based on what is portrayed in these scenes. There are five spatial orientation and mapping questions.

Pattern-solving and matching problems require you to use inductive reasoning to identify common characteristics in a series of visual objects or through information provided. You will be shown several images or pieces of information. Choose the correct object or statement that would logically follow. There are a total of five matching and pattern-solving questions.

You have 25 minutes to answer a total of 20 questions. Start your timer and begin Part 5 now.

Questions 86–90 are decision-making scenarios. You are not required to know police policies and procedures, the applicable law, or law enforcement tactics.

86. You pull over a motorist for speeding. When you check his name on the police computer database, you learn that he has a criminal record for sex offences and possession of child pornography. Based on this information, which of the following statements is your best option?

(A) Search his vehicle to determine if he has any child porn in his possession.
(B) Write him a speeding ticket.
(C) Call for a back-up officer to follow him and see where he goes.
(D) Write him a speeding ticket and then conduct a complete motor vehicle inspection to ensure there are no vehicle defects. You are bound to find something wrong.

87. You attend to a robbery at a convenience store where there are three witnesses and the owner who is visibly upset but uninjured. The owner is screaming at you to go find the suspect—a 15-year-old boy with a knife—who ran west on 12th Avenue five minutes ago. Based on this information, which of the following statements is your best option?

(A) Chase after the suspect, he couldn't have gone too far.
(B) Interview each witness separately and obtain detailed written statements from them.
(C) Calm the owner down and call Victim Services, as the owner has experienced significant trauma.
(D) Obtain a suspect description as quickly as possible and broadcast this information to other police officers in the area.

88. You are in your patrol car driving to a report of a break in and theft of jewelry from a home that occurred yesterday, when you come across a serious motor vehicle collision that just occurred. The driver of one vehicle has a serious laceration to the neck and is bleeding profusely. The driver of the other vehicle is getting out of his vehicle and walking away from you. Based on this information, which of the following statements is your best option?

(A) Arrest the driver who is walking away from the scene.
(B) Call for an ambulance and wait for its arrival before heading to the report of the break and enter.
(C) Immediately attend to the injured driver.
(D) Call for the assistance of a supervisor, you are going to need multiple police units to attend.

89. You stop a motorist for disobeying a red light. You advise him why he's been pulled over and ask him for his driver's licence. He states, "No, the light was yellow, I didn't do anything wrong." Based on this information, which of the following statements is your best option?

   (A) Arrest him for obstructing a police officer in the lawful execution of your duties.
   (B) Call for a cover officer before making your next move.
   (C) Advise the driver that there is a dispute process that he can follow, but he's still required to produce his license to you.
   (D) Write him a ticket for disobeying a yellow light.

90. You and your partner attend to a call of a disturbance on the sidewalk where two males are yelling at one another. You talk to one male, and your partner talks to the other. The male you are talking to was going to sell his car to the other male, they got into a dispute over the price, and the other male pushed him hard twice in the chest and swore at him. The male you are talking to appears to have been drinking. Based on this information, which of the following statements is your best option?

   (A) Talk to your partner and find out what the other male's side of the story is.
   (B) Arrest the male that your partner is talking to for assault.
   (C) Arrest the male that you are talking to for being intoxicated in a public place.
   (D) This is a civil dispute over the price of a car and not a police matter.

---

**Questions 91–95 are syllogisms. For each question, you are provided with a major premise (first statement) and a minor premise (second statement). You must assume that each statement is true. Only one of the four conclusion statements is valid based on the first two statements.**

---

91. Some police officers are females.

   All females are strong-willed.

   (A) Therefore, some police officers are not females.
   (B) Therefore, no strong-willed police officers are males.
   (C) Therefore, some police officers are female.
   (D) Therefore, some police officers are strong-willed.

92. All educational things are useful.

   Some websites are not useful.

   (A) Therefore, some useful things are educational.
   (B) Therefore, some websites are educational.
   (C) Therefore, some websites are not educational.
   (D) No valid conclusion can be made.

93. No convicted person is innocent.

Some young men are convicted persons.

(A) Therefore, some innocent persons are young men.
(B) Therefore, some young men are not innocent.
(C) Therefore, all young men are convicted persons.
(D) Therefore, no convicted persons are young men.

94. Some lawyers are not honest.

All lawyers are human.

(A) Therefore, some lawyers are not human.
(B) Therefore, all humans are not lawyers.
(C) Therefore, some humans are not honest.
(D) Therefore, no human is an honest lawyer.

95. No examination is enjoyable.

Some application processes require an examination.

(A) Therefore, all enjoyment is not an application process.
(B) Therefore, some application processes are not enjoyable.
(C) Therefore, all application processes are not enjoyable.
(D) Therefore, all examinations are not application processes.

Questions 96–97 are spatial orientation and mapping questions and are based solely on the information found in the map below. In this map, all streets are for two-way traffic, unless indicated as one-way, by a one-direction arrow.

**Colder Creek City**

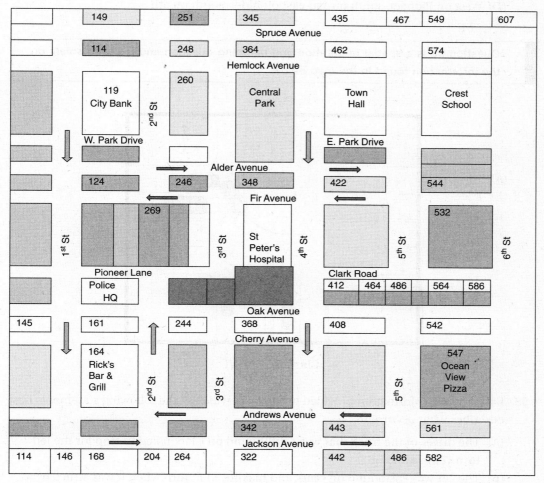

96. You are in your patrol vehicle at the intersection of 2nd Street and Hemlock Ave when you are dispatched to a report of a lost wallet at Ocean View Pizza, 547 Cherry Avenue. Using the map as a reference, what would be the most efficient and most accurate route to this location, while complying with traffic laws?

(A) West on Hemlock, south on 3rd, east on Fir Ave, south on 4th, west on Cherry

(B) South on 2nd, east on Fir, south on 4th, east on Cherry

(C) East on Hemlock, south on 5th, east on Cherry

(D) East on Hemlock, south on 4th, east on Cherry

97. You are in your patrol car in front of Headquarters on Pioneer Lane. You are dispatched to a report of found property, a discarded wallet, at 486 Clark Road. Using the map as a reference, what would be the most efficient and most accurate route to this location, while complying with traffic laws?

(A) East on Pioneer, south on 2nd, east on Oak, north on 4th, east on Clark

(B) East on Pioneer, north on 3rd, east on Fir, south on 4th, east on Clark

(C) East on Pioneer, north on 3rd, east on Alder, south on 5th

(D) West on Pioneer, south on 1st, east on Alder, south on 5th

> Question 98 is a spatial orientation and mapping question and is based solely on the information found in the map below.

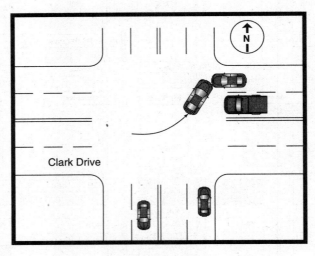

**Clark Drive MVI**

98. Based on the information provided in the map, which of the following statements best describes what occurred?

(A) The driver of the truck that was northbound on Clark failed to stop for the left turn vehicle and hit it.

(B) The car was eastbound on Clark and making a left turn when it was struck by a car westbound in the curb lane on Clark.

(C) The driver of the westbound vehicle failed to stop for through traffic that was eastbound on Clark when it made a left turn.

(D) Eastbound traffic failed to stop for a left turn vehicle, causing a collision.

Question 99 is a spatial orientation and mapping question and is based solely on the information found in the map below.

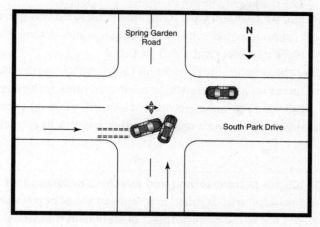

**South Park Drive MVI**

99. Based on the information provided in the map, which of the following statements best describes what occurred?

(A) A vehicle northbound on South Park Drive failed to stop for a red light and struck another vehicle with its driver's side door.

(B) A vehicle eastbound on Spring Garden Road ran a red light and struck a vehicle going the opposite way.

(C) Three vehicles were involved in a t-bone crash. The car on South Park Drive ran a red light.

(D) A vehicle westbound on South Park Drive ran a red light, skidded and crashed into the side of a vehicle travelling southbound on Spring Garden Road.

Question 100 is a spatial orientation and mapping question and is based solely on the information found in the map below.

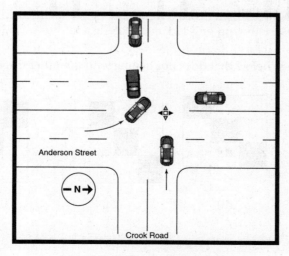

**Anderson Street MVI**

100. Based on the information provided in the map, which of the following statements best describes what occurred?

   (A) A truck that was eastbound on Crook, failed to yield for a left turn vehicle, and hit it on the front driver's side quarter panel.

   (B) The traffic light for east and west traffic on Crook Road was green; a vehicle northbound on Anderson disobeyed a red light while making a left turn and was struck by a truck that was eastbound on Crook.

   (C) The driver of the vehicle southbound on Crook did not notice that the light was red and crashed into a vehicle making a left turn onto Anderson.

   (D) A vehicle eastbound on Anderson made a left turn to travel northbound on Crook. The driver disobeyed a red light and was struck by a truck southbound on Crook.

> Questions 101–105 are pattern-solving and matching problems that require you to identify common characteristics found in a series of visual objects or through information provided. Choose the correct object or statement that would match or complete the pattern. There are a total of five matching and pattern-solving questions.

101. Identify the image below that does not belong with the other three.

   (A)          (B)          (C)          (D)

102. Identify the image below that does not belong with the other three.

   (A)          (B)          (C)          (D)

103. Identify the image below that does not belong with the other three.

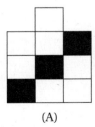  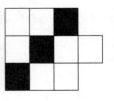 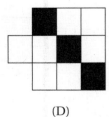

   (A)          (B)          (C)          (D)

104. Select the next image that completes the pattern sequence.

(A)          (B)          (C)          (D)

105. What is the next number in the following pattern?

3, 8, 15, 24, ...

(A) 31

(B) 35

(C) 36

(D) 39

**STOP**  **END OF DIAGNOSTIC EXAM—PART 5**

## PART 6: PROBLEM SOLVING

 **You have 50 minutes to complete Part 6 of the Diagnostic Exam.**

---

### Directions

This section is designed to measure your general mathematical skills. The first 10 questions require you to solve basic mathematical equations. The remaining 20 questions are based on a series of problem-solving statements. Several questions may relate to one specific paragraph.

You are not permitted to use a calculator or any electronic device to assist you in any computation.

You have 50 minutes to answer the following 30 questions. Start your timer and begin Part 6 now.

---

SOLVE THE FOLLOWING MATHEMATICAL EQUATIONS.

106. $63.453 \times 2.13 =$

    (A) 135.15

    (B) 126.92

    (C) 13.51

    (D) 12.692

107. $18.371 - (-3.03) =$

    (A) 15.341

    (B) 21.401

    (C) −15.341

    (D) 13.183

108. $49.028 \div 0.34 =$

    (A) 29.1

    (B) 156.21

    (C) 144.2

    (D) 115.86

109. $39.21 + 16 \div 4 - 23.21 =$

    (A) 24.21

    (B) −9.41

    (C) 13.765

    (D) 20

110. $-74.31 \times -8.04 =$

  (A) −59.74

  (B) 597.45

  (C) −592.74

  (D) 59.741

111. $\dfrac{1}{6} + \dfrac{2}{3} - \dfrac{3}{4} =$

  (A) $\dfrac{1}{3}$

  (B) $\dfrac{4}{9}$

  (C) $\dfrac{3}{4}$

  (D) $\dfrac{1}{12}$

112. $4\dfrac{1}{8} - 2\dfrac{3}{4} =$

  (A) $2\dfrac{3}{4}$

  (B) $1\dfrac{7}{8}$

  (C) $1\dfrac{3}{8}$

  (D) $2\dfrac{1}{4}$

113. $2\dfrac{2}{3} \times 7 =$

  (A) $20\dfrac{1}{7}$

  (B) $18\dfrac{2}{3}$

  (C) $17\dfrac{2}{21}$

  (D) $16\dfrac{2}{9}$

114. $6^3 + 5^3 =$

  (A) $30^9$

  (B) $11^6$

  (C) 216

  (D) 341

115. $(9 \times 3) - 2(45) + 70 =$

(A) 7

(B) 1,195

(C) 49

(D) −16

116. The police department has 45 probationary constables, 67 third class constables, 45 second class constables, and 122 first class constables. What percentage of the police force is comprised of probationary constables?

(A) 12%

(B) 16%

(C) 18%

(D) 22%

117. On four successive days, Constable Morrison drove 56 km, 67 km, 41 km, and 36 km. If the patrol vehicle averages 6 litres of gas per 100 km, approximately how many litres of fuel did the patrol vehicle use during the four days.

(A) 24

(B) 50

(C) 12

(D) Not enough information provided

118. One-half of the police force works in the Patrol Division. One-third of the police agency works in the Investigative Division. What part of the remainder of the police department works somewhere else?

(A) $\dfrac{5}{6}$

(B) $\dfrac{2}{3}$

(C) $\dfrac{3}{12}$

(D) $\dfrac{1}{6}$

119. There are 7 constables, 4 corporals, 3 sergeants, and 1 inspector working at the precinct office. If one person was randomly selected to conduct a departmental survey, what is the probability that a sergeant would be chosen.

(A) $\dfrac{1}{5}$

(B) $\dfrac{1}{3}$

(C) $3\dfrac{3}{12}$

(D) 3:1

120. The ratio of male to female police officers working at the Hankville Police Department is 13:2. If there are 14 females in the department, how many are men?

(A) 251
(B) 91
(C) 61
(D) 101

121. Constable Garrison worked an 11 hour shift. He took his meal break after working for $\frac{1}{3}$ of his shift. How long had he been working before taking his break?

(A) 3 hours, 40 minutes
(B) 3 hours, 30 minutes
(C) 3 hours, 20 minutes
(D) 3 hours, 10 minutes

122. If a large rectangular compound has a perimeter of 150 metres on two sides and 100 metres on the other two sides, how long would it take Officer Cotton to walk the entire perimeter at a rate of 5 km/hour?

(A) 12 minutes
(B) 10 minutes
(C) 8 minutes
(D) 6 minutes

123. Constable Drake responded to an emergency call and drove 3 kilometres in 90 seconds. What was his average speed?

(A) 60 km/h
(B) 90 km/h
(C) 120 km/h
(D) 150 km/h

124. Dorothy the police dispatcher wants to take a trip to the Bahamas and needs to save $1,800. She earns $18 per hour and works 40 hours per week. However, she can only afford to save approximately 25 percent of her weekly paycheque towards the vacation. Approximately how many weeks will Dorothy need to work in order to save enough money to go on the trip?

(A) 9
(B) 10
(C) 11
(D) 12

125. Undercover Officer Jackson paid $45 to purchase half a gram of cocaine powder from the street level dealer. How much would it cost for him to purchase an "8 Ball" which is equal to 3.5 grams?

(A) $228
(B) $285
(C) $315
(D) $355

126. Fraud investigators found that Jim Ponzi had sent three money transactions to an offshore account totalling $735,000. If the first transaction was $75,000 less than $\frac{1}{3}$ of the total, how much was transferred in the first deposit?

(A) $170,000
(B) $245,000
(C) $95,000
(D) $190,000

QUESTIONS 127–128 ARE BASED ON THE INFORMATION CONTAINED IN THE FOLLOWING STATEMENT

Sgt. Drew is the Station NCO and is responsible for approving the laying of criminal charges based on the information contained in a police officer's Report to Crown Counsel (RTCC). He works an 11.5 hour shift and worked four days this week. This week he read 163 RTCCs and approved 129 of these reports for criminal charges.

127. What was the percentage of the total reports read that Sgt. Drew approved for criminal charges?

(A) 70%
(B) 79%
(C) 66%
(D) 75%

128. What is the average number of reports that Sgt. Drew read per hour?

(A) 2.7 per hour
(B) 1.9 per hour
(C) 3.5 per hour
(D) 4.6 per hour

QUESTIONS 129–132 ARE BASED ON THE FOLLOWING INFORMATION

The following table specifies the number of criminal investigations conducted by the OPP Provincial Asset Forfeiture Unit (PAFU), the value of total assets the PAFU seized, and the total value of seized assets that were successfully forfeited to the provincial government from 2007 to 2010.

| OPP ASSET FORFEITURE UNIT 2007–2010 | | | |
| --- | --- | --- | --- |
| YEAR | INVESTIGATIONS | SEIZURES | FORFEITURES |
| 2007 | 599 | $37.5 m | $4.3 m |
| 2008 | 705 | $31.7 m | $6.4 m |
| 2009 | 648 | $44.4 m | $5.3 m |
| 2010 | 498 | $29.6 m | $9.6 m |

129. What was the average number of investigations conducted by the PAFU per year during the four-year period?

(A) 637
(B) 677
(C) 612
(D) 631

130. In 2008, successful forfeitures made up what percentage of total seizures?

(A) 5.2%
(B) 20.2%
(C) 23.6%
(D) 24.7%

131. During the four-year period, the total value of seizures is how much more than the total value of successful forfeitures?

(A) $117.6 m
(B) $232.6 m
(C) $109.5 m
(D) $121.4 m

132. Which year had the best forfeiture to seizure ratio?

(A) 2007
(B) 2008
(C) 2009
(D) 2010

QUESTIONS 133–135 ARE BASED ON THE FOLLOWING INFORMATION

The Toronto Robbery Squad executed a search warrant at the residence of Calvin Reese and located a significant amount of evidence linking him to an armoured car robbery that took place yesterday. In a false ceiling, the police located four duffle bags. Two of the duffle bags contained a total of $431,000 in Canadian cash. The third duffle bag contained $125,000 in U.S. cash. The fourth duffle bag contained $215,000 in U.S. Treasury Bonds and loose U.S. currency.

133. If one of the duffle bags with Canadian currency contained $30,000 more than $\frac{1}{3}$ of the total Canadian cash, how much was in the other bag?

(A) $173,667   → Would be the first Bag.
(B) $143,667
(C) $113,667
(D) $257,334

134. If the U.S. currency (cash and bonds) was worth approx. $1.10 per Canadian dollar. What was the total value (in Canadian currency) of all goods recovered in the search warrant?

    (A) $805,000
    (B) $775,000
    (C) $855,000
    (D) $795,000

135. What percentage of the total value of all goods (in Canadian dollars) did the U.S. Treasury bonds account for?

    (A) 27%
    (B) 29%
    (C) 31%
    (D) 37%

**STOP** END OF DIAGNOSTIC EXAM—PART 6

# ANSWER KEY

## PART 1: Observation and Memorization

| | | | | | | | |
|---|---|---|---|---|---|---|---|
| **1.** | B | **6.** | C | **11.** | C | **16.** | C |
| **2.** | D | **7.** | B | **12.** | D | **17.** | B |
| **3.** | D | **8.** | D | **13.** | A | **18.** | D |
| **4.** | A | **9.** | B | **14.** | D | **19.** | C |
| **5.** | B | **10.** | C | **15.** | D | **20.** | C |

## PART 2: Vocabulary and Mechanics

| | | | | | | | |
|---|---|---|---|---|---|---|---|
| **21.** | B | **29.** | D | **37.** | D | **45.** | B |
| **22.** | B | **30.** | C | **38.** | D | **46.** | C |
| **23.** | A | **31.** | C | **39.** | A | **47.** | B |
| **24.** | C | **32.** | D | **40.** | D | **48.** | A |
| **25.** | D | **33.** | A | **41.** | D | **49.** | B |
| **26.** | A | **34.** | B | **42.** | C | **50.** | D |
| **27.** | B | **35.** | C | **43.** | A | | |
| **28.** | B | **36.** | B | **44.** | C | | |

## PART 3: Grammar

| | | | | | | | |
|---|---|---|---|---|---|---|---|
| **51.** | B | **58.** | A | **65.** | C | **72.** | B |
| **52.** | C | **59.** | C | **66.** | D | **73.** | D |
| **53.** | B | **60.** | D | **67.** | C | **74.** | C |
| **54.** | D | **61.** | A | **68.** | A | **75.** | C |
| **55.** | B | **62.** | C | **69.** | C | | |
| **56.** | C | **63.** | D | **70.** | A | | |
| **57.** | D | **64.** | A | **71.** | A | | |

## PART 4: Reading Comprehension

| | | | |
|---|---|---|---|
| **76.** C | **79.** D | **82.** B | **85.** D |
| **77.** B | **80.** B | **83.** D | |
| **78.** B | **81.** A | **84.** B | |

## PART 5: Judgment and Logic

| | | | |
|---|---|---|---|
| **86.** B | **91.** D | **96.** ~~X~~ D | **101.** B |
| **87.** D | **92.** D | **97.** C | **102.** C |
| **88.** C | **93.** B | **98.** B | **103.** C |
| **89.** C | **94.** C | **99.** D | **104.** C |
| **90.** A | **95.** B | **100.** B | **105.** B |

## PART 6: Problem Solving

| | | | |
|---|---|---|---|
| **106.** A | **114.** D | **122.** D | **130.** B |
| **107.** B | **115.** A | **123.** C | **131.** A |
| **108.** C | **116.** B | **124.** B | **132.** D |
| **109.** D | **117.** C | **125.** C | **133.** A |
| **110.** B | **118.** D | **126.** A | **134.** A |
| **111.** D | **119.** A | **127.** B | **135.** B |
| **112.** C | **120.** B | **128.** C | |
| **113.** B | **121.** A | **129.** C | |

## HOW DID YOU SCORE?

**Part 1: Observation and Memorization**

Strategies that you can use to improve your observation and memorization skills are found in Chapter 6.

Correct Answers: _____/20        Excellent 18–20        Good 15–17        Average 10–14

**Part 2: Vocabulary and Mechanics**

Strategies that you can use to improve your vocabulary, punctuation, and other writing mechanic skills are found in Chapter 7.

Correct Answers: _____/30        Excellent 27–30        Good 23–26        Average 18–22

**Part 3: Grammar**

Strategies that you can use to improve your grammatical skills are found in Chapter 8.

Correct Answers: _____/25        Excellent 22–25        Good 20–22        Average 18–20

**Part 4: Reading Comprehension**

Strategies that you can use to improve your reading comprehension skills are found in Chapter 9.

Correct Answers: _____/10        Excellent 9–10        Good 7–8        Average 5–6

**Part 5: Judgment and Logic**

Strategies that you can use to improve your skills relating to judgment and logic questions are found in Chapter 11.

Correct Answers: _____/20        Excellent 18–20        Good 15–17        Average 10–14

**Part 6: Problem Solving**

Strategies that you can use to improve your mathematical and problem-solving skills are found in Chapter 12.

Correct Answers: _____/30        Excellent 27–30        Good 23–26        Average 18–22

# ANSWERS EXPLAINED

## Part 1: Observation and Memorization

1. **B** There are three beer bottles on the right side of the table.

2. **D** It is unknown what the deceased person has in his left hand. His right arm is on the table, and his left arm is under the table.

3. **D** The roman numeral clock on the wall shows approximately 12:50.

4. **A** On the left side of the table are two bottles of wine, one standing, one on its side, and a half-full glass of wine.

5. **B** There are 11 cards visible. It appears to be a game of Texas Hold 'em Poker. There are five cards dealt on the table, and there is a pair of cards in front of each of the three seats.

6. **C** It is not known how the victim died.

7. **B** There are three sets of hands dealt; three chairs visible; and three types of beverages on the table.

8. **D** On the ledge is a plant behind the fan.

9. **B** The muzzle end of the shotgun is facing towards the right hand side of the picture.

10. **C** The victim is wearing a black golf shirt with a thin white stripe.

11. **C** McLean has a warrant for his arrest for assault causing bodily harm.

12. **D** McLean is the vice-president of the Dusty Knights outlaw motorcycle gang.

13. **A** McLean's last known address was 17673 192A Ave, North Battleford, Saskatchewan.

14. **D** McLean has a criminal record for, among other things, assault, armed robbery, and drug trafficking. You can exclude the other answers through a process of elimination. He does not have a conviction for sexual assault (A), nor theft (B), nor extortion (C).

15. **D** McLean allegedly assaulted Jason Kingsley with a ball-peen hammer. He also assaulted Angelo Cromwell, but his name wasn't one of your choices.

16. **C** Cromwell had a broken left arm and right orbital fracture.

17. **B** McLean has "forever knights, knights forever" tattooed on his right forearm.

18. **D** McLean has several aliases: "David Johnstone," "Mick McLean," and "MC".

19. **C** McLean's previous occupations include being a motorcycle mechanic and a scrap metal dealer.

20. **C** McLean was born on September 12, 1963.

## Part 2: Vocabulary and Mechanics

21. **B** *Strident* means forceful and vocal.

22. **B** *Mundane* means boring and dull.

23. **A** *Inveterate* means chronic and incurable.

24. **C** *Ubiquitous* means omnipresent, or ever-present.

25. **D** *Meticulous* means careful and painstaking.

26. **A** *Pontificate* means to preach and talk on and on.

27. **B** *Recalcitrant* means obstinate and headstrong.

28. **B** *Serendipitous* means opportune and unexpected.

29. **D** *Inane* means absurd and silly.

30. **C** *Emulate* means to imitate and follow.

31. **C** *Seperate* is misspelled. The correct spelling is separate. This is one of the most frequently misspelled words and appears often on entrance exams. For more, see Chapter 7: Spelling.

32. **D** *Handywork* is misspelled. The correct spelling is handiwork. Deceive is spelled correctly—think of the rule "i before e, except after c." Camaraderie, a word with French origins, is also spelled correctly. For more, see Chapter 7: Spelling.

33. **A** *Liason* is misspelled. Remember there are two *i*s in liaison. There are three *e*s in foresee. For susceptible, think of the general rule that if the root word is a complete word, then it usually ends in *able*, if not, then it usually ends in *ible*. For more, see Chapter 7: Spelling.

34. **B** *Intersede* is misspelled. The correct spelling is intercede. For sacrilegious, remember that religious is misspelled. Leisure is an exception to the "i before e" rule. For more, see Chapter 7: Spelling.

35. **C** *Maneouvre* is misspelled. The correct spelling is manoeuvre. You may be tempted to eliminate one of the *r*s in occurrence, or put in an extra *r* in harass, or a *k* in renowned, but they are all correct. For more, see Chapter 7: Spelling.

36. **B** There is no need to put a comma after the word *said*. In this instance, corporal is capitalized because it refers to a title, *Corporal Arnold*. Directions, such as east are not capitalized, and Williams Lake, the name of a place, is capitalized. For more, see Chapter 7: Mechanics and Capitalization.

37. **D** *University* should be capitalized because it refers to a specific place—McGill University. Seasons, such as winter are not capitalized, but languages, such as Spanish and days of the week are. For more, see Chapter 7: Capitalization.

38. **D** The punctuation at the end of the last statement should be a question mark. That is, "Who cares if I lose the case in traffic court?" For more, see Chapter 7: Mechanics.

39. **A** Police Wagon should not be capitalized as it is not a proper noun. The word *and* does not need to be capitalized because the quote is a continuation of a sentence. For more, see Chapter 7: Capitalization.

40. **D** The period at the end of a quoted sentence should be inside the quotation marks. For more, see Chapter 7: Mechanics.

41. **D** *Audacity* means boldness and daring.

42. **C** *Absolve* means to forgive and pardon.

43. **A** *Reproach* means blame and criticism.

44. **C** *Indigent* means poor and needy. *Indignant* means angry, and *indigenous* means native.

45. **B** *Sublime* means uplifting and inspiring.

46. **C** *Bentleys'* should have the apostrophe after the letter *y* showing that the ticket book belongs to him. That is, "he used Constable Bentley's ticket book." For more, see Chapter 7: Mechanics.

47. **B** This is the wrong "led"; it should be the element "lead". For more, see Chapter 8: Homonyms.

48. **A** *Sergeant* should not be capitalized as it is not referring to a specific person's title. The apostrophe placed after the *s* in *constables* is correct in that it shows plural possession of the constables. For more, see Chapter 7: Mechanics.

49. **B** *Principle* is wrong in that it is referring to the school principal. Remember the school principal is your *pal*. For more, see Chapter 8: Homonyms.

50. **D** *Sherrifs* is misspelled. *Centre* should be capitalized because it refers to the name of a specific place and *centre* is the proper Canadian spelling for a place or institution. *Provincial* should not be capitalized, it is not referring to a specific government agency by name, and you do not capitalize after a colon. For more, see Chapter 7: Spelling and Mechanics.

## Part 3: Grammar

51. **B** The preposition *between* should be followed by the objective pronoun (*me*), rather than a subjective pronoun (*I*). For more, see Chapter 8: Sentence Structure.

52. **C** The other options result in a misplaced modifier. For more, see Chapter 8: Sentence Structure.

53. **B** Parallelism is maintained throughout the sentence. The victim "had succumbed" to her injuries, the officers "had tried", and "had done" all they could. The other options contain faulty parallelism and are disjointed. For more see Chapter 8: Faulty Parallelism.

54. **D** This is the only option that maintains subject-verb agreement throughout the statement. For more, see Chapter 8: Subject-Verb Agreement.

55. **B** This is the only statement where commas and apostrophes, which indicate the shortened form of "it is" and possession, are properly placed. For more, see Chapter 8: Mechanics.

56. **C** This is the only sentence that uses the homonyms *apprised* (to be notified) and *breached* (broke free) in their proper context. For more, see Chapter 8: Homonyms.

57. **D** This is the only sentence that uses the homonyms *ensure* (to guarantee) and *illicit* (illegal) in their proper context. For more, see Chapter 8: Homonyms.

58. **A** This is the only sentence with proper subject-verb agreement. *Staff* is a collective noun that is referred to in the singular form. For more, see Chapter 8: Subject-Verb Agreement.

59. **C** This is the only grammatically correct sentence. The other options have faulty parallelism, the sentences are disjointed, or use excessive punctuation. For more, see Chapter 8: Faulty Parallelism.

60. **D** The other sentence options have faulty parallelism or incorrectly use the word *whom*. For more, see Chapter 8: Faulty Parallelism and Other Grammatical Errors.

61. **A** This is the only sentence option with correct use of *it's* (contraction of *it is*) and the homonym *its* (possessive adjective meaning belonging to). For more, see Chapter 8: Homonyms.

62. **C** This is the only sentence with pronoun-antecedent agreement. In this case, the word *neither* creates singular antecedents; therefore, the pronoun must be singular—*himself*. For more, see Chapter 8: Pronoun-Antecedent Agreement.

63. **D** The use of *who* and *whoever* are correct. Who is a pronoun that means what or which persons. Whoever is a pronoun that means whatever person. For more, see Chapter 8: Other Grammatical Errors.

64. **A** This is the only sentence where there is subject-verb agreement between the plural *attributes* and the verb *make*. A semicolon should be used after *officer* to join the dependent and independent clauses. For more, see Chapter 8: Subject-Verb Agreement.

65. **C** This is the appropriate use of the contraction *we're* and the word *either* creates a singular subject; therefore, the correct verb is *is*. For more, see Chapter 8: Subject-Verb Agreement.

66. **D** The term *whose* is the possessive form of who; whereas *who's* is a contraction of who is. For more, see Chapter 8: Other Grammatical Errors.

67. **C** Use *I* when using a first person subjective pronoun (and *me* when using a first person objective pronoun). *Premises* means a building or location, whereas the homonym *premise* means an idea or statement. For more, see Chapter 8: Homonyms and Other Grammatical Errors.

68. **A** This option correctly uses the homonyms *than* (instead of *then*) and *stationary* (instead of *stationery*, which means writing material). For more, see Chapter 8: Homonyms.

69. **C** This option correctly uses the homonyms *effective* (instead of *affective*, which means emotional) and *accept* (instead of *except*, which means excluding). For more, see Chapter 8: Homonyms.

70. **A** *Demure* means modest and reserved.

71. **A** *Criminology* should not be capitalized as it is not a proper noun. The rest of the words are spelled correctly. For more, see Chapter 7: Capitalization.

72. **B** *Colisseum* is misspelled. The correct spelling is coliseum. *Attorneys-general* is correct. It is the plural form of a singular attorney-general. For more, see Chapter 7: Spelling.

73. **D** The word *have* should be capitalized as it is the beginning of a quote. *Themselves* is correct as the plural form of the reflexive third person. For more, see Chapter 7: Capitalization and Chapter 8: Other Grammatical Errors.

74. **C** This is the only grammatically correct sentence that is not disjointed or has faulty parallelism. For more, see Chapter 8: Faulty Parallelism.

75. **C** *Superintendant* is misspelled. The correct spelling is superintendent. You should be able to spell all ranks within a police organization. For more, see Chapter 7: Spelling.

## Part 4: Reading Comprehension

76. **C** The purpose of the extrajudicial measures program in New Brunswick is to keep youth out of the court system. See paragraphs 1, 2.

77. **B** Véronique Essiembre is concerned about the lasting effects of labelling a youth as someone with a criminal record. See paragraphs 9, 10, 11.

78. **B** Seema Poirier suggests that some police officers may not initially support the program because diversion programs create more work for officers, "who already have a lot on their plates." See paragraph 11.

79. **D** Although the acronym CPO is often used for Community Police Office or Community Police Officer, in this article it refers to the Community Programs Officer, who is a civilian member of the RCMP. See paragraph 5.

80. **B** "Breaking the Cycle" refers to identifying at-risk youth early and providing holistic programs for them before they get into serious trouble and end up with criminal records, which perpetuates their problems. See paragraphs 1, 2, 4.

81. **A** The EMS was developed to manage resources and occurrences during major events. See paragraphs 2, 4, 5, 7.

82. **B** The SAMS is not connected to the RCMP Human Resources Management Information System—the EMS system is. See paragraph 5.

83. **D** The earliest date indicated that the SAMS was used in 2009 during President Obama's visit to Ottawa. See paragraph 11.

84. **B** Although the EMS provided several positive functions, Insp. McCarthy specifically mentioned that he was impressed with its ability to schedule and mobilize thousands of officers. See paragraph 6.

85. **D** The coordination of database searches is a function of the SAM system and not EMS. See paragraph 9.

## Part 5: Judgment and Logic

86. **B** Your reason for stopping the suspect is because he violated a traffic law. You have no new information that would give you grounds to search his vehicle, have him followed, or take additional enforcement measures. For more, see Chapter 11: Judgment.

87. **D** There is only a five-minute time delay on the suspect fleeing. You don't have a suspect description, so you need to find out what he looks like quickly, and then broadcast his description to other officers in the area. You can obtain detailed statements later and tend to the victim's emotional concerns after you've obtained the suspect description. It would be useless to run after a suspect five minutes after he fled, he could be anywhere, and you do not know what he looks like. For more, see Chapter 11: Judgment.

88. **C** Although it may be tempting to arrest the driver of the other vehicle who is walking away, preserving life is more important that preserving evidence. This person will

likely die without your immediate assistance. You need to first attend to his serious injury. For more, see Chapter 11: Judgment.

89. **C** You need to use your communication skills to advise the driver that there is a dispute process if he does not agree with you. An arrest may come much later if all other avenues of reasoning have failed. Do not change your ticket based on what the driver states. If you saw him disobey a red light, then that is what you should write him the ticket for. For more, see Chapter 11: Judgment.

90. **A** Before you take any action, you should always try to find out all sides of the story. Your partner may have received completely different information. Although this incident may have started as a civil dispute over the price of a car, a criminal act may have taken place. If a person only appears to have been drinking, it is insufficient to arrest that person for being intoxicated in public. For more, see Chapter 11: Judgment.

91. **D** Rule: Some, All = Some. For more, see Chapter 11: Syllogisms.

92. **D** Rule: No distribution of middle term "useful," therefore, no valid conclusion. For more, see Chapter 11: Syllogisms.

93. **B** Rule: No, Some = Some not (major and minor premise reversed). If no convicted person is innocent (we will just assume this for the sake of this exercise), and some young men are convicted persons, then some young men are convicted persons. For more, see Chapter 11: Syllogisms.

94. **C** Rule: Some, All = Some. If some lawyers are not honest, and all lawyers are human, then some humans are not honest. For more, see Chapter 11: Syllogisms.

95. **B** Rule: No, Some = Some not (major and minor premises reversed). If no examination is enjoyable, and some application processes require an examination, then some application processes are not enjoyable. For more, see Chapter 11: Syllogisms.

96. **C** Use the compass at the top of the map to establish direction. The correct direction, and most efficient route, is to drive east on Hemlock, then turn right and drive south on 4th Street, and then turn left and drive east on Cherry. For more, see Chapter 11: Spatial Orientation.

97. **C** The correct route is to drive east on Pioneer, north on 3rd Street, turn right to drive east on Alder, and then turn right to drive south on 5th Street. Although there appears to be more efficient routes (e.g., driving south on 2nd Street to Oak Street), these would be in violation of one-way roads. Since this is not an emergency call, you would not be justified in disobeying these traffic signs. For more, see Chapter 11: Spatial Orientation.

98. **B** Use the compass to establish north. The car was eastbound, making a left turn to drive north, when it was struck by a westbound vehicle. For more, see Chapter 11: Spatial Orientation.

99. **D** The north indicator is pointing towards the bottom of the diagram. In order to maintain your directional bearings, invert the page so that north points towards the top. The traffic light symbols indicate red for east-west traffic; however, even if you don't recognize that's what the symbol means, you should see that there are skid

marks behind the westbound vehicle and no direction of travel indicated for the eastbound vehicle. For more, see Chapter 11: Spatial Orientation.

100. **B** North is pointing towards the right side of the diagram; therefore, turn the map so that north points towards the top. The light is green for east-west traffic as indicated by the symbol and the direction of vehicles travelling east and west. The southbound vehicle is stationary. The vehicle northbound on Anderson disobeyed the red light. For more, see Chapter 11: Spatial Orientation.

101. **B** In three of the images, the overlapping image creates a third identical image. For example, the two overlapping triangles create a third triangle. This does not occur with image B. For more, see Chapter 11: Patterns.

102. **C** In the lower level window frames, each house has two blank squares per window. In the upper frames, two houses have one blank square and two houses have two blank squares. Only C has no pattern on the chimney. For more, see Chapter 11: Patterns.

103. **C** If you rotate all of the images so that the lone blank square is at the top, you will see that, in all of the patterns except C, the black boxes form a diagonal line from the bottom left corner to the top right. For more, see Chapter 11: Patterns.

104. **C** The black rings create no pattern and are meant to distract your attention. Count the total number of rings in the sequence: 16, 17, 18. C has 19 rings. For more, see Chapter 11: Patterns.

105. **B** The pattern sequence is that each number is squared, minus one. Two squared is four, minus one is three; three squared is nine, minus one is eight, etc. For more, see Chapter 11: Patterns.

## Part 6: Problem Solving

106. **A** First, set up the multiplication equation with the larger number on top. Multiply each bottom row digit with the top row separately. Second, shift one digit to the left for each row being multiplied (see below). Third, total all three rows. Fourth, add five decimal spaces; three spaces for the first number (63.453) and two spaces for the second (2.13).

$$
\begin{array}{r}
63.453 \\
\times \quad 2.13 \\
\end{array}
$$

| | |
|---|---|
| STEP 1 | $190359 = 3 \times 63453$ |
| STEP 2 | $63453 \leftarrow\, = 1 \times 63453$ |
| STEP 3 | $\underline{\quad 126906 \leftarrow\, = 2 \times 63453}$ |
| | $13515489$ |
| STEP 4 | $135.15489 \quad$ Add 5 decimal spaces. |

For more, see Chapter 12: Multiplication & Division.

107. **B** Subtracting a negative integer is the same as addition. When adding numbers with decimals, stack the two numbers to be added in rows and ensure the decimal places align.

$$
\begin{array}{r}
18.371 \\
+\ \ 3.03 \\
\hline
21.401
\end{array}
$$

For more, see Chapter 12: Addition & Subtraction.

108. **C** First, set up the equation in long division format. Start by dividing 34 into 49. Since it only divides once, put a 1 on the quotient (answer) line. Write 34 under the 49 and subtract the difference. The remainder is 15. Next, bring down the 0, which creates 150. Then divide 34 into 150. This may take some trial and error. You can take a good guess though, you know that $3 \times 5 = 15$, therefore $34 \times 5$ will be close to 150. In this case, 5 will be too much, so multiply $34 \times 4 = 136$. Write down the remainder, and bring down the 2. Continue this process until you have finished dividing all the numbers. Since the equation is $49.028 \div 0.34$ and not 34, move the decimal two digits to the right. (i.e., 1.442 becomes 144.2).

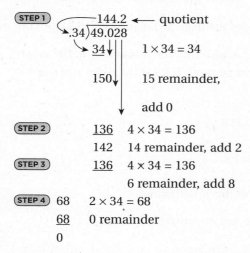

STEP 1
144.2 ← quotient
.34)49.028
34↓    $1 \times 34 = 34$

150↓    15 remainder,

       add 0

STEP 2    136    $4 \times 34 = 136$
          142    14 remainder, add 2
STEP 3    136    $4 \times 34 = 136$
          6 remainder, add 8
STEP 4    68    $2 \times 34 = 68$
          68    0 remainder
          0

For more, see Chapter 12: Multiplication & Division.

109. **D** This is a mathematical order of operations question. Remember the acronym BEDMAS to determine order: Brackets, Exponents, Division, Multiplication, Addition, Subtraction. Since there are no equations within brackets and no exponents (e.g., $4^3$), begin with division.

STEP 1    $16 \div 4 = 4$
STEP 2    $39.21 + 4 = 43.21$
STEP 3    $43.21 - 23.21 = 20$

For more, see Chapter 12: Multiplication & Division.

110. **B** First, set up the multiplication equation in rows as demonstrated in Question 121. Second, add four decimal spaces to the left for your answer. Third, remember that a negative number multiplied by a negative number is a positive number. For more, see Chapter 12: Multiplication & Division.

111. **D** When adding or subtracting fractions, you must ensure that the denominators, the bottom number of the fractions, are equal. In this question, the common denominator of 6, 3, and 4 is 12. For the fraction $\frac{1}{6}$, multiply both the numerator (top number) and denominator by 2, which equals $\frac{2}{12}$. Repeat this process to the remaining fractions so that all the denominators equal 12. Then add and subtract the numerators to obtain the answer.

**STEP 1** $\frac{1}{6} = \frac{2}{12}$    multiply times 2

**STEP 2** $\frac{2}{3} = \frac{8}{12}$    multiply times 4

**STEP 3** $\frac{3}{4} = \frac{9}{12}$    multiply times 3

**STEP 4** $\frac{2}{12} + \frac{8}{12} - \frac{9}{12} = \frac{1}{12}$

For more, see Chapter 12: Fractions.

112. **C** When adding or subtracting mixed numbers (e.g., $4\frac{1}{8}$), you need to ensure not only that they have a common denominator but also that the numerator of the larger number can be subtracted from the lesser number. If it cannot, then you need to borrow from the whole number.

**STEP 1** $4\frac{1}{8} - 2\frac{3}{4}$    common denominator is 8

**STEP 2** $4\frac{1}{8} - 2\frac{6}{8}$    cannot subtract 6 from 1

**STEP 3** $3\frac{9}{8} - 2\frac{6}{8}$    borrow 1 (which is $\frac{8}{8}$ of the whole number)

**STEP 4** $9 - 6 = 3$    subtract fractions, then whole numbers
$3 - 2 = 1$

For more, see Chapter 12: Fractions.

113. **B** When multiplying mixed numbers (e.g., $2\frac{2}{3}$), first convert them to improper fractions (e.g., $\frac{8}{3}$) by multiplying the denominator by the whole number ($3 \times 2$) and then adding the numerator ($6 + 2$). Next, multiply the two numerators together and the two denominators together. Then divide the denominator into the numerator and create a mixed number. For more, see Chapter 12: Multiplying Mixed Numbers.

**STEP 1** $\frac{8}{3} \times \frac{7}{1}$    Convert to improper fractions.

**STEP 2** $= \frac{56}{3}$    Multiply numerators and denominators together.

**STEP 3** $= 18\frac{2}{3}$    Return to mixed number by dividing denominator into numerator to create whole number, with 2 remaining as numerator.

114. **D** When dealing with exponents (e.g., $6^3$) in equations, remember BEDMAS. Therefore, you must deal with exponents before other operations.

(STEP 1) $6^3 = 6 \times 6 \times 6 = 216$
(STEP 2) $5^3 = 5 \times 5 \times 5 = 125$
(STEP 3)    $216 + 125 = 341$

For more, see Chapter 12: Other Operations.

115. **A** Solve multiple-step equations by using the BEDMAS principle. Start with the equations that are within brackets (or parentheses), then multiplication and division, then addition and subtraction. Then solve the equation from left to right.

(STEP 1)     $9 \times 3 = 27$
(STEP 2)     $2 \times 45 = 90$
(STEP 3) $27 - 90 + 70 = 7$

For more, see Chapter 12: Multiplication and Division.

116. **B** This is a two-step problem. First, total the number of police officers in the agency (279). Then divide the number of probationary officers (45) by the total. Remember that $0.10 = \frac{1}{10} = 10\%$.

(STEP 1) $45 + 67 + 45 + 122 = 279$
(STEP 2) $279\overline{)45.000}$ with quotient $.161$
(STEP 3) move decimals   $0.161 = 16\%$

For more, see Chapter 12: Multiplication and Division and Word Problems.

117. **C** This is an algebraic equation. Step one, total the vehicle mileage for the four days. It is known that the vehicle consumes 6 litres of fuel per 100 km. The unknown factor ($x$) is the number of litres the car consumed in 200 km. Therefore, the equation is that $\frac{6}{100} = \frac{x}{200}$. In order to isolate $x$, you must eliminate the denominator fraction. Do this by multiplying the fraction by 200. What you do on one side of the equation, you must do to the other side of the equation.

(STEP 1) $56 + 67 + 41 + 36 = 200$
(STEP 2) Set up equation: $\frac{6}{100} = \frac{x}{200}$.
(STEP 3) Isolate $x$, $(6 \times 200) = 100x$.
(STEP 4) Reduce fraction $\frac{1,200}{100} = x$.
(STEP 5) $x = 12$

Therefore, multiply $6 \times 200$, and then reduce the fraction to make a whole number.

For more, see Chapter 12: Word Problems.

118. **D** This is a three-step equation. First, identify the common denominator (6). Then, add the two fractions to determine total officers working in the Patrol and Investigation Divisions. These two sections account for $\frac{5}{6}$ of the workforce. The $\frac{1}{6}$ remainder work elsewhere.

(STEP 1) $\frac{1}{2} = \frac{3}{6}$

(STEP 2) $\frac{1}{3} = \frac{2}{6}$

(STEP 3) $\frac{3}{6} + \frac{2}{6} = \frac{5}{6}$

(STEP 4) Working elsewhere $= \frac{1}{6}$

For more, see Chapter 12: Word Problems.

119. **A** This is a three-step equation. First, add the total number of officers working in the precinct office (15). Second, create a fraction of sergeants to total officers ($\frac{3}{15}$). Finally, divide the numerator and denominator by 3 to determine the probability of a single sergeant being randomly selected ($x$). For more, see Chapter 12: Word Problems.

120. **B** This question can be set up as an algebraic equation. If the ratio of male-to-female officers is 13:2, then what is $x$ (males), if there are 14 females? You can remove the fractions by multiplying across the equation. Lastly, isolate the $x$ by dividing by 2 on both sides of the equation.

(STEP 1) Set up equation: $\frac{2}{13} = \frac{14}{x}$

(STEP 2) Cross multiply: $\frac{2}{13} \diagup \frac{14}{x}$

(STEP 3) Isolate $x$: $2x = 182$

(STEP 4) Divide both sides by 2: $x = 91$

For more, see Chapter 12: Word Problems and Algebra.

121. **A** The additional complexity of this question is that you need to convert a fraction of an hour to minutes, because $\frac{1}{3}$ of 11 is not a whole number. First, divide 11 by 3 (3.67). Next, convert 0.67 to minutes by creating equal fractions. Lastly, cross-multiply $60 \times 67$. Divide by 100 in order to isolate $x$.

(STEP 1) $11 \div 3 = 3.67$

(STEP 2) Create equation: $\frac{67}{100} = \frac{x}{60}$

(STEP 3) Cross-multiply: $\frac{67}{100} \diagup \frac{x}{60}$

(STEP 4) Isolate $x$: $4{,}020 = 100x$

(STEP 5) Divide both sides by 100: $x = 40.2$

For more, see Chapter 12: Word Problems.

122. **D** The first step is to determine the entire length of the perimeter that Officer Cotton would walk. The perimeter is the sum of all four sides $(2 \times 150) + (2 \times 100) = 500$ m. Second, create the algebraic equation: 5 km/60 minutes = 0.5 km/$x$ minutes. Then, cross-multiply to remove the fractions. Lastly, divide both sides by 5 to isolate $x$.

(STEP 1)   $(2 \times 150) + (2 \times 100) = 500$ m

(STEP 2) Create equation:   $\dfrac{5}{60} = \dfrac{0.5}{x}$

(STEP 3) Cross-multiply:   $5x = 30$

(STEP 4) Isolate $x$: divide both sides by 5

(STEP 5)   $x = 6$

For more, see Chapter 12: Word Problems and Algebra.

123. **C** This is similar to the previous question in that you can determine the speed by converting hours to minutes and using fractions. First, create the equation: 3 km/1.5 minutes (or 90 seconds) = $x$ km/60 minutes (km/h). Then, cross-multiply $3 \times 60$ (180). Divide by 1.5 to isolate $x$.

(STEP 1) Create equation:   $\dfrac{3}{1.50} = \dfrac{x}{60}$

(STEP 2) Cross-multiply:   $180 = 1.5x$

(STEP 3) Isolate $x$: divide both sides by 1.5

(STEP 4)   $x = 120$

For more, see Chapter 12: Word Problems and Algebra.

124. **B** First, determine how much Dorothy makes per week by multiplying her hourly rate times 40 hours per week. Second, multiply her earnings by 0.25, as that is all she can save per week. Finally, divide the total required ($1,800) by her weekly savings ($180).

(STEP 1) Weekly pay:   $18 \times 40 = \$720$

(STEP 2) Savings:   $0.25 \times \$720 = \$180$

(STEP 3) Required:   $\$1,800 \div \$180 = \$10$

For more, see Chapter 12: Word Problems and Multiplication and Division.

125. **C** First, create the equation: $\dfrac{\$45}{0.5\,g} = \dfrac{\$x}{3.5\,g}$. Second, remove the fractions by cross-multiplying. Third, isolate $x$ by dividing.

(STEP 1) Create equation:   $\dfrac{0.5}{45} = \dfrac{3.5}{x}$

(STEP 2) Cross-multiply:   $0.5x = 157.5$

(STEP 3) Isolate $x$: divide both sides by 0.5

(STEP 4) "8 ball" costs   $x = \$315$

For more, see Chapter 12: Word Problems and Algebra.

126. **A** This two-step equation requires you to first find out what one-third of $735,000 is and then to subtract $75,000.

(STEP 1) $735,000 \div 3 = 245,000$
(STEP 2) $245,000 - 75,000 = 170,000$

For more, see Chapter 12: Word Problems and Multiplication and Division.

127. **B** This three-step equation requires you to establish a fraction, or ratio, of read reports to approved reports and then to convert that ratio into a percentage.

(STEP 1) Create equation: $\dfrac{129}{163} = \dfrac{x}{100}$
(STEP 2) Cross-multiply: $12,900 = 163x$
(STEP 3) Divide: $x = 79.14\%$

For more, see Chapter 12: Word Problems and Fractions.

128. **C** In this two-step equation, multiply the number of hours per shift (11.5) times the 4 days he worked (46 hours). Then, divide the total number of reports read (163) by total hours worked (3.543). For more, see Chapter 12: Word Problems and Multiplication and Division.

129. **C** To find the yearly average, add the total investigations for all years (599 + 705 + 648 + 498 = 2,450) and then divide by the number of years (4), which averages 612.5 per year. For more, see Chapter 12: Word Problems and Multiplication and Division.

130. **B** In 2008, the ratio of forfeitures to seizures was $6.4 m to $31.7 m. Create a fraction equation and then cross-multiply to eliminate the fractions. Then, isolate $x$ by dividing by 31.7.

(STEP 1) Create equation: $\dfrac{6.4}{31.7} = \dfrac{x}{100}$
(STEP 2) Cross-multiply: $640 = 31.7x$
(STEP 3) Divide: $x = 20.19\%$

For more, see Chapter 12: Word Problems and Algebra.

131. **A** This three-step question requires you to first add all the seizures during the four years, then add all forfeitures during the same period, and then subtract the difference.

(STEP 1) Total seizures: $143.2 m
(STEP 2) Total forfeitures: $25.6 m
(STEP 3) Subtract difference: $117.6 m

For more, see Chapter 12: Word Problems and Addition and Subtraction.

132. **D** To identify which year had the best forfeiture to seizure ratio, you must find out what the ratio is for each of the four years and then chose the highest ratio (percentage).

(STEP 1) 2007: $\dfrac{4.3}{37.5} = 11.5\%$

(STEP 2) 2008: $\dfrac{6.4}{31.7} = 20.2\%$

(STEP 3) 2009: $\dfrac{5.3}{44.4} = 11.9\%$

(STEP 4) 2010: $\dfrac{9.6}{29.6} = 32.4\%$

For more, see Chapter 12: Word Problems and Multiplication and Division.

133. **A** There are two bags with Canadian cash totalling $431,000. First, divide by 3 to obtain a third. Then, add $30,000 to the total.

(STEP 1) $\dfrac{1}{3}$ cash:  $431,000 \div 3 = 143,667$

(STEP 2) add  $30,000 = \$173,667$

For more, see Chapter 12: Word Problems and Multiplication and Division

134. **A** First, you need to determine the total value of U.S. currency in Canadian dollars by multiplying the total by 1.10 ($374,000). Then, add Canadian cash.

(STEP 1) U.S.:  $125,000 + $215,000
(STEP 2) Convert:  $340,000 × $1.10
(STEP 3) Add:  $374,000 + $431,000

For more, see Chapter 12: Word Problems and Multiplication and Division.

135. **B** The first step is to obtain the Canadian value of U.S. bonds ($236,500). Next, create a fraction using the total value of all goods ($805,000—obtained from previous question) and the value of U.S. bonds ($236,500). Then, convert the fraction to a percentage.

(STEP 1) Convert:  $215,000 × 1.10
(STEP 2) Fraction:  $236,000 ÷ $805,000
(STEP 3) Percent:  0.293 = 29%

For more, see Chapter 12: Word Problems and Multiplication and Division.

# Observation and Memorization

# 6

→ **TEST YOUR MEMORIZATION**

→ **MEMORIZATION**

→ **MNEMONIC DEVICES**

→ **PREPARING FOR MEMORIZATION TASKS**

→ **TIPS FOR OBSERVATION AND MEMORIZATION TASKS**

→ **HAVE I GOT IT RIGHT?**

Being able to accurately observe and recall events is one of the most essential components of police work. Every day, patrol officers are provided with photos of wanted and dangerous offenders and shown vehicle descriptions and licence plate numbers of stolen and suspect vehicles and are expected to be on the lookout for these vehicles and persons. Moreover, police officers must make accurate notes of their observations and involvement in an investigation and then be able to describe in detail their actions often more than a year after the fact. When an officer's recollection of an event is challenged by another witness or contradictory video evidence, an entire trial may be in jeopardy. Therefore, as a police officer it is imperative that you are able to retain information and details about what you have read and witnessed and be able to recount those facts some time later. As a consequence, you can be certain that most police entrance exams will have a visual and written memorization component. For some police agencies, this test may be in the form of viewing a short video clip or series of photographs, reading a "wanted persons" poster, or even being given a short period of time to view a tray displaying various artifacts and then having to recall them later.

This chapter contains a number of proven tips and strategies that you can use during the entrance exam to enhance your memory and recollection of visual and written material. First, assess your memorization competencies by taking the Test Your Memorization evaluation.

# TEST YOUR MEMORIZATION

You have 10 minutes to complete the Test Your Memorization exercise.

## Instructions

1. Study the photograph of a crime scene in Figure 1 below for a maximum of **two minutes** and memorize as much detail about the photograph as possible.

2. You are not permitted to make any written notes or refer back to the photograph when answering subsequent questions.

3. After two minutes have passed, turn the page and read the Wanted Person bulletin (Figure 2). You are only permitted to study the bulletin for **three minutes**.

4. You are not permitted to make any written notes or refer back to the Wanted Person bulletin when answering subsequent questions.

5. Answer the questions in sequential order.

Start your timer and begin the exercise now.

STUDY THE PHOTOGRAPH FOR A MAXIMUM OF TWO MINUTES.

**Figure 1.** Grocery Store Robbery

STUDY THE BULLETIN FOR A MAXIMUM OF THREE MINUTES.

---

**WANTED PERSON BULLETIN**

Name:               CARMONDEZ, Manuel Jesus

Caution:            Armed and Dangerous
                    Flight Risk

Wanted:             Warrant of Arrest for Robbery and Parole Violation

Aliases:            CADENA, Eduardo

Date of Birth:      May 24, 1967

Description:        Hispanic male, 168 cm, 72 kg, slim build, long black hair, brown
                    eyes.

Scars/Marks:        Tattoo skull with red rose on right shoulder; eagle tattoo on left
                    shoulder; "Los Cabos" on back; "Hecho En Mexico" on left chest;
                    5 cm scar on left cheek

History:            Criminal record for theft, drugs, weapons, and sex offences

Occupation:         roofer; construction worker

Address:            St. Thomas Halfway House for Men, 1543 Johnson Ave, Toronto.

CARMONDEZ was identified by video evidence and DNA as the sole person
responsible for the armed robbery with a sawed off shotgun at Barston's Drugs
on 2015-04-21.

CARMONDEZ is currently on parole for a 2008 drug importation offence. He
has failed to return to his residence at St. Thomas halfway house and his
current location is unknown.

CARMONDEZ is considered armed and dangerous and a possible flight risk to
the United States or Mexico.

---

**Figure 2.** Wanted Person Bulletin

QUESTIONS 1–8 RELATE TO INFORMATION PICTURED IN FIGURE 1.

1. What time was this photograph taken?

   (A) 6:20
   (B) 11:50
   (C) 9:15
   (D) 4:30

2. What is the name of the grocery store?

   (A) Hillcrest
   (B) Hillview
   (C) Lakeview
   (D) Lakeside

3. How many police officers are wearing glasses?

   (A) 1
   (B) 2
   (C) 3
   (D) none

4. What is the name of the brand of ice cream displayed on the clock?

   (A) Dairyland
   (B) Dave's
   (C) Peter's
   (D) Doug's

5. What product is advertised on the sign above the awning?

   (A) Pepsi Cola
   (B) Coca Cola
   (C) 7-up
   (D) Sprite

6. What is the address of the store?

   (A) 9070
   (B) 7009
   (C) 7900
   (D) 7090

7. What is leaning against the front steps of the store?

   (A) a wagon
   (B) a pogo stick
   (C) an umbrella
   (D) a bicycle

8. How many advertisements for 7-up are visible?

   (A) 1
   (B) 2
   (C) 3
   (D) 4

QUESTIONS 9–15 RELATE TO INFORMATION PICTURED IN FIGURE 2.

9. What was the alias surname of the wanted person?

   (A) Cabrero
   (B) Carmona
   (C) Cadena
   (D) Condero

10. What does the suspect have tattooed on his chest?

    (A) an eagle
    (B) "Hecho En Mexico"
    (C) "Los Cabos"
    (D) nothing indicated

11. What is the address of the halfway house where the suspect was living?

    (A) 1543 Johnson Ave.
    (B) 1534 Johnston Street
    (C) 5341 Johnson Ave.
    (D) 1534 Johnson Street

12. What is the Warrant of Arrest for?

    (A) Robbery and parole violation
    (B) Drug importation
    (C) Weapons offences
    (D) Theft

13. How tall is the suspect?

    (A) 196 cm
    (B) 168 cm
    (C) 162 cm
    (D) 158 cm

14. What was the name of the pharmacy that the suspect robbed on April 21, 2015?

    (A) Bastion Drugs
    (B) Baron's Drugs
    (C) Barston's Drugs
    (D) Brandon's Drugs

15. What is the suspect's date of birth?

    (A) May 24, 1967
    (B) June 14, 1968
    (C) July 07, 1966
    (D) April 15, 1967

## Answers

1. **D** The clock in the window indicates 4:30.

2. **B** The name of the store is Hillview Grocery.

3. **A** Only one officer is wearing glasses.

4. **C** Peter's Ice Cream is advertised on the clock.

5. **A** Pepsi Cola is advertised above the awning.

6. **B** The address of the grocery store is 7009 and printed above the doorway.

7. **D** There's a bicycle leaning against the stairs.

8. **C** There are three signs advertising 7-up.

9. **C** The alias surname of the wanted person is Cadena.

10. **B** The suspect has "Hecho En Mexico" tattooed on his chest.

11. **A** The address of the halfway house is1543 Johnson Ave.

12. **A** The suspect has an outstanding Warrant of Arrest for Robbery and Parole Violation.

13. **B** The suspect is described as being 168 cm tall.

14. **C** The suspect had robbed Barston's Drugs.

15. **A** The suspect's date of birth is May 24, 1967.

---

### HOW DID YOU SCORE?

Correct Answers: _____/15 Excellent 14–15 Good 11–13 Average 8–10

If your test score is not in the Excellent range, you should focus your study efforts on this chapter to ensure that you improve your visual and written observation and memorization skills.

---

## MEMORIZATION

**TIP**

You can only remember about 7 items in your short-term memory for about 10–15 seconds.

The memorization process involves three steps: encoding, storage, and retrieval. *Encoding* means absorbing information from our environment through our senses (most often visually), and then identifying and categorizing what the stimulus is—"I am looking at the front cover of an entrance exam study guide."

The next step towards memorization is *storage*. Our brains often receive thousands of sensory stimulations every minute, but very little is paid attention. The stimulations that are encoded and given some attention are then transferred into short-term memory. However, even short-term memory is fleeting and holds a very small amount of information for a short period of time. Usually, we can retain only about seven items or fewer for 10–15 seconds before it is gone forever. We frequently use our short-term memory to conduct basic tasks like doing simple addition in our heads (e.g., remembering to carry the one while calculating 14 + 18); remembering the essence of what you read at the start of this sentence (*We frequently use our short-term memory* ...), so that the rest of this sentence makes sense; and remembering what you want to say when someone is talking to you so that you can make an interesting response to her comments.

Nevertheless, short-term memory cannot retain detailed information (e.g., you won't likely remember the first sentence of the previous paragraph), rather it retains significant words or concepts only, and then discards the information soon after. It's like a sticky note in your brain. Unfortunately, all too often we tend to leave important information in our short-term memory and fail to transfer that data to our more enduring long-term memory. How often have you been at a social function and been introduced to people and then forgotten their names as soon as they walk away? Or someone tells you his phone number and it's gone before you get a chance to write it down? When new information is only held in our short-term memory, we have not taken that information through a learning process, and it is soon expunged, never to be recalled. Thus, the learning process allows us to transfer information held in our short-term memory to our more permanent long-term memory. Learning can be accomplished through repetition of information and personal motivation, and it occurs more effectively by giving the new information meaning and associating it to previously acquired knowledge.

Information that is stored in our long-term memories can be categorized as either implicit or explicit. Implicit memories are skills that you have learned that you no longer need to consciously think about when performing those tasks, such as ice-skating or typing. Explicit memories are the retention of conscious facts (e.g., recalling the information that you have studied for a test, the words of our *National Anthem*, or your phone number) and episodic events (e.g., remembering what you did last summer). Some episodic events that have a strong emotional and personal attachment to them are called "flashbulb" memories. These types of memories are long lasting and accurate. They are vivid in your mind, and you can often recall where you were, what you were doing, and what was said at that moment in time. For example, the birth of my children, what I was doing when I first found out about the 9/11 terrorist attacks, and my first confrontation with an armed suspect are all flashbulb memories that I can recall in detail. These types of memories help us understand how our brains function when it comes to the retention and recall of information. Namely, the more important we perceive an event to be, the more emotional attachment we have to an incident, and the more senses that come into play during an event (i.e., auditory, tactile, olfactory, and taste), the greater the level of retention of information surrounding that incident. That is, it is not like I had to make a conscious effort to memorize the circumstances surrounding the births of my children; they were very important and emotional events, so I remember them regardless.

The final step in the memorization process is memory *recall*. Learning new information and storing it in long-term memory is only half the battle—recalling what you have learned can be even more difficult. Chances are you have experienced situations where you have been searching for a word, or an answer to a question, or the name of a person that you know and it is on the tip of your tongue, but you just cannot retrieve it from the recesses of your mind. This tip-of-your-tongue phenomenon is a fairly common occurrence and takes place when either a word exists in a person's lexicon or the person knows the information requested but cannot access it at that point in time.

There are several explanations for why we fail to effectively recall known information. First, often we will be searching for the correct answer when competing plausible alternative choices block our mind from accessing the correct choice. For example, you may recall that the person's name that you met at the house party started with an S, but you can't recall if it is Sonia, Sarah, or Sophia—when, in fact, her name is Sandra. The second factor that may prevent accessing information from memory is that the brain has received insufficient cues to stimulate retrieval. That is, perhaps the context of the information is missing, such as the location or circumstances of where and how the information was first acquired. Third, there may be weak neural connections with the information that is trying to be recalled. In other words, the information that you are searching for has not been accessed frequently, has little value to you, or was not acquired recently. The weaker the neural connection, the more difficult it is to recall. Finally, the strongest correlation between memory and the tip-of-your-tongue phenomenon is age. Regrettably, the older we get, the more frequently this occurs, especially after we reach our 40s. While aging is unavoidable and will inevitably interfere at some level with your ability to recall information, you can employ several strategies to ensure that information is transferred from short-term to long-term memory and that you are able to effectively recall detailed information during your entrance exam.

**TIP**

**Learn at least two mnemonic devices to help you retain information during the memorization portion of your police entrance exam.**

## MNEMONIC DEVICES

Since we tend to be visual learners, most students do fairly well in entrance exams when it comes to remembering what they observed. We cue in to what people are wearing, we notice the baby in the stroller, the kid on the bicycle, and obviously the man wearing a mask while carrying a handgun outside of the bank. If the entrance exam that you are going to take includes watching a video segment, you will likely be able to recall nearly verbatim what the suspect stated because the auditory stimulation adds another layer and location within your brain for memory recall. However, where short-term memories tend to fail is when we have to recall specific written details: What was the plate number on the car? What was the address of the bakery? What was the name of the suspect wanted for robbery, and what was his date of birth? Written words and descriptions are much more difficult to recall than visual images; however, if you practice and master several mnemonic techniques, you will be able to effectively recall this level of detail during your examination.

A mnemonic device refers to any memory technique that aids in information retention. The goal of a mnemonic device is to manipulate large amounts of information into a structure that your brain can more effectively retain than in its original format. Mnemonics are especially effective in recalling specific names, lengthy descriptions, and lists of information—the sort of detail that you will be required to recall in your entrance exam.

## Attention to Detail

Paying attention to detail is critically important during the memory-encoding phase. If you are distracted by other stimuli, such as sounds or invasive thoughts, then encoding of information will be impaired, and the amount of information learned will be reduced. Maintaining attention for a prolonged period while attempting to acquire new information is difficult to do, especially if you are not permitted to make notes. Therefore, you need to concentrate and ensure that your mind stays focused on the information that it is processing and not drifting away to other thoughts. The reason why these types of memory gaps happen is because it is very easy to get distracted when you do not have to concentrate on a task that you are very familiar with. The challenge is to remain attentive throughout the entire task.

One way to stay focused is to bring your own energy and excitement into what you are seeing or reading. Think of a speech or presentation that you have heard by someone with a monotone voice that lacked any emotion and how difficult it was to stay focused on what he or she was saying. However, if you have witnessed a dramatic speaker, who has overemphasized important elements of the speech with strong inflection, emotion, and gestures, those key ideas or statements have likely stayed with you for some time. In the same manner, if you read and observe material with energy and keen interest, more of this new information that you have received will be transferred to long-term memory, and you will have a greater chance of recalling facts later on because of the interest you put into the encoding process in the first place.

## Rote Learning

Rote learning is a foundational technique that most of us have used throughout our entire lives. It is simply the repetition of information until you have acquired and mastered the data. We routinely use this skill in order to memorize phone numbers and addresses, and we have previously used this technique in school to remember multiplication tables and periodic tables and to cram for tests the night before an exam. Rote learning does not require any level of comprehension or a need to understand the complexities or subtleties that may be associated with the new information. It is simply being able to regurgitate the facts when required. Even though rote learning affords the simplest method of recalling facts, it often requires significant repetition to be able to accurately recall a large amount of information. However, if you tried to use this method during the police entrance exam and commit everything that you saw and read to memory via repetition only, you would likely run out of time and have to move on to the next task before being able to learn much of the information. Moreover, since the exams are often structured so that there is an intentional interruption of the memorization process, learning through simple mental repetition of information will likely be significantly degraded. Therefore, you should focus on using more sophisticated mnemonic techniques.

## Visual Image Association

Although we "see" what we read, unless you have a so-called photographic memory you usually do not retain a visual image of these words. In fact, beyond several key words that might jump off a page as you read them, when trying to memorize words or pieces of information you are usually practicing a phonetic loop—hearing in your mind the words repeated over and over. However, a common trait found in individuals who have the ability to memorize and recall vast amounts of information is that they are able to effectively create robust and detailed mental images associated to the data they wish to memorize. The reason why mental images assist in creating stronger memories is that verbal material and images are stored in separate, but linked, locations of the brain.

The most effective method of image association is to use images that you already know and are familiar with. For example, if you are required to remember a suspect's name from a wanted persons bulletin and you already know a person with the same first name, create an image in your mind of the person you know to help you remember. If there are descriptions of that suspect (e.g., scars, marks, and tattoos), then add those features to the person that you already know. Imagery can also help you with recalling names of streets, locations, and other important information. For example, in the Test Your Memorization photograph the name of the grocery store is *Hillview*; therefore, you might picture the store at the base of a large hill. I would not place it on top of the hill because I might accidently remember the name as *Hillcrest* or *Hilltop Grocery*. Likewise, while robbery suspect Carmondez was on parole, he had been living at the St. Thomas Halfway House. I have been to St. Thomas in the U.S. Virgin Islands, so in this case I might picture half a house placed on a beach in St. Thomas.

## "Flashbulb" Moments

The key to memory recall is to make the information that you are reading or observing very important to you. Just like the significant events in your life that are permanently etched into your memory, telling yourself that what you are witnessing matters and is extremely important will also enhance the level of neurological activity and your brain's connection to the event. Allowing yourself to become emotionally attached to the event activates the brain's amygdala region and can have a powerful impact on memory retention. One of the reasons why we occasionally cannot recall a person's name is because we have failed to inform our brain that remembering this person's name was important when we first learned it. If the information is not considered important at the time it is encoded, it will be much more difficult to retrieve later. Therefore, when you are required to learn and recall new information, overemphasize its value and importance and try to attach some deep meaning and

**TIP**

**Memory recall can be greatly enhanced by associating information with mental images you are familiar with.**

**TIP**

**Create your own flashbulb moments—see an event as hugely important—to help you recall information about it.**

significance to it. For example, if you are shown a tray of artifacts, you might want to relate to each piece individually by telling yourself a short story about each item: "The Timex watch looks like the one I gave my dad for Father's Day; the cigarette lighter reminds me of the one that Uncle Jack used before he passed away; the tea cup is like the one that my grandmother used when I visited her as a child" and so on.

## Method of Loci

Method of loci is one of the most famous mnemonic devices and is used to associate information with geographical locations that you are very familiar with. There are several variations of this memory aid, and they may be referred to as memory palaces, Roman rooms, or memory journeys. Regardless, they are all based on the same concept: people have excellent recollection of specific locations they are familiar with. For example, you can undoubtedly describe in detail every room in your home and your daily routine when you get up in the morning. Perhaps you can also list all the major intersections that you cross while driving to work or the various stops that the bus or train makes during your daily travels. Therefore, the premise of method of loci is to associate new material that you are unfamiliar with and place these new pieces of information in specific areas that you know well. Returning to the example of the Wanted Person Bulletin, Carmondez had a criminal record for theft, drugs, weapons, and sex offences. Using method of loci, you could use your morning routine to recall this short list: when you get out of bed, you realize that someone stole your blankets; you are then confronted with a large quantity of cocaine stacked on top of the toilet; next you go to get in the shower and there are guns and knives covering the floor; finally, you go to the sink to brush your teeth and there is a couple having sex on your bathroom vanity counter.

## Acrostic Devices

Creating acronyms from the first letters of key words is an excellent memorization tool. For example, in the police academy we had to remember all of the important police radio codes. The 10-80 codes are used to indicate for what an offender has a criminal record.

| | |
|---|---|
| 10-80: | Record of Violence |
| 10-81: | Record of Robbery |
| 10-82: | Record of Offensive Weapons |
| 10-83: | Record of B&E |
| 10-84: | Record of Theft |
| 10-85: | Record of Drugs |
| 10-86: | Record of Sexual Offence |
| 10-87: | Record of Other Offence |

In order to remember the order of what each code was, we used the first letter of the offence category to create the following sentence: "Violent Robbers Often Break The Door for Sex & Other crimes."

One of the challenges with creating acrostic devices during entrance exams is that you will not have the opportunity to write down key words in order to assemble them into an easy to recall acronym. So unless your list of words or information is relatively short—probably five items or fewer—it will be rather difficult to create an acronym in your head and on the fly. Nevertheless it can be done. In the Wanted Person Bulletin example, you could create several acronyms to remember Carmondez's tattoos and their locations:

"Skull with red rose on right shoulder" could be RRSRS
"Los Cabos on Back" is LCB
"Hecho En Mexico on left chest" is HEMLC.

Whether in a police bulletin or photograph, you will also find acronyms associated with licence plate numbers. However, instead of creating your own acronym from a set of words, you should expand upon preset ones to create a series of words that you will be more likely to remember. For example, if the licence plate number is RTJ-472, you could use the acronym to mean: Returning to Jamaica in 4 weeks and 72 hours.

## Chunking

When faced with large numbers or a large list of items, it is far easier to recall this information if it is broken into smaller chunks of information.

Consider your telephone number. If you were tasked with remembering a ten-digit number, you would probably have little success transferring the number from short- to long-term memory if the number looked like this: 4,192,574,928. However, if you take that same number and set it up like a telephone number (419-257-4928), it is suddenly much easier to remember. The reason is that our brains have been programmed to remember ten-digit numbers using these three sequential chunks of data as opposed to trying to remember the number as 4 billion, 192 million, 574 thousand, 928. Therefore, if you see a ten- or seven-digit number, memorize it like a telephone number, and you will have far greater success. If you are a sports fan, you can combine chunking of numbers with visual image association. That is, 317611 becomes much easier to remember if I think of the number as a collection of jersey numbers of hockey players: Price, Subban, Gallagher.

Similarly, use the chunking method to organize a long list of information. In the Wanted Person Bulletin, there is a lot of information to memorize. Instead of trying to remember a laundry list of details, create manageable chunks of information by placing Carmondez's name and age in one mental file, his description in another, his criminal record in another memory folder, and so on.

## PREPARING FOR MEMORIZATION TASKS
### Train Your Brain

Not only is it important to maintain a healthy brain through diet, exercise, and relaxation, but you should also strive to achieve your optimal brain performance by training your brain to store and retrieve information as efficiently and effectively as possible. Memorization and intellectual proficiency can be enhanced through the frequent performance of skill-challenging mental exercises and games. There are numerous online websites devoted to increasing memorization skills. *Lumosity.com*, for example, is probably the most popular fee-based online site; however, there are also many free websites that provide information and online games devoted to memorization training. But you do not need to sit in front of your computer

**TIP**

Use chunking mnemonic techniques, such as NHL players' jersey numbers, to remember larger strings of numbers.

**TIP**

Science suggests that foods rich in Omega-3 fatty acids are brain foods and enhance memorization performance.

or pay additional expenses to exercise your memorization skills. Here are a few simple and effective strategies that you can do at any time to increase your memorization skills.

### SHOPPING LIST

Write out your shopping list at home and then head to the grocery store. Try to buy everything on your list without looking at it. Only after you are ready to go to the checkout, can you make sure that you've purchased everything. Use mnemonic devices to memorize your list.

### PLATE NUMBERS

While driving, pick the first five vehicle licence plates that you see. Phone home, using your hands-free device of course, and leave a message on your phone of what the plate numbers are. Memorize the plate numbers using mnemonic devices. When you get home, listen to your message and see how accurate you are. If you are having trouble with five, start with three or four.

### PHONE NUMBERS

You probably rarely have to remember people's phone numbers anymore because we have them programmed into our smartphones. Write down the phone numbers of five of your friends and family members and remember them. Test yourself the next day, and see how many you've been able to remember.

### REVERSE MEAL PLAN

Try to remember what you had for dinner over the past week. Unless you make a regular meal plan, this is probably harder than it looks. Go back as many days as you can, and try for improvement the following week.

### DECK OF CARDS

Take a deck of cards and use just two complete suits (e.g., spades and diamonds) and lay them out on a table, face down. Flip over the cards two at a time and then return them face down until you can find a match pair. Once you have made a match, you can remove the pair from the table.

### TIME'S UP

**Read the obituaries to practice remembering names and faces and information about people.**

Entrance exams are timed, and there's nothing worse than remembering an answer to a question only after you have walked out of the exam room. To reduce the number of tip-of-your-tongue situations that are irretrievable when it matters, play timed trivia and memory games like Cranium, Trivial Pursuit, or the multitude of free online timed trivia games at *www.purposegames.com*

### SOLEMN REMEMBRANCE

Find the obituaries in your local newspaper and randomly select five people who have passed away. Study their photos and read the write-up about them. Use visual image association techniques to remember their names. Clip the obituary column and fold it up so that just the photograph is showing. Put the columns away for a few days and then look at the photos again. Do you remember their names? What can you say about each person? In the meantime, hopefully you will have learned something positive about an important member of your community.

## TIPS FOR OBSERVATION AND MEMORIZATION TASKS

When you get to the memorization components of your entrance exams, the following tips and strategies may also assist in ensuring that you capture important details.

### Be Methodical

Witnesses to serious crimes are often understandably faulted for having tunnel vision in that they will see the obvious threat, such as the man carrying the shotgun, but completely miss other important details, like whether the suspect was bald. As a police witness, your goal is to expand your field of vision and take in everything that is in front of you. Therefore, when presented with a photograph, start from one side or the top and work your way slowly across the photograph. Look for every minute detail—nothing should be considered too trivial. Make certain that you have completely scanned the photograph and tried to remember every detail before time runs out.

### Read Everything

When being shown a photograph, drawing, or collection of artifacts, there will undoubtedly be written material: brand names of products, advertising, company names, street signs, and licence plate numbers. Make a mental note of all of them.

### Keep Track of the Time

If there is a digital or analog clock, a wrist or pocket watch, or even a sundial shown somewhere in the image, you can be certain that you will be asked what the indicated time was. The same can be said for the date.

### Count on It

If there is more than one of anything, make a mental note of it. For example, you may be asked not only about obvious things like the number of police officers standing in the picture, but also more subtle details like the number of traffic signs, cars, bullet casings, and so forth.

### Note Anything That's Unusual

If something looks odd or out of place in the picture, it is there for a reason, and you will likely be questioned whether you made a mental note of it.

### Recall W5&H

As the saying goes, every picture tells a story or is worth a thousand words. Your goal is to study the image and elicit the story by asking yourself who is involved, what, when, and where did this happen, why did this occur, and how did it happen? This level of critical analysis is needed so that you are prepared to answer all questions that may be posed to you.

## Use Mnemonic Devices

For the vast majority of individuals, it will be impossible to memorize everything that is written down verbatim—especially for things like wanted posters, officer safety bulletins, or short narratives about a crime occurrence. Rather than stress about trying to memorize so much detail, use the mnemonic strategies that you have been practicing to break the information down into manageable pieces.

## Write It Down

As mentioned, you will likely be distracted for a short period of time between the observation phase of the exam and the recollection phase. Therefore, as soon as you have the opportunity to write down what you observed, do so. Although the goal is to transfer as much of what you saw and read from short-term to long-term memory, stress, interference, and distractions may have negatively impacted that process. Therefore, write down as much as you can as soon as permitted before retention of the information dissipates.

Before continuing to the next chapter, study the photograph and read the *Suspect for Identification* bulletin. Use mnemonic devices to assist in remembering your observations, and then answer the review questions that follow—just to make sure that you have got it right.

## HAVE I GOT IT RIGHT?

 **You have six minutes to complete the exercise.**

### Instructions

1. Study the photograph of a crime scene on the following page (Figure 3) for a maximum of one minute and memorize as much detail about the photograph as possible.

2. You are not permitted to make any written notes or refer back to the photograph when answering the subsequent questions.

3. After one minute has passed, turn the page and read the *Suspect for Identification* bulletin (Figure 4). You are only permitted to study the bulletin for two minutes.

4. You are not permitted to make any written notes or refer back to the bulletin when answering the subsequent questions.

5. Answer the questions in sequential order.

Start your timer and begin the exercise now.

STUDY THE PHOTOGRAPH FOR A MAXIMUM OF ONE MINUTE.

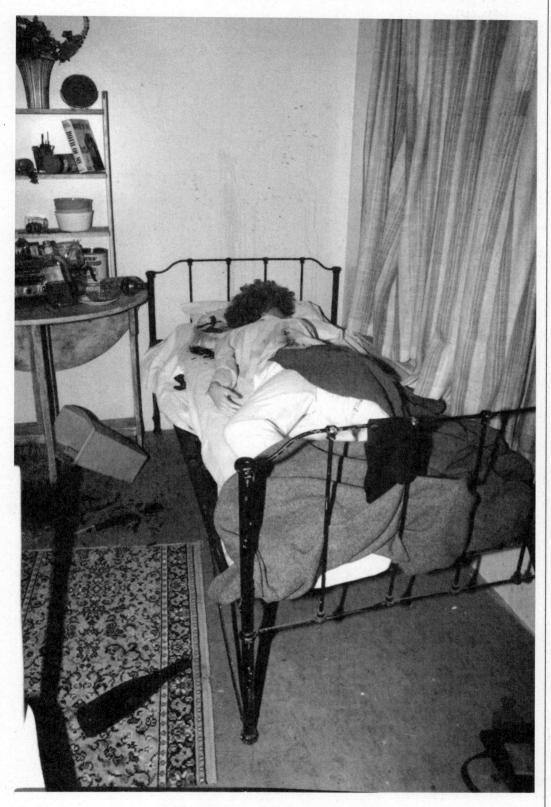

**Figure 3.** Rooming House Murder

STUDY THE BULLETIN BELOW FOR A MAXIMUM OF TWO MINUTES.

## SUSPECT
## FOR IDENTIFICATION

DATE & TIME: 2015-June-11 at 1910 hours

LOCATION: Javabuck Coffee, 2532 18th Street, Scarborough, Ont

VIDEO AVAILABLE: Yes

SUSPECT DESCRIPTION: Caucasian male in his 20s, wearing a black balaclava, blue and white striped hoodie, blue jeans, white runners, and wearing brown gloves

STOLEN: $194.65 in $20 and $10 bills and coins from cash drawer of till

WEAPON: blue handled jacknife with a 4 inch folding blade

VEHICLE: Suspect fled scene in a dark blue 2002 Dodge Neon, 4 door, partial plate obtained: RK?-3?5

DETAILS: At approximately 1710 hours the male suspect entered the coffee shop and approached the victim employee at the front counter. The suspect asked for the manager and the victim said that the manager was in the back room. The suspect jumped over the counter and produced a knife yelling, "I'm robbing you, jackass!" The suspect then told the victim, "open the till, or I'll carve you." The victim opened the cash register as the suspect removed his gloves and grabbed the bills and coins from the drawer. The suspect then leapt back over the counter, leaving his gloves by the till and ran out of the cafe. As the suspect left, he yelled, "Try to follow me and I'll gut you, I swear." The suspect then jumped into a Neon and drove away. The victim was only able to get a partial plate.

**Figure 4.** Suspect for Identification Bulletin

QUESTIONS 1–4 RELATE TO THE CONTENTS OF THE PHOTOGRAPH IN FIGURE 3.

1. What item is placed on the top shelf situated against the wall?

   (A) book
   (B) bowl
   (C) vase
   (D) radio

2. What was the position of the victim when she was found?

   (A) lying on her stomach
   (B) lying on her back
   (C) lying on her left side
   (D) lying on her right side

3. What item is underneath the tipped garbage can?

   (A) glasses
   (B) bible
   (C) comb
   (D) knife

4. How many vertical railings are between the outside posts of the headboard?

   (A) 2
   (B) 3
   (C) 4
   (D) 5

QUESTION 5–10 RELATE TO THE CONTENTS OF THE SUSPECT FOR IDENTIFICATION BULLETIN IN FIGURE 4.

5. At what time did the robbery occur?

   (A) 1,946 hours
   (B) 1,701 hours
   (C) 1,510 hours
   (D) 1,710 hours

6. What is the correct order of letters and numbers on the licence plate that the victim could recall?

   (A) RK?-3?5
   (B) K?R-5?3
   (C) R??- 5?5
   (D) KR?-3?5

7. Which of the following statements did the suspect make verbatim?

   (A) "Open the till, or I'll gut you."
   (B) "Open the till, or I'll carve you."
   (C) "Open the till, jackass!"
   (D) "I'll gut and carve you, jackass."

8. According to the bulletin, what was the year, make, and model of the getaway car?

    (A) 2001 Chrysler Neon

    (B) 2010 Dodge Neon

    (C) 2002 Dodge Neon

    (D) 2002 Chrysler Neon

9. What was the value of cash stolen in the robbery?

    (A) $194.65

    (B) $156.49

    (C) $196.45

    (D) $195.64

10. What is the address of Javabuck Coffee?

    (A) 5323 16th Street, Scarborough

    (B) 2532 18th Street, Scarborough

    (C) 2852 18th Ave, Scarborough

    (D) 2352 16th Street, Scarborough

## Answers

1. **C** A vase and small round mirror are on the top shelf.

2. **B** The victim is on her back. Her thumbs are pointing up.

3. **A** There's a pair of black glasses underneath the tipped garbage can.

4. **C** There are four vertical railings between the headboard posts.

5. **D** The robbery occurred at 1710 hours.

6. **A** The witness recalled the plate as RK?-3?5.

7. **B** The suspect said, "Open the till, or I'll carve you."

8. **C** The car is a 2002 Dodge Neon.

9. **A** A total of $194.65 was stolen in the robbery.

10. **B** The address of the crime is 2532 18th Street, Scarborough.

# Mechanics of Writing and Vocabulary

7

→ **TEST YOUR KNOWLEDGE**

→ **SPELLING**

→ **CAPITALIZATION**

→ **PUNCTUATION**

→ **VOCABULARY**

→ **HAVE I GOT IT RIGHT?**

Catching crooks and putting bad guys in jail is exciting and the reason why most people want to become police officers, but the arrest of a suspect often comes with a heavy burden—the mountain of paperwork that follows. If you are the assigned officer or lead investigator on a file, then you will become tasked with writing the majority of the report; the other officers involved in the case only have to explain their specific actions. The assigned officer must provide a chronological narrative of the whole criminal event, including a summarization of witness and suspect statements, and provide details regarding any evidence that was seized and processed. If, for example, you caught a suspect breaking into a residence, you would likely spend about three hours writing a report. If you arrested an impaired driver at a motor vehicle collision, you can increase the time to approximately five hours. Moreover, if search warrants need to be written, then you can more than double the amount of time required for any investigation. Needless to say, it's imperative that police officers possess strong written communication skills, because they spend a significant portion of every shift writing reports.

Since effective writing skills are a must in policing, most police entrance exams devote considerable space towards evaluating these competencies. Not only will you likely have to identify misspelled words and proper word usage through multiple-choice questions, but you will likely also be required to write paragraphs, or even an essay, and will lose points for any spelling mistakes or other grammatical errors.

Effective written communication skills begin with the basics: proper spelling, capitalization and punctuation (known as the mechanics of writing), and word usage (or vocabulary). This chapter covers these essential components of writing and provides methods to improve your scores in these areas. Begin by completing the Test Your Knowledge assessment.

# TEST YOUR KNOWLEDGE

 You have 10 minutes to complete this exercise.

---

**Instructions**

Indicate whether the underlined portions of the following statements contain any errors in vocabulary, spelling, punctuation, or capitalization.

---

1. The <u>Sergeant</u> was trying to <u>decipher</u> if the name given to him by the suspect was actually an <u>alias</u>.

   (A) Sergeant
   (B) decipher
   (C) alias
   (D) no error

2. It was pretty <u>humorous</u> that Constable Evans showed such a lack of good <u>judgment</u> on this <u>occasion</u>.

   (A) humorous
   (B) judgment
   (C) occasion
   (D) no error

3. The <u>Emergency Response Team</u> members found themselves in an <u>awful</u> dilemma. Officer Jones asked, "Should we enter the room immediately and <u>suprise</u> the suspect, or continue negotiations?"

   (A) Emergency Response Team
   (B) awful
   (C) suprise
   (D) no error

4. If we wanted to <u>succeed</u> in the <u>endeavour</u>, we would need to <u>seperate</u> the truth from speculation.

   (A) succeed
   (B) endeavour
   (C) seperate
   (D) no error

5. The district <u>analyst</u> said, <u>"the</u> crime rate is beginning to decline in the Collingwood <u>neighbourhood</u>."

   (A) analyst
   (B) "the
   (C) neighbourhood
   (D) no error

6. Constable Forman asked, "Surely this must be a temporary assignment, and not something permanent."

   (A) "Surely
   (B) temporary
   (C) permanent."
   (D) no error

7. It's important that police officers posses common sense and excellent decision-making skills; although, these intangible qualities are sometimes difficult to define.

   (A) It's
   (B) posses
   (C) intangible
   (D) no error

8. It occurred to Constable Hollingsdale that it was irrelevant whether his field trainer was young or old, as long as she provided the guidance and assistance he needed.

   (A) occurred
   (B) irrelevant
   (C) old,
   (D) no error

9. The high-calibre assault rifle was concealed in a false ceiling in the neighbours basement suite.

   (A) high-calibre
   (B) ceiling
   (C) neighbours
   (D) no error

10. The prosecutor said that mr. James Hill should not receive bail because his treacherous behaviour was a threat to the community.

    (A) prosecutor
    (B) mr.
    (C) receive
    (D) treacherous

11. The suspect drove the stolen car South on Winchester Street and crashed the vehicle into Uncle Jim's Family Market.

    (A) South
    (B) Street
    (C) vehicle
    (D) no error

12. Master Corporal James raised a glass and shouted out as he made his salute, "To Her Majesty the Queen."

    (A) Master Corporal
    (B) "To
    (C) Queen."
    (D) no error

13. <u>Basically</u>, the Toronto Police Department's policy on pursuits has several <u>idiosyncrasies</u> that make it unique from that of other <u>jurisdictions</u>.

(A) Basically
(B) idiosyncrasies
(C) jurisdictions
(D) no error

14. <u>Apparently</u>, the young officer had left his <u>goverment</u> issued identification on the counter in the <u>restaurant</u>.

(A) Apparently,
(B) goverment
(C) restaurant
(D) no error

15. The new <u>lieutenant</u> appreciated the positive and <u>pejorative</u> evaluations that he had received from his peers that <u>assisted</u> him in obtaining the promotion.

(A) lieutenant
(B) pejorative
(C) assisted
(D) no errors

## Answers

1. **A** "Sergeant" should not be capitalized.

2. **D** *No error*—correct Canadian spelling of judgment.

3. **C** The Emergency Response Team members found themselves in an awful dilemma. Officer Jones asked, "Should we enter the room immediately and **surprise** the suspect, or continue negotiations?"

4. **C** If we wanted to succeed in the endeavour, we would need to **separate** the truth from speculation.

5. **B** Capitalize the beginning of a quoted statement.

6. **C** Constable Forman asked a question and, therefore, her statement should have ended with a question mark.

7. **B** It's important that police officers **possess** common sense and excellent decision-making skills; although, these intangible qualities are sometimes difficult to define.

8. **D** *No error*—**occurred** and **irrelevant** are spelled correctly.

9. **C** An apostrophe is required in "neighbours" to show possession.

10. **B** Titles of person's names are capitalized.

11. **A** Directions are not capitalized.

12. **C** James had shouted his salute; therefore, the statement should have ended with an exclamation mark. The title of "Her Majesty the Queen" is capitalized correctly.

13. **D** *No error*—**idiosyncrasies** is spelled correctly.

14. **B** Apparently, the young officer had left his **government** issued identification on the counter in the restaurant.

15. **B** Misuse of the word pejorative, which means disapproving, harsh, and scornful, is hardly the type of evaluation that would assist someone in getting promoted.

---

### HOW DID YOU SCORE?

Correct Answers: _____ /15    Excellent 14–15    Good 11–13    Average 8–10

If your test score is not in the Excellent range, you should focus your study efforts on this chapter to ensure that you improve your spelling, mechanics, and vocabulary skills.

---

## SPELLING

Effective communication skills begin with being able to spell properly. Few things will draw the negative attention of supervisors more quickly than a constable's report that is written poorly and riddled with spelling mistakes. Many police reports are now written at computer workstations that have software that will check spelling, however, most police organizations still use many forms and documents that need to be completed manually.

The first step in becoming proficient at spelling is to know and follow the basic rules of spelling that apply to the English language. Of course with every rule, there is usually an exception to that rule. These exceptions often create problems because it is more than likely that these troublesome words will appear in police entrance exams. Therefore, not only do you need to learn the basic rules of spelling, but also the one off exceptions. Below are the essential rules of spelling and their common exceptions.

 **TIP**

**Learn the exceptions to the rule: *i before e, except after c.***

### Essentials of Spelling

**RULE 1.** When spelling a word that has an *i* and *e* combination, the rule is: *i before e except after c.* For example, alien, ambient, and chief follow the *i* before *e* rule; however, ceiling, deceit, and receive follow the rule's basic exception.

Unfortunately, there are a number of exceptions to this general rule:

**Exceptions:**

1. When the *i* and *e* combination make a long *a* sound.
   *Example:*
   **weigh, sleigh, and neighbour**
2. When the *i* and *e* combination makes a long *i* sound.
   *Example*:
   **feisty, heist, and height**
3. When the *i* is used as an unstressed vowel.
   *Example:*
   **foreign, forfeit, and counterfeit**
4. There are several words where *i* and *e* follow *c*. Most notable are science, efficient, sufficient, and any word that ends in *cy* that is made plural.
   *Example:*
   **bureaucracies, inconsistencies, and frequencies**

**RULE 2.** When adding a suffix to a root word that ends with a *y* that is preceded by a consonant, change the *y* to an *i*.

> *Example:*
> families, studied, and replies

> **Exception:**
> If the suffix begins with an *i* (i.e., *ing*, or *ish*), then the *y* is retained.

> *Example:*
> replying, tidying, and carrying

**RULE 3.** When adding a suffix to a root word that ends with a *y* that is preceded by a vowel, then the *y* is retained.

> *Example:*
> annoying, conveying, and deployable

**RULE 4.** When adding a suffix that begins with a vowel or *y* to a root word that ends with a short vowel sound and a consonant, double the last consonant.

> *Example:*
> runny, hopping, and rotten

**RULE 5.** When adding a suffix that begins with a vowel or *y* to a root word that ends with an *e*, drop the *e* before adding the suffix.

> *Example:*
> continuous, coinciding, and tasty

> **Exceptions:**
> 1. If the root word ends in *ce* or *ge* and the consonant is "soft," then the *e* is retained.
>    > *Example:*
>    > acknowledgement, advantageous, and enforceable
> 2. If the root word ends in a double *e*, then the *e* is retained.
>    > *Example:*
>    > fleeing and agreeing

**RULE 6.** When adding a suffix that begins with a vowel, double the final consonant of the root word if it is preceded by a single vowel.

> *Example:*
> beginning, committed, and regrettable

> **Exceptions:**
> 1. If there is more than one vowel before the final consonant, do not double the last consonant.
>    > *Example:*
>    > bailed, pooling, and sailing
> 2. If the root word has more than one syllable and the stress does not fall on the last syllable, do not double the final consonant.
>    > *Example:*
>    > benefited, blistering, and quivered
> 3. If the root word has only one syllable, but the stress changes with the addition of the suffix, do not double the final consonant.
>    > *Example:*
>    > deference, preference, and reference

**RULE 7.** The Canadian spelling of root words that end with the consonants *l* or *p* and are preceded by a vowel, the final consonant is doubled when adding a suffix that begins with a vowel.

> *Example:*
>
> **cancelled, totalled, and worshipped**

See below for more examples of differences between the Canadian and American spelling of words.

## Plural Nouns

Errors in spelling sometimes occur when attempting to write a word in its plural form. The following rules will assist you in spelling plural nouns.

**RULE 1.** If the noun ends in a *y* and is preceded by a vowel, add an *s*.

> *Example:*
>
> **attorneys, obeys, and plays**

**RULE 2.** If the noun ends in a *y* and is preceded by a consonant, add *ies*.

> *Example:*
>
> **juries, ladies, and theories**

**RULE 3.** If the noun ends with an *o*, add *es*.

> *Example:*
>
> **potatoes, tomatoes, and zeroes**
>
> There are some notable exceptions to this rule.
>
> *Example:*
>
> **photos, stereos, and videos**

**RULE 4.** If the noun ends with a *ch, s, sh,* or *x*, add *es*.

> *Example:*
>
> **boxes, churches, and stashes**

**RULE 5.** If the noun ends in *f* or *fe*, change to *ves*. For example: knives, selves, and wolves. There are also some notable exceptions to this rule.

> *Example:*
>
> **chiefs, mischiefs, and safes**

**RULE 6.** For compound nouns, the first word is made plural.

> *Example:*
>
> **attorneys general, mothers-in-law, and passers-by**

**RULE 7.** Greek root words that end in *is*, change to *es*.

> *Example:*
>
> **analyses, crises, and synopses**

**RULE 8.** Latin root words that end in *us*, change to *i*.

> *Example:*
>
> **fungi, syllabi, and stimuli**

**RULE 9.** Latin root words that end in *a*, change to *ae*.

> *Example:*
>
> **antennae, larvae, and vertebrae**

**RULE 10.** Some nouns do not change between the singular and plural. This is especially true of wildlife, but there are many others. Here are the top 20:

| | | | | |
|---|---|---|---|---|
| advice | elk | information | luggage | sheep |
| aircraft | equipment | furniture | moose | shorts |
| bison | evidence | jewellery | pants | silver |
| deer | gold | legislation | salmon | wood |

## Words Ending in *Able* or *Ible*

In determining whether a word ends with *able* or *ible*, first consider that there are more than 900 words that end with *able* but only approximately 200 that end with *ible*. Although the odds are stacked in your favour of using *able*, there are several rules to follow to ensure proper spelling.

**RULE 1.** If the root word is able to stand on its own as a complete word, then the ending of the words is spelled with *able*.

*Example:*

acceptable, dependable, and understandable

**Exceptions:**

accessible, convertible, corruptible, digestible, extendible, forcible, flexible, and suggestible.

**RULE 2.** If the root words ends with an *e*, whether the *e* needs to be dropped or not, the ending of the word is spelled with *able*.

*Example:*

changeable, desirable, and likeable

**Exceptions:**

collapsible, defensible, reducible, responsible, submersible, submergible, and reversible

Below is a list of 50 of the most commonly used words that end in *ible*.

| | | | |
|---|---|---|---|
| accessible | discernible | incomprehensible | reprehensible |
| admissible | divisible | incredible | resistible |
| audible | edible | indelible | responsible |
| collapsible | eligible | indestructible | reversible |
| compatible | extendible | intelligible | sensible |
| comprehensible | fallible | invincible | submersible |
| contemptible | feasible | invisible | suggestible |
| convertible | flexible | legible | susceptible |
| credible | forcible | negligible | tangible |
| deductible | implausible | perceptible | terrible |
| defensible | impossible | permissible | visible |
| digestible | inaccessible | plausible | |
| destructible | incompatible | reducible | |

## Words Ending in *Ance* and *Ence*

The ending of these words often sounds very similar, and it's often difficult to discern the spelling of the word just by sounding it out. Fortunately, there are a couple of rules that will help you spell these words.

**RULE 1.** If the root word is from a verb that ends in *ear, ure,* or *y,* then the ending of the word is spelled with *ance.*

> *Example:*
> appearance, compliance, and endurance

**RULE 2.** If the root word is from a verb that ends in *ate,* then the ending of the word is spelled with *ance.*

> *Example:*
> deviance, hesitance, and intolerance

**RULE 3.** If the root word is from a verb that ends in *ere,* then the ending of the word is spelled with *ence.*

> *Example:*
> adherence, interference, and reverence
>
> **Exceptions:**
> perseverance and severance

**RULE 4.** If the root word ends with a soft *ce* or *ge,* then the ending of the word is spelled with *ence.*

> *Example:*
> belligerence, complacence, and indulgence

## Words Ending in *Ary, Ery,* and *Ory*

There are several rules to assist you in deciding how to spell the endings of these words.

**RULE 1.** Words ending with the spelling *ery* often exist as nouns on their own without the suffix.

> *Example:*
> bribery, delivery, and robbery
>
> **Exceptions:**
> accessory, depository, and inventory (to name a few)

**RULE 2.** Words ending with the spelling *ory* are often preceded by the letters *at.*

> *Example:*
> conservatory, inflammatory, and laboratory

**RULE 3.** If the first part of the word cannot exist on its own without the suffix, then the ending is usually spelled *ary.*

> *Example:*
> military, ordinary, and temporary
>
> **Exceptions:**
> celery, fiery, and query (to name a few)

## Words Ending in *Cede*, *Ceed*, and *Sede*

**TIP**

*cede, ceed, or sede?*
*1 word ends with sede:*
• *supersede*
*3 words end with ceed:*
• *exceed*
• *proceed*
• *succeed*

Another troublesome set of words are those that end with a "seed" sound. There are no rules regarding the spelling of these verbs; however, you are fortunate in that there are only a few words to learn. There is only one word that ends with *sede*—supersede. There are only three verbs that end with *ceed*—exceed, proceed, and succeed. However, in the word procedure the middle *e* is dropped. There are seven remaining verbs that end with *ede*: accede, cede, concede, intercede, precede, recede, and secede.

The list below contains many of the words that are frequently misspelled, especially in a law enforcement environment. Once you've mastered this list, there are many online sources that contain sample practice spelling quizzes and lists of difficult words. Take advantage of these sources since many are free to download and print.

## 200 COMMONLY MISSPELLED WORDS

| | | | |
|---|---|---|---|
| absence | corollary | independent | probably |
| absorption | cough | indispensable | professional |
| accelerate | criticize | inedible | proverbial |
| acceptable | curriculum | innocuous | provincial |
| accessible | deceive | intercede | proficient |
| accessory | definitely | interpretation | psychology |
| accidentally | desperate | interrupted | pursue |
| accommodate | difference | invigorate | realize |
| achieve | dilapidated | irrelevant | receive |
| acquaintance | dilemma | irresistible | recognize |
| acquit | disingenuous | irritable | reference |
| across | disappear | laboratory | rendezvous |
| address | diarrhea | leisure | renowned |
| advice | drunkenness | lieutenant | repertoire |
| advisable | duly | liaison | rhyme |
| aggressive | dysfunction | library | rhythm |
| alcohol | easily | losing | sacrilegious |
| anecdote | ecstasy | maintenance | secretary |
| anomaly | either | manoeuvre | seize |
| apparent | embarrass | marriage | seizure |
| argument | environment | millennium | separate |
| asphalt | equipped | miscellaneous | sergeant |
| asterisk | exaggerate | mischievous | sheriff |
| athlete | exceed | misspell | sincerely |
| auxiliary | except | necessary | similar |

| | | | |
|---|---|---|---|
| awful | excerpt | neighbour | siren |
| basically | exhilarate | neither | speech |
| becoming | existence | noticeable | studying |
| besiege | experience | occasion | susceptible |
| bookkeeper | familiar | occurrence | succeed |
| breathe | fascinating | offered | tariff |
| brilliant | February | often | temporary |
| burglary | fiery | operate | through |
| bureaucracy | foreign | ought | threshold |
| calendar | fluorescent | parallel | tortuous |
| caffeine | fluoride | parliament | tragedy |
| camaraderie | foresee | pastime | trying |
| camouflage | generally | particularly | truly |
| ceiling | government | peculiar | until |
| cemetery | grammar | pejorative | unusual |
| certain | grievous | perceive | vaccinate |
| chief | guarantee | perennial | vacillate |
| citizen | heroin | perseverance | vague |
| collaborate | hygiene | persuade | vicious |
| collectable | hypocrisy | phenomenon | village |
| committee | identity | possess | warrant |
| concede | identification | possible | Wednesday |
| consensus | imitation | practical | weird |
| constable | immediately | presence | whether |
| convenience | incident | privilege | withhold |

## CAPITALIZATION

Although proper capitalization may seem like a relatively small part of the overall mechanics of spelling and writing, it's very important that you know when, and just as important to know when not, to use capitals. Whether you are tasked in a police entrance exam with identifying errors in a paragraph or writing your own narrative, the misuse of capitalization is an area where marks can easily be gained or lost. Below are rules regarding the mechanics of capitalization.

**RULE 1.** Capitalize the first word of a sentence and after a period, exclamation mark, or question mark. On some occasions, you also capitalize after a colon (see "Colons").

**RULE 2.** Capitalize the first word of a direct quote that is a complete sentence.
   *Example:*
   The chief said, "**We** will be implementing the new intelligence-led initiative next month."

**Do not capitalize directions and seasons.**

**Exception.** Do not capitalize a portion of a quote that is an incomplete sentence.

*Example:*

The chief said that he was going to implement the "new intelligence-led initiative" sometime next month.

**RULE 3.** Capitalize the first word of a fragmented sentence in a direct quote.

*Example:*

"It's fine with me," I said. then I added, "As long as I don't have to work weekends."

**RULE 4.** Capitalize personal names, nicknames, and their preceding titles.

*Example:*

Mr. David Jones, The Golden Bear, and Mayor Dianne Watts

**RULE 5.** Capitalize specific governments and institutions.

*Example:*

the Supreme Court of Canada, the Parliament Buildings, and Correctional Services of Canada.

**RULE 6.** Capitalize languages, religion, and races.

*Example:*

Cantonese, Christian, and Chinese

**RULE 7.** Capitalize calendar months, days of the week, and holidays; but not seasons.

*Example:*

Thanksgiving, Wednesday, and October; do not capitalize spring

**RULE 8.** Capitalize geographical locations and regions, but do not capitalize directions.

*Example:*

Prince Edward Island, Rideau Canal, and Main Street; but do not capitalize north.

**RULE 9.** Capitalize words when they are used as part of a proper name. For example, "lake", "college", and "river" are only capitalized when they form specific locations:

Sproat Lake, Langara College, and Fraser River.

**RULE 10.** Capitalize the names of books, magazines, journals, films, newspapers and copyrighted names.

*Example:*

*Anne of Green Gables*, Maclean's, *Canadian Journal of Criminology and Criminal Justice*, the *Toronto Star*, and Molson Canadian beer.

## PUNCTUATION

### Apostrophe

The apostrophe is used to indicate possessions, contractions, and omissions in words.

**RULE 1.** Use the apostrophe to indicate possession. For singular nouns and pronouns use *s* (apostrophe *s*). For plural nouns ending in *s*, add the apostrophe after the *s*. For compound words, add *s* to the last word.

*Examples:*

The attorney general's media release will occur this afternoon.

The four juveniles' parents were contacted by the police to come to headquarters.

Officer Janzen said, "It is someone else's turn to complete the arrest booking sheet."

**RULE 2.** Use the apostrophe to indicate contractions and omissions.

*Examples:*

It is = it's

He will = he'll

Class of 1984 = Class of '84

It is nine "on the clock" = it's nine o'clock

**RULE 3.** Use the apostrophe to indicate plural forms of letters and abbreviations.

*Examples:*

I was told to "watch my p's and q's" around Officer Green.

This bright student has obtained M.A.'s from two separate universities.

**Exception.**

Either *'s* or *s* is acceptable for plural numbers.

*Example:*

Jim said he consumed so many drugs during the 1960's (or 1960s) that now he has hardly any recollection of that time.

## Colon

The colon is used to introduce a list, statement, or quotation. It is also used to identify time and is used in formal salutations.

**RULE 1.** Use a colon to introduce a list.

*Example:*

Constable Wong had everything he needed for his presentation to the community policing volunteers: laptop, speakers, projector, and cables.

**RULE 2.** Use a colon to direct attention to a quotation, statement, or summary that follows an introductory sentence.

*Example:*

We should take to heart what U.S. president John F. Kennedy stated: "Ask not what your country can do for you, ask what you can do for your country."

**RULE 3.** Use a colon to separate two main clauses when the second clause restates or explains the first.

*Example:*

The acting sergeant performed poorly in his first week: he failed to notify his supervisor of a serious incident, and he let half the squad go home early on Friday night.

**RULE 4.** Use a colon in the salutation section of a formal business letter.

*Example:*

Dear Sergeant James:

Please accept this letter as my formal request to apply for transfer to District 9, Watch 3.

**RULE 5.** Use the colon to indicate hours and minutes.

*Example:*

The witness said the shooting happened at 5:37 p.m.

**Exception.**

Do not use the colon for indicating time on the 24-hour clock.

*Example:*

Cst. Rider wrote in his occurrence report that the shooting occurred at approximately 1735 hours.

# Comma

There are numerous situations in writing where a comma should be used; however, one of the problems that frequently occurs in writing is that commas are overused or misused. A comma allows the reader to pause and briefly reflect on what he just read. However, the misuse of a comma can significantly alter the meaning of the sentence. Consider the following examples:

Let's eat Dad. (Dad should be worried).

Let's eat, Dad. (Dad is happy it's dinner time).

**RULE 1.** Use a comma after each item in a series of three or more.

*Example:*

The strange burglary suspects broke into the house and stole jewellery, cash, electronic devices, liquor, and meat out of the freezer.

**RULE 2.** Use a comma to begin a direct quote within a sentence.

*Example:*

Officer Smith said, "Bart Dawson, you're under arrest for robbery."

**RULE 3.** Use a comma when you join two clauses with a coordinating conjunction (e.g., and, but, nor, for).

*Example:*

Constable Singh has finished writing the report, but Constable Marks is still tagging the evidence.

**RULE 4.** Use a comma to indicate a pause when it is necessary to ensure the meaning of the sentence.

*Example:*

Remember, "Those who can, do; those who can't, teach."

**RULE 5.** Use commas to indicate parenthetical expressions and contrasted elements.

*Examples:*

The Drug Squad, supervised by Sergeant Richmond, had the highest number of arrests in recent years.

Unlike previous years, the Drug Squad was the top producing section in the department this year.

**RULE 6.** Use commas to separate the day of the month from the year.

*Example:*

Officer Dale wrote the original report on January 31, 2015, and submitted it for review two days later.

**Exception.**

If the day of the month is not included, then no comma is required.

*Example:*

February 2015 was a good month.

**RULE 7.** Use a comma between multiple adjectives not joined by "and".

*Example:*

The suspect was a tall, heavy-set, and menacing person.

**RULE 8.** Use a comma before and after interrupting words such as therefore and however.

*Example:*

All of Officer Statham's paperwork was done, therefore, he would be able to leave on time.

**RULE 9.** Use a comma when beginning sentences with introductory words such as "well," "no," or "yes".

*Example:*

No, that won't be necessary.

**RULE 10.** Use commas for addresses, titles used after a person's name, and informal letter salutations and complimentary closures.

*Examples:*

312 Main Street, Vancouver, British Columbia.

Martin Goldberg, Ph.D. is a faculty member of our university.

Dear John,

Best regards,

## Dash

The dash—also known as the "em dash" because it is the width of the letter "m"—is used in writing to indicate a sudden change in thought, introduce a series, and provide a parenthetical element.

**RULE 1.** Use a dash to indicate a sudden change of thought.

*Example:*

The suspect was wearing a green shirt—or was it blue?

**RULE 2.** Use a dash to indicate an abrupt break in a sentence.

*Example:*

The Officer in Charge could not let the disturbance escalate—people were about to get hurt.

**RULE 3.** Use a dash in place of parentheses to give the clause greater emphasis.

*Example:*

Everyone thought that the harassment policy training was worthwhile—even the seasoned veteran members—and they would be able to apply some of the information that they learned.

## Ellipsis Marks

Ellipsis dots, or three periods in succession, are used in writing to indicate omissions or hesitations. Obviously, it would be rare to use an ellipsis in a police report or narrative. The only exception would be where confidential information was intentionally redacted or excluded from a report and you specifically indicater that it has been removed.

**RULE 1.** Use an ellipsis mark to indicate hesitation by the writer.

*Example:*

As the suspect approached, I couldn't decide which level of force to use: my pistol, baton, pepper spray .... (The fourth ellipsis is the period at the end of the sentence.)

**RULE 2.** Use an ellipsis mark to indicate that the writer's thoughts trail off.

*Example:*

"What's the best thing about working for that police department? I'll tell you, it's.... Hey, did you see the Canucks game last night?"

**RULE 3.** Use an ellipsis mark to indicate omissions within a direct quotation. These are used to shorten the length of the quote, hopefully without changing the essence of the statement. Use brackets to show that the ellipsis was not in the original text or quote [...].

*Example:*

Dick Cheney said, "I think the key that happened on 9/11 is we went from considering terrorist attacks as a law enforcement problem to considering terrorist attacks, especially on the scale we have on 9/11, as being an act of war." This could be shortened to, "I think the key that happened on 9/11 is we went from considering terrorist attacks as a law enforcement problem to considering terrorist attacks [...] as being an act of war."

## Exclamation Mark

Exclamation marks are used to indicate a strong emotional response, such as surprise or anger.

*Example:*

As the new recruit was recklessly racing to the call, the frightened field trainer yelled out, "Slow down, before you kill us both!"

**RULE 1.** Do not overuse an exclamation point in a narrative as it will lose its impact.

**RULE 2.** Do not use a question mark, comma, or period after an exclamation mark.

## Hyphen

The hyphen is used to join compound words and phrases and to eliminate confusion between similarly spelled words that have different meanings.

**RULE 1.** Use a hyphen for compound adjectives that precede a noun.

*Examples:*

first-class service

year-end reports

not-for-profit agency

**RULE 2.** Use a hyphen for compound numbers from twenty-one to ninety-nine, with fractions, and when compounding numbers with words.

*Examples:*

seventy-fifth

one-third

six-year-old

**RULE 3.** Use a hyphen in compound words composed of two or more nouns.

*Examples:*

attorney-general

father-in-law

merry-go-round

**RULE 4.** Use a hyphen when adding the following prefixes: "ex-", "self-", "all-", and "great-", and with the suffix "-elect".

> *Examples:*
> ex-chief
> all-purpose
> great-grandmother
> mayor-elect

**RULE 5.** Use a hyphen when adding a prefix to a proper name.

> *Examples:*
> pro-Canadian
> mid-February
> un-American

**RULE 6.** Use a hyphen to eliminate confusion of words that are spelled the same but have different meanings.

> *Examples:*
> re-count (to count again) and recount (to describe events)
> re-press (to press again) and repress (to suppress)
> re-cover (to cover again) and recover (to get better)

**RULE 7.** Use a hyphen when the prefix ends with a vowel and the word begins with the same vowel.

> *Examples:*
> re-enter
> co-owner
> multi-institutional
> **Exceptions**:
> coordinate, cooperate

## Parentheses

Parentheses are commonly used in writing to indicate supplemental or illustrative material within a sentence, and to enclose numbers and letters that are used for enumeration.

**RULE 1.** Use parentheses (which are always used in pairs) to enclose a clause that is not directly relevant to the main statement or that adds supplemental information.

> *Example:*
> Constable Martin sent the exhibits (blood-stained shirt, knife, and the victim's running shoes) to the forensic lab for DNA analysis.

**RULE 2.** Use parentheses to enclose letters or numbers for enumeration purposes.

> *Example:*
> The successful applicant for the Traffic Section posting will be selected based on **(1)** knowledge of the *Motor Vehicle Act* legislation, **(2)** motorcycle riding proficiency, **(3)** previous impaired driving investigations, and **(4)** collision investigation experience.

# Period

The period is the most common punctuation mark and is used in writing to indicate the end of a sentence. It is also used for abbreviations.

**RULE 1.** Use a period at the end of a sentence that does not contain strong emotion and is not asking a question.

*Example:*

If nothing else, police work is always interesting.

**RULE 2.** Use a period at the end of an abbreviation or after initials.

*Example:*

a.m., Mr., etc. (*et cetera*, meaning "and so forth"), e.g. (*exempli gratia*, meaning "for example"), and Arthur P. Gilmore

**Exception.**

A period is not required between abbreviations that are acronyms, or names of organizations and national or international agencies.

*Example:*

RCMP, CBC, and NHL.

# Question Mark

The question mark is used to indicate direct, but not indirect, questions.

**RULE 1.** Use a question mark to indicate a direct question, but not an indirect question.

*Example:*

Direct question: The sergeant asked, "Who started the brawl inside the pub?"

Indirect question (no question mark): Officer Sanderson told Officer Franklin that the sergeant wanted to know who started the brawl in the pub.

**RULE 2.** When a declarative statement is made that contains a direct question, no comma or period follows the question mark.

*Example:*

"Who started the brawl?" the sergeant asked.

# Quotation Marks

Quotation marks are used to indicate direct quotes or passages written by others, to identify titles, and to emphasize words or phrases.

**RULE 1.** Use quotation marks to set off and enclose direct quotes.

*Example:*

As we approached the nightclub brawl, my partner said, "We are going to need more back up."

**RULE 2.** Punctuation marks are placed inside of quotation marks.

*Example:*

Constable Davis asked, "Are you actually going ahead with this flawed Operations Plan?"

**Exception.**

Do not place question marks inside of the quotation if they do not make up part of the quotation.

*Example:*

What did the suspect mean when he said, "I knew you would be knocking on my door soon"?

**RULE 3.** Use a single quotation mark inside a double quotation mark when you have a quote within another quotation.

*Example:*

Sergeant Erickson asked, "Did Constable Davis really question my decision and say, 'Are you actually going ahead with this'?"

**RULE 4.** Use quotation marks to indicate emphasized words, colloquial sayings, ironic words, and words used in a special context.

*Examples:*

It was positive to hear that the young recruit was not going to "cop out" of working late on the fraud investigation.

The emotionally disturbed man, who was armed with a knife, gave the officer a telling "thousand yard stare."

The thief claimed that he had only "borrowed" the neighbour's lawn mower.

**RULE 5.** Use quotation marks to indicate the titles of articles in periodicals, essays, songs, and movies. Quotation marks can also be used for titles of books, periodicals, journals, and newspapers, however, italics are preferred.

*Examples:*

Led Zeppelin's "Ramble On" is one of my favourite classic-rock tunes.

I found the article "Green Greed" in the RCMP *Gazette* magazine a very interesting account of organized crime's exploitation of natural resources.

Many felt that the *Toronto Advocate's* story "Police rarely get their man" was a piece of one-sided reporting.

## Semicolon

Use the semicolon to join two independent clauses that are closely related and not linked by a coordinating conjunction and to separate items within a list that also contains commas.

**RULE 1.** Use a semicolon to link two independent clauses of equal grammatical rank that are related in meaning. That is, you may use a semicolon between two clauses where you can also separate them by a period.

*Example:*

If the barricaded suspect advances on us, we will use force; if the suspect stays where he is, we will continue to negotiate.

**RULE 2.** Do not use a semicolon to link an independent clause to a dependent clause—a comma is appropriate here.

*Example:*

Although it may take years of physical training and dedication to become a member of the Emergency Response Team, the effort will pay off in the long run.

**RULE 3.** Use a semicolon between conjunctive adverbs (e.g., "however" and "therefore") and conjunctive transitional phrases (e.g., "on the other hand").

*Example:*

The Emergency Response Team was prepared to make an entry; however, they decided to wait until confirmation for the use of the flash bang distraction device was confirmed.

**TIP**

Use a colon, not a semicolon, to introduce a list of items.

**RULE 4.** Use a semicolon to separate a series of items that contain commas within the clause.

> ***Example:***
>
> The police board is usually comprised of the following: the chair, who is the mayor of the municipality; the chief of the police department; a lawyer, of good standing in the community; a business person; a community advocate; and a representative appointed by the provincial government.

---

### IMPROVING VOCABULARY

1. Read daily.
2. Read from multiple sources.
3. Look up unfamiliar words.
4. Use a dictionary.
5. Learn synonyms and antonyms of words.
6. Keep a list of troublesome words.
7. Play word games and puzzles.
8. Participate in online blogs.
9. Download vocab-building apps.
10. Write more often.

---

## VOCABULARY

There are about 200,000 words in the English language; however, many people use as few as 2,000 words in their conversational vocabulary. By the time you graduate from high school, you will have acquired a reading vocabulary of at least 20,000 words. The problem is that unless you read or hear the context of words on at least an occasional basis, you may tend to forget their meaning and have difficulty retrieving them to use in conversation and writing.

It is important to build a fairly large and expansive vocabulary so that not only are you able to understand the conversation and writing of others but you are also able to communicate your ideas and points of view effectively. Police entrance exams tend to have a significant number of vocabulary questions to ensure that you have strong written communication skills.

In preparing for the exam, you should build the strength of your vocabulary from a policing perspective. That is, it is important that you are able to recognize and converse in words that are associated with the profession. For the entrance exam, there is little use in discovering new words and their meaning from the medical field, for example. Therefore, you should focus on learning new words from sources within the social science disciplines (e.g., criminology, sociology, and law) by following current events.

## Strategies for Improving Vocabulary

### READ EVERY DAY

The first step in building your vocabulary is to read as often as you can. It sounds simple enough, but reading takes time away from other activities, such as watching TV, spending time with friends, playing X-Box, and surfing the net. Although you will always broaden your vocabulary by watching TV or through social contact, it will be limited in scope, and it would take a very long time to learn relatively few words. Set aside time each day to read. For example, you could read the newspaper in the morning, a journal at lunch, and engross yourself in a nonfiction book in the evening.

### READ FROM A VARIETY OF SOURCES

Don't focus on one source of material such as newspapers or books; instead, find enjoyment in reading by selecting literature from a variety of mediums. You want to expand your vocabulary in an enjoyable way and not have it feel like dreaded work. Sources to consider: newspapers that are professional or business oriented, such as the *Globe and Mail*; news and general interest magazines, such as *Maclean's*; academic journals and textbooks, for instance *Canadian Criminal Justice* (Griffiths, 2007), that critically explore policing and the criminal justice system; and both fiction and nonfiction works that both entertain and inform.

## LOOK UP UNFAMILIAR WORDS

As you spend time reading through your spectrum of material, make note of words that you do not recognize or are unsure of their precise meaning. Stop and look up the word using an online dictionary or thesaurus, or "go old school" and dust off your parents' hardcopy. Find out what the word means and the context within which it is used. You will be able to recall the word and its meaning more readily if you can associate it with a narrative that you just read and put it into context.

## USE A DICTIONARY

Although you will be using a dictionary or thesaurus to look up the meaning of unknown words, you should also spend some time each week reading through a dictionary. You will come across unfamiliar words much more frequently by using a dictionary than from any other source. Dictionaries also provide a word's part of speech (adjective, noun, etc.) and its proper pronunciation, and most dictionaries also provide an example of the correct use of the word in a sentence.

## LEARN SYNONYMS AND ANTONYMS OF WORDS

In addition to learning the proper meaning of a new word, spend the extra effort to discover the word's synonyms and antonyms. Beyond thesauruses and dictionaries, most word processing programs can quickly provide this information with the click of the mouse. Many police entrance exams contain multiple-choice questions that provide an uncommon word and then ask you to identify its synonym or antonym.

## KEEP A LIST

Just as you should keep a list of words that are difficult to spell, you should also have an ongoing list of new words and their meanings. Make flashcards, keep a small notebook, or use sticky notes that you can keep beside your computer monitor or the living room couch so that you can refer to them during breaks in the hockey game. Always keep with you a stack of flashcards that you can refer to throughout the day. After you have mastered one list of words and definitions, start a new one; you should be continuously building the scope and strength of your vocabulary.

## PLAY WORD GAMES AND PUZZLES

Word puzzles, such as crosswords, word jumbles, and word search games can be found in daily newspapers, magazines, puzzle books, and free online sources. They often use uncommon words to keep their games challenging and to maintain your interest. Other word games such as Scrabble, Boggle, and Word Whomp are available as board games or online. These word games and puzzles not only build your vocabulary and enhance your problem-solving and critical-thinking skills but also improve memory and recall.

### PARTICIPATE IN ONLINE BLOGS

Keep abreast of current events, people's opinions, and subject-specific news by following and participating in online forums and blogs. There are Canadian police-related blogs such as Saskatoon Police Service's "cops and bloggers" (*http://copsandbloggers.ca/*), and many Canadian police agencies have a Twitter account and are on Facebook. Your objective is to find police-related stories and information that contain words with which you may have previously been unfamiliar.

### DOWNLOAD VOCABULARY-BUILDING APPS

There are many free dictionary and vocabulary-based apps that you can download to your tablet or smartphone. For example, for devices that use the Android operating system, there are more than 200 free apps that are designed to build vocabulary skills. These interactive and multimedia applications often incorporate game playing and skill development. Many also have the ability to become increasingly challenging according to your level of progress.

Established dictionary publishers such as Merriam-Webster and Oxford Dictionaries have their own websites and downloadable apps that host a variety of games and quizzes. In addition, you can sign up to be e-mailed their "Word of the Day" or receive information via daily Twitter feeds.

### WRITE MORE OFTEN

One of the most important strategies in developing and expanding your vocabulary skills is to practice writing. You don't necessarily need to take on extra writing assignments at work or school (people might think that there's something wrong with you if you do), but you should at least start by writing more emails, whether at work or to your friends and family. Although it seems that people rarely write emails in complete sentences, you should focus on constructing grammatically correct emails that use complete sentences and incorporate a robust vocabulary (otherwise U-L B SOL, and won't do GR8 on the entrance exam; QQ). By writing frequently and using your new words in well-constructed sentences, you will find that you are steadily enhancing your vocabulary skills.

Before continuing to the next chapter, answer the 10 multiple-choice review questions below—just to make sure that you have got it right.

## HAVE I GOT IT RIGHT?

 **You have 5 minutes to complete the exercise.**

IN QUESTIONS 1–3, CHOOSE THE SYNONYM OF THE UNDERLINED WORD.

1. The <u>recalcitrant</u> youth were disobeying police orders to disperse and starting to damage property.

   (A) obstreperous
   (B) disingenuous
   (C) deleterious
   (D) ubiquitous

2. The murderer was unrepentant when found guilty of committing these <u>egregious</u> criminal acts.

   (A) sedulous
   (B) salubrious
   (C) ethereal
   (D) flagrant

3. Constable Garnett could not <u>assuage</u> the anger of the distraught woman that had just received her second violation ticket in two days.

   (A) juxtapose
   (B) placate
   (C) languish
   (D) imperil

IN QUESTIONS 4–5, CHOOSE THE ANTONYM OF THE UNDERLINED WORD.

4. Despite intense cross examination by the defence lawyer, Constable Arlington was <u>steadfast</u> in her recollection of events.

   (A) surfeit
   (B) convalesce
   (C) oscillate
   (D) insolent

5. Sergeant Harbrace asked <u>solicitous</u> questions regarding the injured officer's welfare.

   (A) esoteric
   (B) irascible
   (C) truculent
   (D) callous

IN QUESTIONS 6–10, IDENTIFY WHICH OF THE UNDERLINED WORDS ARE MISSPELLED OR IF THERE ARE ANY ERRORS IN PUNCTUATION.

6. It is <u>truly</u> <u>regretable</u> that the suspect was not convicted of being an <u>accessary </u>to murdering his <u>neighbour</u>.

   (A) truly
   (B) regretable
   (C) accessary
   (D) neighbour
   (E) no error

7. <u>Auxillary</u> Constable Stark said, "<u>Let</u> me check my <u>calendar</u> to see if I'm <u>scheduled</u> to work that day."

   (A) Auxillary
   (B) Let
   (C) calendar
   (D) scheduled
   (E) no error

8. The suspect was charged with <u>forcible</u> confinement, assault <u>causing</u> <u>grevious</u> bodily harm, and <u>extortion</u>.

    (A) forcible

    (B) causing

    (C) grevious

    (D) extortion

    (E) no error

9. "Where did my Blackberry get moved to<u>?</u>" demanded Sergeant Jaxson. He then <u>proceded</u> to tell me that he's already lost some <u>jewellery</u> this week—his wedding ring.

    (A) ?"

    (B) proceded

    (C) jewellery

    (D) —

    (E) No error

10. Even though writing was one of the <u>notable</u> skills in his impressive <u>repertoire</u>, it didn't seem <u>feasable</u> that Constable Nelson would complete the <u>occurrence</u> report so quickly.

    (A) notable

    (B) repertoire

    (C) feasable

    (D) occurrence

    (E) no error

## Answers

1. **A** obstreperous and recalcitrant.

2. **D** egregious and flagrant.

3. **B** assuage and placate.

4. **C** oscillate.

5. **D** callous.

6. **B** See Essentials of Spelling, words ending in *able*, Rule 1.

7. **A** See 200 Commonly Misspelled Words.

8. **C** See 200 Commonly Misspelled Words.

9. **B** See Essentials of Spelling, words ending in *ceed*.

10. **C** See Essentials of Spelling, words ending in *ible*.

# Grammar and Sentence Structure

8

→ **TEST YOUR KNOWLEDGE**

→ **HOMONYMS**

→ **SENTENCE STRUCTURE**

→ **OTHER GRAMMATICAL ERRORS**

→ **HAVE I GOT IT RIGHT?**

As a prospective police officer, it is imperative that you are able to demonstrate that you possess a strong command of the English language, especially in written communication. Police entrance exams typically test your ability to correctly answer questions relating to a variety of grammatical areas. The previous chapter highlighted frequently misspelled words and punctuation errors, which can be relatively easy to spot because you are generally looking for just one thing. However, in this chapter you will examine the more complex area of grammatical errors associated with word usage and sentence structure. Sentence structure can be challenging in that you must ensure that there are no errors throughout the entire sentence and not just with individual words. Fortunately, there are a number of straightforward rules and tips that you can use to ensure proper word usage and sentence structure. Begin by completing the *Test Your Knowledge* assessment.

## TEST YOUR KNOWLEDGE

 **You have 10 minutes to complete this exercise.**

> Select the correct response to the underlined portions of the following statements.

1. Neither Cst. Johnson nor Cpl. Davis ____ available tomorrow night.

    (A) were

    (B) is

    (C) are

    (D) won't be

2. Since the suspect was wounded during the gun battle, the police _____ been able to track his location sooner.

   (A) would of
   (B) should have
   (C) could of
   (D) has

3. The police hockey team ___ still without a loss.

   (A) will be
   (B) are
   (C) is
   (D) were

4. It's important to keep the chief _____ of the unfolding hostage situation on Main Street.

   (A) apprised
   (B) appraised
   (C) appeased
   (D) apposed

5. The Emergency Response Team entered the suite because the hostage appeared to be in _____ danger.

   (A) immanent
   (B) immortal
   (C) imposable
   (D) imminent

6. The chief, along with his two deputies, _____ expected to attend the press conference.

   (A) are
   (B) were
   (C) is
   (D) shall be

7. Every applicant must do ____ best in order to pass all recruitment stages.

   (A) his
   (B) there
   (C) they're
   (D) their

8. The police dog wagged ___ tail.

   (A) it's
   (B) i'ts
   (C) its
   (D) its'

9. The sergeant said he will hire _____ is most qualified.

    (A) whomever
    (B) whoever
    (C) whomsoever
    (D) who

10. The pimp was arrested for operating an _____ brothel.

    (A) elicit
    (B) eclectic
    (C) impudent
    (D) illicit

11. When working long tours of duty, some police members are known to _____ down for a few minutes to grab a short rest.

    (A) lay
    (B) lie
    (C) have lain
    (D) laid

12. The officers felt it was _____ duty to keep hunting for the suspect until they found him.

    (A) there
    (B) they're
    (C) those
    (D) their

13. The sergeant wanted to know _____ police car was observed speeding along Marine Drive without its emergency equipment activated.

    (A) whose
    (B) who is
    (C) whomever's
    (D) who's

14. Last weekend, three youths flipped their canoe and _____ in Grey Lake.

    (A) did drown
    (B) drowned
    (C) drown
    (D) had drown

15. The officers attended a lecture that was taught by ___ FBI agent.

    (A) an
    (B) its
    (C) it's
    (D) a

## Answers

1. **B** Neither Cst. Johnson nor Cpl. Davis **is** available tomorrow night.

2. **B** Since the suspect was wounded during the gun battle, the police **should have** been able to track his location sooner.

3. **C** The police hockey team **is** still without a loss.

4. **A** It's important to keep the chief **apprised** of the unfolding hostage situation on Main Street.

5. **D** The Emergency Response Team entered the suite because the hostage appeared to be in **imminent** danger.

6. **C** The chief, along with his two deputies, **is** expected to attend the press conference.

7. **A** Every applicant must do **his (or her)** best in order to pass all recruitment stages.

8. **C** The police dog wagged **its** tail.

9. **B** The sergeant said he will hire **whoever** is most qualified.

10. **D** The pimp was arrested for operating an **illicit** brothel.

11. **C** When working long tours of duty, some police members are known to **have lain** down for a few minutes to grab a short rest.

12. **D** The officers felt it was **their** duty to keep hunting for the suspect until they found him.

13. **A** The sergeant wanted to know **whose** police car was observed speeding along Marine Drive without its emergency equipment activated.

14. **B** Last weekend, three youths flipped their canoe and **drowned** in Grey Lake.

15. **A** The officers attended a lecture that was taught by **an** FBI agent.

| HOW DID YOU SCORE? |
|---|
| Correct Answers: _____/15    Excellent 14–15    Good 11–13    Average 8–10 |
| If your test score is not in the Excellent range, you should focus your study efforts on this chapter to ensure that you understand key grammatical rules. |

## HOMONYMS

**TIP**

Misuse of homonyms—such as *their, there,* and *they're*—are one of the most common grammatical errors.

One of the most common grammatical errors that we make involves the misuse of homonyms—where two or more words sound similar but have different spellings and meanings. We tend to rely on computer word processing programmes to capture and auto-correct the mistakes we make; however, most computer programmes do not indicate when you use a word in the wrong context. For example, I once wrote a report stating that a victim was severely beaten and had slipped into a "comma." Although it was a tragic incident, my supervisor did enjoy pointing out the error and asked whether the victim had run afoul of any other punctuation marks. Similarly, I have read several reports where drug dealers have been in possession of "heroine" or police officers have searched a "premise" looking for a suspect. Since homonyms are used in the wrong context so frequently, they often appear in police entrance exams. You, however, can avoid many of these types of pitfalls by learning these 50 common homonym errors.

## Accept / Except

*Accept* is a verb that means to receive something.

*Except* is a preposition that means to exclude or leave out.

> Officer Jones was told not to *accept* free meals at his favourite restaurant.
>
> Everyone displayed a high level of dress and deportment, *except* Constable Smith.

## Adverse / Averse

*Adverse* is an adjective that means harmful or unfavourable.

*Averse* is an adjective that means a feeling of repugnance or something being distasteful.

> The *adverse* effects of crack cocaine abuse are well known.
>
> Some police officers have a strong *averse* reaction to attending sudden death calls.

## Advice / Advise

*Advice* is a noun that means a recommendation or information.

*Advise* is a verb that means to caution, warn, or consult.

> The police officer *advised* the motorist to slow down in the school zone.
>
> The motorist accepted that *advice.*

## Affect / Effect

*Affect* is used both as a verb meaning to produce an influence and as a noun as an aspect of an emotion.

*Effect* is used both as a verb meaning to bring about or to cause and as a noun meaning the consequence or impact.

> How does the increased crime rate in Toronto *affect* policing strategies?
>
> The woman displayed little *affect* when the police officer told her that her husband was killed in a car accident.
>
> The sergeant's rant appeared to have little motivational *effect*.
>
> Hopefully the tougher impaired driving laws will *effect* change in people's behaviour.

## A lot / Alot / Allot

*A lot* is a phrase meaning to a considerable degree and frequently.

*Alot* is not a word—do not use it.

*Allot* is a verb meaning to assign as a share or portion.

> Officer Roth said he could not leave early as he had *a lot* of paperwork to complete.
>
> The supervisor decided to *allot* each member of the squad his fair share of wagon duty.

## Allusion / Illusion

*Allusion* is a noun meaning a direct reference to something.

An *illusion* is a noun meaning a misleading appearance.

> The discipline officer made an *allusion* to the lack of ethics training he had received.
>
> The perceived reduction in crime was a short-lived *illusion*.

## Already / All Ready

*Already* is an adverb meaning previously.

*All ready* are two words that together mean entirely ready.

> The motorist had *already* been given a warning last week; this time he was getting a ticket.

> When the supervisor arrived, the Emergency Response Team was *all ready* to enter the suspect's house.

## Altogether / All together

*Altogether* is an adverb meaning completely or entirely.

*All together* are two words meaning together in a group.

> The constable was *altogether* exhausted at the end of his overtime shift.

> The Crowd Control Unit was *all together* and prepared to deploy.

## Anyway / Anyways

*Anyway* is an adverb that means regardless or in any event.

*Anyways* is not a word—do not use it.

> Officer Joe was told to wait for backup before entering the premises, but he went in *anyway*.

## Appraise / Apprise

*Appraise* is a verb that means to estimate or to set the value of something.

*Apprise* is a verb that means to give notice and to tell.

> The stolen watch had an *appraised* value of $1,200.

> The sergeant wanted to be *apprised* of any serious calls in her area.

## Boarder / Border

*Boarder* is a noun meaning one who is provided with lodging and meals, or a snow or skate boarder.

*Border* is a noun that means an outer part or edge, or a boundary.

> I didn't know that Corporal Johns was both a skier and snow *boarder*.

> The Canadian *Border* Services Agency officials caught the suspect trying to enter the country illegally.

## Bloc / Block

*Bloc* is a noun that means a group of persons or companies or nations.

*Block* is used both as a verb meaning to obstruct or prevent and a noun meaning group of things or a solid piece.

> The Black *Bloc* anarchists were set on starting a riot during the 2010 Winter Olympics.

> One of the police officers was hit in the head with a cinder *block* during the disturbance.

## Breach / Breech

*Breach* is a noun meaning a gap or violation or a verb meaning to break or violate.

*Breech* is a noun meaning a type of pants, lower parts, or the back end of a firearm barrel.

> The suspect was able to *breach* police containment and escape.

> The traffic cops were used to wearing *breeches* while riding motorcycles.

## Casual / Causal

*Casual* is an adjective meaning informal and occasional and is also a noun meaning temporary employee.

*Causal* is an adjective relating to the cause or causation of something.

> The Police Ball is never a *casual* dress event.

> There is considerable disagreement whether there is a *causal* relationship between Taser use and in-custody deaths.

## Canvas / Canvass

*Canvas* is a noun meaning a type of cloth used to make sails and tents.

*Canvass* is a verb that means to go through, or to solicit for information.

> The thief stole a large *canvas* awning.

> After the bank robbery, the police *canvassed* the area for witnesses and video evidence.

## Capital / Capitol

*Capital* is an adjective meaning very significant or excellent, the most serious, and punishable by death. It is also a noun meaning the stock and the city serving as government.

*Capitol* is a noun that refers to a state government building in the United States.

> Every news story involving a serial killer re-ignites the debate over *capital* punishment in Canada.

> The legislators met at the Washington *Capitol* building.

## Censor / Censure — *criticize*

*Censor* is a verb that means to check the acceptability of or to delete inappropriate material and a noun that describes a person who does this.

*Censure* is a verb the means to criticize or blame and a noun that means a reprimand.

> The *censor* concluded that the pornographic movie was illegal because it violated community standards.

> The officer was *censured* for speaking publicly about the criminal investigation without permission from his supervisor.

## Cite / Site / Sight

*Cite* is a verb meaning to call upon to reference and to quote an authority.

*Site* is a noun meaning a place, specific location, or area around a building.

*Sight* is a noun meaning the act or process of seeing or something to see, and a verb meaning to aim or look through.

> People often *cite* Sir Robert Peel's Principles when discussing the foundation of policing in Canada.

> During the hostage-taking incident, a police officer was assigned to determine a *site* for a command post.

> Proper *sight* alignment is essential in proficient target shooting.

## Coma / Comma

*Coma* is a noun meaning profound unconsciousness.

*Comma* is a punctuation mark.

> The severely assaulted victim slipped into a *coma*.

> The police officer mistakenly wrote in his report that the victim had slipped into a *"comma."*

## Compliment / Complement

*Complement* is a noun that means something that adds to or makes complete.

*Compliment* is a noun that means an expression of respect, appreciation, or honour.

> The forged hat *complements* the officer's uniform.

> The victim *complimented* the officer for the level of compassion she showed.

## Councillor / Counsellor

*Councillor* is a noun that means a member of a council.

*Counsellor* is a noun that means an adviser or lawyer.

> The mayor and a *councillor* attended the police board meeting.

> The accused was instructed to speak to his *counsellor* prior to making a statement.

## Cue / Queue

*Cue* is a noun meaning a signal or prompt or a wooden stick used to play billiards.

*Queue* is a noun meaning a waiting line or a temporary storage area for processing work.

> The Emergency Response Team waited for the undercover police officer's *cue* before executing the take down.

> The newly hired police recruits had to form a long *queue* and wait more than two hours before being issued their new uniforms.

## Desert / Dessert

*Desert* is a noun that means an arid land and is a verb that means to abandon or leave.

*Dessert* is a noun that means a sweet dish.

> The officer was reprimanded for *deserting* his position during the riot.

> You must try Angela's *desserts*—they're the best!

## Discreet / Discrete

*Discreet* is an adjective that means being prudent, tactful, and unnoticeable.

*Discrete* is an adjective that means being distinct or finite.

> The undercover officer working surveillance had to be *discreet* so that he would not draw attention to himself.

> There is a *discrete* number of police recruit positions available at any given time.

## Elicit / Illicit

*Elicit* is a verb that means to bring out or draw forth.

*Illicit* is an adjective meaning unlawful or illegal.

> The police officer was tactful in her ability to *elicit* a confession from the suspect.

> The apartment building was well known for the *illicit* activity that occurred on its premises.

## Eligible / Legible

*Eligible* is an adjective meaning the person is qualified or worthy of something.

*Legible* is an adjective that means something is capable of being read.

Most police officers must have patrol experience before they are *eligible* for detective work.

It is essential that police officers make *legible* entries in their notebooks.

## Ensure / Insure

*Ensure* is a verb that means to guarantee or make certain.

*Insure* is a verb that means to obtain insurance or to take appropriate precautions.

The heavy police presence at the football game was to *ensure* the safety of the fans.

People are advised to *insure* their valuable property in the event it is stolen.

## Flair / Flare

*Flair* is a noun that means a special talent or inclination towards something.

*Flare* is a noun that means a fire used to attract attention and a verb that means to spread out.

The tenacious beat officer had a *flair* for making street-level drug arrests.

The emergency road *flares* are kept in the trunk of the sergeant's patrol vehicle.

## Heroin / Heroine

*Heroin* is a noun that means an illegal opiate.

*Heroine* is a noun that describes a woman who is admired for her achievements.

Cocaine and *heroin* addiction have ruined countless lives.

The woman who saved the young child from the burning building was a real-life *heroine*.

## Hoard / Horde

*Hoard* is a noun that means a cache of stored things and a verb that means to keep and to save up.

*Horde* is a noun that means a crowd.

The emergency workers had a difficult time accessing the elderly male's suite as he had a *hoard* of old newspapers and magazines stacked to the ceiling.

The melee broke out when a *horde* of intoxicated young men went on a rampage in the streets.

## Immanent / Imminent

*Immanent* is an adjective meaning inherent.

*Imminent* is an adjective that means something is about to occur.

Compassion for those less fortunate is an *immanent* quality that many police recruiters look for in applicants.

The police evacuated the building believing that the risk of an explosion was *imminent*.

## Inequity / Iniquity

*Inequity* is a noun that means unfairness.

*Iniquity* is a noun that means wickedness or sin.

It was a great *inequity* to see the murderer set free on a technicality.

The terrorist bombing was an *iniquity* that tore into the consciousness of society.

## Incident / Incidence

*Incident* is a noun that means an occurrence or something of importance.

*Incidence* means the rate of occurrence or the arrival of something at a surface.

> There were many serious *incidents* occurring in the area this month.

> There was a high *incidence* of crime along Main Street this month.

## Its / It's

*Its* is an adjective meaning belonging to or shows possession.

*It's* is a contraction of "it is".

> Vancouver saw *its* international reputation bruised during the Stanley Cup riot.

> After completing the test, *it's* important to review your answers before submitting your exam.

## Loose / Lose

*Loose* is an adjective that means slack and not tight.

*Lose* is a verb that means to suffer loss of, or to misplace.

> The prisoner was able to escape because the handcuffs were too *loose*.

> Police sports teams hate to *lose* to firefighter sports teams.

## Patience / Patients

*Patience* is a noun that means to be patient and tolerant.

*Patients* is the plural form of the noun patient meaning a person under treatment or medical care.

> Working surveillance requires a great deal of *patience* as there may be many long hours of inactivity.

> The break-in at the doctor's office meant that he had to cancel several appointments with his *patients* that morning.

## Pedal / Peddle

*Pedal* is a verb that means to operate levers with your feet and a noun that means a device activated by the foot.

*Peddle* is a verb that means to sell or offer for sale goods and wares.

> The motorist advised the officer that he crashed his car because his gas *pedal* was stuck.

> Police quickly caught up to the man trying to *peddle* stolen goods.

## Personal / Personnel

*Personal* is an adjective relating to a person or individual or meaning private.

*Personnel* is a noun that means a body of persons, usually referring to employment and staff.

> The pre-employment background questionnaire asked numerous *personal* questions.

> There were more than 100 police *personnel* assigned to the mass demonstration.

## Precede / Proceed

*Precede* is a verb that means to come before, to be ahead of.

*Proceed* is a verb that means to continue or to move forward.

The fight in the stands appears to be the significant event that *preceded* the riot.

The police chief wanted to *proceed* with implementing the new crime-fighting strategy, despite some vocal opposition.

## Premise / Premises

*Premise* is a noun that means a proposition or inference.

*Premises* is a noun that means a building or part of a building.

The defence lawyer put forward a *premise* that it was impossible for his client to have committed the crime as he would have needed to be in two places at the same time.

The fugitive squad methodically searched each room of the *premises* for the wanted suspect.

## Prescribe / Proscribe

*Prescribe* is a verb that means to write a prescription or to provide direction with authority.

*Proscribe* is a verb that means to prohibit or to condemn as unlawful.

The law *prescribes* that using a firearm during an offence requires a mandatory minimum prison sentence.

Bumper-surfing is a *proscribed* act because of the inherent danger associated with hanging onto a moving vehicle while riding a skateboard.

## Principal / Principle

*Principal* is an adjective that means the most important and a noun that means the head school administrator.

*Principle* is a noun that means a rule, doctrine, or the primary source.

School Liaison Officer Jackson spoke to the *principal* at length about the troublesome youth.

Police officers are trained to consider the "one-plus-one" *principle* when deciding upon an appropriate level of force to use when confronting a suspect.

## Right / Rite / Write

*Right* is an adjective that means correct, a noun that means something that one is entitled, an adverb that means precisely, and a verb that means to do justice.

*Rite* is a noun that means a ceremony or practice.

*Write* is a verb that means to form letters, words, or symbols with a pen or pencil.

The protestors believed it was their *right* to spray paint the storefront window.

The grueling hill climb was a *rite* of passage for the recruits on their first day at the police academy.

Although most police officers now type their reports, they still need to *write* legibly in their notebooks.

## Stationary / Stationery

*Stationary* is an adjective meaning motionless or not moving.

*Stationery* is a noun that refers to writing materials such as paper, pens, and envelopes.

The officers at the ceremony stood at attention, *stationary* for half an hour.

Once the computers stopped working, it was time to break out the *stationery* and write the reports the old-fashioned way.

## Than / Then

*Than* is a conjunction and preposition that is used to compare or indicate a difference.

*Then* can be used as a noun, adjective, or adverb that indicates time or order.

> Police officers have been heard to say, "I would rather be judged by twelve, *than* carried by six."

> The patrol officers started their day with a parade briefing, and *then* they went for coffee.

## Their / There / They're

*Their* is an adjective that means the possessive form of they.

*There* is an adverb meaning a place or location.

*They're* is a contraction of "they are."

> The vacationers were distraught over having *their* wallets stolen from the lockers.

> The officer drew his firearm and yelled at the suspect, "Stop right *there!*"

> The store owner pointed to the youths and said, "*They're* nothing but trouble."

## Threw / Through

*Threw* is the past tense of the verb *throw*.

*Through* is a preposition that means the passage of something from one point (or side) to another point (including time).

> The suspect *threw* down his weapon when challenged by the police officers.

> The suspect's bullet had passed *through* the victim's chest and exited his lower back.

## To / Too / Two

*To* is a preposition that is used to indicate movement or action and an adverb that means to indicate direction.

*Two* is the number between one and three.

*Too* is an adverb that means also, besides, or to a degree.

> The police officers were dispatched *to* the robbery in progress.

> Police officers driving "Code *Two,*" means driving without lights and siren activated.

> The Office of the Police Complaints Commission determined that the officer had not used *too* much force when he arrested the suspect.

## Weak / Week

*Weak* is an adjective that means lacks strength or skill or is inefficient.

*Week* is a noun that means a 7-day period.

> The battered victim was almost too *weak* to call 911.

> It has been almost a *week* since the last robbery in the area.

## Were / We're/ Where

*Were* is the past tense of the verb *to be*.

*We're* is a contraction of "we are."

*Where* is an adverb meaning to, at, or in what place, or what situation.

> The detectives *were* finally able to get some rest once the suspect was arrested.

> The Field Training Officer told the new recruit, "*We're* going out for dinner after work, and we expect you to join us."

> The new recruit didn't know *where* to look for the Health and Safety forms.

# SENTENCE STRUCTURE

Homonym errors are relatively easy to spot in sentences. However, it can be more difficult to identify and correct structural issues. Faulty subject-verb and pronoun-antecedent agreement and faulty parallelism are the most common grammatical errors. Understanding and following the grammatical rules below will help you make your way through the grammatical minefields (or "mind fields") that are often sprinkled throughout police entrance exams.

## Subject–Verb Agreement

In each sentence, you must ensure that the subject and the verb are always in agreement in number and person. Although this may seem like a daunting journey back to Grade 9 English, identifying faulty subject-verb agreement is not challenging if you remember to follow and practice these rules.

**RULE 1.** If the subject is singular, then the verb must be singular, and if the subject is plural, then the verb must also be plural.

> **Example:**
> The male police officers *are* getting new lockers next week, but Cst. Brown *has* identified his already.

In this example the subject in the first part of the sentence is plural—*the male police officers*—therefore, the form of "to be" must also be plural—*are*. In the second half of the sentence, *Cst. Brown* is singular, so the verb "have" must also be singular—*has*.

However, it is not always easy to tell whether the subject is singular or plural. For instance, collective nouns are usually referred to in the singular form even though they are plural in meaning.

> **Examples:**
> The jury gave *its* verdict. The crowd *was* agitated and began throwing rocks at the police officers.

| COLLECTIVE NOUNS | | |
|---|---|---|
| Audience | Flock | Jury |
| Class | Group | Staff |
| Crowd | Herd | Team |

In addition, there are a few nouns that appear to be plural, but are referred to in the singular form (e.g., mathematics, news, statistics).

> **Example:**
> The officer could tell from the look on the doctor's face that the news *was* bad.

**RULE 2.** If two singular subjects are connected by *either, neither, or,* or *nor* then the verb is singular.

> **Example:**
> Either Cst. Andrews or Cst. Jones *is* assigned to drive the wagon today.

**TIP**

Refer to collective nouns, such as "staff", in the singular form.

**TIP**

Although politically incorrect, stating that everybody must do "his" own work is grammatically correct.

**RULE 3.** If *either* and *neither* are the subjects, the verbs take a singular form.

*Example:*

Although the reporters wanted to speak to the chief and the superintendent, neither of them *is* available right now.

**RULE 4.** The pronouns *anybody, anyone, everyone, everybody, someone,* and *somebody* are singular and require singular verbs.

*Example:*

To be successful, everybody must do *his* (or *her*) own studying. Although this may not sound politically correct, it is grammatically correct.

**RULE 5.** Ignore intervening words that create distance between the subject and the verb. The key is to isolate the subject and the verb to ensure agreement.

*Example:*

The new police chief, who was met by numerous citizens, officers, and reporters, *was* visibly nervous on the first day on the job.

**RULE 6.** Use singular verbs for nations, cities, companies, organizations, and compositions, such as books and films.

*Example:*

The RCMP *is* one of the most recognized symbols of Canada.

**RULE 7.** Use a singular verb for uncountable nouns, sums of money, or periods of time.

*Example:*

Four years *is* too short of a prison sentence for taking someone's life.

## Pronoun–Antecedent Agreement

A similar grammatical error that frequently occurs is when pronouns fail to be in agreement with their antecedents in number, gender, and person. Pronouns are words that replace nouns, and antecedents are the words that they replace.

*Example:*

Constable Richards accidently discharged his firearm into the ceiling of the locker room.

In the example, "Constable Richards" is the antecedent, and "his" is the pronoun that replaces the noun.

Unfortunately, pronoun-antecedent agreement is rarely so obvious—especially on police entrance exams.

*Example:*

Constable Ryan is the only one of the team members who always wears his hat.

In this example, the antecedent is "one" and "his" is the pronoun. It would be incorrect in this situation to state "their hat."

There are many different types of pronouns, and the list below highlights just a few of them. *First person* means that a person is speaking or writing about themselves; *second person* means that someone is speaking or writing about you; and *third person* means that someone is speaking or writing about someone not present.

| EXAMPLES OF PRONOUNS | SINGULAR | PLURAL |
|---|---|---|
| Personal first person | I<br>me | we<br>us |
| Personal second person | you | you |
| Personal third person | she, her, he,<br>him, it | they<br>them |
| Reflexive first person | myself | ourselves |
| Reflexive second person | yourself | yourselves |
| Reflexive third person | himself, herself, itself | themselves |
| Demonstrative | this<br>that | these<br>those |
| Possessive | my, mine,<br>your, yours,<br>his, her, hers, its | our, ours,<br>your, yours,<br>their, theirs |

**TIP**

Identify faulty parallelism in sentence structure by reading sentences out loud.

## Faulty Parallelism

Faulty parallelism is the failure to match various grammatical structures (e.g., clauses, nouns, verbs, adjectives, etc.) that are found in the same sentence. That is, elements in a sentence that have the same function or express similar ideas should be grammatically parallel, or grammatically matched. These grammatical structures must remain in the same form (e.g., tense) throughout the sentence. Below are five rules of parallelism to be followed to ensure correct sentence structure.

**RULE 1.** Use parallel elements to express parallel ideas. That is, balance nouns with nouns, prepositions with prepositions, and so on.

FAULTY PARALLELISM: Officer Garnet likes running, swimming, and going for a workout.

PARALLEL STRUCTURE: Officer Garnet likes running, swimming, and working out.

**RULE 2.** When a sentence includes a series of items, match grammatical structures for the items listed.

FAULTY PARALLELISM: Constable Johnson is an adult, divorced, and has a young son. (noun, adjective, verbal phrase)

PARALLEL STRUCTURE: Constable Johnson is an adult, a divorcee, and the mother of a young son. (noun, noun, noun)

**RULE 3.** When there is more than one verb in a sentence, their tenses must remain the same.

FAULTY PARALLELISM: The chief wrote the speech during the morning's boring Senior Management Team meeting, and it was delivered by him later that night at the Board of Trade dinner. (active verb and passive verb)

PARALLEL STRUCTURE: The chief wrote the speech during the morning's boring Senior Management Team meeting and delivered it that night at the Board of Trade dinner. (both verbs are active)

**RULE 4.** Correlatives (e.g., *both ... and*; *not only ... but also*; *whether ... or*) connect parallel structures. In addition, the first correlative must be used immediately before the parallel element.

>FAULTY PARALLELISM: *Not only* did the thief steal the computer and electronics, *but also* the jewellery was stolen.
>
>PARALLEL STRUCTURE: *Not only* did the thief steal the computer and electronics, *but* he *also* stole the jewellery.
>
>FAULTY PARALLELISM: Constable Ryan was *both* asked to work late tomorrow night *and* to work overtime this weekend.
>
>PARALLEL STRUCTURE: Constable Ryan was asked *both* to work late tomorrow night *and* to work overtime this weekend.

**RULE 5.** "Who", "whom", or "which" clauses must precede "and who", "and whom", or "and which".

>FAULTY PARALLELISM: Officer Fraser was one that spent many years working in the Traffic Section *and who* also worked in the Major Crime Section.
>
>PARALLEL STRUCTURE: Officer Fraser was one *who* spent many years working in the Traffic Section *and who* also worked in the Major Crime Section.

## OTHER GRAMMATICAL ERRORS

Below are ten frequently misused pronouns, abbreviations, and slang words that also may be found in police entrance exams.

## Could of / Would of / Should of

These phrases are all slang—do not use any of them.

>The correct phrases are: *could have, would have, and should have.*
>
>The officers *should have* obtained a search warrant before searching the basement for a grow-op.

## i.e. / e.g. / etc.

The abbreviation *i.e.* is Latin for *id est*, which means "that is."

>The abbreviation *e.g.* is Latin for *exempli gratia*, which means "for example."
>
>A comma always follows both *i.e.* and *e.g.*
>
>The abbreviation *etc.* is Latin for *et cetera*, which means "and so forth."
>
>The RCMP officer looked professional in her red serge (*i.e.*, dress uniform).
>
>The suspect's flop house was full of stolen property (*e.g.*, computers, DVD players, game consoles, *etc.*).

## Imply / Infer

*Imply* is a verb that means to hint or to indirectly indicate something.

*Infer* is a verb that means to draw a conclusion based on the information one has.

>On the witness stand, the officer asked the defence counsel, "Are you trying to *imply* that I fabricated my evidence?"
>
>The defence lawyer apologized to the officer and stated, "No, I'm not implying that at all, and I'm sorry if that's what you *inferred*."

## Infact / In fact

*Infact* is not a word—do not use it.

*In fact* is a phrase meaning in truth.

> The patrol officer ran the car's serial numbers on CPIC and confirmed that the vehicle was *in fact* stolen.

## Irregardless / Regardless

*Irregardless* is not a word—do not use it.

*Regardless* is an adverb that means despite everything.

> The witness stated that the suspect was an Asian female, *regardless* of what the other witnesses stated.

## Less / Fewer

*Less* is used to denote matters of degree, expressions of time or amount, and modifies collective nouns (e.g., money).

*Fewer* is used to denote countable items, people, and modifies plural nouns.

> This year there is *less* violent crime in the downtown core than in the previous two years. Ironically, there are *fewer* officers working in the downtown core than in the previous two years.

## Me / I

*I* is the first person singular subject pronoun and refers to the person performing the action of a verb.

*Me* refers to the person that the action of a verb is being done to.

The decision of whether to use "me" or "I" can be confusing, especially since they are often used incorrectly when combined with another pronoun or name by using "and" or "or."

The reason for the confusion is that sometimes "you and I" is correct and sometimes "you and me" is correct. The difference is whether "you and I" are performing the action or whether "you and me" are the subject of the action. An effective tip is to drop the "you" (or other pronoun or name) when reading the sentence, and the correct word will become more obvious.

> CORRECT: Constable Jefferson and I are going to the gun range this afternoon.
> INCORRECT: Constable Jefferson and me are going to the gun range.
> CORRECT: The chief gave Constable Franklin and me the Award of Merit.
> INCORRECT: The chief gave Constable Franklin and I the Award of Merit.

**Exception**:

If a sentence uses a preposition such as "between", it must be followed by an indirect object pronoun (e.g., *me*, *him*, *her*, and *us*) rather than a subjective pronoun (e.g., *I*, *he*, *she*, and *we*).

> CORRECT: The superintendent stated that the Homicide Squad position was between Officer Jones and me.
> INCORRECT: The superintendent stated that the Homicide Squad position was between Officer Jones and I.

**TIP**

**You and I, or You and Me?**
If you can't decide which to use, drop the "you and"—it will be obvious.

## That / Which / Who

*That* and *which* refer to groups or things. "That" introduces essential clauses, meaning that if no words were to follow "that," it would be an incomplete sentence. Conversely, "which" introduces nonessential clauses. A nonessential clause is often separated by commas.

*Who* refers to people.

Officer Parsons was one of the members of the entire squad *that* recently received a Chief Constable's Award.

Officer Parsons is a member of Squad 9, *which* recently received a Chief Constable's Award.

Officer Parsons, *who* along with his entire team recently received a Chief Constable's Award, is a member of Squad 9.

## Who / Whom

*Who* is a pronoun that means what or which persons.

*Whom* is the objective form of who.

**Who or Whom? When deciding whether to use *who* or *whom* substitute *he* or *him* to respond to the statement.**

> **REMEMBER:** When deciding whether to use *who* or *whom* substitute *he* or *him* to respond to the statement.

*Example:*

*Who/Whom* was arrested for robbery last night?

*He/Him* was arrested.

Thus, the correct phrase is "Who was arrested for robbery last night?"

The constable asked his sergeant, "To *who/whom* shall I send the transfer request to?

Send it to *he/him.*

Again, when you apply this strategy, "To whom" is obvious as the correct response.

## Whoever / Whomever

*Whoever* is a pronoun that means whatever person.

*Whomever* is the objective form of whoever.

The rules for *whoever* and *whomever* are the same as *who* and *whom.*

*Example:*

Officer Davidson was clearly upset when he barked out, "*Whoever/Whomever* used this patrol car last left it looking like a pig's sty!"

*He/Him* used the patrol car last.

The correct response is *whoever.*

The recruiting officer stated to his supervisor, "I think we should hire *whoever/whomever* you recommend."

You recommend *he/him.*

The correct response is *whomever.*

Before continuing to the next chapter, answer the 10 multiple-choice review questions below—just to make sure that you have got it right.

# HAVE I GOT IT RIGHT?

 **You have 5 minutes to complete the exercise.**

1. _____ shall I say is calling?

    (A) Who
    (B) Whom
    (C) Whose
    (D) Who's

2. Constable Charlesworth and ___ are attending the conference.

    (A) me
    (B) I
    (C) myself
    (D) mine

3. When one has been working in the Youth Squad as long as Constable Relish has, _____ to think that all teenagers _____bad.

    (A) he starts / is
    (B) one starts / are
    (C) you start / are
    (D) one starts / is

4. Motorola announced _____ releasing a new police radio system next year.

    (A) it is
    (B) they are
    (C) itself is
    (D) their

5. The jail guards or Constable Major ____ responsible for the suspect escaping.

    (A) is
    (B) are
    (C) were
    (D) where

6. During the night, the lone officer checking the perimeter of the building said, "I wish my partner _____ here."

    (A) was
    (B) is
    (C) were
    (D) are

7. This will be just between you and ___.

   (A) myself
   (B) I
   (C) me
   (D) mine

8. The intoxicated man _____ fell off the balcony nearly died from his injuries.

   (A) himself
   (B) who
   (C) which
   (D) that

9. The sergeant advised the squad, "Everybody attending the conference must complete ____ own travel expense form."

   (A) its
   (B) his
   (C) they're
   (D) their

10. Officer Montrose was tasked with establishing a _____ for the Command Post during the barricaded person incident.

    (A) cite
    (B) site
    (C) sight
    (D) seight

## Answers

1. **A** Who/Whom: *He* = *who.*

2. **B** Me/I: Drop the "you".

3. **B** Faulty Parallelism.

4. **A** Subject-Verb Agreement: Rule 6.

5. **A** Subject-Verb Agreement: Rule 2.

6. **C** Past Subjunctive Mood.

7. **C** Me/I: Exception "between."

8. **B** That/Which/Who: *Who* = people.

9. **B** Subject-Verb Agreement: Rule 4.

10. **B** Homonyms #16.

# Reading Comprehension

# 9

→ **TEST YOUR READING COMPREHENSION**
→ **IMPROVING READING COMPREHENSION SKILLS**
→ **POLICE ENTRANCE EXAM STRATEGIES**
→ **HAVE I GOT IT RIGHT?**

Just as a considerable portion of every police officer's day is devoted to report writing, nearly an equal percentage of time is spent reading through reports, gleaning essential information from documents for the purpose of furthering an investigation, or creating an action plan. For example, if you and your partner were dispatched to a call of a domestic disturbance at a residence, you would want to know how many times the police have previously been to that address and what the outcomes of those incidents were. While en route to these types of calls, you will be able to access databanks, including records management systems, and read through other police officers' reports directly from the laptop of your police car. You will want to arm yourself with as much information about the occupants of the address, and what has occurred on previous occasions, prior to your arrival at the front door. In order to accomplish this, you need to be able to efficiently scan through reports, gather salient facts, and organize them in chronological order so that you can create a timeline of events in your own mind. Then you must remember these key details when you speak to the occupants.

Therefore, as you prepare to enter the police selection process, it is imperative that you recognize the need to possess a high level of reading comprehension. Robust reading comprehension means much more than simply understanding the meaning of words. It also means understanding words in the context of the sentence, paragraph, and the entire document in which they are written. In addition, reading comprehension includes the ability to conduct an ongoing critical assessment of what you are reading. Finally, reading comprehension means retaining key facts about documents and being able to accurately recall the main points some time later.

Most police entrance exams require you to demonstrate a high level of reading comprehension. Complete the exercise below in order to assess your ability to read through documents and garner key facts efficiently.

# TEST YOUR READING COMPREHENSION

 You have 15 minutes to complete this exercise.

Read the following nine-paragraph excerpt from a longitudinal research study relating to attitudes and perceptions of recruit police officers and how these cognitions may evolve over the course of recruit training.

You may refer back to the reading material when searching for answers; however, keep in mind that you have just 15 minutes to answer the ten questions. The paragraphs for this article are numbered so that you can refer to them when analysing your answers.

### Perceptions, Attitudes and Career Orientations of Recruit Police Officers

1 Police agencies spend considerable resources recruiting, screening, and training police officers with the objective that the individuals they hire will become valuable employees, committed to the goals of the organization. However, predicting future behaviour is a difficult task. As a result, recruiters often turn to personality attributes to assist in their predictions. Generally, police agencies prefer candidates who can demonstrate they are reliable, honest, patient, and emotionally stable. However, even successfully identifying these basic characteristics does not necessarily indicate an individual's future performance. As a result, recruiters have looked to other gauges of reliability, such as age and education.

2 Research into police recruiting practices shows a trend by police agencies to seek prospective employees that are more mature and possess higher levels of postsecondary education. Furthermore, there appears to be a desire to hire employees with previous police experience or those with policing backgrounds in their immediate families. The demographical composition of recruits in the current analysis appears to support these assertions: 44% were 30 years of age or older; 83% were 25 years or older; 41% of recruits had completed a four-year university degree or higher; 10% had previous police experience; and 21% had family members who were police officers.

3 The conventional wisdom behind hiring older recruits is the belief that, with age, comes maturity and life experience, thus making for better police officers. For example, Ellis et al. (1991: 112) found that senior officers and field training officers believed that recruits possessing the most "life experience" would make successful transitions from recruit to competent street-level police officers. However, these opinions were without empirical validation, and as Decker and Huckabee (2002: 795) concluded, the common assumption that older recruits make better police officers has been based primarily on intuition and not grounded in research.

4 Similarly, research results relating to whether recruits who possess higher levels of education make better police officers are varied. Some research indicates that officers who are highly educated become less satisfied with their careers the longer they

remain in patrol functions (Dantzker, 1992), while other studies suggest that recruits having college degrees demonstrated better work performance and ethical behaviour than those who are less educated (Tyre & Braunstein, 1992).

5   The belief that having police members in the family background creates a higher probability of recruit success is another perception that appears to be based more on common sense than quantitative data. For instance, Chan (2003: 206) discovered no statistical difference in recruits' increasingly negative occupational views irrespective of age, gender, ethnicity, or having family members in policing.

6   The findings of this study are not intended to show whether recruits that are older, better educated, or have family members in policing make better police officers. Rather, the purpose was to determine whether significant differences in perceptions between these groups and the entire recruit population existed, and whether changes in perceptions among these groups are significant. It is believed that substantial differences or changes in perceptions during training serve as a red flag, indicating that a recruit's initial occupational perceptions were not realistic. Haarr (2005) found that one of the key reasons recruits and junior officers drop out of policing is because of unmet or unrealistic career perceptions and expectations. Furthermore, theories relating to police cynicism and a negative police culture also focus on unmet career expectations (Niederhoffer, 1967; Van Maanen, 1973). However, the current analysis revealed only slight differences in initial perceptions of policing and few changes in perceptions between groups. The only noteworthy differences that were consistently demonstrated were from police recruits with previous police experience. In other words, the interactive effects upon recruit attitudes, perceptions and expectations, age, education, or having police in the family are negligible. Therefore, since the majority of recruits displayed realistic expectations of training and police work regardless of demographic differences, the implications of this research are that it may not be necessary for recruiters to place such a heavy emphasis on searching for prospective employees possessing these background attributes.

7   The relative homogeneity of initial recruit perceptions and the fact that these views change very little during training reveals that recruits possess realistic career expectations prior to arrival at the Police Academy. This demonstrates that recruiting officers are ensuring that successful applicants have a very good understanding of the nature of police work. If recruiting staff did not enforce this aspect in their rigid selection criteria, then the Police Academy would undoubtedly see higher rates of recruits dropping out.

8   Regardless of the recruiting staff's level of commitment, the study does reveal a few areas where recruiters and trainers could do more to ensure that some of the realities of policing are better known. For example, more females might be interested in pursuing a career in policing if they were made aware that most female police officers do not view the job to be as challenging as they initially feared. Police agencies also need to further explore the reasons why female recruits do not believe there will be as many opportunities for career advancement as they originally thought. In addition, although many applicants state that they would like to enter a career in policing because they want to make a difference, they should be aware that this is not a goal that is easily accomplished. This was perhaps the single biggest attitudinal change that occurred during training; fortunately, this change in expectations did not manifest itself in high drop-out rates.

**9** Finally, the study found few differences in the initial perceptions of recruits based on age, gender, race, education, or previous life experiences, and few areas where these demographic variables influenced changes in attitudes and perceptions during training. Recruits graduated from the JIBC Police Academy with positive evaluations of training, indicating they felt well-prepared to start their new careers. Opportunities for future research involve more detailed comparative analysis of other police academy training programmes so that police trainers can be provided with the knowledge required to deliver the most professional, comprehensive, and realistic training, ensuring that recruits are best prepared to face the challenges of their new career.

> **Read the questions below and write out your answers on a separate piece of paper. You may refer back to the narrative, but remember, the clock is ticking!**

1. According to the study, what are the three demographical factors that police recruiters occasionally examine when attempting to determine whether a candidate will make a good officer?

2. In this study, what is the percentage of recruits who are 25 years of age or older?

3. What is the percentage of recruits who have family members who have worked as police officers?

4. What are the findings of Chan (2003) and Decker and Huckabee (2002) regarding the age of police recruits?

5. What does homogeneity mean?

6. What did Haarr (2005) find as one of the main reasons why recruits and junior officers leave policing?

7. What did the study find in relation to the changes in perceptions of policing among female recruits?

8. According to the study, among all recruits, what is perhaps the biggest single change in their attitudes and perceptions?

9. Who are the two researchers that examined police culture and police cynicism more than forty years ago?

10. What is the overall finding of the study in relation to changes in recruit attitudes and perceptions of policing?

## Answers

1. Age, education, and previous police experience or policing in their family's background (para. 1, 2).

2. 83% were 25 years or older (para. 2).

3. 21% had family members who were police officers (para. 2).

4. Decker and Huckabee (2002) concluded that the common assumption that older recruits make better police officers has been based primarily on intuition and not grounded in research. Chan (2003) found that age of the officer made no difference in terms of negative attitudes towards policing (para. 3, 5).

5. Paragraph 7 discusses the homogeneity of police recruit perceptions and that they changed very little. If you did not know what the word means, you could figure it out from the context of the previous paragraphs—the recruits had similar perceptions despite demographical differences. In addition, the prefix *homo* means "same." Therefore, the term *homogeneity* is synonymous with sameness and uniformity.

6. Haarr's (2005) study revealed that junior officers quit policing because of unmet or unrealistic career perceptions and expectations (para. 6).

7. Female police officers do not view the job to be as challenging as they initially feared, and female recruits do not believe there will be as many opportunities for career advancement as they originally thought (para. 8).

8. Most recruits discovered that they would not be able to make a difference in the lives of others as much as they originally perceived (para. 8).

9. Niederhoffer (1967) and Van Maanen (1973) examined police culture and police cynicism (para. 6).

10. The study found few differences in the initial perceptions of recruits based on age, gender, race, education, or previous life experiences, and few areas where these demographic variables influenced changes in attitudes and perceptions during training (para. 9).

| HOW DID YOU SCORE? | | | |
| --- | --- | --- | --- |
| Correct Answers: _____/10 | Excellent 9–10 | Good 7–8 | Average 5–6 |

## IMPROVING READING COMPREHENSION SKILLS

If you were unable to answer all of the questions within the 15 minute time frame, or you did not score in the Excellent range, then you should apply the strategies below to increase your efficiency at reading comprehension.

Reading comprehension is just like the many other skills that people possess. Some are just more natural at it than others—they can pick up a book and be fully engaged and immersed in a story right away and breeze through a lengthy novel in just a couple of days. For others, it is a struggle to read much more than an article in a magazine. But reading proficiency is not indicative of how intelligent you are. Some people just do not like having to read—they see it as work, think it is boring, or would rather be informed and entertained via some other medium. If you fall into the latter category, you are unfortunately in good company—bookstores are going out of business every day. Nevertheless, this is an aptitude that you will need to demonstrate during the application process. However, if you do find reading and reading comprehension a challenge, you can greatly improve your reading comprehension skills by applying each of the following techniques.

## Read

Just as reading is an excellent strategy for improving your vocabulary, dedicating time each day to focus on reading also greatly enhances your level of reading comprehension. Unfortunately, there is no quick fix method to improving your reading comprehension. It simply requires you to practice reading often. However, you can be efficient in this manner by reading the types and lengths of documents that you may find on your exam. That is, reading a romance novel will not assist you in preparing for the length of document, type of vocabulary, and style of writing that you might expect to find in a police report. Instead, read shorter stories and articles, since you will not likely have to read a passage that is more than 1,500 words for any police exam.

**Read journals and articles that interest you and are less than 1,500 words.**

The key to increasing your level of comprehension begins by reading for enjoyment—read about subjects that interest you. Whether it is fashion, current events, sports, politics, or law that appeals to you, find magazines, short stories, or journals that pique your interests. It is a good idea to also read police-related journals and magazines, such as *Blue Line Magazine* (*Blueline.ca*) and the *RCMP Gazette Magazine* (*www.rcmp-grc.gc.ca/gazette*), as they will not only increase your policing vocabulary but also your spectrum of knowledge relating to current police issues.

There are regional and national newspapers (many available online and in print) that can not only assist in developing reading comprehension but also provide insight into current events relating to policing in your community, regionally, and nationally. The best newspapers for practicing reading comprehension are those published in broadsheet format (e.g., *The Vancouver Sun*, *The Ottawa Citizen*, and *The Globe and Mail*). Avoid tabloid format newspapers as the length of articles are usually quite short and lack detailed critical analysis and description of a particular news story.

**Read regional newspapers and magazines to stay informed of current events in your community.**

## Write Notes

One of the best ways to retain key information is to make notes. When you read an important fact, make note of it in the margin or on a scrap piece of paper. For the entrance exam, ask beforehand if you can use additional paper for making notes or if you can write on the back pages of the test document itself. Your goal is to use note taking as a means to increase your level of reading comprehension.

Practice note taking by using documents or articles that you can mark up and are approximately 10 paragraphs long. For your first practice run, take more notes than you think you will need in order to retain all of the key facts. Draw boxes, use arrows, circle events, and write specific details in the margin. Use multiple colours of highlighters to help identify and categorize key information. For example, highlight text in yellow that relates to one key point or character, then highlight key text relating to the second point or character with a green marker, and so forth. On a separate piece of paper, make notes about specific events, timelines, key facts, and statistics. Identify all individuals that are introduced, their relationship to the each other, and their context within the passage. It is important to tie or link related pieces of information together as they will be easier to recall later and help you organize your thoughts. For example, if you are reading a police narrative that relates to a motor vehicle collision, arrange your notes so that they categorize and link people and vehicles together. That is, first, identify who was the driver of the at-fault vehicle. Then, identify the driver's injuries, which vehicle he or she was driving, the vehicle's direction of travel, any damage to that vehicle, and whether there were any other occupants of that vehicle. After you have established these facts, you can move onto identifying and linking the driver and occupants of other vehicles. Often this information will not be provided to you in a clear and logical manner, and it will be your task to not only make sense of the narrative but also to summarize details of the incident in a coherent fashion.

After you have completed making your notes, put the article and notes away for a full 24 hours. The next day, review your notes and see if you can recall all specific details about the article. Reread the article and see if you missed any points. If you failed to recall specific facts, then you need to take more notes or more detailed notes relating to a specific event or person.

**TIP**

Check the effectiveness of your note-taking abilities by reviewing your notes a day later and try to recall the key facts in the article.

## Note-Taking Exercise

Read the following fictional example of a brief police occurrence report and practice taking notes by circling the key information, use arrows to link details to individuals, and write out pertinent notes on a separate piece of paper in the manner described above.

**Theft Report Incident Number: 2015-672411**

On 2015-May-24 at approximately 1930 hours, WILLIAMS was working as a store security officer for Paris Drugs, located at 3469 E. 4th Ave, Edmonton. At that time he observed a 35-year-old Caucasian male enter the store, later identified as SIEGAL, who was wearing a black and white button-up shirt, green khaki pants, and black shoes. SIEGAL walked over to the camera department and appeared nervous, glancing at the store surveillance cameras mounted in the ceiling. He then began looking at the selection of MP3 players, cameras, and smartphones. WILLIAMS observed SIEGAL pick up a Jaxi MP3 player and put it on a counter near the camera section. SIEGAL then asked the sales representative JEFFERSON who was behind the counter about the Nikon camera that was displayed on the wall behind her. As JEFFERSON turned around to select the camera, WILLIAMS observed SIEGAL pick up the MP3 player and conceal it under his shirt, just under his left arm. SIEGAL then turned and proceeded to walk out of the store, walking past two available cashiers without making any attempt to pay. WILLIAMS followed SIEGAL onto E. 4th Ave and in the 3500 block he stopped SIEGAL and informed him that he was a store security officer and that SIEGAL was under arrest for theft under $5,000.

SIEGAL immediately turned and ran onto the street and was struck by a vehicle in the eastbound lane driven by HOPKINS. SIEGAL was struck by the vehicle's front passenger side bumper on his left leg and landed on the hood of the car. WILLIAMS called 911 from his cellphone and asked for the police and an ambulance to attend.

At 1945 hours, Constable FURBAN attended 3500 E. 4th Avenue in regards to the MVI and theft report. FURBAN spoke to WILLIAMS who advised him of the details. FURBAN asked SIEGAL if he was hurt. SIEGAL said he thought his leg was broken. FURBAN told SIEGAL he was under arrest for theft and read him his Charter rights from an issued card. FURBAN asked him if he understood his rights, SIEGAL replied, "Yes." FURBAN asked him if he wanted to call a lawyer, SIEGAL winced in pain, "I need a doctor, you idiot!"

FURBAN then searched SIEGAL and located the MP3 player, still in its packaging, inside his shirt on the left hand side. The MP3 player was valued at $69.99. The property was photographed for evidence and returned to Paris Drugs.

The vehicle involved was a 2012 Chrysler X2. The registered owner is the driver. Damage to the front bumper and hood is estimated at $900. A separate report into the motor vehicle collision is filed under 2015-672419.

SIEGAL had no money or ID on him. FURBAN confirmed the identify of SIEGAL through CPIC police database based on physical description: 5'11", 175 lb, brown eyes, tattoo of a rose on the right side of his neck, star on the outside corner of his left eye, and skull and snake tattoo on his left forearm. SIEGAL had no outstanding warrants. FURBAN issued SIEGAL a Federal Appearance Notice for Theft Under $5,000, requiring him to appear in court on June 30, 2015. SIEGAL was then transported to Royal Alexandra Hospital for examination of a possible tibia fracture.

What notes did you make regarding the theft and misfortune of Mr. Siegal? Did you identify all of the individuals involved and what their roles were? Did you link key pieces of information and evidence? The notes that I would make regarding this incident would be as follows:

---

**Notes:** Theft Under $5,000 15-672411

- May 24, 1930 hrs
- Paris Drugs—3469 E. 4th Ave
- Susp: SIEGAL, white/male 35, 5'11", 175 lb, brn eyes
- b & w button-up shirt, khaki pants, black shoes
- Tattoos: rose—right neck, star—left eye, skull and snake left forearm
- Stolen: Jaxi MP3 Player, in pkg, $69.99, conceal left side inside shirt
- Photographed & returned to store
- Injured left tibia—poss fracture—Royal Alexandra Hosp.
- WILLIAMS—Store security, observed theft, arrest, call 911
- HOPKINS—R/O & Driver of vehicle
- Veh: 2012 Chrysler X2. Damage—ft p/side bumper and hood est. $900. MVA15-672419.
- Cst. FURBAN—Attend 1945, Arrest, Charter—Lawyer? "I need a doctor, idiot". Search—seized MP3, photograph, returned.
- Fed App Notice—June 30

---

## Critical Analysis—W5H

Improving your level of reading comprehension requires more than simply reading the contents of documents and articles. It also requires you to conduct an ongoing critical analysis of what you are reading—the W5H (Who, What, When, Where, Why, and How). Begin by asking yourself what is the purpose of the article. Often the title of the article states the key message that the author wants to relate. If not the title, then the introductory paragraph usually summarizes the main aspects of the document. Police reports often begin with a synopsis, which are usually less than 200 words in length and provide the reader with a high-level overview of the circumstances of the event.

As you read each paragraph ask yourself, "What is the purpose of this paragraph?" If the author has taken the time to write it, hopefully there is a specific point or piece of information

**TIP**

Critical Analysis = W5H.

- Who
- What
- Where
- When
- Why
- How

that the author wants to impart. Often a paragraph will begin with that key piece of information, and the rest of the sentences provide supporting material and are there to flesh out each idea.

Critical analysis also means creating questions in your mind as you begin to read the passage. If, for example, the title of the article is, "Green Greed: Organized Crime's Exploitation of Natural Resources," there should be a number of questions that you would want answered as you read the article. What organized crime groups are we talking about? What natural resources are being exploited and how is this occurring? Where is this taking place and how long has it been going on? What are the police doing about it? Creating questions takes you from simply reading the text to analyzing it. Does the author make a statement and then provide sound supporting documentation to make a compelling case, or is the argument weak, flawed, or lack clarity? Does the story provide a balanced perspective; are there alternate points of view that are not mentioned? By continuously asking yourself these types of questions, you will be able to capture the salient points of the article and be able to recall them later.

**TIP**

Stay focused on a passage by immersing yourself in the story.

## Summarize

After you have read an article, taken succinct notes, and applied sufficient analytical vigour to ensure that all W5H questions have been answered, wait a day and then explain the article to another person. Whether you are talking to your parents, life partner, or buddy, strike up a conversation about the article you read and see if you can summarize the narrative in a two- to three-minute synopsis. Explain what it was about and why it was interesting, identify the main characters and facts, and discuss whether the author made a persuasive argument. After you have completed the exercise with your unsuspecting acquaintance (victim), review the article to determine the strength of your summarization skills.

## POLICE ENTRANCE EXAM STRATEGIES

When the time comes to write your police entrance exam, hopefully you will have applied the tools suggested above and have worked diligently at becoming proficient at extracting and retaining key information from various articles. Use the following tactics to incorporate these skills on examination day.

## Read the Directions

It's been stated before in previous chapters but it bears repeating here—there are multiple entrance exam formats used by police agencies across Canada; some do not even have a reading comprehension component. However, for those that do, there are many variations and distinctions between them. Therefore, you need to know exactly what the expectation of the examiner is. For example, try to determine whether you are expected to answer several multiple-choice questions pertaining to several short passages. Are you expected to summarize a lengthy narrative, or are you required to do something else? Make sure you understand the directions before you proceed.

## Read the Questions First

A simple, yet effective, strategy is to carefully read all of the questions that pertain to the narrative before you actually read it. Reading the questions in advance will provide you with the tools to critically analyze the document as you search for the answers to the questions while reading. It will keep you focused and on track. As you read the article and find a statement that either fully or partially answers the question, indicate either in the margin or on a separate piece of paper that you have located the answer to one of the questions (e.g., if a statement relates to the third question, write "Q3" in the margin beside it).

## Manage Your Time

Effective time management is critical when you are answering reading comprehension questions. The format of examinations are intentionally structured so that time is of the essence, and there will be little opportunity to spend additional time on any particular subject area. Thus, the most important task for you when tackling reading comprehension questions is to ensure that you are reading through the material at an efficient speed and not spending excessive time rereading the passages while searching for answers to questions.

As you prepare for the types of questions found in the reading comprehension portions of police entrance exams, it's important to spend the time to read often, with a critical eye, and armed with the questions in advance, so that you can be certain that you have identified, captured, and retained the essential information relating to comprehension examination questions.

Before continuing to the next chapter, read the article below and answer the five corresponding multiple-choice questions—just to make sure that you have got it right.

## HAVE I GOT IT RIGHT?

 **You have 7 minutes to complete the exercise.**

**Nunavut Says No**
By Mallory Procunier

1 As part of its corporate social responsibility, Canada Post has partnered with the RCMP, the Sûreté du Québec (SQ) and other law enforcement agencies in Québec to prevent contraband items from being mailed to the North.

2 Through the postal inspection project, Canada Post's postal inspectors team up with police officers and police dogs to examine parcels for anything that seems out of the ordinary. If they find a suspicious package, informed officers are able to determine if it's drugs or alcohol destined for a northern community.

3 "The law enforcement community recognized that, especially in some of those dry areas where alcohol is prohibited, we had to help retrieve those items," says Rita Estwick, senior postal inspector at Canada Post. "We recognize, collectively, the negative impact that this has on a northern community."

4 The inspection project is based in Montréal at Canada Post's second-largest sorting facility—where most of the mail headed north passes through.

5 When the project first began in 1999 after being proposed by the law enforcement community, it only happened once or twice a year. Since then, the partnership has strengthened, and inspections now occur almost every other month, benefiting all those involved. The RCMP's Aboriginal Combined Forces Special Enforcement Unit in Québec is taking a lead role in co-ordinating the project.

6 "It provides us with some protection for our folks who handle certain mail and helps us contribute to the communities where this particular contraband is headed," says Ted Upshaw, chief postal inspector for Canada Post.

7 And by being present when postal inspectors find contraband items, law enforcement agencies can get a head start on an investigation.

8 Ret. C/Supt. Steve McVarnock, the former commanding officer of RCMP in Nunavut, has witnessed the project grow in his territory. He says despite the fact that the public is aware of the inspection project, members still find a lot of drugs and alcohol coming through the system—more than $5 million in the last two years alone.

9 "When I equate that to a return on investment for what we've probably stopped from occurring in terms of violence and the money we've redirected to the community, it's probably had a significant return on investment," McVarnock says.

10 And at the community level, members in Nunavut are seeing a staggering effect.

11 "In a couple of the communities, the nurses have spoken to the members about seeing patients coming in with withdrawal symptoms because of the interdiction," says Insp. Frank Gallagher, operations support officer for RCMP in Iqaluit.

12 It's also helping community members focus on what's important in their lives and what money should be spent on instead of drugs and alcohol.

13 "It has reduced incidents of crime in that people are not buying and selling illicit drugs within the community and, therefore, they may have more money for food," says Supt. Hilton Smee, who heads criminal operations for the territory.

14 McVarnock says the initiative has had great success in Nunavut, because the only way in and out is by air.

15 "In other provinces or territories, you have road networks and there are many ways to get contraband into communities," McVarnock says.

16 Upshaw understands the importance of keeping drugs and alcohol out of northern communities, having served 28 years with the RCMP in northern Vancouver Island.

17 "There are days we wish we had more capacity to be able to keep contraband out, but I also know the RCMP wishes it had more capacity to put more resources in another place," Upshaw says.

18 And for an organization that has 69,000 employees, 6,500 offices, and a presence in every Canadian community, Canada Post recognizes the critical part it plays in helping keep communities safe.

19 "Anytime we can work with our partners and are able to take these things out, then we've provided an increased safety to the community and the members who serve in that area," Upshaw says.

*The above article is reprinted courtesy of the RCMP Gazette, as published in Vol. 75, No. 2, 2013.*

1. What is the position of Ted Upshaw?

   (A) Aboriginal Combined Forces Special Enforcement Unit Coordinator
   (B) Chief Postal Inspector, Canada Post
   (C) Chief Superintendent RCMP
   (D) Senior Postal Inspector, Canada Post

2. What agencies partnered with the RCMP to prevent contraband from reaching the north?

   (A) Combined Forces Special Enforcement Unit
   (B) Ontario Provincial Police and Montréal Police
   (C) Nunavut Regional Police and Canada Post
   (D) Canada Post and the Sûreté du Québec

3. Why was the project more successful in Nunavut than other northern communities?

   (A) The people of Nunavut were more cooperative with the police keeping out contraband.
   (B) There is no road access to Nunavut.
   (C) People in other northern communities do not trust the RCMP.
   (D) Nunavut was specifically targeted at the Montréal sorting station.

4. What was the value of illegal alcohol and drugs that has been found coming into Nunavut over the past two years?

   (A) $1 million
   (B) $3 million
   (C) $5 million
   (D) $7 million

5. According to the article, which organization has 69,000 employees?

   (A) Canada Post
   (B) RCMP
   (C) Sûreté du Québec
   (D) Ontario Provincial Police

## Answers

Hopefully, as previously suggested, you completed this exercise by reading the questions prior to reading the article; you made notes of key facts, statistics, and the roles associated to various individuals; and you asked yourself questions relating to the article as you proceeded to read through it. You were given a short time frame to answer the questions so that you would not have very much time to reread and search through the article for the answers.

1. **B** Ted Upshaw is the Chief Postal Inspector, Canada Post (para. 6).

2. **D** Canada Post and the Sûreté du Québec partnered with the RCMP to prevent contraband from reaching the north (para. 1).

3. **B** The project was more successful in Nunavut than other northern communities because there is no road access to Nunavut (paras. 14, 15).

4. **C** The value of illegal alcohol and drugs that has been found coming into Nunavut over the past two years is $5 million (para. 8).

5. **A** According to the article, Canada Post has 69,000 employees (para. 18).

# Essay Composition

# 10

→ **ESSAY PLANNING**
→ **ESSAY WRITING**
→ **ESSAY EDIT AND REVIEW**
→ **ENTRANCE EXAM ESSAY TIPS**
→ **SUMMARIZATION TASKS**
→ **SUMMARIZATION EXERCISE**

While movies and TV shows glamourize the action and excitement of police work, the reality is that much of police officers' days are spent compiling detailed reports relating to the various calls that they have attended. Therefore, a significant portion of most police entrance exams are devoted to assessing your proficiency at expository or essay writing. Some examinations may only require you to respond to several questions with paragraph-length answers; however, other exams may provide you with a broader topic and give you an hour or longer to compose a comprehensive essay. Regardless of the length of the essay that you'll be required to write, there are a number of steps that you can follow to create concise, persuasive, and well-written narratives so that you can achieve the highest marks possible.

## ESSAY PLANNING

## Understand the Question

Read the question and circle or underline key points. Carefully consider what is being asked of you. If you are asked to *compare*, you should be examining similarities and differences of two or more ideas (that are often in contrast with each other). If the essay topic requires you to *discuss* an issue, you should set out a number of key points pertaining to the subject in a logical manner. If you are being asked to *evaluate* a topic, you should assess the strengths and weaknesses of a proposition. Furthermore, essay questions may relate to current issues in policing that are global in nature (e.g., "Discuss how police resources should address the increase in incidents of driving while impaired by drugs"), or questions may relate to a specific region or city (e.g., "Evaluate whether police resources in the Lower Mainland of British Columbia should amalgamate and create a regional police force").

**TIP**

**Prepare for possible essay topics by becoming familiar with current policing issues in your community.**

## Develop an Outline

When you get to the essay portion of an entrance exam, you will likely feel a twinge of anxiety—"Where do I begin?" "What should I say first?" or, "Crap, I only have 30 minutes to write this essay!" It is important that you do not panic; instead, spend a few minutes organizing your thoughts and making a rough outline of your ideas. Usually you will be provided with additional paper to use for making notes, or you can make notes in the pages of another booklet that is handed out in advance. If you write notes in the booklet, ensure that whatever notes you make are crossed off so as not to be mistaken as your actual answer.

The first step in developing an outline is to create a central theme for your essay. Your theme must address the question posed or assigned. If, for example, the essay assignment is to evaluate whether police resources in the Lower Mainland of British Columbia should amalgamate and create a regional police force, then your theme or central idea must specifically address the task. In this assignment, your theme might be that you are in favour of such a proposition.

The second step in developing an outline is to brainstorm and come up with as many ideas or points that will support your central idea. Do not go into too much detail, simply write down keywords or phrases that relate to each point. In the regionalization of policing example, your task is to evaluate the proposed idea; therefore, you should develop several key points that support this position. However, you should also provide a balanced perspective and acknowledge several points to articulate why some individuals may be opposed to the plan. In this situation, you would come up with a brief list of pros and cons and then select the best points that support the position and several counterpoints. The notes below provide an example of the outline that you might create if this was your essay assignment.

**TIP**

**Essay Outline**

- **Develop theme**
- **Introduction—overview**
- **Brainstorm key ideas**
- **Rank by importance**
- **Include counterpoints**
- **Conclusion—summary**

---

**Outline:** Regionalization of Policing in Lower Mainland

**Theme:** Support regionalization

**Intro:** What would regionalization mean? Key points for and against:

**Pros**
- standardized recruitment and training
- economies of scale for smaller municipalities
- enhanced communication and information sharing
- increased public safety in region

**Cons**
- start-up costs
- loss of control of police for small cities
- VPD takes over?

**Conclusion:** Public safety trumps all other arguments

---

The final step in preparing an outline is to arrange your points in a logical order. Depending on the type of essay that has been assigned, there are a variety of methods by which you can arrange the points that you will be discussing. For instance, you may wish to arrange your ideas in chronological order, such as creating a timeline of significant events. Another method is to create an information funnel by commencing with a general subject (e.g., technology has improved policing in the past 25 years) and increasingly honing the focus of your discussion to a specific concept or idea as you progress through the essay (e.g., new technologies associated to DNA detection and suspect identification have improved the effectiveness of police investigations over the past 25 years). Finally, the most common approach is to arrange your subject matter in an order of climax—commence with the least important point or persuasive fact and progressively build the essay so that you finish with your best or most compelling statement. The manner in which your outline is formatted will, in some respects, be determined by the nature of the assigned essay topic and your personal preference. The key is to get your best points across in a logical and succinct manner.

## Manage Your Time

As discussed in Chapter 4, effective time management is a key component in essay composition. Approximately one-quarter of your allotted time should be spent preparing the outline for your paper. You do not need to write the outline out in detail, but you should list the points that you are going to make, arrange them in a logical order, and make notes to assist in your opening statement and conclusion.

About half of your time should be dedicated to writing the actual essay. A well thought-out and detailed paragraph may take anywhere from five to ten minutes to write. Therefore, if you are given one hour to write an essay, this means you only have about 30 minutes to actually write the essay itself. If your essay contains an introductory paragraph, three paragraphs covering the main body of the essay and a conclusion, you only have six minutes to write each paragraph.

The final quarter of your time should be spent editing and revising your essay. This period should be used checking for spelling errors, ensuring that the assignment question or statement is properly answered, evaluating the clarity of your response, checking that you have effective transitions between paragraphs, and confirming the persuasiveness of your conclusion.

## ESSAY WRITING

The purpose of an essay is to create a persuasive statement through a series of closely related paragraphs that support a central idea or theme. For most police entrance exams, you will be limited by time constraints and will not have sufficient time to explore these themes in great detail. Do not waste time thinking about how to craft a masterful composition. You will not have much time, and your marker is more interested in discovering whether you can write an essay that presents and supports a position in a logical and methodical manner rather than your ability to construct beautiful flowing prose. Focus on writing cogently and succinctly—getting right to the point.

Your narrative should follow the basic structure outlined below so that your message is methodically sound and properly conveyed:

1. **Introduction.**
   - State what you are going to write about; identify the task.
   - State your central theme (thesis). State the specific perspective your essay is taking. That is, are you arguing for or against something, comparing, evaluating, explaining, or doing something else?
2. **Essay Body.**
   - Identify key points that support your central theme and provide material or examples to demonstrate each point.
   - Use a separate paragraph or sentence for each major point.
3. **Conclusion.**
   - Summarize what you just wrote, but in a different way from the introduction.

**TIP**

**Essay Time Management**
- ¼ time preparing outline
- ½ time writing essay
- ¼ time editing & revising

## Introduction

The introductory paragraph provides a concise summary of the main points that you will raise. Do not go into too much detail in this section as you will then be repeating yourself in the body of the essay. Rather than starting with lengthy complex sentences, begin with short sentences that highlight the key points that you will be raising. The introductory paragraph provides clarity to the subject matter or question that has been posed, the central theme of your response, and the supporting points that you will develop in your essay. You may wish to start with a general statement about the topic and then identify the key points that you will be discussing. The example below illustrates the introduction that you might use if your essay topic is to evaluate regionalization of police resources in the Lower Mainland.

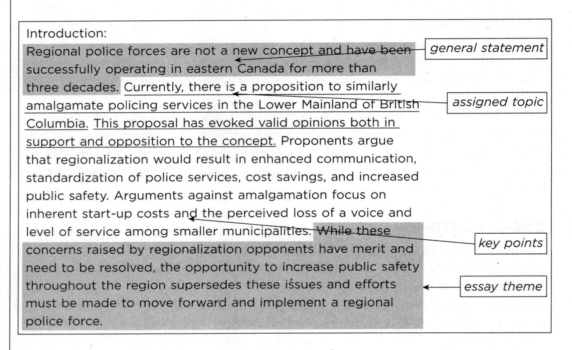

Introduction:

Regional police forces are not a new concept and have been [*general statement*] successfully operating in eastern Canada for more than three decades. Currently, there is a proposition to similarly [*assigned topic*] amalgamate policing services in the Lower Mainland of British Columbia. This proposal has evoked valid opinions both in support and opposition to the concept. Proponents argue that regionalization would result in enhanced communication, standardization of police services, cost savings, and increased public safety. Arguments against amalgamation focus on inherent start-up costs and the perceived loss of a voice and level of service among smaller municipalities. While these [*key points*] concerns raised by regionalization opponents have merit and need to be resolved, the opportunity to increase public safety throughout the region supersedes these issues and efforts [*essay theme*] must be made to move forward and implement a regional police force.

## Essay Body

After you have written the introduction, the next step is to provide several coherent paragraphs that support the central theme of your essay. By the time you start to write the body of the essay, you will have already used your outline to decide on the key points that you will develop and the order in which you will present them. Each paragraph should relate specific details about each of the key points that support the central theme. That is, every paragraph should have a singular focus and follow an individual area of thought that expands in one direction only. Each new topic should always begin with a new paragraph.

Each paragraph should be closely structured to that of an essay itself. It should have an opening statement that promotes the main topic of the paragraph and how it supports the overall theme of the essay. Subsequent sentences within that paragraph, likewise, should support the paragraph's main idea or topic. Additionally, a paragraph can be further developed with sentences that provide specific examples used to illustrate the paragraph's theme. If sentences in a paragraph are not closely related, it will lack cohesion, and the reader may lose comprehension of what you are trying to state.

Finally, a paragraph should conclude with a statement that provides a final observation relating to the theme of the paragraph and allow for a natural transition to the next. The example below demonstrates the constituent elements of a paragraph.

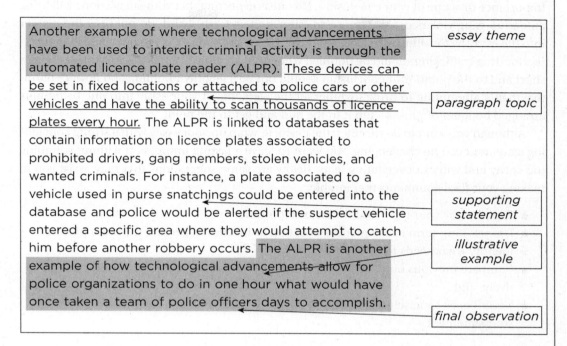

Another example of where technological advancements have been used to interdict criminal activity is through the automated licence plate reader (ALPR). *essay theme*

These devices can be set in fixed locations or attached to police cars or other vehicles and have the ability to scan thousands of licence plates every hour. *paragraph topic*

The ALPR is linked to databases that contain information on licence plates associated to prohibited drivers, gang members, stolen vehicles, and wanted criminals. For instance, a plate associated to a vehicle used in purse snatchings could be entered into the database and police would be alerted if the suspect vehicle entered a specific area where they would attempt to catch him before another robbery occurs. *supporting statement* / *illustrative example*

The ALPR is another example of how technological advancements allow for police organizations to do in one hour what would have once taken a team of police officers days to accomplish. *final observation*

One of the difficulties that some people face in trying to write essays is that they are unsure of how to make an essay flow. A smooth, flowing essay can be achieved by effective use of transitions between sentences within a paragraph and transitions from one paragraph to the next. Transitional expressions help the essay flow more smoothly by showing the connection and relationship between concepts; this can be as simple as one word or it could be an entire phrase. Some examples of transitional words and phrases are "additionally", "furthermore", and "all things considered".

## Conclusion

Your concluding paragraph is your last chance to impress upon your marker that you have strong expository writing communication skills and that you can organize and express your point of view in a well thought-out and logical manner. The impression that you create in your conclusion will stay with the marker for some time and likely have the greatest influence on his or her perception of your writing abilities. Therefore, it is critical that your conclusion does not simply regurgitate the contents of your introduction or restate your main idea. Nevertheless, your conclusion should contain the following elements:

- Brief restatement of the assigned topic,
- Usage of similar or same words found in assignment,
- Summary of your theme/point of view/argument,
- Highlighted key points,
- Restatement of most important point,
- Acknowledgement of key counterpoints, and
- A memorable statement.

**TIP**

**Transitional expressions, such as "in addition," help essays flow more smoothly from one sentence or paragraph to the next.**

**TIP**

**Your conclusion will create a lasting impression of your writing skills—ensure that it is a positive one.**

There are several elements that should not be included in your conclusion. First, you should never introduce new ideas or concepts. The marker has already assimilated the main points that you have presented in the body of the essay. Second, you should not overstate the importance or scope of your conclusion. No one is expecting that your suggestions will bring an end to gang violence, solve drug addiction, and so forth. Third, do not drag the marker into the essay by finishing with a question. That is, do not state, "Do you not agree that penalties for drug trafficking should be doubled when sold to youth?" Finally, keep your sentences short and to the point. Your conclusion should not be a lengthy rambling and flowery narrative that is attempting to bring together all the elements of your essay into one beautifully arranged bouquet of proses—nip it in the bud and get to the point.

Although you want to be succinct, the desire to wrap up your essay with a strong concluding statement can be challenging. You want to leave a lasting impression without sounding too corny and without overstating facts. Below are some suggestions that may assist you in making your final comments memorable:

- Explain why your topic and theme is important;
- Discuss long-term consequences of action or inaction regarding the main point;
- Identify what needs to be done next;
- Compare previous outcomes involving similar situations, either positively or negatively; and
- Describe, as concisely as possible, a powerful image that can easily be connected to your statement.

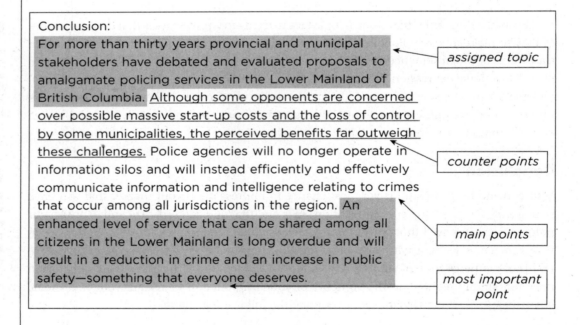

## ESSAY EDIT AND REVIEW

The final quarter of the time allotted to write your exam's essay should be spent reviewing and editing your work. During this time, you need to conduct a comprehensive review of your essay's content and structure, make any changes necessary, and proofread for any grammatical errors.

The first task of the review process is to assess your essay for completeness by ensuring that you have addressed the assignment in its entirety. For example, was the assignment a two part question and you have only answered the first half? Furthermore, did you fully understand what was being asked or did you misinterpret the question? Unfortunately, it is fairly common for individuals to lose marks on writing assignments because they did not fully answer the question presented.

The second step of the review process is to ensure that the structure of the essay is complete. This starts with making certain that the introduction contains a clear thesis statement or central theme and identifies the perspective that your essay discusses. Next, be certain that each paragraph contains a topic sentence, and that each subsequent sentence in the paragraph relates to that topic. Edit any sentence that does not have parallel structure and effective transitional phrases. Finally, amend any sentence that is overly wordy or awkwardly stated or does not provide the material in a compelling and effective manner.

The last stage of the review process is to proofread your essay for spelling, punctuation, and grammatical errors. Spelling errors can be as simple as forgetting to use the plural term of a word, writing "there" when you meant "their", or missing a word entirely. When writing an essay under time limitations, it is easy to forget to write out articles and conjunctions, such as "a", "as", and "the". When it comes to writing an essay during your police entrance exam, it is essential that you already possess a high level of comprehension and proficiency in English grammar and the mechanics of writing, and that you are able to identify and correct your own errors.

**TIP**

**Do not lose valuable marks because you misspelled a challenging or unique word—only use words that you are confident in spelling.**

## ENTRANCE EXAM ESSAY TIPS
### Write Legibly

It is important that the marker of your essay clearly understands the message that you are trying to get across. The proliferation of computers and word processing programs has resulted in our rarely having to handwrite more than a sentence or two at any given time. You will likely lose considerable marks if your essay looks more like a lengthy prescription from your doctor and the marker is spending all her time trying to decipher what you wrote. Therefore, if your handwriting is messy, you may need to slow down and focus on writing clearly, or you may need to print your essay.

### Double Space Your Essay

Unless directed otherwise, double space your essay so that when you are making edits and revisions, you can do so relatively easily. This way you will not be making too much of a mess, and you will not be writing vertically down the margins or using arrows and sending the marker on a wild goose chase trying to connect your sentences and paragraphs.

### Write Complete Sentences

Do not write in bullet point form. Even if you are rushed for time, it is better to write in full sentences that are grammatically correct in structure and word usage. Furthermore, you should avoid using abbreviations and contractions as they fail to meet academic essay expectations.

## Use Words You Know

Use words that you are familiar with in terms of their context and meaning. In daily speech, we often hear people using words in the wrong context, but these errors are even more glaring if they are used in writing because it is undeniable that the person does not know what the word means. For instance, the word "chronic" means long-lasting and enduring, but it is often incorrectly used to mean very bad. Likewise, homonyms are frequently misused (see Chapter 8) in speech; however, one can usually avoid detection because the correct word sounds the same as the misused one. For example, the error is more obvious if you were to write, "A street crime unit could focus on all types of *elicit* behaviour."

## Do Not Use Clichés

When writing an essay, do not be tempted to make your narrative appear more profound by inserting a well-known statement or saying. These phrases are actually tiresome clichés and should be permanently retired. Remember, when writing an essay, you want to present your work in a professional and academic way. Here are some clichés that you should avoid, and appropriate alternative suggestions:

- CLICHÉ: the root of the matter
  INSTEAD, USE: the essential cause or the reason
- CLICHÉ: rule of thumb
  INSTEAD, USE: guide
- CLICHÉ: there's more than one way to skin a cat
  INSTEAD, USE: there are plausible alternatives

## Do Not Use First Person

Do not write your essays in the first person by stating, "I think that police agencies in the Lower Mainland should amalgamate and create a regional force." The marker knows you wrote the paper and that it is your opinion. The essay will come across more professionally if you simply delete "I think that ..." and start with "Police agencies in the Lower Mainland... ."

## Check Marking Scheme

When you are tasked with responding to a question or statement in an essay format, one of the first things that you should do is determine the number of marks associated with the various components of the writing assignment. That is, identifying or developing key points may be more heavily weighted than ensuring that your essay meets length requirements or is presented in a logical way. In addition, you will undoubtedly be deducted marks for each spelling, grammatical, and punctuation error.

## SUMMARIZATION TASKS

Several police agencies now require that as part of the examination process you must read through an assortment of witness statements regarding an incident such as a crime, motor vehicle collision, or other police call and then condense this information into a lucid synopsis of the event. This type of testing is highly valuable in that it tests your level of reading comprehension, critical analysis, and essay composition skills.

When an officer has been designated as the "assigned unit" regarding a police incident, it means that he or she is responsible for compiling witness statements and the evidence of other police officers and then assembling it into one logical and comprehensive report. This can be a daunting task as witnesses tend to provide disjointed accounts of events and the information will likely not be provided in chronological order.

The most important task in compiling any police report is to create a synopsis at the beginning so that another police officer who subsequently looks at the report will quickly obtain an accurate overview of the most important circumstances of the event. Thus, the synopsis must capture the essential elements of the incident and be presented in a logical and coherent way.

The first step in writing a synopsis is to assemble the facts in chronological order. Namely, the report needs to detail what happened from the first event to the last.

The second challenge is to make sure that you are being succinct, yet not to the point of excluding essential information. Typically, a synopsis should be no more than 200 words in length, while still encapsulating all the critical details of the event. In other words, the *who*, *what*, *where*, *when*, *why*, and *how* (W5H) must all be obtained and presented in a cohesive manner.

## SUMMARIZATION EXERCISE

> The following narrative provides you with an opportunity to practice your summarization skills. Read through the various statements and then prepare a synopsis of the event, using a maximum of 150 words.

### STATEMENT OF WITNESS BOURKIN

My name is Justin Bourkin, and I am the owner of the Greezy Spoon restaurant. Today, the guy that the police arrested was eating in my restaurant. He had ordered the seafood special, and he also had a bottle of wine, Uncorked Red. He had some pie for dessert. His bill was $46.87.

At 5:30 p.m. he came up to me to pay his bill. He said he would pay with his Dinette Club charge card and handed it to me. He told me to make the bill an even $50. He wasn't much of a tipper—cheap guy. I tried to use the card but I kept getting a "Declined" message on the computer. He made me try three times, but I kept getting the same message. So I phoned the number on the back of the card, and I was told by the operator that the card was stolen and to call police. I went to call police, and he grabbed the card and ran out the back door of my restaurant. I chased him outside and yelled, "Stop thief." There was lots of people, but I didn't see anybody do anything so I went back inside and called 911. About 10 minutes later a police officer came and told me that they caught the guy and asked me for a statement. I know what the guy looks like, I would know if I saw him again. The officer was nice, but said I probably won't get my $50 back. I hope he goes to jail.

**TIP**

Practice your summarization skills by reading a magazine article and then creating a 150- to 200-word synopsis.

**STATEMENT OF WITNESS MCKENZIE**

My name is Andrew McKenzie, and I'm 35 years old. Today, I was sitting outside Big-Bucks Coffee shop enjoying a latte when I saw this guy who looked like he was about 50 with grey hair and a beard run out the back of my favourite restaurant, the Greezy Spoon. I then saw Justin the owner chase after him, and he was yelling "Thief, thief, help me somebody!" I ran across the street and caught up to the guy a block away. He was sweating profusely and smelled like booze. I told him to stop, and he turned around. I told him he had stolen from the restaurant. He said he did not and started to walk away. I decided to make a citizen's arrest. I grabbed him by the arm, and he pulled away from me. I am a part-time judo instructor and used a leg sweep combined with a hip throw to take him to the ground. I then used a kata-kesa-gatame hold to keep him pinned to the ground. It was about that time that I saw a police car driving by, and he stopped and arrested the man. I have a small scrape on my knee from when I took him to the ground. I think he might have some injuries. I don't consider myself a hero, I think anyone would do this in the situation. Thank you.

**EVIDENCE OF CONSTABLE CHANG**

On 2015-May-24, I was on duty and in uniform assigned to patrol. At approximately 1735 hrs I was dispatched to a report of a Fraud at the Greezy Spoon restaurant at 3143 E. Pemberton Street, and the suspect had fled on foot with a two-minute time delay. When I was approximately one block east of the premises, I observed a male, later identified as witness McKenzie, holding down on the sidewalk another male, later identified as suspect Tremblay. I stopped and exited the police car and asked what was happening. McKenzie stated that he was having a coffee across the street when he saw "Justin" running after the suspect yelling for help and stop thief. At 1740 hrs I arrested Tremblay and handcuffed him and searched him, locating a Dinette Club credit card in the name of Jorge Coulsen located in his front left pocket. I then read Tremblay his Charter rights from a card. He said he understood and didn't want to call a lawyer. I noticed that Tremblay had minor scrapes on his left knee and chin, which McKenzie said happened when he threw him to the ground. I then attended the Greezy Spoon restaurant and obtained a written statement from the victim. I confirmed that the credit card was stolen and tagged it in the property office for evidence. Tremblay was lodged in the jail at 1800 hrs.

The essential elements pertaining to this fraud can be gleaned from the officer's and witnesses' statements by detailing the W5H of this incident.

**Who:**
Constable Chang—Arresting Officer
Bourkin—Victim, owner of Greezy Spoon
Coulsen—Victim, owner of stolen credit card
McKenzie—witness, detained suspect
Tremblay—Suspect

**What:**
Fraud—possession and use of a stolen credit card.
Suspect obtained a meal by false pretences and attempted to use a stolen credit card to pay. Suspect was detained by a citizen who came to the aid of the victim.
Suspect and witness received minor scrapes during scuffle.

Value of fraud—$46.87

**Where:**

Fraud—3143 E. Pemberton Street

Arrest—3200 E. Pemberton Street (1 block east)

**When:**

Fraud—2015-May-24 at 1730 hrs

Detention—1735 hrs

Arrest—1740 hrs

**Why:**

Why Tremblay committed the crime is unknown and, in this case, irrelevant.

**How:**

Tremblay committed the fraud by obtaining food without any intention of actually paying and by attempting to use a stolen credit card.

Before you read the synopsis provided below, spend 10 minutes writing your own summary of the above fraud event. Remember to keep the paragraph under 150 words, while capturing the most important facts provided by the witnesses and Officer Chang. After you have written the summary, count the words to be sure that there are less than 150 and make sure that the sentences flow and are written in chronological order.

## Synopsis

_____

_____

_____

_____

_____

_____

_____

_____

_____

_____

_____

_____

_____

## FRAUD SYNOPSIS

On 2015-May-24 at approx. 1730 hrs, suspect Tremblay committed fraud at the Greezy Spoon restaurant located at 3143 E. Pemberton Street by attempting to pay for a meal and liquor valued at $46.87 with a stolen credit card. Tremblay presented a Dinnette Club card, in the name of Coulsen, to restaurant owner Bourkin. The card was declined, and Bourkin called the credit card company who advised it was reported stolen. Tremblay took the card back and ran out the restaurant with Bourkin chasing behind calling for help. McKenzie witnessed the incident and detained Tremblay a block away. Constable Chang responded to the call and observed McKenzie holding Tremblay on the ground. Tremblay was arrested and searched, the stolen card seized, and Tremblay was lodged in cells.

(127 words)

# Judgment and Logic

**11**

→ **TEST YOUR KNOWLEDGE**

→ **DECISION MAKING**

→ **SYLLOGISMS**

→ **WORD LOGIC PROBLEMS**

→ **INDUCTIVE REASONING**

→ **SPATIAL ORIENTATION AND MAPPING**

→ **TRAVEL TIME TASKS**

→ **CLASSIFICATION**

→ **PATTERN SERIES**

→ **HAVE I GOT IT RIGHT?**

Police entrance exams are cognitive ability tests designed to assess basic skills such as memory, reading comprehension, and grammatical proficiency. Research has shown that when these types of tests are properly developed and administered, they are valid predictors of recruit performance not only during their academic training at a police academy but also in their future success as police officers. However, there are a significant number of police organizations that use police entrance exams to further assess more complex competencies such as logical thought processes and abstract reasoning through the use of various IQ brainteasers and logic questions. Successfully passing IQ questions can be like learning a party trick—if you spend enough time learning the concepts and premises that many IQ questions are based upon, you might be able to impress your friends with this skill but may have little practical application in the real (policing) world. Unfortunately, since there is no standardized testing procedure across the country, you are well-advised to learn and practice answering these types of questions.

Police entrance exams use a variety of tests to measure complex cognitive abilities, the most common being decision-making scenarios, syllogisms, abstract reasoning, spatial orientation, pattern solving, and math problems. The first five processes are examined here, and math problems are the focus of Chapter 12.

In order to evaluate your proficiency at logic and decision-making questions, begin by completing the Test Your Knowledge assessment.

# TEST YOUR KNOWLEDGE

 **You have 20 minutes to answer a total of 15 questions. Start your timer and begin now.**

In the following three decision-making scenarios, you are on duty as a police officer. For these questions you are not required to know police policy and procedures, the applicable law, or law enforcement tactics.

1. A citizen phoned in a complaint that a mother spanked her 4-year-old child in a parking lot. You locate the mother, and she admits to spanking her after the child pulled away from her grasp, ran into the street, and was almost struck by a vehicle. Based on this information, which of the following statements is your best option?

   (A) Arrest the mother for assaulting the child.
   (B) Speak to the complainant and find out what else was observed regarding the actions of the mother.
   (C) Apprehend the child under the Protection of Children Act and turn the child over to the Ministry of Child and Family Development.
   (D) Write the mother a ticket for allowing a person in her care to enter a roadway when unsafe.

2. A store owner calls saying that a man is protesting in front of his store and blocking the entrance. You attend and speak to the protestor who says that the store's shoes are made by young child-slaves working in dangerous factories in Bangladesh. Based on this information, which of the following statements is your best option?

   (A) Advise the protestor that he cannot prevent shoppers from entering the store and provide alternative ways that he could lawfully protest.
   (B) Advise the protestor that you support his point of view, but that he cannot prevent people from accessing the store.
   (C) Take a statement from the protestor and investigate further to determine if his claim is true.
   (D) Arrest the protestor for obstruction and breach of the peace.

3. You are driving across town outside of your assigned area to meet up with another officer to arrest a man in his home for an assault that occurred at a bar last week. While outside your patrol area, you see a woman standing on a street corner waving her arms and saying, "Help, police!" No one has reported a crime in the area. Based on this information, which of the following statements is your best option?

   (A) Stop your car, talk to the woman, and investigate the incident fully.
   (B) This is outside your assigned area, you must let an officer assigned to the area deal with it. Call dispatch on your radio and advise that there's a woman screaming and provide the location where you saw her.

(C) Stop and tell the woman that you will call for another officer to come and assist her as this is not your assigned area.

(D) Stop your car, advise dispatch of the situation, and tell dispatch that you will advise as soon as you know more information.

> **Questions 4–6 are syllogisms. For each question, you are provided with a major premise (first statement) and a minor premise (second statement). You must assume that each statement is true. Only one of the four conclusion statements is valid based on the first two statements.**

4. No police officers are morticians.

   All Danish people are police officers.

   (A) Therefore, some police officers are not Danish morticians.
   (B) Therefore, some police officers are not Danish people.
   (C) Therefore, some Danish people are not morticians.
   (D) Therefore, all morticians are not Danish people.

5. Some police officers are friendly persons.

   All friendly persons are persons who value others.

   (A) Therefore, some persons who value others are police officers.
   (B) Therefore, some police officers are persons who value others.
   (C) Therefore, some nonfriendly persons are not police officers.
   (D) No logical conclusion can be made.

6. No lawyers are honest people.

   Some honest people are trustworthy.

   (A) Therefore, some honest people are not lawyers.
   (B) Therefore, all lawyers are not honest.
   (C) Therefore, some trustworthy people are not lawyers.
   (D) Therefore, no lawyers are trustworthy.

> **Questions 7–10 are abstract reasoning questions that are common to cognitive aptitude segments of police entrance exams.**

7. Police dog Sabre weighs more than police dog Rex. Nitro weighs more than Chase but less than Justice. Chase weighs more than Rex. Justice weighs less than Sabre. List the dogs in order of weight from heaviest to lightest.

   (A) Sabre, Justice, Nitro, Chase, Rex
   (B) Justice, Sabre, Chase, Nitro, Rex
   (C) Sabre, Nitro, Rex, Chase, Justice
   (D) Sabre, Chase, Nitro, Justice, Rex

8. Which of the following numbers does not belong in the sequence?

18 23 19 28 20 32 21

(A) 18
(B) 21
(C) 28
(D) 32

9. Complete the comparison. Phoenix is to Saber-toothed Tiger as Centaur is to

(A) Dragon
(B) Dodo bird
(C) Medussa
(D) Unicorn

10. If 40 percent of farks are carks and 50 percent of carks are shrinkarks, what percent of farks are shrinkarks?

(A) 60%
(B) 20%
(C) 50%
(D) more information required

Questions 11 and 12 are spatial orientation and mapping questions and are based solely on the information found in Figures 1 and 2.

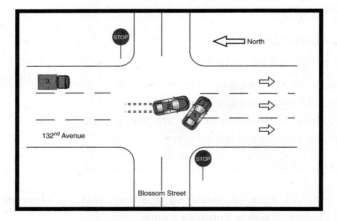

**Figure 1.** Blossom Street MVI

11. Based on the information provided in Figure 1, which of the following statements best describes what occurred?

(A) Vehicle 1 was northbound on 132nd Ave when it changed lanes and cut off Vehicle 2 causing an accident.
(B) Vehicle 1 was northbound on Blossom St failed to stop at a stop sign, and was struck by Vehicle 2 eastbound on 132nd Avenue.
(C) Vehicle 1 eastbound on Blossom St failed to stop for a stop sign and was struck by Vehicle 2 southbound on 132nd Ave.

(D) Vehicle 2 was southbound on 132nd Ave and failed to yield to Vehicle 1 westbound on Blossom St.

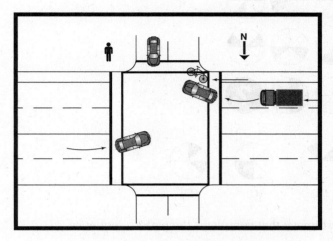

**Figure 2.** Cyclist Struck MVI

12. Based on the information provided in Figure 2, which of the following statements best describes what occurred?

(A) The witness was standing on the northeast corner of the intersection and observed the vehicle turn right into the path of the bicyclist.

(B) The bicyclist was westbound on the road when a car made a right turn into him.

(C) The car turned southbound and struck the eastbound bicyclist.

(D) The car turned northbound into the path of the westbound bicyclist.

> Questions 13–15 are pattern-solving and matching problems that require you to identify common characteristics found in a series of visual objects or through information provided. Choose the correct object or statement that would match or complete the pattern.

13. Identify the image that should come next in the sequence.

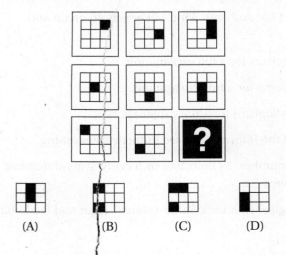

14. Select the next image that completes the pattern sequence.

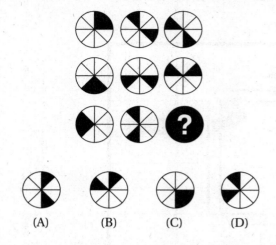

    (A)       (B)       (C)       (D)

15. Select the next image that completes the pattern sequence.

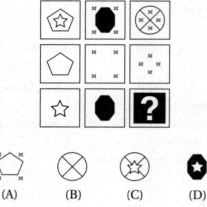

    (A)       (B)       (C)       (D)

## Answers

1. **B** Arresting the mother or seizing the child would be a measure of last resort—get all the facts first.

2. **A** Never take sides or express your personal opinion as it could lead to further conflict. Provide alternatives and arrest as a last resort.

3. **D** You have a primary duty to protect life and limb. Find out what's going on and advise dispatch.

4. **C** Rule: No, All = Some not. See Syllogisms for a full explanation.

5. **B** Rule: Some, All = Some. See Syllogisms for a full explanation.

6. **C** Rule: No, Some = Some not. See Syllogisms for a full explanation.

7. **A** This can be solved by drawing out the information; see Inductive Reasoning.

8. **D** 18 increases by one every second number; 23 increases by 5 every second number. 32 did not belong as it should have been 33.

9. **B** Phoenix and Centaur are mythological creatures, Saber-toothed Tiger and Dodo bird are extinct creatures.

10. **B** This can be solved by creating a diagram and inserting the silly-named creatures; see Inductive Reasoning.

11. **C** Rotate diagram so north is facing top of your page.

12. **C** Rotate diagram so north is facing top of your page.

13. **B** The pattern in each row goes from left to right, each square by itself then combined on the right.

14. **A** The pattern in each row goes from left to right, each slice of pie starts together, then two spaces apart, then four spaces apart.

15. **B** Each column goes from top to bottom, the two symbols are combined at the top and then into separate images below.

---

## HOW DID YOU SCORE?

Correct Answers: _____/15     Excellent 14–15     Good 11–13     Average 8–10

If your test score is not in the Excellent range, you should focus on this chapter to ensure that you improve your skills relating to rational decision making, syllogism solving, abstract reasoning, spatial orientation, and pattern solving.

---

## DECISION MAKING

The decision-making scenarios discussed in this section are those that you will be required to make either after reading a short narrative and then being presented with several courses of action, or based on your observations of video-based scenarios. For example, in the province of Ontario, all police applicants to either the Ontario Provincial Police (OPP) or any of the municipal police agencies must pass the Behavioural Personnel Assessment Device (BPAD), which is a 20-minute exercise that involves watching a series of short scenarios on a TV monitor and then providing a verbal response to each one.

Before examining several hypothetical scenarios, it is worth revisiting the common law duties of a police officer, which are to:

- Preserve the peace,
- Prevent crime, and
- Protect life and property.

This list should be viewed in ascending order—the protection of life is always the ultimate mandate of a police officer. That is, protection of life and limb are paramount whether this is a result of the actions of another, self-inflicted, accident, or an act of god. Furthermore, in 1829 Sir Robert Peel created the London's Metropolitan police and stated that the basic mission of the police is to prevent crime and disorder. He also said that the use of force (which includes simply placing someone under arrest) should always be a last resort and used only when the exercise of persuasion, advice, and warning fail. Therefore, you should always have these basic tenets in the back of your mind prior to making a decision about any police situation.

There are countless scenarios that may be presented in examination questions but generally they fall within several nonexclusive categories: a verbal conflict, an information-gathering task, an informing task, and an ethical decision. Usually there is more than one of these

**TIP**

**Police Decision-Making Priority:**
1. **Protect Life and Limb**
2. **Prevent Crime**
3. **Keep the Peace**

elements built into each task. The following are examples of the types of scenarios that you may face, the challenges presented, and the competencies that you would be expected to exhibit in these situations.

## Scenario—Traffic Stop

In these situations, the driver may not want to produce a licence, will not sign the ticket, or disagrees with your observations of the violation.

Challenges: conflict, noncompliance, tension escalation, no respect for the law, hostility, stress.

Expected Behaviour:

- De-escalate—acknowledge that the person is upset, and he or she has a right to disagree with you.
- Inform—advise the person that he or she can dispute the ticket.
- Be adaptable—depending on seriousness of offence, you may not have to write a ticket to get the desired effect (discretion).
- Professionalism—maintain professional language and conduct throughout.

## Scenario—Dispute

It may be a dispute between neighbours over dog droppings on each other's lawns, a customer who is dissatisfied with a product, or a mom who wants you to arrest her teenage son for smoking marijuana at a party on the weekend. In these cases, it should be evident (or explained to you) that either no crime has been committed or arresting in not a viable option.

Challenges: conflict, one party will want police to take action (arrest); disputants will expect police to solve problem.

Expected Behaviour:

- Neutrality—do not take sides in civil disputes.
- Keep the peace—one of the police's primary mandates.
- Information gathering—get to the core of what the problem is from both sides.
- Problem solving—identify plausible options and offer solutions.

## Scenario—Ethical Conduct

The situation may involve your observation of another police officer (e.g., you saw an officer drive impaired) or your confrontation with a situation (e.g., you are offered free tickets from a home owner to a NHL game for arresting theft suspect).

Challenges: loyalty, honour, integrity

Expected Behaviour:

- Information gathering—what is the policy around accepting gifts?
- Informing—advise supervisor of observed ethical behaviour.
- Ethical decision—what behaviour would offend community standard?

Regardless of the scenario itself, you will be able to demonstrate sound judgment and rational decision-making skills if you are professional, remain calm, listen to people, collect all relevant information thoroughly, are adaptable, are ethical, and make decisions based on a reasonable assessment of all options presented to you.

# SYLLOGISMS

A syllogism is a form of deductive reasoning in which a logical conclusion is supported by two premise statements. Being able to draw a logical conclusion based on two (sometimes nonsensical) premise statements may demonstrate one's proficiency at solving syllogisms; however, the skill has little to do with one's competency as a police officer. Nevertheless, several police organizations continue to incorporate syllogisms as a component of the application process. For example, one of the initial assessments that applicants to the OPP, or any of the municipal departments in the province of Ontario, must pass is the Police Analytical Thinking Inventory (PATI). The PATI is a 90-question multiple-choice exam that assesses deductive reasoning, inductive reasoning, and quantitative reasoning. Deductive reasoning is tested through the use of syllogisms and travel time tests. Unfortunately, it is not just Ontario that uses syllogisms as part of their battery of tests. If, for example, you are an applicant to one of the police agencies that uses the Wonderlic or similar IQ tests, then you will also likely be exposed to several syllogism questions during the entrance examination process.

Each syllogism has three main components: a major premise, a minor premise, and a conclusion. The conclusion must logically flow from the major and minor premises. Consider the following syllogism:

> MAJOR PREMISE: All compassionate people want to help less fortunate people.
> MINOR PREMISE: All police officers are compassionate people.
> CONCLUSION: All police officers want to help less fortunate people.

The major term of the major premise forms the predicate of the concluding statement. In this case, the predicate is wanting *to help less fortunate people*. The minor term in the minor premise forms the subject of the concluding statement. In this example, the subject is *police officers*. Finally, the term that is common in both the major and minor premises is called the *middle term*. In this example, *compassionate people* is the middle term.

There are also four possible expressions for each of the two premises and the concluding statement. The first is a universal affirmative statement (e.g., *All police officers are compassionate*). The second type of premise is a universal negative (e.g., *No criminal is innocent*). The third expression is a particular affirmative (e.g., *Some police officers are lawyers*). The final expression is a particular negative (e.g., *Some judges are not in touch with reality*). By applying the following rules to the four expressions of major and minor premises, the correct conclusion should be clear.

**RULE ONE.** Always assume that the statements in the major premise and minor premise are true even if you know that not to be the case. Syllogisms are exercises in abstract reasoning and may include nonsensical terms or obvious untruths. The goal is to determine if a logical and valid conclusion can be derived based on assuming the truthfulness of the first two statements.

**RULE TWO.** The middle term must appear in both the major premise and minor premise, but not in the conclusion.

> *Example:*
> No honest people are **liars** (middle term).
> Some **liars** (middle term) are lawyers.
> Some lawyers are not honest people.

**TIP**

In syllogisms, premise statements may be factually incorrect, or nonsensical, yet reach a logical conclusion.

**RULE THREE.** When both premises are affirmative, the conclusion cannot be negative (can only be *all* or *some*).

> *Example:*
> *All men are mortal.*
> *James is a man.*
> *Therefore, James is mortal.*

**RULE FOUR.** When both premises are particular (e.g., *some* and *some not*), then no logical conclusion can be derived.

> *Example:*
> *Some police officers are detectives.*
> *Some detectives exercise regularly.*
> It is an invalid conclusion to state *some police officers exercise regularly* because the officers may not belong to the group of detectives that exercise regularly.

**RULE FIVE.** When only one premise is negative, the conclusion must also be negative.

> *Example:*
> *No man is perfect.*
> *Some men are sergeants.*
> *Some sergeants are not perfect.*

**RULE SIX.** When both premises are negative (e.g., *some not* and *no*, etc.), then no logical conclusion can be derived.

> *Example:*
> *No man is perfect.*
> *Some men are not sergeants.*

In this example, to conclude *some non-sergeants are not perfect* would be an invalid conclusion.

**RULE SEVEN.** The middle term must be distributed (used as a universal or particular statement) at least once in either the major or minor premises; otherwise, no conclusion can be derived. In the example below, *police dogs* is the middle term, but are not distributed (*all*, *some*, etc.) in either the major or minor premises.

> *Example:*
> *All animals are police dogs.*
> *No horses are police dogs.*

Therefore, no logical conclusion can be reached. For example, it is invalid to conclude that horses are not animals.

**RULE EIGHT.** If either the major premise or minor premise is particular (e.g, *some As are Bs*), then the conclusion must also be particular (i.e., conclude with *some*).

> *Example:*
> *Some members of the Emergency Response Team are hockey players.*
> *All hockey players think that one day they are going to "The Show."*
> *Some Emergency Response Team members think that one day they are going to "The Show."*

## Syllogism Expressions and Conclusions

The Table below provides a quick reference chart for determining the valid conclusion based on whether the major and minor premise statements are universal affirmative, negative, or particular.

| MAJOR | MINOR | CONCLUSION |
|---|---|---|
| All | All | All / Some ✓ |
| All | Some | Several possible valid conclusions |
| Some | All | Some |
| Some | Some | No valid conclusion |
| Some | No | Some not |
| No | No | No valid conclusion |
| No | All | No (major and minor reversed) |
| No | Some | Some not (major and minor reversed) |
| All | No | No |

## Eliminate the Middle Term

When it comes to solving syllogisms, it's beneficial to eliminate the middle term when determining if a valid conclusion can be derived from the two premise statements.

> **Example:**
> Premise 1: *Some clocks are Uzliamaque.*
> Premise 2: *No Uzliamaque is effective.*
> Eliminate Middle Term: *Uzliamaque* (It does not matter if you do not know what it means—no one does.)
> Conclusion: *Some clocks are not effective.* (refer to the list above)

**TIP**

Solve most syllogisms by removing the portion of the statement that's repeated in the first and second line.

## Venn Diagrams

In the late 1800s, British philosopher John Venn realized that logical concepts were far easier to grasp if one could visualize them through drawings. Thus, by using three circles to represent each premise and the conclusion, and then assessing the extent to which they intersect or overlap, you can determine whether a given syllogism is valid or not. Universal affirmative statements are represented as one circle (the subject) inside of another circle (the predicate). Universal negative statements are represented as two mutually exclusive, nonoverlapping circles. Particular statements are represented as two intersecting circles, each with an area in common and exclusive to the other circle(s).

> **Example:** Universal Affirmative Statements
> Premise 1: *All pistols are weapons.*
> Premise 2: *All weapons are dangerous.*
> Conclusion: *All pistols are dangerous.*

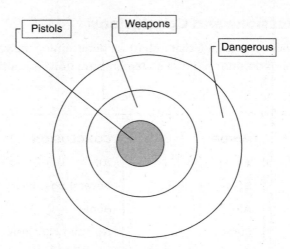

**Venn Diagram—Affirmative Statement**

*Example:* Particular Statements

Premise 1: *Some police officers are detectives.*

Premise 2: *All detectives are excellent communicators.*

Conclusion: *Some police officers are excellent communicators.*

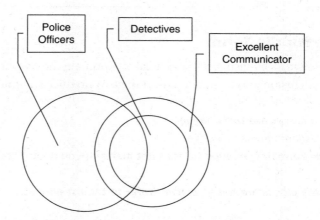

**Venn Diagram—Particular Statement**

## WORD LOGIC PROBLEMS

Categorical syllogisms are the most common form of deductive reasoning questions; however, there are many other similar logic invoking scenarios that require you to interpret and work through various statements. In these types of logic questions, you will be provided with a narrative or a set of statements and then you will have to determine if the conclusion is true or false or select the correct response from a group of statements.

Consider the following statements:

The police station is two blocks east of city hall.

The market is one block west of the police station.

Based on these two statements, which of the following is true?

 (A) City hall is west of the market.
 (B) The police station is to the west of city hall.
 (C) The market is west of city hall.
 (D) City hall is to the east of the police station.

**Answer: A**

The market is one block west of the police station. City hall is two blocks west of the police station, so city hall is west of the market.

Often these types of questions are a lot more complicated. Rather than try to perform mental gymnastics, if you were to quickly sketch out each statement, the answer would be self-evident.

**STEP 1** The police station is two blocks east of city hall.

Begin by drawing a compass with north at the top. It follows that west is to the left and east is to the right. If you have trouble remembering if west is on the left or right, think of British Columbia as the "Left Coast" (often politically) of Canada.

Next, draw city hall and indicate two blocks to the east and draw the police station.

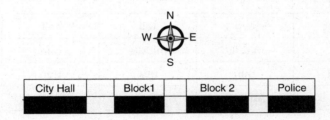

**STEP 2** The market is one block west of the police station.

Next, indicate on your drawing that the market is one block to the west of the police station.

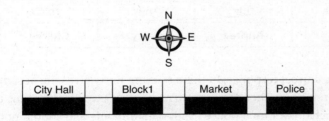

**STEP 3** Compare your sketch to the four options. Only choice A is correct.

Some logic problems can best be solved by creating a grid to identify commonality and linkages between statements and variables (people, dates, locations, etc.) and to eliminate variables that do not apply or support the conclusion. For example, some police entrance exams may ask you to identify whether a witness statement is correct based on the strength of commonalities between other witness descriptions. This, in fact would be a potentially misleading police tactic if it were actually used because witness accounts are known to be quite inaccurate and subject to a "groupthink" mentality. Police officers should never assume the validity of a suspect description based solely on a majority-rules mindset. Nevertheless, for the purposes of these types of exercises only, you may be asked to identify which witness account is likely to be most accurate.

*Example:*

Andrea, Barry, Charlie, and Denise are witnesses to a robbery. Each of them gave varying descriptions of the suspect. Andrea said he was average height, thin, and middle-aged. Barry said he was tall, thin, and middle-aged. Charlie said he was tall, thin, and young, and Denise said he was tall, of average weight, and middle-aged. Which description is probably right?

(STEP 1) Create a grid or table. List the four individuals on one axis and list the suspects defining features on the other.

| Height | | | | |
|---|---|---|---|---|
| Age | | | | |
| Build | | | | |
| | Andrea | Barry | Charlie | Denise |

(STEP 2) Plot descriptions based upon the statements by each of the witnesses.

| Height | avg | tall | tall | tall |
|---|---|---|---|---|
| Age | middle | middle | young | middle |
| Build | thin | thin | thin | avg |
| | Andrea | Barry | Charlie | Denise |

(STEP 3) Find the strongest commonalities. Circle the elements that appear most frequently.

| Height | avg | tall | tall | tall |
|---|---|---|---|---|
| Age | middle | middle | young | middle |
| Build | thin | thin | thin | avg |
| | Andrea | Barry | Charlie | Denise |

(STEP 4) Identify the correct response. In this situation, Barry gives the description that is most frequently repeated. Therefore, the answer is B. It's worth repeating, however, that this is the correct answer for a police exam scenario only and should not be taken to infer that's how a good police investigator would solely make decisions regarding what a suspect looked like.

## INDUCTIVE REASONING

In addition to syllogisms, many police entrance exams also include an assortment of other abstract reasoning exercises as a means of discovering your ability to solve problems. Examples include pattern solving, logic problems, spatial orientation, number series, and analogies. While syllogisms are an example of deductive reasoning, the following categories of questions are examples of inductive reasoning exercises, where you are required to recognize similarities between concepts, shapes, and patterns and then come to valid conclusions without being provided with prior knowledge.

## Analogies

Analogies are used to make comparisons or inferences between two like subjects or things.

*Example:*

Pistol is to police officer as axe is to lumberjack.

The analogy is a tool used by each occupation. However, rarely will the analogy be so self-evident, so there are several steps that you can use to solve the question.

**(STEP 1)** **Identify the relationship.**

The analogous question will most likely be provided in one of two possible ways. The first method is to provide you with two words, separated by a colon, and then require you to choose from a list of words that are formatted in the same manner and identify the pairing that has the same relationship.

**TIP**

Solve analogous statements by identifying and generalizing word relationships.

*Example:*

Overbearing: Subservient

(A) Casual: Unpremeditated

(B) Harsh: Exacting

(C) Trusting: Suspicious

(D) Pedestrian: Vehicular

The second method of creating the analogous question is to provide the first pair of words, and then provide the first half of the second pair of words in the form of an incomplete sentence. You would then be required to choose the appropriate response from a list of words.

*Example:*

Ferry is to captain as airplane is to

(A) mechanic

(B) stewardess

(C) air traffic controller

(D) pilot

In the first example, the relationship that exists between the words *overbearing* and *subservient* is that they are both adjectives usually used to describe a person; therefore, they require you to identify the meaning of these two words. Overbearing means trying to control other people. Subservient means overly willing to obey other people. In the second example, the relationship is that a ferry is a mode of transportation and the captain is responsible for navigating the craft.

**(STEP 2)** **Generalize the relationship.**

In the first example the relationship is that overbearing and subservient are antonyms, or opposites. Obviously, a significant requirement to solving analogous questions is to possess strong grammatical skills so that you will know the meaning of most words. In the second example, the generalization that you can make is that you will want to match a mode of transportation (aircraft) with the person who is responsible for its navigation.

**Make the match.**

In the first example, you are looking for another pair of antonyms. Options A and B will not suffice since *casual* and *unpremeditated* are synonymous as are *harsh* and *exacting*. Option D is also not valid since the relationship between *pedestrian* and *vehicular* is not synonymous or antonymous and their relationship is not known without intervening words (e.g., roadway travel). However, *trusting* and *suspicious* are antonyms; therefore, the answer is C. In the second example, just as the captain is responsible for the ferry's navigation, the pilot is responsible for the aircraft's navigation. The air traffic controller can assist in that regard, but that person does not actually fly the plane.

## Number Series

Number series questions require you to know less about math and more about finding out what the sequence of numbers is. You will usually be provided with a series of numbers, most likely from four to eight, that often start with the smallest number on the left and the largest number on the right. For these types of questions, there is always a pattern to the values indicated. It may take several steps to identify what that pattern is.

*Example:*

**Consider this number series: 14, 28, 23, 46, 41, 82, ... What number should come next?**

(A) 52

(B) 67

(C) 77

(D) 121

STEP 1 **Pair first numbers.**

Start with the number on the left and discover what its relationship is to the number beside it. In this example, the pair is 14 and 28. The difference between 28 and 14 is 14; therefore, the relationship between the numbers is that 28 is 14 more than 14, or 14 multiplied by 2.

STEP 2 **Move right.**

Do not jump to the next pair of numbers, instead look to the number immediately to the right and identify what the relationship is. In this instance 23 is 5 less than 28. There is no other obvious relationship.

STEP 3 **Repeat.**

Continue this process until a pattern emerges. It will often take four or more numbers before a sequence is identified. In the example provided, the following number is 46, which is 23 times 2. Now you can identify at least one pattern.

**Do not stop.**

Keep repeating this process until you have gone through all the numbers. In our example, you know that every second number is double the number before it, however, what is less obvious is what the next number should be. The next number is 41, which is 5 less than 46. Now you have a second pattern in the series. It then follows that 41 multiplied by 2 equals 82, which is the next number in the sequence.

**STEP 5** **Complete the sequence.**

Following the sequence identified, after doubling the previous value, the next step is to subtract 5. Therefore, the next number is 77, which is option C.

## SPATIAL ORIENTATION AND MAPPING

Spatial orientation and mapping questions require you to study a street-view map or a diagram of a traffic intersection and then make decisions based on statements provided and the information that is visually portrayed in these scenes. In addition, travel time tests are another analytical thinking exercise that combine spatial orientation with basic mathematical skills and require you to calculate how long it would take to get from one location on a map to another.

## Mapping

Mapping questions will place you at a specific location and require you to make your way to a dispatched call via the most efficient route. You will be advised to follow all rules of the road, unless specifically advised that it is an emergency situation and you can disregard traffic laws, such as one-way streets. Another objective of mapping questions is to determine whether you can correctly identify direction of travel. That is, are you travelling northbound or eastbound in order to get to the call?

### SUSPICIOUS PERSON

*Example:*

You are in your patrol car in front of Headquarters on Young Street. You are dispatched to a report of a suspicious male hanging around the north side of the library. Using the map below of Port Walnut as a reference, what would be the most efficient and accurate route to this location, while complying with all traffic laws?

(A) Drive south on Young, east on 7th Ave, and left onto Main St.

(B) Drive north on Young, west on 7th Ave, south onto Madison St.

(C) Drive east on Young, north on 7th Ave, west onto Main St.

(D) Drive east on Young, north on 7th Ave, left onto Madison St.

**TIP**

Always rotate maps so that north is pointing towards the top of your page.

**Port Walnut**

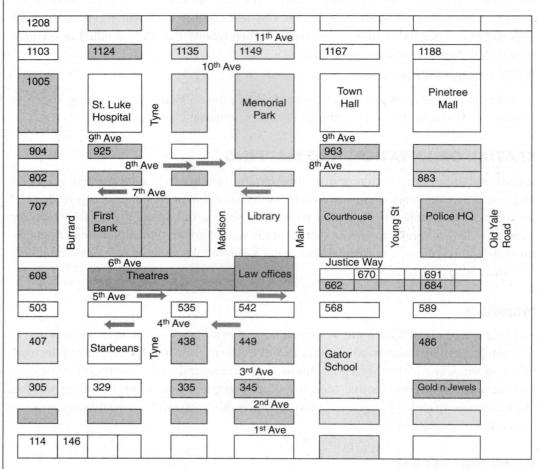

Solving these types of mapping questions is an easy two-step process.

**STEP 1   Face north.**

You will have a much easier time trying to figure out in which direction you need to drive if you orient the map so that north is facing towards the top of your page. We have been trained since elementary school to look at maps this way. Although the map will have a compass indicating which direction is north, one of the tricks that is often used in these kinds of questions is that north will not be facing towards the top of the page. Therefore, look at the compass first and turn your map so that north faces towards the top.

**STEP 2   Trace the route.**

When tracing the route, it is important that you read the instructions carefully. For example, what side of the building have you been dispatched to? Are you permitted to ignore traffic control devices, such as one-way direction signs?

**STEP 3   Match the route.**

The final step is to match the visual route that you traced with one of the options provided. Use the process of elimination and double check the route to ensure you have identified the correct response—your options will likely all look very similar. In this particular example, you are dispatched to a suspicious male hanging around the north side of the library; therefore, you must attend that location on Madison Ave. Option B has the directions all wrong, so D is the correct response.

When dealing with maps that show only a specific intersection, which is usually in the context of a motor vehicle collision, the same principles apply. First, ensure that north is at the top of the page so that you can determine which direction vehicles, bicycles, and pedestrians were traveling. Second, use the process of elimination for each of the options presented to determine the correct sequence of events.

## MOTOR VEHICLE INCIDENT

### Example:

Using the information provided in the diagram below, which of the following statements best describes what occurred?

(A) A vehicle was north on Montrose when it disobeyed a stop sign and was struck by an eastbound car and a westbound car almost simultaneously.

(B) A vehicle that was northbound on Burd Avenue struck an eastbound car that failed to stop for a stop sign. The southbound vehicle also struck the eastbound vehicle.

(C) A vehicle southbound on Burd Avenue struck a westbound car that failed to stop for a stop sign. The westbound car was also struck by a northbound vehicle.

(D) A car that was turning from Burd Avenue onto Montrose disobeyed a stop sign and was struck by a northbound vehicle and a southbound vehicle.

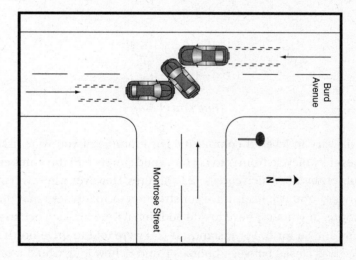

To solve this spatial orientation question, the first step is to rotate the diagram so that north faces the top of the page. Then, go through each of the options step by step.

Option A begins by stating that a "vehicle was north on Montrose... ." You can eliminate this option since Montrose runs east-west.

Option B states that "a vehicle that was northbound on Burd Avenue struck an eastbound car." This option can also be eliminated because the car on Montrose was travelling west as it entered the T-intersection.

Option C states that "a vehicle southbound on Burd Avenue struck a westbound car that failed to stop for a stop sign. The westbound car was also struck by a northbound vehicle." This is awkwardly worded, but it is a factual representation of what is drawn.

Option D states that a "car that was turning from Burd Avenue onto Montrose." From the diagram, we can see that the vehicle is turning from Montrose onto Burd. Thus, you can also eliminate this option.

Therefore, the correct response is C.

## TRAVEL TIME TASKS

Some entrance exams use travel time tasks as a means of evaluating your deductive reasoning skills. In the example below, the lines between each bubble represent one city block; therefore, travelling from bubbles A to D is three blocks. You will likely be advised that you are to travel by car, bicycle, or on foot or a combination thereof. Each mode of transportation will have a different length of time associated with it. For this exercise, travel times per block are as follows:

Police Car: 1 minute
Bicycle: 2.5 minutes
On Foot: 4 minutes

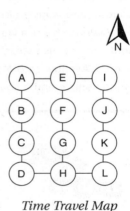

*Time Travel Map*

Questions will vary in level of complexity. For example, if you were asked how long it would take to travel by bicycle from A to L, you would simply add the number of blocks travelled (5) and multiply by 2.5, which equals 12.5 minutes. However, rarely will these challenges be so straightforward. You will likely have construction or roadblocks that prevent you from taking a direct route, or you may have to add additional time for each occurrence where you change directions and so forth. For instance, if you were told to drive north from bubble H to E, but the road was closed between bubbles F and E, how long would it take you to drive to E, if you had to add an additional 30 seconds for each turn you made?

To answer this question, you would first count the total number of blocks that you would have to travel (5) and then add the number of times that you changed direction (3) adding 30 seconds each time. Therefore, it would take you 6.5 minutes to drive from H to E (see diagram on page 215). Additionally, if you were advised that you could cross the roadblock between F and E on foot, would it be quicker to drive around or walk the last block? In this case, there are three blocks to drive, with the extra 90 seconds for each turn, which is 4.5 minutes of travel time. If you walked through the road closure, it would take you 4 minutes total; therefore, it would be quicker to walk.

**TIP**

In travel time tasks, trace routes and calculate times to ensure you arrive at the most efficient route.

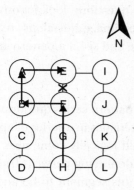

*Time Travel Roadblock*

## CLASSIFICATION

Classification problems measure your ability to organize several items, whether they be shapes, pictures, numbers, or words, and find similarities and differences between them. In classification questions, you will typically be shown four or more images and then be required to identify which one of those images does not maintain a relationship between the others and, therefore, does not belong with the group, or, alternatively, which two images are a match. For example, you may be shown several mug shots of suspects and be asked to identify which two individuals are the same, or conversely which one of the four mug shots is not of the same person.

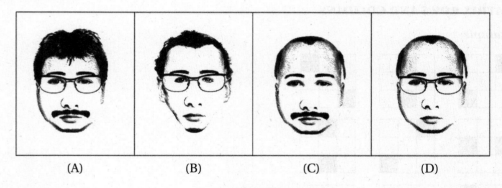

(A)          (B)          (C)          (D)

*Suspect Mug Shots*

In the previous diagram, for example, you might be asked which one of these individuals is not the same suspect. There are certain features that you should be looking for that will always be the same if they are the same person:

- Eyes—although they may sometimes be disguised by a patch or glasses,
- Nose,
- Jaw line,
- Ears, and
- Lips—although the mouth may have different shapes if the suspect is smiling or not.

In other words, do not pay attention to hair lines, hair styles, beards, moustaches, or whether the suspects are wearing hats or glasses. The eyes will usually help you the most in making your match.

For other types of classification questions, look for other commonalities that may not be immediately obvious. Especially for image questions, try counting the number of various lines and shapes within each image and see if a pattern emerges.

## PATTERN SERIES

Similar to classification problems, pattern series questions require you to use inductive reasoning to identify common characteristics in a series of apparently ambiguous visual objects and then decide what shape should logically come next. Once again, despite your level of intelligence, if you have not tried identifying patterns from visual objects since you were in elementary school, you may find this segment to be another challenging aspect of police entrance exams. Fortunately, as with most other logic problems, once you have learned the rules and strategies that apply to these types of questions, you will find them relatively easy to solve.

### Rule One: Scan All Figures

Whether you are attempting to complete an image classification exercise, where you are required to identify the image that does not belong, or the more complex three-row by three-column image matrices, where you are required to complete the ninth image in the sequence, the same rule applies—scan all the images and all the rows and columns to identify the potential pattern. For example, in a 3 × 3 image matrix, the pattern may be based on each row, or each column, or both.

### MATRIX ROWS AND COLUMNS

*Example:*

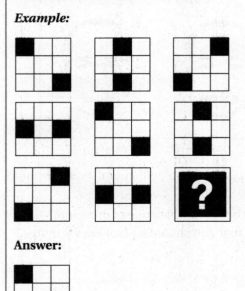

**Answer:**

In this example, the pattern sequence is found in both the rows and the columns. Starting at the top left-hand pattern, the blacked out squares move clockwise one position as you move across the row. This sequence is repeated for the second and third rows. However, you could come to the same conclusion if you went column by column, except the squares move one position counterclockwise from top to bottom. Therefore, when looking for pattern sequences, ensure that you look both row by row and column by column to reveal the sequence.

## Rule Two: Progression

As you scan a pattern and look at the various images, one of the most common sequences will be an increase or decrease between adjacent images in position, size, or number. As in the example above, the progression was a change in the position of the black squares either clockwise or counterclockwise from one image to the next.

**PROGRESSION**

*Example:*

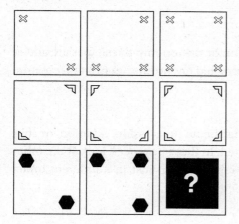

**Answer:**

In this basic example above, there is obviously a progression in the number and location of images within each row.

## Rule Three: Addition and Subtraction

In these types of patterns, a shape or image from one column or row is added to or subtracted from the next column or row to produce the third image.

## ADDITION AND SUBTRACTION

*Example:*

**Answer:**

●

In this instance, whether you look at the left column or the top row, the shapes are added together in the middle row and column, and then subtracted on the bottom row and column.

## Rule Four: Complete the Set

Sometimes when you look at a row of shapes there may be no progression, addition, or subtraction of images, and they may appear to be unrelated. In these instances, look at the other two rows and determine whether these images are repeated, but just in a different order. These are examples where you are required to complete the set.

**COMPLETE THE SET**

*Example:*

**Answer:**

In this example, looking at each row individually does not indicate the pattern sequence; however, by looking at all three rows, you can identify that for each row there are two outlines of shapes that are the same and a different shape that is filled in black. The outlined and filled-in shapes then change with each row. Therefore, to complete the set, the final image must be a filled-in shape that has not yet been used—the square.

## Rule Five: Image Transformation

On occasion the first image and the third image may appear somewhat related, but the middle image doesn't seem to belong. This middle image may be indicative of a specific function that changes the form of the first image to the third. That is, it may flip the first image on its vertical axis, horizontal axis, invert the image, and so on.

**IMAGE TRANSFORMATION**

*Example:*

**Answer:**

In this example, the vertical bar in the first row indicates that the image is rotated on a vertical axis, so that a mirror image is produced. On the second row, the horizontal bar indicates that the image is to be flipped on its horizontal access. The final t-shaped bars indicate that the image is rotated both horizontally and vertically.

> **TIP**
>
> When solving patterns, focus on the following:
> - Complete a set of shapes
> - Progression in size, number, and direction of shapes
> - Image transformation clues
> - Ignore irrelevant shapes

## Rule Six: Ignore Irrelevant Images

As the patterns become more complicated, one of the methods that is often used to throw you off is to include irrelevant images in the pattern, trying to make you focus on something that doesn't seem to fit instead of ignoring it and seeing the pattern around it. For example, it is possible that only one or two of the images per square are distributed in each row, while the rest are "white noise" distractions.

**IRRELEVANT IMAGES**

*Example:*

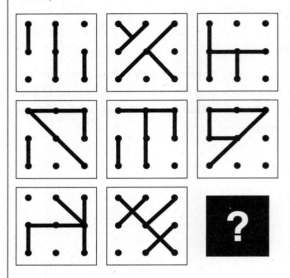

**Answer:**

In this case, the only constant among all the images is that the centre bar rotates clockwise on its axis. Therefore, it is irrelevant where all the other bars are located. The only relevant image in the sequence is that the centre bar has rotated back to the vertical position.

## Rule Seven: Multiple Rules

Finally, complex patterns often have more than one set of rules that apply to the entire matrix. For example, over the course of the three rows, the images may change in shape, progression, and number. In these instances, identifying just a single sequence will be insufficient to solving the pattern, and you may have to test several hypotheses.

## MULTIPLE SETS

*Example:*

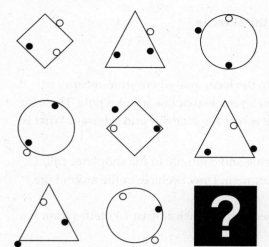

**Answer:**

In this example there are several rules at play:

- Complete the set—the diamond shape completes the third shape that is consistent in each row.
- Progression—the pair of black circles inside the shape changes in each row, with the other two shapes having a black and white circle inside each of them.
- Irrelevant images—each shape has a black or white circle placed in a random location outside of each shape. In addition, the location of the circles inside the shape are also randomly placed.

Before continuing to the next chapter, answer the 10 multiple-choice review questions below—just to make sure that you have got it right.

# HAVE I GOT IT RIGHT?

 **You have 7 minutes to complete the exercise.**

1. You are driving along Main Street en route to the local mall where store security is detaining a shoplifter when you come across a vehicle that has struck a pole. There are no injuries, but live electrical wires are lying across the roadway and sidewalk. What is your next course of action?

   (A) Ask dispatch to send electrical engineering and continue to the shoplifter call.
   (B) Call for an ambulance and the fire department. Direct vehicle traffic around the collision scene.
   (C) Advise dispatch of the problem. Keep pedestrians back at least 10 metres from the wires.
   (D) Protect the public by locating the power junction box and disabling the electricity.

2. You are writing a driver a ticket for disobeying a "no U turn" sign when a citizen approaches you and states that just around the corner is a very intoxicated male fumbling with his keys and that he appears to be trying to start his vehicle.

   (A) Ask the citizen for the plate number and vehicle description and broadcast the information to other units in the area; continue to write the ticket.
   (B) Obtain a description of the suspect and the vehicle, advise dispatch, ask the witness to remain there in case a statement is needed, return licence and registration to the violator, investigate allegation.
   (C) The citizen is probably a friend of the violator and this is likely some ploy to get you to stop writing the ticket and let him go.
   (D) Tell the violator and witness to follow you around the corner so that you can investigate the citizen's claim.

QUESTIONS 3–4 ARE SYLLOGISMS. FOR EACH QUESTION, YOU MUST ASSUME THAT EACH STATEMENT IS TRUE.

3. Some criminals are members of the 604 Gang.

   No 604 Gang members live in Alberta.

   (A) Therefore, some 604 Gang members are criminal.
   (B) Therefore, some criminals do not live in Alberta.
   (C) Therefore, no Albertans are gang members.
   (D) Therefore, all 604 Gang members not living in Alberta are criminals.

4. Some Canadians are wealthy.

   All poor people are Canadians.

   (A) Therefore, some poor people are wealthy.
   (B) Therefore, some Canadians are poor people.
   (C) Therefore, some Canadians are not wealthy.
   (D) Therefore, all poor people are not Canadians.

5. What is the next number in the sequence?

   28 41 55 70 86 103

   (A) 134
   (B) 127
   (C) 123
   (D) 121

6. Constable Mark was looking at his collection of foreign police officer shoulder flashes and realized that all of them were blue, except two; all of them were green, except two; and all of them were brown, except two. How many foreign police officer shoulder flashes does Constable Mark have?

   (A) 9
   (B) 6
   (C) 4
   (D) 3

7. Complete the comparison.

 is to  as  is to...

   (A)            (B)            (C)            (D)

8. Complete the comparison.

   Montréal is to 76 as Calgary is to

   (A) 104
   (B) 49
   (C) 91
   (D) 88

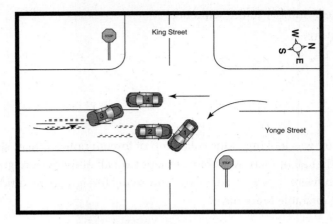

**Yonge & King MVI**

9. Based on the information provided in the image above, which of the following statements best describes what occurred?

   (A) Vehicle 1 made a left turn in front of Vehicle 2 that was eastbound on Yonge Street. Vehicle 2 braked and skid into Vehicle 1. At the same time, Vehicle 3 braked and skid into oncoming traffic and slid into Vehicle 4.

   (B) Vehicle 1 was southbound on Yonge Street, made a left turn into oncoming vehicle 2. Vehicle 2 braked to avoid collision but skid into Vehicle 1. Vehicle 3 was eastbound on Yonge and tried to avoid the collision but skid into oncoming traffic and was hit by Vehicle 4.

   (C) Vehicle 2 was northbound on Yonge Street when Vehicle 1 turned left in front of it. Vehicle 2 braked and skid into Vehicle 1. Vehicle 3 was behind Vehicle 2 and braked to avoid collision but skid into oncoming Vehicle 4 that was southbound on Yonge Street.

   (D) Vehicle 1 was southbound on Yonge Street, made a left turn to proceed westbound on King Street, turning in front of Vehicle 2 that was northbound on Yonge Street. Vehicle 2 braked and skid into Vehicle 1. Vehicle 3 attempted to avoid collision and braked and skid into oncoming traffic and was hit by Vehicle 4.

10. Select the next image that completes the pattern sequence.

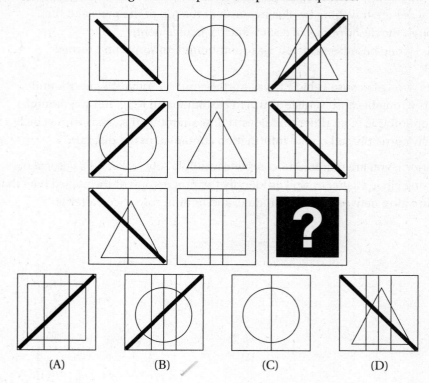

(A)          (B)          (C)          (D)

## Answers

1. **C** Public safety is always your top priority. A downed high-voltage wire is a far greater risk to pedestrians than motorists. Call for assistance and keep pedestrians back from the wires.

2. **B** Impaired driving kills hundreds of people each year in Canada and, therefore, is a much higher priority than a minor traffic offence. However, before heading off on a wild goose chase, quickly obtain the suspect and vehicle description from the witness, and his own particulars in the event a statement is needed from him. The possibility that this is a ruse by an accomplice of the violator is remote, and in any event, you have his particulars if you need to track him down later and complete the ticket.

3. **B** Rule: Some, No = Some Not; see Syllogisms.

4. **A** Rule: Some, All = Some; see Syllogisms.

5. **D** Add 13, 14, 15, 16, 17, then 18 to previous number; see Number Series.

6. **D** Mark has three shoulder flashes; he only has one of each colour. This is best solved by sketching the statement.

7. **C** This is a visual analogy, but can be solved in the same way as the others—identify and generalize the relationship. In this case, the relationship is a three-sided shape is to a four-sided shape as a six-sided shape is to an eight-sided shape. See Analogies.

8. **D** The analogy in this instance is that Montréal hosted the Olympics in 1976, and Calgary was the host city for the Olympics in 1988.

9. **C** This mapping and spatial recognition assignment requires you to recognize which direction vehicles are travelling by placing north at the top of the page and then reading through the descriptions of each vehicle's involvement.

- Option A is wrong because vehicle 1 was southbound on Yonge and turned eastbound.
- Option B is wrong because vehicle 3 was northbound on Yonge, not eastbound.
- Option D is wrong because vehicle 1 turned eastbound on King, not westbound.
- Although option C is in an order that doesn't flow smoothly (i.e., start with vehicle 1), it is factually correct based on the information contained in the diagram.

10. **B** In this pattern, you are required to complete multiple sets (1, 2, and 3 vertical bars and the missing circle shape) as well as identify the progression of the angled bars that alternated direction between the top, middle, and bottom rows. See Patterns.

# Problem Solving

12

- → TEST YOUR KNOWLEDGE
- → BASIC MATHEMATICAL OPERATIONS
- → ORDER OF OPERATIONS
- → DECIMALS
- → FRACTIONS
- → GEOMETRY
- → ALGEBRAIC EQUATIONS
- → WORD PROBLEMS
- → HAVE I GOT IT RIGHT?

Although police officers are not required to possess an actuarial degree, there is an expectation that officers can demonstrate sufficient mathematical skills to be able to conduct basic calculations and solve simple math problems. Fortunately, mathematical problem solving generally accounts for less than a quarter of the content of most police entrance exams, and the majority of the problems that you would face are at a Grade 10 equivalency or lower.

Begin by completing the Test Your Knowledge assessment to measure your mathematical proficiency.

## TEST YOUR KNOWLEDGE

**You have 30 minutes to answer the following 20 questions.**

The first 13 questions require you to solve basic mathematical equations. The remaining 7 questions are based on a series of problem-solving statements. Do not use a calculator or any electronic device; however, you may use scrap paper for notes and calculations.

Start your timer and begin now.

1. Find the quotient of 41,607 ÷ 23.

   (A) 0.00055
   (B) 919
   (C) 1,919
   (D) 1,809

2. Express the sum of $\frac{22}{5} + \frac{11}{5}$.

   (A) $\frac{55}{2}$

   (B) $\frac{33}{5}$

   (C) $\frac{165}{2}$

   (D) $\frac{33}{25}$

3. Calculate $23 + 10 + 15 + 11 \times 23$.

   (A) 267
   (B) 301
   (C) 1,168
   (D) 1,357

4. What is the product of $23.46 \times 42.3$?

   (A) 768.23
   (B) 992.358
   (C) 6,323.38
   (D) 1,043.438

5. What is $\frac{2}{7}$ divided by $\frac{4}{8}$?

   (A) $\frac{1}{7}$

   (B) $\frac{4}{7}$

   (C) $\frac{8}{14}$

   (D) $\frac{2}{18}$

6. Find the sum of $\frac{2}{9} + \frac{3}{2}$.

   (A) $\frac{5}{6}$

   (B) $-\frac{23}{18}$

   (C) $2\frac{5}{11}$

   (D) $1\frac{13}{18}$

7. Solve $52.9 + 117 \div 3 - 13.74$.

   (A) 78.16
   (B) −5.29
   (C) 57.93
   (D) 31.457

8. Find the quotient of $180.18 \div 4.95$.

   (A) 67.327
   (B) 29.624
   (C) 36.4
   (D) 44.74

9. Find the product of $2\frac{5}{8} \times 9$.

   (A) $16\frac{3}{4}$

   (B) $23\frac{5}{8}$

   (C) $18\frac{5}{8}$

   (D) $21\frac{1}{2}$

10. Solve $\frac{3}{8} - \frac{1}{24} + \frac{2}{3}$.

    (A) $2\frac{3}{8}$

    (B) $\frac{13}{24}$

    (C) 1

    (D) None of the above

11. Solve for the variable $y$. $\frac{4}{5}y = 120$.

(A) 80

(B) 96

(C) 134

(D) 150

12. Solve for the variable $y$. $3(y - 8) = 33$.

(A) 13

(B) −13

(C) 19

(D) $\frac{11}{33}$

13. Solve for the ratio $y$. $9 : 3 = y : 11$.

(A) 29

(B) 33

(C) 43

(D) 3.66

14. If a highway patrol car is driven at an average speed of 95 kilometres per hour for 45 minutes, approximately how far will it have travelled?

(A) 53 kilometres

(B) 66 kilometres

(C) 71 kilometres

(D) 83 kilometres

15. The Calgary Police Department located a large illegal marijuana grow operation filling the interior of a warehouse on the outskirts of town. The rectangular warehouse was 150 m by 45 m. What was the total area, in square metres, of the grow op.

(A) 390 m$^2$

(B) 6,750 m$^2$

(C) 7,540 m$^2$

(D) 1,990 m$^2$

16. If Constable Basra wrote eight speeding tickets in three hours, approximately how many tickets could she write in eleven hours if she maintained the same pace?

(A) 24

(B) 29

(C) 31

(D) 37

17. The chief was concerned about the amount of racial diversity in the demographics of the police department. Out of 800 members, she found that 447 were Caucasian, 129 were South Asian, 93 were Asian, 52 were Hispanic, 47 were of African descent, and 32 were Aboriginal. What percentage of the department is of Aboriginal ancestry?

    (A) 4%
    (B) 6%
    (C) 7%
    (D) 8%

18. Constable Tang and Constable Rodriguez recorded the most arrests in their squad last year. Together, the two officers had 96 arrests; however, Constable Tang had twice as many arrests as Constable Rodriguez. How many arrests did Constable Tang make?

    (A) 56
    (B) 75
    (C) 48
    (D) 64

19. Four constables calculated that they have an average of eight years of service. Constable Armundson has five years, Cantterra has six years, and Jamieson has 13 years. How many years of service does Constable Ryan have?

    (A) 6
    (B) 7
    (C) 8
    (D) 9

20. Constable Derry had to pick up a prisoner in a neighbouring city. She drove 80 km/h driving to the city and 70 km/h driving back. She drove a total of four hours without stopping. What is the approximate distance between the two cities?

    (A) 176 km
    (B) 149 km
    (C) 137 km
    (D) 124 km

## Answers

1. **D** The quotient of $41{,}607 \div 23 = 1{,}809$; see Division.

2. **B** The sum of $\dfrac{22}{5} + \dfrac{11}{5} = \dfrac{33}{5}$; see Adding and Subtracting Fractions.

3. **B** The sum of $23 + 10 + 15 + 11 \times 23 = 301$; see Order of Operations and Multiplication.

4. **B** The product of $23.46 \times 42.3 = 992.358$; see Multiplication; Decimals.

5. **C** The quotient of $\dfrac{2}{7} \div \dfrac{4}{8} = \dfrac{8}{14}$; see Multiplying and Dividing Fractions.

6. **D** The sum of $\dfrac{2}{9} + \dfrac{3}{2} = 1\dfrac{13}{18}$; see Adding and Subtracting Fractions.

7. **A** $52.9 + 117 \div 3 - 13.74 = 78.16$; see Order of Operations.

8. **C** The quotient of $180.18 \div 4.95 = 36.4$; see Division; Decimals.

9. **B** The product of $2\frac{5}{8} \times 9 = 23\frac{5}{8}$; see Multiplying and Dividing Fractions.

10. **C** $\frac{3}{8} - \frac{1}{24} + \frac{2}{3} = \frac{24}{24} = 1$; see Adding and Subtracting Fractions.

11. **D** $\frac{4}{5}y = 120$. $y = 150$; see Algebra.

12. **C** $3(y - 8) = 33$. $y = 19$; see Algebra.

13. **B** $9 : 3 = y : 11$. $y = 33$; see Algebra.

14. **C** $\frac{95}{60} = \frac{x}{45}$. $x = 71.25$; see Algebra; Word Problems.

15. **B** Area $= l \times w$. $150 \times 45 = 6{,}750$ m²; see Area and Volumes.

16. **B** $\frac{8}{3} = \frac{x}{11}$. $x = 29.3$; see Algebra; Word Problems.

17. **A** $\frac{33}{805} = \frac{x}{100}$. $x = 4.09$; see Algebra; Word Problems.

18. **D** $x + 2x = 96$. $x = 32$; see Algebra; Word Problems.

19. **C** $(5 + 6 + 13 + x) / 4 = 8$; $x = 8$; see Algebra; Word Problems.

20. **B** $\frac{x}{80} + \frac{x}{70} = 4$; $x = 149.3$; see Algebra; Word Problems.

---

### HOW DID YOU SCORE?

Correct Answers: _____/20        Excellent 18–20        Good 15–17        Average 12–14

If your test score is not in the Excellent range, then you should focus your study efforts on this chapter to ensure that you understand the essential rules of arithmetic and algebra.

---

## BASIC MATHEMATICAL OPERATIONS
## Addition

The most basic math operation is adding two or more values (numbers) together in order to obtain a total value. The first step when adding large numerical values is to make sure that the columns representing their values are properly aligned. That is, if you are asked to provide the sum of 4,510 and 1,630, you would begin by stacking the two values vertically (see *Table 1*). The second step is to add the value of the vertical columns together, beginning on the right with the ones column. Record the sum of each column below the equation and move to the next column. If, however, the sum of a column exceeds 9, write down the ones value in that column and indicate in the next column to the left of the ten value of that number. For example, in the hundreds column of Figure 1, 500 plus 600 equals 1,100, however, only 1 is placed below in the hundreds column, and the other 1 is added to the thousands column.

## Table 1. Value of Numbers

| Thousands | Hundreds | Tens | Ones |
|:---:|:---:|:---:|:---:|
| 4 | 5 | 1 | 0 |
| 1 | 6 | 3 | 0 |

$$
\begin{array}{r}
^1 4\,5\,1\,0 \\
+\ 1\,6\,3\,0 \\
\hline
6\,^11\,4\,0
\end{array}
$$

**Figure 1.** Addition

## Subtraction

Subtracting numbers is set up in the same manner as addition in that you stack one set of numbers above the other. However, when subtracting, always place the greater number on top of the lower one. Also, in subtraction, you can only calculate the difference between two values at once. That is, you cannot calculate the difference between three or more numbers (e.g., 916 – 213 – 415) in one step.

When subtracting, if the number on top in one of the columns is less than the corresponding number below, you must borrow 1 from the column to the left. In the example in Figure 2, the 3 in the tens column is less than the 5 below it, so 1 must be borrowed from the hundreds column. The 3 then becomes a 13. If the number in the column that you need to borrow from is a 0, then you need to move one column further to the left to borrow. The 0 then becomes a 9 for your calculations.

$$
\begin{array}{r}
2\ \overset{5}{6}\,^13\,7 \\
-\ 1\,5\,5\,3 \\
\hline
1\,0\,8\,4
\end{array}
$$

**Figure 2.** Subtraction

## Multiplication

You will not be permitted to use calculators or other electronic devices while taking any police entrance exam. Therefore, in order to complete any of the multiplication questions, at the very least you must know the multiplication table from zero to 10 in advance.

Solving multiplication problems involves using a multistep process. The first step of multiplication is to arrange the two sets of numbers in the same manner as you would if you were subtracting them—stacked one above the other, with the greater number on top. The next step is to multiply the bottom number on the right with all the numbers above, moving from right to left. For example, if you were to find the product of 278 × 12, you would arrange the two numbers as shown in Figure 3.

**Figure 3.** Multiplication Step

**TIP**

Calculators are not permitted in police entrance exams. Therefore, at a minimum memorize multiplication tables from 0 to 10.

**STEP 1** In this example, the first step is to calculate $2 \times 278$. Since $2 \times 8 = 16$, you would write the 6 in the ones column and carry the 1 to the tens column. $2 \times 7 = 14$, plus the 1 that was carried $= 15$. Write the 5 in the tens column and carry the 1 to the hundreds column. Finally, $2 \times 2 = 4$, plus 1 that was carried $= 5$. Therefore the product of the first step equals 556. See Figure 4.

$$
\begin{array}{r}
2\ 7\ 8 \\
\times\quad\ 1\ 2 \\
\hline
5\ 5\ 6 \\
2\ 7\ 8\ 0 \\
\end{array}
$$

**Figure 4.** Multiplication Step Two

**STEP 2** Drop a row beneath the first product line, add a zero to the right-hand ones column and repeat Step One. See Figure 4.

**STEP 3** The final step, as indicated in Figure 5, is to add the numbers in all the columns to determine your final product. If the number being multiplied was even larger (e.g., $278 \times 212$), repeat Step Two before doing Step Three, adding another zero to each line.

$$
\begin{array}{r}
2\ 7\ 8 \\
\times\quad\ 1\ 2 \\
\hline
5\ 5\ 6 \\
+\ 2\ 7\ 8\ 0 \\
\hline
3\ 3\ 3\ 6 \\
\end{array}
$$

**Figure 5.** Multiplication Product

## Division

Solving a division problem usually involves more steps than the other basic math operations; however, this does not mean that these questions are more difficult. If you pay attention to detail and follow each step required, you will find that division problems simply involve a series of repeated multiplication and subtraction exercises.

**STEP 1** Make sure that you read the question carefully and lay the equation out properly. For example, $126 \div 14$ will result in a much different answer than $14 \div 126$. Usually you will be asked to divide the larger number by the smaller number (e.g., 126 divided by $14 = 9$). In this case, 126 is the dividend, 14 is the divisor, and 9 is the quotient. This can be expressed in several ways: $126 \div 14$, $14\overline{)126}$, or $\dfrac{126}{14}$. To set up an equation for long division, place the dividend inside the long division bracket and the divisor outside the bracket on the left side. See Figure 6.

$$
3\ 2\overline{)9\ 1\ 5}
$$

**Figure 6.** Division Step One

**STEP 2** Determine how many times the divisor will divide into the dividend. This will usually take some trial and error, especially when dealing with larger numbers because it will not always be readily apparent. Start by estimating the number of times and then use a piece of scrap paper to find out the number of times without going over the dividend. In this example, you could round the divisor to 30 and see how many times it divides into 90, which is 3. Unfortunately, the divisor is 32 and the first two numbers of the dividend are 91—so no luck for a simple solution. Therefore, it will only divide twice and you will have a large remainder. Place a 2 on top of the bracket, above the 1, as the first number of your quotient. See Figure 7.

$$\begin{array}{r} 2\phantom{99} \\ 3\,2\,\overline{)\,9\ 1\ 5} \end{array}$$

**Figure 7.** Division Step Two

**STEP 3** As demonstrated in Figure 8, multiply the first number in the quotient by the divisor and write the number below the first numbers of the dividend. Next, subtract the difference between the two numbers in order to determine the remainder. In this example there is 27 remaining.

$$\begin{array}{r} 2\phantom{99} \\ 3\,2\,\overline{)\,9\ 1\ 5} \\ -6\ 4\phantom{9} \\ \hline 2\ 7\phantom{9} \end{array}$$

**Figure 8.** Division Step Three

**STEP 4** Bring the number down to the remainder from the next column to the right. In this example, drop down 5 from the ones column to join the remainder to make 275. See Figure 9. Next determine how many times 32 goes into 275. We know that number will be large since 27 almost divides into 32. Again, you could estimate 9; however, you would see the result is too high (288); thus, you would use 8.

$$\begin{array}{r} 2\ 8\phantom{9} \\ 3\,2\,\overline{)\,9\ 1\ 5} \\ -6\ 4\downarrow \\ \hline 2\ 7\ 5 \end{array}$$

**Figure 9.** Division Step Four

**STEP 5** The final step of the problem is to determine if the number divides evenly into the dividend or if there is a remainder. In this example, $8 \times 32 = 256$. This is then subtracted from 275, which leaves a remainder of 19. See Figure 10. The remainder, which is less than a whole number, can be indicated as a fraction $\left(\dfrac{19}{32}\right)$ or a decimal (0.6). However, unless specifically requested to write the remainder as a fraction or decimal, the correct expression of the quotient in this example is 28r19.

$$\begin{array}{r} 2\ 8\ R = 19 \\ 3\,2\,\overline{)\,9\ 1\ 5} \\ -6\ 4\downarrow \\ \hline 2\ 7\ 5 \\ -2\ 5\ 6 \\ \hline 1\ 9 \end{array}$$

**Figure 10.** Division Step Five

## Exponents

An exponent is the small number above a base number that tells you how many times to multiply the base number. For example, $2^3 = 2 \times 2 \times 2 = 8$. In this example, the base number is 2, and the exponent is $^3$. If the exponent is a two, we say that the base number is "squared"; if it is a three, we state the base number is "cubed"; and anything else is the base number is "to the power of" whatever the value of the exponent is.

There are a few rules to remember when dealing with exponents and basic math equations. First, you can multiply exponents together, but only if the base numbers are the same. In this case, you would add the values of the two exponents together (e.g., $3^2 \times 3^3 = 3^{2+3} = 3^5$ = 243). Second, even if the base numbers are the same, you cannot conduct addition of values with exponents without first simplifying. (e.g., $3^2 + 3^3 = 9 + 27 = 36$). Third, any number to the power of zero is equal to 1 (e.g., $4^0 = 1$). Finally, if the exponent is a negative number (e.g., $3^{-2}$), then in order to simplify you remove the negative from the exponent by taking the inverse of the power (e.g., $3^{-2} = \dfrac{1}{3^2} = \dfrac{1}{9}$).

## ORDER OF OPERATIONS

**TIP**

**Use BEDMAS to remember order of operations:
Brackets
Exponents
Division
Multiplication
Addition
Subtraction**

Some entrance exams may present multiple-operation problems. In these cases, if you fail to follow the proper order of operations, you will come up with varying, and incorrect, results. Since it is a fairly common mistake to not follow the order of operations, some police entrance exams may put in their multiple-choice responses answers that you may have obtained if you followed the wrong order. Consider, for example, the following equation:

$$24 + 14 \times 9 - 87 = ?$$

If you solved each step from left to right it would be $24 + 14 = 38$; $38 \times 9 = 342$; $342 - 87 = 255$. However, if you decided to do all the addition and subtraction first, then multiplication, the result would be –2,964. Therefore, in order to prevent confusion and inconsistent results there are established rules pertaining to the order of operations when solving multistage questions. The best way to remember these rules is to memorize the mnemonic **BEDMAS**.

---

1. **Brackets**

2. **Exponents**

3. **Division and Multiplication (from left to right—whichever comes first)**

4. **Addition and Subtraction (from left to right—whichever comes first)**

---

In the example above, since there are no numbers inside brackets and there are no exponents (e.g., $4^3$) to simplify, the first task will be to solve $14 \times 9$ (which equals 126). The next step is to start at the left and add $24 + 126 = 150$ and then subtract $87 = 63$.

As another example, in order to solve the following equation, you need to complete the following steps:

$$(3 \times 2)^2 + 12 - 8 \div 2$$

**STEP 1** Brackets $(3 \times 2) = 6$

**STEP 2** Exponents $6^2 = 36$

**STEP 3** Division 8 ÷ 2 = 4

**STEP 4** Addition/Subtraction 36 + 12 − 4 = 44

## DECIMALS

Decimals are less than whole numbers. For example 5.5 means 5 and one-half of a whole number. If you were going to print half of a whole number, you would usually put a zero in front, which is 0.5. However, you could put an infinite number of zeroes on the right side of the 5, and the value of the number would not change. That is, 0.5 = 0.50000. Just as whole numbers can reach an infinite amount, so too can decimals. For example, one-third is represented as 0.3333 (with the 3s repeating forever). Decimals can also be added, subtracted, multiplied, and divided like whole numbers, and just like whole numbers, it is critical to make sure that the numbers are properly aligned when completing the calculations. For example, if you were going to add 10.012 + 0.997, you must have the columns line up by the decimal point.

| 100s | 10s | 1s | . | 10ths | 100ths | 1,000ths |
|---|---|---|---|---|---|---|
|  | 1 | 0 | . | 0 | 1 | 2 |
| + |  | 0 | . | 9 | 9 | 7 |
| 1 |  | 1 | . | 0 | 0 | 9 |

## Percentages

For most calculations, percentages are best represented as decimals. For example, 25% is equal to 0.25 (and is also represented as the fraction $\frac{25}{100}$, or reduced to $\frac{1}{4}$). Therefore, when you are required to calculate the percentage of a value, first convert the percentage to a decimal. For example, if the bill for a meal was $57.00 (no police discount) and you wanted to calculate a 15% tip, multiply the total cost by 0.15 ($57.00 × 0.15 = $8.55).

## Multiplying Decimals

When multiplying decimals, place the number with the most digits on top (it may not be the largest number). There is no need to align the decimals when stacking the two numbers. Multiply the numbers as usual, however, you will need to add the number of decimal places after completing the multiplication. For example, to solve 3.401 × 2.76 take the following steps.

**STEP 1** Stack the numbers one on top of the other. Do not try to align decimal places.

$$
\begin{array}{r}
3.401 \\
\times\ 2.76 \\
\end{array}
$$

**STEP 2** Complete the multiplication equation as described above (see Multiplication).

$$
\begin{array}{r}
3.401 \\
\times\ 2.76 \\
\hline
20406 \\
238070 \\
+\ 680200 \\
\hline
938676 \\
\end{array}
$$

**TIP**

When multiplying decimals that are less than 1, the product will be an even smaller number.

**STEP 3** In order to place the decimal point in the correct location, add the total number of decimal places that each number has. For example, 3.401 has three decimal places to the right of the 3 and 2.76 has two decimal places, for a combined total of five decimal places. Now count five places to the left of the product and insert the decimal point.

$$9.38676$$

## Dividing Decimals

Dividing decimals is a little more complicated than decimal multiplication. If the dividend (the number inside the long division bracket) has a decimal, then you align the quotient (your answer) with the decimal place. However, if the divisor also has a decimal, you must move the decimal place in the divisor to the right, in order to remove it from the equation. You then move the decimal place in the dividend an equal number of places to the right. For example, if you were to find the quotient for 148.41 ÷ 9.7, you would move the decimal place to the right in both numbers.

The next step would be to solve the equation using long division as previously described.

## FRACTIONS

Fractions and decimals refer to parts of a number that are less than a whole number. A fraction can be presented as a decimal, and vice versa. For example, the fraction $\frac{3}{4}$ is also represented as 0.75.

Just like whole numbers, fractions can be added, subtracted, multiplied, and divided. There are two parts to a fraction; the numerator is the top part of the fraction, and the denominator is the bottom. If the numerator is an exact multiple of the denominator, then the fraction can be displayed as a whole number. That is, $\frac{16}{16}$ is 1, and $\frac{32}{16} = 2$. Furthermore, fractions can be reduced or simplified if necessary. For example, $\frac{3}{9}$ can be reduced to $\frac{1}{3}$. This is accomplished by dividing both the numerator and the denominator by 3. When fractions are reduced, the value of the fraction doesn't change. Finally, fractions can also be displayed as improper fractions, (e.g., $\frac{21}{4}$) where the numerator exceeds the value of the denominator, and as mixed numbers that have a whole number attached to the fraction (e.g., $\frac{21}{4} = 5\frac{1}{4}$).

**TIP**

Fractions must first have a common denominator before they can be added or subtracted.

## Adding and Subtracting Fractions

To add or subtract fractions, you need to make sure that the fractions have common denominators. That is, you cannot simply add $\frac{3}{8}$ and $\frac{2}{6}$ together; you must first establish their lowest common denominator.

**STEP 1** Lowest common denominator of $\frac{3}{8}$ and $\frac{2}{6}$ = 24.

$$8 \times 3 = 24$$
$$6 \times 4 = 24$$

**STEP 2** What you do to the denominator, you must also do to the numerator. That is, after multiplying the denominator (8) by 3 to become 24, you must multiply the numerator by the same amount so as not to change the value of the fraction.

$$3 \times 3 = 9$$
$$2 \times 4 = 8$$

**STEP 3** Add the values of the numerators together. The denominator does not change in value.

$$\frac{9}{24} + \frac{8}{24} = \frac{17}{24}$$

You can add and subtract mixed numbers as long as the denominators are the same. In instances where you are subtracting mixed numbers, you may need to borrow from the whole number in order to complete the equation. For example, if you are to solve $7\frac{2}{9} - 4\frac{7}{9}$ you cannot simply subtract 7 from 2. Instead you must first convert $7\frac{2}{9}$ into an improper fraction.

**STEP 1** Borrow from the whole number. Remember that in this example, $\frac{9}{9}$ is equal to 1.

Therefore, borrow 1 whole number from $7\frac{2}{9}$, which becomes an improper fraction $6\frac{11}{9}$

**STEP 2** Subtract the fractions first, then whole numbers, and calculate the difference.

$$\begin{array}{r} 6\frac{11}{9} \\ - \ 4\frac{1}{9} \\ \hline 2\frac{4}{9} \end{array}$$

## Multiplying and Dividing Fractions

It is easier to multiply and divide fractions than to add or subtract them in that you do not need to find a common denominator in order to complete the equation. When multiplying

**TIP**

Fractions do not need a common denominator in order to be multiplied or divided.

two fractions, the two numerators are multiplied and then the two denominators are multiplied. For example, to find the product of $\frac{3}{4} \times \frac{4}{9}$ requires the following:

**STEP 1** Multiply numerators: $3 \times 4 = 12$

**STEP 2** Multiply denominators: $4 \times 9 = 36$

**STEP 3** Reduce the fraction: $\frac{12}{36}$ is reduced to $\frac{1}{3}$ by dividing the numerator and denominator by 12.

When multiplying fractions, you may be able to reduce the size of the numbers to be multiplied by cross-cancelling the fractions prior to multiplying. That is, $\frac{5}{24} \times \frac{8}{15}$ can be reduced by cross-dividing common multiples of the numerator of one fraction by the denominator of the other and vice versa.

**STEP 1** Determine if the numerator of the first fraction can be reduced with the denominator of the second fraction. In this case they both divide by 5.

$$\frac{\overset{1}{\cancel{5}}}{24} \times \frac{8}{\cancel{15}^{3}}$$

**STEP 2** Determine if the denominator of the first fraction can be divided by a factor of the numerator of the second fraction. In this case they both divide by 8.

$$\frac{1}{\underset{3}{\cancel{24}}} \times \frac{\cancel{8}^{1}}{3}$$

**STEP 3** Multiply the reduced fractions.

$$\frac{1}{3} \times \frac{1}{3} = \frac{1}{9}$$

## Multiplying Mixed Numbers

When multiplying mixed numbers, you must first convert them into improper fractions. If, for example, you were to multiply $6\frac{2}{3} \times 4\frac{1}{8}$, you would first convert each fraction to an improper one.

**STEP 1** $6\frac{2}{3}$, $6 \times 3$ (denominator) $+ 2$ (numerator) $= 20$ to create an improper fraction $\frac{20}{3}$.

**STEP 2** Repeat with second fraction, $4\frac{1}{8}$, $(4 \times 8) + 1 = 33$ to create the second improper fraction $\frac{33}{8}$.

**STEP 3** Reduce fractions before multiplying, $\frac{20}{3} \times \frac{33}{8}$ becomes $\frac{5}{1} \times \frac{11}{2}$.

**STEP 4** Multiply numerators $(5 \times 11)$ and denominators $(1 \times 2) = \frac{55}{2}$.

**STEP 5** Convert back to a mixed number (divide numerator by denominator) $= 27\frac{1}{2}$.

## Dividing Fractions

When you consider how many steps there are to calculating long division, the prospect of dividing fractions may appear dreadful; however, it is actually very easy. Simply invert the numerator and denominator of the second fraction and multiply the equation. For example, $\frac{2}{9} \div \frac{4}{5}$ becomes $\frac{2}{9} \times \frac{5}{4}$.

**STEP 1** Cross reduce fractions: $\frac{1}{9} \times \frac{5}{2}$

**STEP 2** Multiply fractions: $\frac{1}{9} \times \frac{5}{2} = \frac{5}{18}$

## GEOMETRY

Having to find the area of a square, rectangle, or triangle will likely be uncommon in most police entrance exams; calculating the volume of a prism or cylinder is an even more remote possibility. Nevertheless, these types of math questions may surface from time to time, so it is better to be prepared than caught off guard.

## Perimeter

Finding the perimeter of something means calculating the total distance around the outside edges of the specific area or region. A perimeter can be obtained for virtually any shape, such as a square, triangle, rectangle, or parallelogram. Calculating the perimeter may be as simple as adding together all the provided lengths of a given object. For example, in the figure below, the lengths of the triangle are given. Therefore, the perimeter is (8 cm + 10 cm + 6 cm) = 24 cm.

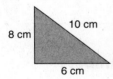

However, all of the lengths are rarely provided to you when having to make your calculations, but the missing values are usually easy enough to find. For example, a square has four equal length sides; therefore, even if only one length is provided, the perimeter is equal to the length of one side ×4. Similarly, in a rectangle, the lengths of two sides are equal, as well as the measurement of two widths. Therefore, the perimeter of a rectangle = 2 × length + 2 × width. For example, in the figure below, the perimeter is (2 × 10 cm + 2 × 5 cm) = 30 cm.

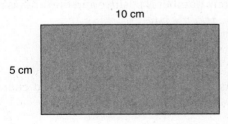

## Area

Calculating the area of a specific area or region means finding out what the size of the surface area is. For example, if you wanted to put new flooring in the police Report Writing room, which is 8 m × 5 m, and you wanted to use 1 m × 1 m square pieces of carpet, you could literally count out the square tiles and place them one by one, as indicated in the figure below. In this case, you would need 40 square 1 m × 1 m pieces of carpet in order to cover the surface area. However, a much more efficient method of determining the number of tiles would be to multiply the length (8 m) by the width (5 m) and come up with the same result, 40 square metres, or 40 m². Therefore, in order to determine the square area of a rectangle or square surface, multiply length times width (e.g., 5 m × 8 m = 40 m²).

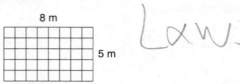

## Volume

Volume is used to determine the amount of room inside a three-dimensional space. For example, how many cube boxes could fit inside a container truck or warehouse? Here, you must not only determine the two-dimensional surface area but also multiply the height of an object. In other words, the volume of a space is determined by multiplying the length × width × height. Thus, to determine the volume capacity of the intermodal transport container in the figure below, you would multiply the length (12 m) by the width (2.5 m) by the height (2.5 m) = 75 cubic metres, or 75 m³.

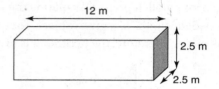

## Working with Negative Numbers

Sometimes you may be required to complete basic math operations using negative numbers. There are several rules that you must remember when adding, subtracting, multiplying, and dividing negative numbers.

### ADDING

If both numbers are negative, then you add the numbers together and maintain the negative sign (e.g., −2 + −8 = −10). If one number is positive and the other is negative, then you subtract from the larger value (e.g., −15 + 7 = −8).

### SUBTRACTING

When subtracting numbers, change the minus to add, and change the sign of the second number (e.g., 8 − −3 is converted to 8 + 3 = 11).

### MULTIPLICATION AND DIVISION

Whether multiplying or dividing, if the two numbers are both negative, the answer is always positive. If one of the numbers is negative and the other is positive, the answer is always negative (e.g, −5 × −5 = 25; however, 5 × −5 = −25).

## ALGEBRAIC EQUATIONS

Algebraic equations are not common in most police entrance exams, but the word problems on these exams often require that you build an equation where you have to solve for an unknown variable. A variable means that a letter (e.g., $y$) has replaced a number. For example, in the equation $8 - y = 5$, it is pretty obvious that $y = 3$. When solving an algebraic equation, the goal is to simplify the equation so that the variable stands alone on one side of the equal sign. The important tip to remember is that what you do to one side of the equation, you must also do to the other. In the example below, in order to isolate the variable, you need to subtract 25 on the left side, so you must do the same on the right side of the equation.

$$
\begin{aligned}
y + 25 &= 42 \\
-25 &= -25 \\
y &= 17
\end{aligned}
$$

Regardless of how complicated the equation, the same principle of reciprocating calculations from one side of the equation to the other applies. Consider the following example: $6y + 18 = 54$. Using two steps, this can be solved by simplifying the equation in order to isolate $y$.

**TIP**

Algebraic Equations: Always add or subtract values before multiplying or dividing.

**STEP 1** Always do addition or subtraction first. Remove the 18 from the left side of the equation by subtracting the value on both sides.

$$
\begin{aligned}
6y + 18 &= 54 \\
-18 &= -18 \\
6y &= 36
\end{aligned}
$$

**STEP 2** Remember that $6y = 6 \times y$. Therefore, remove the multiples of $y$ by dividing by 6.

$$
\begin{aligned}
6y &= 54 \\
\div 6 & \quad \div 6 \\
y &= 9
\end{aligned}
$$

The same rule applies for fractions. To solve the equation $\frac{2}{3}y - 6 = 90$ you must multiply the fraction $\frac{2}{3}$ by its reciprocal $\frac{3}{2}$.

**STEP 1** Remove 6 by adding the value to both sides of the equation.

$$
\begin{aligned}
\frac{2}{3}y - 6 &= 90 \\
+6 &= +6 \\
\frac{2}{3}y &= 96
\end{aligned}
$$

**STEP 2** Multiply $\frac{2}{3}$ by its reciprocal on both sides of the equation.

$$
\begin{aligned}
\frac{2}{3}y &= 96 \\
\times \frac{3}{2} & \quad \times \frac{3}{2} \\
y &= 144
\end{aligned}
$$

If an equation has several multiples of the same variable, they can be added or subtracted. For example, $5y + 2y = 49$ can be simplified to $7y = 49$. In this instance, $y = 7$. Furthermore, if there are multiples of a variable on either side of an equation, they can be added or subtracted to be brought to the same side. For example, if the equation was $5y = 49 - 2y$, the $2y$ could be added on the right and then on the left as well, so $7y = 49$.

## WORD PROBLEMS

By far the most common math questions that you will face in a police entrance exam are those posed in the form of a sentence in which you are required to build an equation in order to find a solution. The difficulty with these types of questions is not necessarily based on how challenging the math question is, rather the challenge is usually creating the proper mathematical formula that is representative of the problem posed.

### Basic Math Questions

The simplest form of word problems require you to perform basic math equations such as addition and multiplication. For example, you might have to calculate the total value of goods stolen in a break and enter when provided with a list such as the one below.

| PROPERTY STOLEN SMITH RESIDENCE | | |
|---|---|---|
| **# OF ITEMS** | **ARTICLE** | **VALUE** |
| 1 | Watch | $350 |
| 3 | Gold Coins | $150 each |
| 2 | Earrings | $500 each |
| 1 | TV | $900 |
| 1 | Laptop | $1,200 |

The key in obtaining the correct answer is to pay attention to the multiples of any specific item and calculate the multiple values first and then add all the total losses together.

### Ratio and Percent Questions

Word problems that task you with determining a ratio or percentage of a value can all be solved in the same way—by converting the numbers into fractions. For example, if Constable Jacob had a 2 : 5 conviction to arrest ratio, how many convictions should she have if she made 70 arrests last year?

**STEP 1** Convert this to an algebraic equation.

$$\frac{2}{5} = \frac{x}{70}$$

**STEP 2** Multiply $\frac{x}{70}$ by its reciprocal to isolate $x$.

**TIP**

Always confirm your answers by replacing the variable with your answer and checking the equation.

**STEP 3** What you do to one side, you must do to the other.

$$\frac{2}{5} \times \frac{70}{1} = x$$

**STEP 4** Simplify.

$$\frac{140}{5} = x$$

$$28 = x$$

Therefore, at a 2 : 5 ratio, Constable Jacob should obtain 28 convictions if she made 70 arrests.

Similarly, if you are asked to find a percentage in a word question, you could construct the equation the same way. For example, if 30% of the police department's 800 employees lived within the city limits, then how many lived outside?

**STEP 1** Convert the question to an algebraic equation using fractions, remember that $30\% = \frac{30}{100}$.

$$\frac{30}{100} = \frac{x}{800}$$

**STEP 2** Isolate the $x$ by multiplying $\frac{x}{800}$ by its reciprocal.

**STEP 3** What you do to one side, you must do to the other.

$$\frac{30}{100} \times \frac{800}{1} = x$$

**STEP 4** Simplify.

$$\frac{30}{1} \times \frac{8}{1} = x$$

$$x = 240$$

**STEP 5** Do not forget what the question is asking—here you calculated the number for the 30% that live inside the city; however, the question is how many live outside.

Therefore, 800 − 240 = 560 live outside the city limits.

## Building the Equation

Sometimes the types of questions previously described are asked in a slightly different way, making them appear to be more complex. For example, Test Your Knowledge Question 18 states that Constable Tang had twice as many arrests as Constable Rodriguez and together they made 96 arrests. To solve this equation you do not need to create two unknown variables because we know that Tang has twice as many as Rodriguez has. Instead, we need to show that whatever the number Rodriguez had, plus twice that number, are equal to 96. So how do you calculate that equation?

**STEP 1** Build the equation.

$$x + 2x = 96$$

**STEP 2** Add like variables together.

$$3x = 96$$

**STEP 3** Isolate $x$.

$$x = \frac{96}{3}$$

$$x = 32$$

**STEP 4** Remember that the question is how many arrests did Tang make? Twice the number that Rodriguez made = 64.

## Time / Distance Questions

If you are posed with questions that require you to calculate how long a task took, how far someone travelled in a given time, or how many events occurred in a specific time, there are three elements to consider: rate, events, and time. For example, speed is usually calculated at distance/time (kilometres/hour), and typing proficiency is stated as words/minute. Therefore, you can usually structure these types of word problems and solve for $x$ through the use of fractions. If, for example, a problem stated that Constable Van der Zwaag drove at 120 km/h for 75 minutes and asked how far she had driven during that time, you could construct the equation as follows:

**STEP 1** Construct the equation. Since the question is asking you to compare two different measurements of time, you must convert them to the same units. It is much simpler to convert an hour to minutes than vice versa.

$$\frac{120}{60} = \frac{x}{75}$$

**STEP 2** Isolate the $x$ by multiplying $\frac{x}{75}$ by its reciprocal.

**STEP 3** What you do to one side, you must do to the other.

$$\frac{120}{60} \times \frac{75}{1} = x$$

**STEP 4** Simplify.

$$2 \times 75 = x$$

$$x = 150 \text{ kilometres}$$

Test Your Knowledge Question 20 is probably the most difficult type of word problem that you will face in any police entrance exam. The challenge with this question is being able to accurately construct an equation that answers the question. In this problem, Constable Derry had to pick up a prisoner in a neighbouring city and she drove 80 km/h driving to the city and 70 km/h driving back. We know that she drove for a total of four hours without stopping. You are asked to calculate the approximate distance between the two cities. The problem is that you do not know how long it took her to drive either to the other city or back, just that

**TIP**

When calculating time/distance equations, use minutes as your common measurement of time.

$speed = \dfrac{distance}{time}$

the total was four hours. Therefore, in this scenario let $x$ be the distance travelled between the two cities at a specific rate of speed and that the combination of these two variables equals four hours.

**STEP 1** Construct the equation. We know that distance/speed to the city, plus distance/speed coming back = 4 hours. Therefore,

$$\frac{x}{80} + \frac{x}{70} = 4$$

**STEP 2** Find common denominators for 80 and 70. Since they are multiples of 10 you can determine that, $7 \times 80$ and $8 \times 70$ both equal 560. Remember to also multiply the numerators by 7 and 8, respectively. Therefore,

$$\frac{7x}{560} + \frac{8x}{560} = 4$$

$$\frac{15x}{560} = 4$$

**STEP 3** Isolate $x$ by multiplying $\frac{15x}{560}$ by its reciprocal. Therefore, what you do to one side, you must do to the other. Thus,

$$x = 2{,}240 \div 15$$

$$x = 149.3 \text{ km.}$$

Before continuing to the next chapter, answer the 10 multiple-choice review questions below—just to make sure that you have got it right.

## HAVE I GOT IT RIGHT?

 **You have 8 minutes to complete the exercise.**

1.  What is the sum of $\frac{2}{7} + \frac{3}{4}$?

    (A) $\frac{5}{6}$

    (B) $2\frac{2}{3}$

    (C) $1\frac{1}{28}$

    (D) $1\frac{3}{14}$

2. What is the product of $5\dfrac{7}{13} \times 7\dfrac{3}{8}$ ?

(A) 35

(B) $40\dfrac{11}{13}$

(C) 47

(D) $13\dfrac{9}{52}$

3. What is the value of $y$: $\dfrac{2}{11}y - 11 = 7$?

(A) 99

(B) 23

(C) 77

(D) 69

4. What is the product of $-23.45 \times 32.2$?

(A) $-831.17$

(B) $732.09$

(C) $754.29$

(D) $-755.09$

5. Find the quotient of $96.48 \div 13.4$?

(A) $97.21$

(B) $7.98$

(C) $17.92$

(D) $7.20$

6. What is the volume of space inside the police exhibit locker?

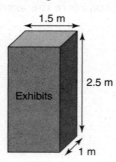

(A) $5.75 \text{ m}^2$

(B) $7.25 \text{ m}^3$

(C) $3.75 \text{ m}^3$

(D) $4.75 \text{ m}^3$

7. The police department has an annual budget of $16.5 million. If 95% of the budget pays for employee wages and benefits, how much is left over for other costs?

   (A) $695,000
   (B) $825,000
   (C) $875,000
   (D) $1.2 million

8. Constable Dosanjh responded to an emergency call and drove 5 kilometres in 2 minutes and 30 seconds. What was his average speed?

   (A) 100 km/h
   (B) 120 km/h
   (C) 140 km/h
   (D) 160 km/h

9. Constable Davidson took the Sergeant's qualifying exam. There were 75 questions in total, and he only got 5 questions wrong. What was his ratio of correct to incorrect responses?

   (A) 15 : 1
   (B) 75 : 5
   (C) 14 : 1
   (D) 17 : 2

10. Two-thirds of the police department's 300 personnel are Caucasian, one-fifth are Asian, and the remainder are of various other races. How many members would be in the "other races" category?

   (A) 40
   (B) 47
   (C) 53
   (D) 67

## Answers

1. **C** see Adding Fractions.

2. **B** see Multiplying Fractions.

3. **A** see Algebra.

4. **D** see Multiplying Decimals; Working with Negative Numbers.

5. **D** see Dividing Decimals.

6. **C** see Basic Geometry—Volume.

7. **B** $16.5 \times 0.95 = 15.675$; $16.5 - 15.675 = 0.825$; see Percentages.

8. **B** $\dfrac{x}{60} = \dfrac{5}{2.5}$; see Word Problems—Time/Distance.

9. **C** 70 correct / 5 incorrect; $\dfrac{70}{5} = 14:1$; see Ratio and Percent Questions.

10. **A** $\dfrac{1}{5} + \dfrac{2}{3} = \dfrac{13}{15}$; $\dfrac{2}{15} = \dfrac{x}{300}$; see Adding Fractions; Word Problems.

# 13

# Next Steps

→ **WHAT'S NEXT?**
→ **ASSESSMENT CENTRES**
→ **INTEGRITY TESTING**
→ **MEDICAL TESTS**
→ **PSYCHOMETRIC ASSESSMENTS**
→ **THE INTERVIEW**

## WHAT'S NEXT?

If you have made it to this stage of the application process, congratulations are in order. By now you will have already successfully passed the entrance exam and physical testing; many of the applicants that you are competing against will have already been screened out of the process. As you move into the next stages you may have to pass one or more interviews, engage in role-playing scenarios, obtain medical clearance, and pass psychometric and integrity evaluations.

Preparing for these next processes is not the same as preparing to take the entrance exam—there are no practice exams that you can take to better your score. Instead, this section of the guide focuses on providing you with as much information about the various processes themselves, offering insight into what assessors should be looking for, and offering you some tips and strategies that you can use in order to demonstrate in the most effective way possible that you possess the knowledge, skills, and abilities that make you an excellent police officer candidate.

## ASSESSMENT CENTRES

In many other police jurisdictions, especially in the United Kingdom, assessment centres have been part of police officer selection processes since the 1950s; however, with the exception of municipal police agencies in British Columbia and the Canadian Armed Forces Military Police, no other police organizations in Canada currently use the complete assessment centre method. There are three main components to the police officer recruitment assessment centre: (1) a group discussion, (2) role-playing scenarios, and (3) a supervisor's interview.

The Justice Institute of BC (JIBC) police constable assessment centre takes approximately five hours to complete, and you will be required to be involved in a leaderless group discussion, several role-playing exercises, and a sergeant's interview. Throughout the day you will be monitored by one or more assessors in each scenario and during the group discussion. The assessors will be making notes and looking to see how well you demonstrate specific competencies. Each situation that you are involved in is independently scored and then the evaluators will meet the following day to determine an overall combined score. Within a few days of the assessment centre evaluation, a recruiting officer will contact you and provide you with your score, which will be between 0 and 5, and may also include a half-score. The table below explains the assessment centre scoring matrix. Most police agencies require a score of 3 or higher in order to continue on in the recruitment process.

| ASSESSMENT CENTRE SCORING MATRIX | |
|---|---|
| Excellent (Perfect) | 5 |
| A great deal of ability shown | 4+ |
| Well above average | 4 |
| Above average | 4− |
| Slightly above average | 3+ |
| Average (Competent) | 3 |
| Slightly below average | 3− |
| Below average | 2+ |
| Well below average | 2 |
| Poor | 1 |
| No opportunity to observe | 0 |

## Total Competencies Assessed

Since assessors are evaluating the degree to which you demonstrate specific competencies, it is important that you have an understanding of what the competencies are, and specifically what they will be evaluating.

1. **Analytical skills.** The degree to which you gather all possible information that is relevant to a scenario. You do not have to be a trained investigator, but you should be asking probing questions, such as, "Can you tell me more about what happened?" or "I want to make sure that I clearly understand your situation." You will want to ask for information from all parties or participants, listen to the facts carefully, and analyze the situation from everyone's point of view.

2. **Diligence.** Your work ethic will be assessed in terms of the degree to which you are disciplined in meeting deadlines and consistently working hard. You will be placed in multiple situations throughout the assessment centre day and be required to make decisions, answer questions, and resolve issues in a timely manner. You should continuously strive for excellence during each exercise.

3. **Decision making.** You need to be able to demonstrate that you make rational decisions by weighing the pros and cons of options available, and that you make sound decisions based on an assessment of all available facts. Although you should show initiative and creativity in your decisions, they must be realistic and supported by the facts elicited. Most importantly, you must make a decision and take action; failure to decide on a course of action is considered a fatal flaw.

4. **Integrity.** Throughout the assessment process, demonstrate honesty and fairness; show dignity, respect, and compassion for others; and demonstrate honourable

intentions and motives in all of your actions. You will have to make the right decision if faced with having to choose between loyalty and integrity.

5. **Interpersonal skills**. It is very important that you demonstrate strong interpersonal communication skills at every opportunity. This means demonstrating sensitivity and empathy, listening carefully to what you are being told, maintaining eye contact, paraphrasing, showing interest and compassion, using tension-reducing language and gestures, calming volatile situations by being tactful and diplomatic, and showing individuals that you are taking their concerns seriously.

6. **Judgment**. Show that you possess common sense and a high level of situational awareness. Instead of having tunnel vision and only focusing on what is in front of you, show that you are vigilant to unusual events and other actions occurring around you. Show that you are also willing to make decisions, without having had the opportunity to obtain all the facts, and still take appropriate action in emergency situations based on the limited information you have received.

7. **Maturity**. It is essential that you demonstrate that you are an emotionally well-adjusted person. Try to show that you have learned through experience, can recover from mistakes, and can appreciate the consequences of your actions or inaction.

8. **Oral communication skills**. Ensure that you express your ideas and knowledge in a clear and concise manner. Whether in a group or one-on-one situations, your voice must be calm, yet speak with authority and confidence. Make statements that are articulate, logical, and easy to comprehend. Ask appropriate questions and provide logical and insightful answers when asked. You must also be able to accurately relay information that has been provided to you.

9. **Presence**. Demonstrate command presence through your body language, voice, gestures, the way you dress, and your professionalism. Show confidence by staying calm and taking charge in high-pressure situations. Show that you are not afraid to assert yourself and confront difficult situations. Your actions will demonstrate that you are confident in your own abilities and judgment.

10. **Teamwork**. Police work is about working together with partners to solve problems. Therefore, during the assessment centre day you will have to collaborate with others on projects that are competing for the same job as you. Therefore, you will need to seek input from other applicants, encourage input and participation, give everyone an equal voice, share information, and not come across as overbearing or domineering.

11. **Tolerance**. The assessment centre day is intentionally stressful. The assessors will be closely monitoring your ability to stay calm under stressful conditions. They want to make sure that you do not react negatively even if you are taunted or provoked. You do not want to engage in heated arguments nor do you want to shut down completely. Therefore, demonstrate positive stress management strategies by showing that tense situations do not negatively impact your performance. In addition, show tolerance by respecting other people's culture, race, sexual orientations, and attitudes. Show that you are able to work effectively with diverse backgrounds and communities.

## Group Discussion

When applicants think about assessment centres, they often focus on the role-playing exercises that they will be involved in; however, the group discussion exercise is an important

**TIP**

The key is not to solve the problem on your own but to come up with intelligent and meaningful contributions.

component of the overall assessment. During this exercise, you will be with a group, ranging from four to eight other candidates, in a room that also contains up to an equal number of evaluators. The evaluators will not be part of the discussion and are solely there to observe and mark all of your performances. The group will be provided with an issue or problem.

## Group Discussion Competencies Assessed

The purpose of this exercise is for you to showcase your interpersonal skills relating to leadership, teamwork, and problem solving. Specifically, the following competencies will be assessed.

1. **Persuasion**. Your ability to demonstrate initiative and influence the decisions of others and to have others adopt your proposed course of action.
2. **Teamwork**. Your ability to work together to find solutions, as opposed to being competitive with other team members.
3. **Analytical skills**. Your ability to listen to the opinions of others but to think independently and offer constructive input and strategic analysis of the opinions of others. This includes your ability to identify practical solutions.
4. **Interpersonal skills**. Your ability to communicate effectively with the group. You need to demonstrate that you value the opinions of others, listen to what other candidates have to say, showing professionalism and emotional intelligence (i.e., to truly appreciate the feelings and emotions of others).
5. **Decision making**. If appropriate, your ability to lead the team in coming to a decision on the best course of action to solve the problem after all opinions and options have been taken into consideration.

## Group Discussion Strategies

To make a positive impression in the group discussion exercise, you should consider a number of courses of action.

First, you must become involved in the discussion throughout the exercise. You cannot be a wallflower and act as a silent or minimal participant. You are expected to be active and make well-informed and thoughtful comments that demonstrate your analytical skills and that you contribute to the overall discussion.

Second, be supportive and considerate of the opinions of all participants but look for opportunities to challenge comments (in a professional way) that you may disagree with and have alternative options or opinions that can be more strongly supported. Build on the statements of others. For example, you could say, "I really agree with what Jane has put forward, and further to that I would also add that ... (say something remarkable here)." You should receive a higher score if you can have a positive influence on the outcome of the discussion.

Third, be yourself. This is a theme that will be repeated throughout the assessment centre evaluations and the rest of the application process. If you are not being true to your own personality, your comments and opinions will come across as manufactured or disingenuous, and you will not be able to sustain your act throughout the entire day. For example, if you are not a natural leader in group situations, do not try to be—the exercise is a leaderless group discussion, you are not required to take charge of the discussion in order to get high marks. In fact, your actions may be interpreted by the assessors as being confrontational, controlling, and overbearing if you do not assume this role in a natural way. That is, there may be others in the group who have extensive experience in leading group meetings and discussions and are a natural fit. Do not think that you have to challenge this person in that role in order to get a higher score.

## Role-Play Exercises

At the assessment centre you will be required to engage in at least two role-playing scenarios where you will play the role of a police officer who has been given an assignment. During each scenario, you will meet with one or more actors who will play the role of a suspect, complainant, victim, or witness to an event. You are not required to know the law or the police agency's policies and procedures in advance; however, prior to the scenario commencing, an assessor may give you a piece of paper that explains the law or policy that relates specifically to the scenario that is about to unfold—read it carefully and remember what it says.

The scenarios will be timed, approximately 20 minutes in length, and you will be provided with a set of instructions prior to the commencement of the scenario. Read the instructions carefully and make sure that you know the details of the instructions before you begin. If you are allowed to ask questions before the role-play exercise begins, do so.

## Role-Play Competencies Assessed

The purpose of role-play exercises is for you to demonstrate your interpersonal skills relating to problem confrontation, oral communication, problem solving, and decision making. Specifically, the following competencies will be assessed.

1. **Fact finding**. The main purpose of many of the role-play exercises is to determine whether you possess basic investigational and observational techniques. Did you ask sufficient questions to elicit information and determine a set of facts? Have you overlooked or failed to surface critical information that was available to you? Did you make actual observations that either supported or were in conflict with information that was being offered to you? Did you make a valid conclusion based on your observations and fact finding?

2. **Interpersonal communication skills**. You need to be an effective listener and demonstrate that you understand and appreciate what the person is saying. Practice active listening skills by summarizing what a person is saying from time to time. For example, you could say, "So what you are saying Mr. Jones is that you are extremely upset that your neighbour has put his yard trimmings in your driveway and is refusing to remove them?" Use nonverbal communication by maintaining eye contact and nodding occasionally to show that you are interested in what the person is saying. Make sure that your body language shows that you are not closed up or disinterested, keep your hands out of your pockets and do not cross your arms. Show empathy and compassion and take people's claims seriously, no matter how trivial they may appear.

3. **Oral communication skills**. In role-play exercises, you must be able to speak in a calm and clear voice. In many situations, you will be required to de-escalate tension by talking to people and calming them down. You need to be able to effectively explain to individuals what the policy or law states about their behaviour or wishes. You might also be required to inform an individual of tragic news in a compassionate way, yet ensuring that all relevant information is provided to the individual. Oral communications skills are about being able to articulate information effectively, promote your point of view in a positive manner, persuade others, resolve conflict, and justify your actions.

4. **Adaptability**. In some role-play scenarios, you may discover that what you had pre-conceived as the method to address the problem has shifted because you have discovered new information. In these situations, you need to demonstrate flexibility and open-mindedness and that you can give consideration to new information and adjust your behaviour accordingly. For example, if you were to speak to a landlord about a tenant who refused to pay the rent and the landlord said the tenant "threatened" him, you would begin an investigation into a threatening complaint. However, if you then talked to the tenant who said that he has threatened to take legal action against the landlord because the landlord has cut off the tenant's electricity and hot water in the suite because the landlord said his showers were too long and he drained all the hot water, your perception of the situation would change. You would need to realize that this is no longer a criminal complaint but now a civil matter and would require you to adapt your plan of action based on this new information.

5. **Stress tolerance**. Your ability to cope with stressful situations will be challenged during role-play scenarios more so than in any other exercise. Actors may be extremely vocal and confrontational with you. You may have information thrown at you from multiple sources, such as two people engaged in an argument when you arrive on scene, and you need to assess the situation and be effective at de-escalating the tension rather than contributing to it. The assessors may want to see how you react if someone were to insult you, or refuse to follow your directions, or is incapable of communicating with you effectively because of a physical or mental disability. How will you react in these situations? What would be the first thing you would do if confronted by a woman screaming hysterically that her two-year-old child has gone missing out front of her home?

6. **Analytical skills**. This is really your ability to maintain an open mind and continuously assess the situation as you work towards identifying the problem based on the information that you are able to elicit. After you have fully assessed the circumstances, you then need to develop practical and constructive solutions. What would you do if, for example, you attended a restaurant where a customer was refusing to pay for an expensive dinner because he stated that he was not satisfied with the service or quality of the meal? In this situation, you might want to find out how much the bill was. Does the customer even have the means to pay? What did the customer not like about the meal; was it just one thing, did he order dessert, alcohol, and so forth? What are some options available to you? Is the customer willing to pay for the portion of the meal that was acceptable? Using your investigative skills, you need to determine if the customer is just trying to get a free meal, has a legitimate complaint, is intoxicated, or if something else is going on.

7. **Decision making**. A competency that is similar to analytical skills is your decision-making ability. The main difference is that analytical skills only require you to correctly identify the problem or issue; however, decision-making skills require you to accurately interpret all the facts presented to you and then to have the confidence to make a decision on your course of action and stick to it. The key in these situations is to be certain that you are not making a premature decision because you have not accurately identified the true problem or collected all the facts. However, it is equally important that you do actually make a decision. If you are presented with a dilemma and you have completed your fact-finding exercise, you must make a decision. You cannot simply throw the information back at the actor or actors and say, "Here's the

situation, and I'll let you decide what you're going to do about it." In some situations the scenario may be civil in nature, meaning that no offence has been committed and therefore no police action needs to take place. Nevertheless, even in these situations you can still present options and solutions and make a strong recommendation for a course of action.

8. **Persuasion**. Once you have used your analytical skills to determine what the problem is and made a decision on your course of action, on some occasions you will have to persuade a reluctant individual to comply with your directions. Managing the behaviour of others is a skill. The first step is to explain all the facts and reason with the individual. Next, provide the subject with options and what the consequences of those options might be. For example, if a person was ordered by a bar manager to leave a licenced premises because he has been harassing the customers and you were called in, what persuasive techniques could you use before resorting to dragging the person out in handcuffs? Persuasion techniques could include explaining the law—that he has to leave if directed by the manager—and providing consequences: he could spend the night in jail, be charged with an offence, would have to retain a lawyer, would have to spend time going to court, and may endure possible embarrassment to reputation and family. Alternatively, he could get up and leave as directed. Finally, if persuasive techniques are ineffective, then you must let the person know that you are prepared to take other steps to ensure that your directions are complied with—be unequivocal.

## Examples of Role-Play Scenarios

The role-play scenarios that you will encounter at an assessment centre change frequently from one cohort to the next and, more importantly, are dynamic and subject to change during the course of each scenario based on an actor's response to the behaviour that the candidate is exhibiting. Therefore, even on the same day, two separate candidates will likely experience dissimilar scenarios because they tend to play out differently based simply on the fluidity of the interactions between the candidate and the actor. In other words, there is little value going over a list of all the different scenarios that you may encounter and then providing a detailed step-by-step course of action for you to take as you work through each scenario. Nevertheless, rather than a detailed review of specific scenarios, let's examine the types of encounters you may experience and identify the competencies that assessors will want to see you exhibit in these types of situations.

1. **Investigation**. In these situations you will be responding to a crime that has taken place (e.g., home was broken into and the owner has just come home, a robbery has taken place, a victim reports a date-rape sexual assault). Evaluators will be assessing your fact-finding and observation skills. That is, when did this occur, are there any witnesses, what crime occurred, where did this occur, and who is the victim? Assessors will also be grading your communication and interpersonal skills, watching to see if you show compassion and sensitivity, and assessing whether you can overcome language barriers or effectively communicate with individuals from a different cultural background, ethnicity, or sexual orientation.

2. **Controlling situation**. In controlling role-play exercises, you will be dealing with a confrontational person where the anger is either directed at you, such as an angry motorist who does not want a ticket, or where two or more people are engaged in a

dispute, such as a domestic situation that is on the verge of turning violent, and you are called upon to intervene. In these scenarios, assessors are evaluating your stress tolerance, analytical and decision-making skills, persuasion skills, and conflict and problem-solving skills.

3. **Problem resolution**. In these types of situations, there is less of a potential for violence present as in a controlling situation, but there is still a significant conflict that you must address. Examples may include a neighbour dispute, landlord-tenant dispute, customer-service provider dispute, or a citizen's complaint about another police officer's behaviour or attitude. Assessors will be evaluating your analytical, decision-making, persuasive, and interpersonal communication skills. That is, you must identify the needs of all parties involved, be a good listener and communicator, and develop a reasonable solution to the problem.

4. **Decisiveness required**. In some situations, you may be required to act quickly and with decisive authority. Examples include a rapidly escalating situation where violence may erupt if you do not intervene with authority. Assessors will be evaluating whether you can use your judgment to act in an emergent situation when perhaps all the facts are not yet known, but the situation demands action. Other competencies assessed in these types of scenarios include your presence, confidence, and level of maturity.

5. **Notification**. Other types of scenarios may require that you pass along information to other police officers or that you inform a citizen of a police matter or death notification. In these situations, you need to demonstrate robust oral and written communication skills and very strong interpersonal skills. For example, in a death notification scenario, not only do you need to show empathy and compassion and on occasion even take physical control of an individual, but you must also be certain that you copied down the information correctly and are completely accurate in passing the information along to the deceased's loved ones. There are few things worse than the recipient of a death notification being misinformed.

6. **Integrity**. On occasion, a scenario may have a component where your integrity and professional conduct are challenged. In these cases, your partner may accept some small amount of "graft" for a police favour (e.g., ripping up a ticket for a friend, accepting a free meal, or something similar). Obviously assessors will watch you carefully to see how you deal with this: Did you challenge your partner, are you going to inform your supervisor, or do you agree with your partner that this a minor technical indiscretion that everyone does? Standing up for your values of honesty and integrity are difficult when you need to confront a co-worker about apparent misconduct. Your oral and interpersonal communication skills will be put to the test.

## Role-Play Exercise Strategies

As mentioned, there is nothing to be gained by going through each possible role-play scenario and developing a scripted protocol to follow for each example. These situations are far too dynamic, and one of the key objectives in the assessment centre process is to see how adaptable you are to a changing situation and whether or not you can think on your feet. Providing you with too much guidance would actually be detrimental to your ability to react quickly to an unfolding scenario as you would be thinking too much about your mentally prepared script and not reacting appropriately to the situation. Instead, the following are more generalized strategies that you can apply in many situations and thereby demonstrate your competencies effectively.

First, always read the instructions before each exercise carefully. This includes paying special attention to any information relating to police policy or the law—the assessors are providing you with this because it will likely come into play during the scenario. If you are required to pass along some information, make notes if you can, you do not want to get the information wrong.

Second, focus on how you are presenting yourself. It is okay and expected that you will be a little nervous; however, you do not want to allow personal stress to inhibit your performance. You want to be calm and professional in your voice and mannerisms. Do not fidget around or pick at your fingers and nails or constantly run your fingers through your hair. Consider what your body position looks like—are you rigid and cold, are your arms crossed and uninviting, or do you appear relaxed in your stance, but with your hands outside of your pockets? Remember that confidence, effective stress management, and officer presence are key competencies that assessors will be looking for and evaluating.

Third, use active listening strategies when fact gathering. There are several elements to being an active listener. First, have an open and unbiased mindset. Do not predetermine that you are not going to agree with this actor's point of view, he or she just might be right and change your opinion. Show empathy to the individual. What they are telling you is extremely important to them. Perhaps they have been frustrated for years with the neighbour and the dog droppings on his lawn were the "straws that broke the camel's back." Try to use language that does not come across as blaming. Instead of saying, "You are wrong for not removing your garbage from your neighbour's driveway." Perhaps say, "I see that you are very upset with your neighbour and that you have placed your garbage in your neighbour's driveway." If you use the first statement, the subject will likely shut down and not talk to you anymore or become further enraged because you have already made up your mind who is at fault. The alternative statement fosters open communication by allowing the subject to agree with you and further explain why he's upset. Paraphrasing what the subject says is an excellent way of demonstrating understanding and clarity. By occasionally summing up what the subject has stated and paraphrasing comments back to him, it proves to the complainant that you are in fact listening to his position and also allows for any misunderstandings to be corrected.

Fourth, anticipate that actors will be upset, even to the point of being hysterical, and may vent and swear at you. Your goal is to calm the individual down and discover the problem. You cannot do that effectively if the person is yelling, swearing, and going off on a rant. You may want to initially allow the actor to blow off some steam and then, by your own professional words and calming hand gestures, get the person to settle down so that you can find out what is enraging him.

**TIP**

To gain compliance from a resistant person:
1. Ask why
2. Educate
3. Present options

Finally, use persuasion skills as an effective way to deal with a noncompliant person. The first step in dealing with a noncompliant individual is to ask the person why they are being resistant. For example, in the case of a protestor, the person may feel that she has a moral, legal, or ethical right to do so. The second step is to educate the resistive person as to what her lawful authority is and more importantly what she is prohibited from doing under the law. Of course, this piece will only come into play if you were informed about the law prior to the scenario's commencement. Advising the noncompliant person about her legal obligations re-asserts your professional presence and lawful authority to direct and control her behaviour. The final step is to be a negotiator and present options and what the consequences of the options will be. For the unlawful protestor who, for example, is on private property, perhaps you have advised her where she can lawfully protest, or other means by which she can demonstrate her objections just as effectively, and what will happen to her in terms of arrest and charges if she does not comply and leave the property. This allows the person to fully weigh options presented to him and the consequences of failing to comply.

## B-PAD

If you are applying to any police agency in the province of Ontario (except the RCMP), once you have successfully completed the Police Analytical Thinking Inventory (PATI), the Written Communication Test (WCT), and the Physical Readiness Evaluation for Police (PREP) test, you must successfully pass the Behavioural Personnel Assessment Device (B-PAD). The B-PAD assessment takes only about 30 minutes to complete, and rather than a role-play exercise with live actors and evaluators, you will be required to view eight video clips on a monitor that represent critical situations police officers respond to every day. The video is shown in first person, as if you are the officer at the scene. At some point, the video will pause and the word "respond" will appear on the monitor. You will then have approximately 45 seconds to respond as if you were talking to the individuals on the screen. In these situations, you may be required to issue commands, ask questions, solicit information, or offer advice.

The scenarios used in the B-PAD assessment will be similar to those used in assessment centres. For example, you may be required to deal with an emotionally disturbed person or angry motorist, conduct a death notification, or solve a neighbour dispute. The one key difference is that since live actors are not used, the B-PAD scenarios are not dynamic. There will not be an ongoing fluid interaction between you and an actor that will evolve based on what you say and do. Therefore, the assessment will be primarily based on your initial verbal responses to each situation. The most important thing for you to do is to keep talking. It may sound easy enough, but if no one is talking back to you, it can be difficult to ask questions or give directions for up to a minute. The competencies that will be assessed are also comparable to those evaluated using the assessment centre method, such as judgment, interpersonal communication skills, and problem solving. Each competency is assigned a score from one to four, with a four indicating the highest level of competence. If you successfully pass the B-PAD, your mark will be valid for three years. If you are not successful, you will have to wait six months before being eligible to take the test again.

**TIP**

**Q: How to pass the polygraph?**

**A: Be truthful at every stage of the application process.**

## INTEGRITY TESTING

Many police organizations in Canada, such as Vancouver, Calgary, Halifax Regional, and the RCMP, require you to successfully pass a polygraph examination before an offer of employment is made. One notable exception is the polygraph is not a requirement for police agencies in Ontario.

Remember that police agencies are not looking for men and women who have never made mistakes, done things that they are not proud of, or would rather forget. Nearly everyone has done something in his or her life that he or she regrets; the real question is have you owned up to your mistakes and changed your behaviour? Police officers do not need to be blemish free, but they do need to be accountable, honest, trustworthy, and scrupulous. If you are trying to lie your way onto the police department, you are starting off on shaky ground, and no agency wants you to work for them. In other words, start the application process by admitting mistakes that you have made while completing your background questionnaire and during your preliminary interview. If the police agency is still interested in you after you have already confessed to past indiscretions, then you can go into the polygraph with a clean conscience and worry free.

The polygraph examination process may take between two and four hours depending on the examiner. The standard procedure is that you will meet with the polygraph examiner who will conduct an in-depth interview with you and ask you questions based on your responses to your previously submitted background questionnaire and potential issues that have surfaced during background checks and interviews with associates and former co-workers. In addition, your responses to any earlier interview that you may have already conducted with the police service will be reviewed. This interview is usually the longest part of the process and may take several hours.

After the interview, the examiner will then offer a polygraph examination. If you agree to participate, you will be seated in a chair and hooked up to several sensors. A standard blood pressure cuff will be placed on your upper arm to measure blood pressure and heart rate, two pneumographs, which are rubber tubes filled with air, will be placed around your chest and abdomen to measure your respiration rate, and two metal plates will be attached to your fingertips to measure galvanic skin resistance, which is essentially the amount of sweat in your fingers.

The questions that you will be asked will not be a surprise as you will likely have already answered these questions, probably more than once, in your background questionnaire or interview. Therefore, it is your physiological responses to these questions, rather than the questions themselves that are at issue. The purpose of the instrument is to assist in identifying whether you are providing any deceptive answers based on minute involuntary physiological responses to these questions.

I'm sure that by now you know the purpose of this section is not to teach you how to "beat the lie detector." If that is your goal, there are sites on the Internet that offer—for a fee—advice on so-called countermeasures that you can use in order to pass a polygraph. First, I have no interest in helping you lie and cheat in order to become a police officer. Second, my colleagues who are polygraph examiners are all well aware of the various tricks that people have tried in order to have a deceptive answer go undetected. Hopefully you do not think that you can "trick" the polygraph by counting backwards by seven while trying to respond to a question, or by squeezing the thumbtack hidden in your shoe against your big toe when you are asked a control question, or by biting your tongue while answering questions. It is very obvious when individuals are trying to use these false tactics. Moreover, if the examiner suspects that you are being deceptive and trying to use countermeasures, the test will be stopped immediately, you will be sent on your way, and not only will you be unsuccessful in your current application, but it is unlikely any other police agency will ever accept you once it is known that you attempted countermeasures during a polygraph.

A lesser known integrity test device is the computer voice stress analyzer (CVSA), which has been in use since the mid-1980s; however, there is only a handful of police agencies in Canada that currently use it. The CVSA measure changes in voice patterns called microtremors that are said to be caused by the stress of trying to be deceptive. Despite the claims of manufacturers of these products, there have been no independent studies that have shown much confidence in the validity or reliability of CVSA test results. In fact, the American Polygraph Association strongly questions the validity of the CVSA, and a recent independent study commissioned by the U.S. National Institute of Justice found that the CVSA correctly detected lies about drug use in only 15 percent of cases. Even worser, it recorded a significant number of false positive results—wrongly concluding that a person who stated that he or she had not

**TIP**

Polygraph countermeasures do not work, and if your use of them is discovered, it will get you banned from every police agency in Canada.

used drugs was lying, when urinalysis proved otherwise. As a result of these and similar findings, the number of agencies in Canada using the CVSA has been on a steady decline.

## MEDICAL TESTS

As with all stages of the application process, there is no nationwide standardized policy for medical clearance. However, the Ontario Association of Chiefs of Police has agreed to medical standards for all applicants in the province and have produced a complete list of medical requirements. For example, if you have cardiovascular conditions such as sustained hypertension with systolic pressure greater than 170 mm Hg or diastolic pressure greater than 110 mm Hg, or nervous system conditions such as Parkinsons Disease or Tourette's Syndrome, renal disorders that require you to be on dialysis, or even diabetes in some cases will disqualify you from being a police officer in the province.

As part of the comprehensive physical examination process, you will also be required to meet minimum standards for hearing and vision. As mentioned in Chapter 2, some agencies will require that you download a vision report from the police department and then take the report to a qualified ophthalmologist or optometrist for completion. Other police agencies provide the basic vision testing "in house," using the city's dedicated service provider. Typical minimum vision standards are

- **Uncorrected vision**—20/40 with both eyes open, with any one eye no worse than 20/100 (other agencies are 30/60 with both eyes open).
- **Corrected vision**—20/20 with both eyes open, with any one eye no worse than 20/40 (others are correctable to 20/30 with both eyes).
- **Colour perception**—Pass the Farnsworth D-15 colour blindness tests without the use of any corrective lenses.
- **Laser eye surgery**—Most police agencies will allow you to have had corrective laser eye surgery (e.g., LASIK, LASEK, or PRK); however, you typically have to wait 3–6 months after the surgery before taking the police eye exam.

The minimum hearing requirements for many police forces across the country indicate that hearing loss can be no greater than 30 decibels (dB) in the 500–3,000 Hz frequency range in both ears. Some agencies are more relaxed and allow for hearing loss no greater than 30 dB in the worst ear in the range of 500–2,900 Hz frequency and no more than 50 dB in the worst ear at 3,000 Hz. Once again, Ontario's provincially standardized requirements test four-frequency averages (500, 1,000, 2,000, 3,000 Hz) and stipulate that none shall exceed 35 dB and at 4,000 Hz the hearing loss shall not exceed 45 dB.

## PSYCHOMETRIC ASSESSMENTS

Since the 1950s, psychological and psychiatric screening procedures have been a standard component of the police recruitment process. Often referred to as a clinical assessment of personality this process typically includes a combination of psychometric pencil-and-paper tests and a psychological interview. These tests measure a multitude of characteristics, such as skills, values, and personality traits and identifies weaknesses in an individual's personality that may interfere with his or her ability to function effectively as a police officer. For instance, this could include lack of empathy, antisocial attitudes, a lack of emotional intelligence, phobia personality, and so forth.

Just as denying an individual employment solely because of a physical disability constitutes prohibited grounds for discrimination, denying a person employment because of a mental disability also constitutes discrimination in Canada. Therefore, clinical psychological assessments cannot be the only determinant of suitability but may be used as part of the overall assessment to determine whether an applicant is suitable for employment or not. Below are the most common psychometric assessment tools used in Canada and the personality characteristics that they hope to identify.

**TIP**

Do not try to study, identify patterns, or overanalyze psychometric testing questions. Simply answer the questions honestly and straightforwardly.

## Millon Clinical Multiaxial Inventory (MCMI-III)

The Millon Clinical Multiaxial Inventory-III (MCMI-III) is a psychological assessment tool composed of 175 true/false questions intended to provide information on potential psychopathic tendencies in the applicant. The test uses four scales, including personality disorder scales and clinical syndrome scales, to identify mental disorders. Although the test was specifically designed to be administered in clinical settings, such as in treatment centres for individuals previously diagnosed with existing mental health illnesses, it has shown to be a strong predictor of specific disorders outlined in the DSM-IV. Thus, psychologists often administer the test in the general population. Several police agencies in Alberta, such as Medicine Hat and Camrose police departments, currently use the MCMI-III.

## Minnesota Multiphasic Personality Inventory (MMPI-2)

The Minnesota Multiphasic Personality Inventory-2 (MMPI-2) is the most widely used psychometric test of adult personality and psychopathology in both the general population and by police agencies, specifically. For example, it is used for all applicants in the province of Ontario, several agencies in Alberta, and all recruits prior to graduation at the Atlantic Police Academy.

The MMPI-2 consists of 567 true/false questions and may take from three to four hours to complete the written test. The tests contains 10 major clinical scales and a host of subscales designed to assist in the assessment of a wide range of clinical conditions. For example, there are scales designed to measure an individual's preoccupation with his or her health, level of depression, emotionality, paranoia, trust, anxiety, social introversion, schizophrenia, and even energy level.

As with most psychometric testing, an interview with a qualified psychologist follows the written test. In Ontario, for example, the psychological interview usually lasts from one-and-a-half to two hours. After the interview, the psychologist will then write a report for the police organization that will be used towards compiling an overall suitability assessment picture.

## Six Factor Personality Questionnaire (SFPQ)

Applicants to the RCMP and those in Saskatchewan are required to complete the Six Factor Personality Questionnaire (SFPQ). The test was developed by SIGMA Assessment Systems and consists of 108 statements used to identify and evaluate several personality characteristics. The test uses Likert-type scales (e.g., "strongly disagree" at one end of the scale and "strongly agree" at the other end) and are designed to measure the following personality characteristics:

- **Agreeableness**—abasement, even-tempered, good-natured
- **Extroversion**—affiliation, dominance, exhibition
- **Independence**—autonomy, individualism, self-reliance
- **Industriousness**—achievement, seriousness, endurance
- **Methodicalness**—cognitive structure, deliberateness, order
- **Openness to experience**—change, understanding, breadth of interest

Obviously, individuals who are shown to be sociable, persuasive, and assertive will score better than those who are identified as being uncommunicative, introverted and unapproachable.

Regardless of which one of the psychometric tests listed above you will be required to complete during the application process, they all have a common purpose: risk management. That is, agencies want to know now, before it is too late, whether you possess any mental health issues or personality traits that could potentially result in your being nondeployable for an extended period of time, or being involved in one or more situations that would damage the reputation of the police organization or result in law suits being filed against the police department. Police organizations realize that virtually everyone has something in their character or personality that may be considered a blemish or flaw—the concern is whether or not that blemish will splatter across the front page of a newspaper one day.

## THE INTERVIEW

**Prepare for the interview by learning key facts about your police agency and city.**

As you make your way through the application process, you will likely have to participate in more than one interview along the way—perhaps a preliminary interview with a recruiting detective or an interview with a sergeant at the assessment centre. However, the most important interview will occur in the final stages and will be conducted before a senior sergeant or a commissioned officer (inspector rank or higher).

## Preparing for the Interview

The first step in preparing for a police interview is to gain background knowledge about the police organization and the community or region that you are applying to work for. You want to demonstrate your ambition to become a member of this particular agency and that you know and care a great deal about it. You should be prepared to answer the following questions:

### KNOW YOUR POLICE SERVICE

- How many police officers work for the agency?
- Who is the chief and what do you know about him or her?
- How many districts or divisions are there and could you locate them on a map?
- What is the Mission Statement of the police service?
- What are the major crime and disorder challenges facing the organization?

### KNOW YOUR COMMUNITY

- What is the population of the city or region that the police agency is responsible for policing (if you are applying to the RCMP or a provincial police service you might consider examples of some of the communities that these services police)?

- Who is the mayor of the city?
- What are the main social and economic issues in the city or region?

## KNOW YOUR ACCOMPLISHMENTS

The purpose of the interview is for you to showcase your accomplishments and to demonstrate to the employer that you possess the skills, abilities, and competencies that they are looking for in a police constable. The interviewers expect that you will sell yourself and speak of your abilities in a confident and assertive manner. Having said that, there is a fine line between being confident and not coming across as arrogant or overstating your abilities; therefore, ensure that you are being upbeat and making statements that are condescending towards others—including your competition.

## KNOW YOUR COMPETENCIES

Police organizations seek individuals who possess specific skills or competencies that have been shown to be essential attributes of the occupation. Some of these qualities will have already been elicited in the entrance exam or other stages of the application process, but it is important that you are able to demonstrate and provide examples of these competencies during the interview itself. Personal aptitudes that you may want to promote include: reliability, attention to detail, adaptability, interpersonal skills, problem-solving skills, and integrity.

## Interview Questions

There are four primary types of questions that you may be asked during an interview: (1) general interest questions; (2) occupational questions; (3) situational questions; and (4) behaviour descriptive questions. The purpose of these types of questions, example questions, and responses that you should consider are discussed below.

## GENERAL INTEREST QUESTIONS

General interest questions are commonly used as an ice breaker at the beginning of the interview and are often used to put you, the interviewee, at ease. They are generally considered soft lob questions because you should be able to easily speak to the subject and, with some practice, knock your answer "out of the park." An example question could be, "Why are you interested in a career in policing?"

## OCCUPATIONAL QUESTIONS

Occupational questions are used to determine your level of organizational awareness and commitment to policing.

Occupational questions that you might encounter are for the purpose of satisfying the interviewer that you are aware of the specific challenges of police work:

- "Are you willing to work shiftwork, including weekends and holidays, and miss family functions and special occasions?"
- "Are you willing to stand in the rain or snow up to several hours at a time while directing traffic?"

- "Are you willing to use physical force in the performance of your duties, up to and including deadly force if necessary?"

## HYPOTHETICAL / SITUATIONAL INTERVIEW QUESTIONS

Situational questions focus on informing the interviewer how you would act in various hypothetical situations. You will not need to know the law or policies and procedures of the police agency. Instead, the questions will be generic enough that you will be able to identify a course of action based on a logical assessment of the facts and information provided to you. After the hypothetical situation is presented to you, you will then be asked to describe in detail what you would do in this circumstance.

When answering situational questions, an effective strategy to use is to identify which competency is being assessed and then recount a personal experience that relates to this competency. Consider, for example, the following scenario: You and your partner eat at a local pizzeria. When you go to pay for your bill, the manager says, "It's on the house; you guys keep the riff raff from coming into my restaurant." In this situation, the competencies being assessed are accountability and integrity. Therefore, you should not only lay out the various options—accept the offer, pay the bill anyway, leave a large tip to cover your portion of the meal—and the potential consequences of following through with each option, but you could also relate a similar experience in your life where you faced an ethical dilemma and what decision you made at that time. This technique will demonstrate that you can not only logically evaluate a hypothetical situation and identify courses of action but also associate these scenarios to specific competencies because you have first-hand knowledge and experience in handling these types of situations.

**TIP**

**Prepare for BDI questions by associating core competencies with examples in your own life.**

## BEHAVIOUR DESCRIPTIVE INTERVIEW QUESTIONS

The behaviour descriptive interview (BDI) format has become increasingly popular as part of the employment interview process for almost all professions. The premise behind the BDI follows the adage that past behaviour is the best indicator of future performance. Therefore, if you can provide specific examples of past experiences where you have demonstrated the desired competencies of a police officer, then there is an enhanced degree of predictability that you will be able to demonstrate those skills and abilities in the future. The following is an example of a BDI question that seeks to assess your problem-solving abilities: "Describe a time when you identified a problem either at work or in another setting and the procedures you followed to find a solution."

In this instance, you will need to identify and describe the problem that you faced, detail the steps that you took to solve it, and articulate the outcome. One of the challenges associated with BDI questions is knowing how much detail and time you should commit during the interview in describing the problem and detailing the actions that you took.

Use the acronym STAR (situation, task, action, result) as an effective means to address a BDI question.

**BDI Questions**

*Situation*
*Task*
*Action*
*Result*

- **Situation**—Start by clearly describing the context of the issue. For example, describe your role or responsibility at the time, where this took place, who was involved, and what the important details that influenced your decision were.
- **Task**—Describe a specific task that you were assigned to do or that you had assigned someone else to do. What was it about this task that was unique or challenging and what did it require for completion?

- **Action**—In this section, you need to provide specific details regarding the actions that you took in this situation. For example, what skills or techniques did you employ in order to address the challenges and resolve the problem? Ensure that you state what you did, specifically. The majority of your answer should be spent explaining your actions in detail.

- **Result**—End your example by summarizing the outcome of your actions. Stress what you accomplished and what the effect of your solution was on the situation. The more profound and lasting the effect, the more weight the interviewer will attribute to your example. This is a step that is often overlooked by the interviewee when asked a BDI question. It is very important to remember to explain the outcome of your situation in order to receive maximum marks for that question.

When using the STAR framework to answer a BDI question, you should use the following as a guide to determine how much time to spend on each portion of your answer:

- Situation and Task—20 percent,
- Action—60 percent, and
- Result—20 percent.

Choosing a BDI example can be a difficult task. You should try to use work-related examples, but academic and social examples are also acceptable if nothing else fits. Identify examples that were especially challenging; overcoming a minor dilemma or encounter will not carry much weight. Also, recent examples are preferable to historical ones. Demonstrating that you have recently used the specific skills and competencies addressed in the question will be scored more favourably. Nevertheless, if you have a very strong example that is more than three or four years old, use it if you believe it will have a greater impact than more recent examples.

## The Interview

Even though it is natural to feel some anxiety and nervousness on the day of the interview, if you have followed the steps above in preparing for this day, you should be able to keep those emotions suppressed and walk into the interview with a high level of confidence knowing that you are well-prepared to answer any question. Making your best impression in an interview starts with being rested and alert, which means getting a good night's sleep the night before. On the evening prior to the interview plan a healthy distraction to keep your mind off the interview. If you are "cramming" the night before and dwelling on possible questions and responses, you will probably have a restless sleep.

On the day of the interview, begin with a light meal, free your calendar of any possible distractions, and plan your schedule so that you arrive well in advance of your interview time slot so that and you are not feeling additional stress about getting to the police station on time.

Dress for your success in the police organization by wearing professional and conservative business attire. Men should wear a suit and tie, and women should wear a business suit or dress. You want your attire to complement the professional image that you want to portray, so ensure that your suit or dress is not too bright or flamboyant as it will become a distraction and likely a topic of discussion—you want the interviewers to focus on you, not your clothes.

There are just two things that you should bring with you to the interview: a pen and a small bottle of water. If you are allowed to make notes there will be a pad of paper and pen (which may or may not work) on the table in front of you. Use the pen to jot down some key points when formulating a response to a question. For example, if you are asked a BDI question, you may want to write down STAR so that you can refer to each of the points when providing your answer. Also, taking a moment to write out some notes when you are asked a question will give you additional time to come up with an answer that does not appear to be a drawn out pause.

Having a bottle of water with you will help in case you get a dry mouth or lump in your throat and taking a sip of water allows you to clear your throat. More importantly, when you are asked a question, taking a short pause to have a drink of water before answering also gives you a few extra seconds to think about your response.

When you are called into the interview room, make sure that you greet each of the interviewers individually. If you are carrying anything, keep it in your left hand so that your right hand is free to shake the hand of each interviewer. Use a firm handshake, but don't crush the interviewer's hand. Conversely, you don't want the interviewers to feel like they are shaking hands with a floppy dead fish. Also, you will be a little nervous so make certain that your hands are not dripping in sweat when you are called into the interview. When you greet each interviewer, make eye contact with the person while shaking hands, smile, and be courteous. Thank them for giving you the opportunity to interview for the police agency.

The interview will commence with the interviewer going over basic housekeeping items: how long the interview will last, how many questions there will be, and whether or not you can make notes, ask questions to be repeated, and so forth. Depending on the police agency, the interview may take anywhere from one to three hours. In order to be fair to all participants, each interview will have a maximum time limit and a set number of questions. You should try to find out in advance how long the interview is anticipated to last and how many questions there will be. As a rule of thumb, you should only take about seven minutes to respond to any question; however, if you can determine the number of interview questions and the maximum allowable time beforehand, then you can adjust the length of your responses accordingly.

Listen to each question carefully. You do not want to talk for five minutes only to find out that you misunderstood the question. Also, some questions may have more than one part, ensure that you recognize multipart questions and that you answer all parts of the question. Make notes for multipart questions so that you can refer back and be certain that you have answered the question completely.

### INTERVIEW DO LIST

- Be well-prepared
- Dress professionally
- Be enthusiastic
- Be confident
- Listen carefully
- Speak in a clear voice
- Ask clarifying questions
- Make notes
- Provide detailed answers
- Demonstrate you key skills and abilities

If you do not understand the question, you will likely be permitted to ask for clarification or for the interviewer to repeat the question. Again, this technique also gives you a few extra seconds to think about your answer if needed. However, do this only once or twice at the maximum as the interviewer will think that either you are not a good listener or you are using this as a stall tactic.

If you are asked a question and you draw a blank, do not panic. Collect your thoughts, write out some notes, and try to formulate a response. If still nothing is coming to mind, most agencies will not penalize you for asking to come back to that question later (although it may affect the interviewer's perception of your stress tolerance competencies). Therefore, this should only be done as a last resort, and you should never do it more than once in an interview.

Remember to let your personality shine through by being enthusiastic in your responses. Demonstrate that you are passionate about a career in policing, that you are well-prepared to take on the challenges of the occupation, and that you will add value to the organization. Speak in a calm and clear voice and do not rush through your answers.

When responding to questions, you will typically be looking at the top of the interviewer's head as he or she will be making extensive notes of your answers. If you notice that the interviewer is not making any notes at all, it may mean that you are rambling, or that he or she has already heard enough information, or it may also mean that you are off-track in your response. You can take this as a clue to either stop talking or perhaps ask for the question to be repeated to ensure that you have not missed a key part of the question. Since you can speak much faster than an interviewer can make notes, you will frequently find that the interviewer will continue writing after you have finished talking. After you have finished your response, sit quietly, collect your thoughts, and wait for the next question.

> **INTERVIEW DO NOT LIST**
> - Dress casually
> - Wear strong cologne/perfume
> - Chew gum
> - Slouch or slump in your chair
> - Speak too quickly
> - Try to remember responses verbatim
> - Use slang, colloquial, or unprofessional language
> - Repeat the same example for multiple questions
> - Get flustered
> - Hold back—this is your chance to shine

Almost every interview will end with what is commonly referred to as the "Why you?" question. This is your opportunity to make a lasting impression by covering all of the key attributes, competencies, and achievements that you possess that make you an ideal candidate. It is important that you provide specific detail of your abilities. That is, not only should you say that you are a team player who is highly ethical and works well under pressure and will add value to the organization with your depth of skills that cover a broad spectrum of competencies, you also need to back up each statement with specific examples. For instance, if you state that you are a highly ethical person, do not simply stop there, instead provide an example to illustrate an ethical dilemma that you were once involved in, the decision that you made, and what the outcome was.

Finally, since this will likely be the last question during the interview, your response will be the one that resonates with the interviewer or panel members after you leave the room. Even if you think you had a subpar answer on an earlier question, a strong final answer that clearly lays out in a compelling manner why you should be selected ahead of other applicants may have a halo effect and positively influence the scores on earlier questions.

After the interview is over, you may have the opportunity to ask questions. You may ask when you should expect to hear from the police department, but I would advise against asking further questions. Instead, take the opportunity to once again thank them for allowing you to compete for the police constable's position and restate that you know you have so much to offer the organization and will make them proud to have you as a new employee. After you leave the interview, the interviewer or panel members will immediately score your interview and forward their results to the recruiting section. Hopefully, as a result of your planning, dedication and being able to effectively showcase your skills, you will be contacted by the police agency within a few days to congratulate you and offer you employment as a police constable.

# Model Practice Exams

14

→ **MODEL EXAM ONE: ALBERTA COMMUNICATION TEST (ACT)**

→ **MODEL EXAM TWO: ONTARIO'S POLICE ANALYTICAL THINKING INVENTORY (PATI)**

→ **MODEL EXAM THREE: RCMP POLICE APTITUDE TEST (RPAT)**

→ **MODEL EXAM FOUR: SASKATCHEWAN SIGMA EXAM**

→ **MODEL EXAM FIVE: VANCOUVER POLICE DEPARTMENT INTAKE EXAM**

→ **MODEL EXAM SIX: WINNIPEG POLICE SERVICE WRITTEN TEST**

Each practice exam is a near replication of the format used by each of the identified police agencies. The structure for each practice exam reflects the number of questions, the competencies assessed, and the total time allotted for each exam. These six practice exams vary in style and content in order to provide you with a comprehensive spectrum of examination formats that you can expect from different police agencies across Canada.

Obviously, the questions contained within these practice examinations are not the actual questions that you will find on any of the entrance exams; however, they will prepare you for the types of questions that you can expect to see when you actually write the test. Furthermore, even though you have been provided with the most current format used by these police agencies, each organization is subject to change the format of its exams without notice. Therefore, before you write the exam, contact the recruiting section of the police agency that you are applying to and ask about the length of the exam, the number of questions that you can expect, and the format used (e.g., multiple choice, short answer, observation exercises). Most agencies will at least provide you with a basic framework that you can expect to see.

Before you begin, remove the attached Answer Sheets at the front section of each practice exam to record your answers. Ensure that the answers you provide on each sheet corresponds with the question number for the particular practice exam. An Answer Key and detailed explanations are at the end of each of the practice exams.

Finally, be sure to record the time it takes you to complete each segment of each exam so that you are certain you can complete each section within the allotted time.

If you have studied all the chapters in this guide and completed these practice exams, you will be well-prepared to take any police entrance exam, anywhere in Canada.

Good luck!

# Model Exam One: Alberta Communication Test (ACT)

The Alberta Communication Test (ACT) is one of three written entrance requirements for police applicants to municipal police departments in the province of Alberta. Immediately after completing the ACT, applicants must write an hour-long expository essay on a subject that will be provided at that time. On a separate date, applicants must also complete the Alberta Police Cognitive Abilities Test (APCAT), which is a 120-question multiple-choice exam that covers competencies such as observation, memory, judgment, and logic. These competencies are covered in other practice exams, such as the PATI, and therefore are not replicated here.

The ACT is comprised of 134 multiple-choice questions and takes 90 minutes to complete. The ACT measures three different competencies: vocabulary, spelling skills, and grammar.

| ALBERTA ACT FORMAT | | | |
|---|---|---|---|
| **SECTION** | **COMPETENCY** | **QUESTIONS** | **TIME ALLOWED** |
| Part 1 | Vocabulary | 40 | 20 minutes |
| Part 2 | Spelling | 50 | 30 minutes |
| Part 3 | Grammar | 44 | 40 minutes |
| | Total | 134 | 1.5 hours |

# ANSWER SHEET
## Model Exam One

### PART 1: Vocabulary

1. Ⓐ Ⓑ Ⓒ Ⓓ
2. Ⓐ Ⓑ Ⓒ Ⓓ
3. Ⓐ Ⓑ Ⓒ Ⓓ
4. Ⓐ Ⓑ Ⓒ Ⓓ
5. Ⓐ Ⓑ Ⓒ Ⓓ
6. Ⓐ Ⓑ Ⓒ Ⓓ
7. Ⓐ Ⓑ Ⓒ Ⓓ
8. Ⓐ Ⓑ Ⓒ Ⓓ
9. Ⓐ Ⓑ Ⓒ Ⓓ
10. Ⓐ Ⓑ Ⓒ Ⓓ

11. Ⓐ Ⓑ Ⓒ Ⓓ
12. Ⓐ Ⓑ Ⓒ Ⓓ
13. Ⓐ Ⓑ Ⓒ Ⓓ
14. Ⓐ Ⓑ Ⓒ Ⓓ
15. Ⓐ Ⓑ Ⓒ Ⓓ
16. Ⓐ Ⓑ Ⓒ Ⓓ
17. Ⓐ Ⓑ Ⓒ Ⓓ
18. Ⓐ Ⓑ Ⓒ Ⓓ
19. Ⓐ Ⓑ Ⓒ Ⓓ
20. Ⓐ Ⓑ Ⓒ Ⓓ

21. Ⓐ Ⓑ Ⓒ Ⓓ
22. Ⓐ Ⓑ Ⓒ Ⓓ
23. Ⓐ Ⓑ Ⓒ Ⓓ
24. Ⓐ Ⓑ Ⓒ Ⓓ
25. Ⓐ Ⓑ Ⓒ Ⓓ
26. Ⓐ Ⓑ Ⓒ Ⓓ
27. Ⓐ Ⓑ Ⓒ Ⓓ
28. Ⓐ Ⓑ Ⓒ Ⓓ
29. Ⓐ Ⓑ Ⓒ Ⓓ
30. Ⓐ Ⓑ Ⓒ Ⓓ

31. Ⓐ Ⓑ Ⓒ Ⓓ
32. Ⓐ Ⓑ Ⓒ Ⓓ
33. Ⓐ Ⓑ Ⓒ Ⓓ
34. Ⓐ Ⓑ Ⓒ Ⓓ
35. Ⓐ Ⓑ Ⓒ Ⓓ
36. Ⓐ Ⓑ Ⓒ Ⓓ
37. Ⓐ Ⓑ Ⓒ Ⓓ
38. Ⓐ Ⓑ Ⓒ Ⓓ
39. Ⓐ Ⓑ Ⓒ Ⓓ
40. Ⓐ Ⓑ Ⓒ Ⓓ

### PART 2: Spelling

41. Ⓐ Ⓑ Ⓒ Ⓓ
42. Ⓐ Ⓑ Ⓒ Ⓓ
43. Ⓐ Ⓑ Ⓒ Ⓓ
44. Ⓐ Ⓑ Ⓒ Ⓓ
45. Ⓐ Ⓑ Ⓒ Ⓓ
46. Ⓐ Ⓑ Ⓒ Ⓓ
47. Ⓐ Ⓑ Ⓒ Ⓓ
48. Ⓐ Ⓑ Ⓒ Ⓓ
49. Ⓐ Ⓑ Ⓒ Ⓓ
50. Ⓐ Ⓑ Ⓒ Ⓓ
51. Ⓐ Ⓑ Ⓒ Ⓓ
52. Ⓐ Ⓑ Ⓒ Ⓓ
53. Ⓐ Ⓑ Ⓒ Ⓓ

54. Ⓐ Ⓑ Ⓒ Ⓓ
55. Ⓐ Ⓑ Ⓒ Ⓓ
56. Ⓐ Ⓑ Ⓒ Ⓓ
57. Ⓐ Ⓑ Ⓒ Ⓓ
58. Ⓐ Ⓑ Ⓒ Ⓓ
59. Ⓐ Ⓑ Ⓒ Ⓓ
60. Ⓐ Ⓑ Ⓒ Ⓓ
61. Ⓐ Ⓑ Ⓒ Ⓓ
62. Ⓐ Ⓑ Ⓒ Ⓓ
63. Ⓐ Ⓑ Ⓒ Ⓓ
64. Ⓐ Ⓑ Ⓒ Ⓓ
65. Ⓐ Ⓑ Ⓒ Ⓓ
66. Ⓐ Ⓑ Ⓒ Ⓓ

67. Ⓐ Ⓑ Ⓒ Ⓓ
68. Ⓐ Ⓑ Ⓒ Ⓓ
69. Ⓐ Ⓑ Ⓒ Ⓓ
70. Ⓐ Ⓑ Ⓒ Ⓓ
71. Ⓐ Ⓑ Ⓒ Ⓓ
72. Ⓐ Ⓑ Ⓒ Ⓓ
73. Ⓐ Ⓑ Ⓒ Ⓓ
74. Ⓐ Ⓑ Ⓒ Ⓓ
75. Ⓐ Ⓑ Ⓒ Ⓓ
76. Ⓐ Ⓑ Ⓒ Ⓓ
77. Ⓐ Ⓑ Ⓒ Ⓓ
78. Ⓐ Ⓑ Ⓒ Ⓓ
79. Ⓐ Ⓑ Ⓒ Ⓓ

80. Ⓐ Ⓑ Ⓒ Ⓓ
81. Ⓐ Ⓑ Ⓒ Ⓓ
82. Ⓐ Ⓑ Ⓒ Ⓓ
83. Ⓐ Ⓑ Ⓒ Ⓓ
84. Ⓐ Ⓑ Ⓒ Ⓓ
85. Ⓐ Ⓑ Ⓒ Ⓓ
86. Ⓐ Ⓑ Ⓒ Ⓓ
87. Ⓐ Ⓑ Ⓒ Ⓓ
88. Ⓐ Ⓑ Ⓒ Ⓓ
89. Ⓐ Ⓑ Ⓒ Ⓓ
90. Ⓐ Ⓑ Ⓒ Ⓓ

## PART 3: Grammar

91. Ⓐ Ⓑ Ⓒ Ⓓ
92. Ⓐ Ⓑ Ⓒ Ⓓ
93. Ⓐ Ⓑ Ⓒ Ⓓ
94. Ⓐ Ⓑ Ⓒ Ⓓ
95. Ⓐ Ⓑ Ⓒ Ⓓ
96. Ⓐ Ⓑ Ⓒ Ⓓ
97. Ⓐ Ⓑ Ⓒ Ⓓ
98. Ⓐ Ⓑ Ⓒ Ⓓ
99. Ⓐ Ⓑ Ⓒ Ⓓ
100. Ⓐ Ⓑ Ⓒ Ⓓ
101. Ⓐ Ⓑ Ⓒ Ⓓ

102. Ⓐ Ⓑ Ⓒ Ⓓ
103. Ⓐ Ⓑ Ⓒ Ⓓ
104. Ⓐ Ⓑ Ⓒ Ⓓ
105. Ⓐ Ⓑ Ⓒ Ⓓ
106. Ⓐ Ⓑ Ⓒ Ⓓ
107. Ⓐ Ⓑ Ⓒ Ⓓ
108. Ⓐ Ⓑ Ⓒ Ⓓ
109. Ⓐ Ⓑ Ⓒ Ⓓ
110. Ⓐ Ⓑ Ⓒ Ⓓ
111. Ⓐ Ⓑ Ⓒ Ⓓ
112. Ⓐ Ⓑ Ⓒ Ⓓ

113. Ⓐ Ⓑ Ⓒ Ⓓ
114. Ⓐ Ⓑ Ⓒ Ⓓ
115. Ⓐ Ⓑ Ⓒ Ⓓ
116. Ⓐ Ⓑ Ⓒ Ⓓ
117. Ⓐ Ⓑ Ⓒ Ⓓ
118. Ⓐ Ⓑ Ⓒ Ⓓ
119. Ⓐ Ⓑ Ⓒ Ⓓ
120. Ⓐ Ⓑ Ⓒ Ⓓ
121. Ⓐ Ⓑ Ⓒ Ⓓ
122. Ⓐ Ⓑ Ⓒ Ⓓ
123. Ⓐ Ⓑ Ⓒ Ⓓ

124. Ⓐ Ⓑ Ⓒ Ⓓ
125. Ⓐ Ⓑ Ⓒ Ⓓ
126. Ⓐ Ⓑ Ⓒ Ⓓ
127. Ⓐ Ⓑ Ⓒ Ⓓ
128. Ⓐ Ⓑ Ⓒ Ⓓ
129. Ⓐ Ⓑ Ⓒ Ⓓ
130. Ⓐ Ⓑ Ⓒ Ⓓ
131. Ⓐ Ⓑ Ⓒ Ⓓ
132. Ⓐ Ⓑ Ⓒ Ⓓ
133. Ⓐ Ⓑ Ⓒ Ⓓ
134. Ⓐ Ⓑ Ⓒ Ⓓ

# PART 1: VOCABULARY

 You have 20 minutes to complete the following 40 questions.

1. Which of the following words means *meliorate*? — *To help*

   (A) improve
   (B) insolent
   (C) gloomy
   (D) fragile

2. Which of the following words means *castigate*?

   (A) iniquitous
   (B) admonish — *warn*
   (C) bide
   (D) aggravate

3. Which of the following terms means the opposite of *strident*? — *noisy*

   (A) spurious
   (B) clamorous
   (C) gentle
   (D) arcane

4. Having to inform the mother of her son's death was a terrible burden for the officer to bear.

   In which of the following sentences does the word *bear* have the same meaning as in the sentence above?

   (A) The doctor informed the woman that she would be unable to bear any more children.
   (B) The suspect's alibi did bear further examination.
   (C) Officer Jensen could not bear to see another careless driver injure innocent people caused by texting and driving.
   (D) Criminals must bear responsibility for their actions.

5. Which word best completes the following sentence?

   Prior to releasing the police report to the media, sensitive information was _____ from the document.

   (A) enacted
   (B) redacted
   (C) dedacted
   (D) undacted

6. Which word best completes the following sentence?

   The judge told the convicted thief that he was fortunate because he was allowing him to serve all three of his prison sentences _____.

   (A) austerely
   (B) consecutively  — one by one
   (C) pragmatically
   (D) concurrently

7. Which of the following words is not synonymous with the word *putative*?

   (A) ostensible
   (B) reputed
   (C) pedantic
   (D) purported

8. Which underlined word in the following sentences is used in the wrong context?

   (A) Officer Grant informed his peers that he was not <u>bemused</u> by the shaving cream on the door handle prank.
   (B) Officer Daniels was an excellent interviewer because he always showed compassion and was able to <u>commiserate</u> with just about anyone.
   (C) Officer Janice was very <u>meticulous</u> and known for her attention to detail when writing search warrants.
   (D) Officer Hunter felt that the <u>recalcitrant</u> youth was not going to be rehabilitated by such a light sentence.

9. If the staff sergeant was known for his narcissistic behaviour, it means that he was known to be_____.

   (A) astute
   (B) moody
   (C) self-absorbed
   (D) eccentric — Strange?

10. Which of the following is an antonym for the word *genial*?

    (A) amiable
    (B) inhospitable
    (C) menial
    (D) evasive

11. The word *pedestrian* usually means a person who is walking, but it also means_____.

    (A) uncompromising
    (B) quaint
    (C) lucid
    (D) ordinary

12. Which underlined word in the following sentences is used in the wrong context?

  (A) Officer Green was perturbed by the youth at the beach who were openly <u>flouting</u> the liquor laws.

  (B) The motorist's pleas for mercy had no <u>affect</u> on Constable Christensen's decision to write a ticket.

  (C) Constable Martens was <u>vehement</u> in his denial that he was the one who damaged the police car.

  (D) The defence lawyer suggested that Detective Prasad had offered his client an <u>enticement</u> in order to gain a confession.

13. Which underlined word in the following sentences is used in the wrong context?

  (A) The family that had been victims of a break and enter <u>complimented</u> Constable Merriott for arresting the suspect and returning their property.

  (B) The police were called to attend the town hall meeting because of the <u>obstreperous</u> behaviour of a small group of protestors.

  (C) The Health and Safety representative was under no <u>allusion</u> that the patrol officers would take his lecture on personal hygiene seriously.

  (D) The sex offender was obviously a <u>misogynist</u> because of the way he spoke so disparagingly towards women.

14. Which underlined word in the following sentences is used in the wrong context?

  (A) Police officers are trained to be <u>weary</u> of the risks associated with traffic stops.

  (B) Officer Stewart demonstrated her investigative <u>acumen</u> by correctly speculating where the fugitive suspect would take refuge.

  (C) The young offender was hoping that the fact that this was only his second conviction would <u>mitigate</u> the severity of the judge's sentence.

  (D) The home owners were extremely upset they were victims of a break in twice this year, and Constable Boardman spent considerable time with them to <u>mollify</u> their concerns.

15. Which of the following words means *immature*?

  (A) knave
  (B) neophyte
  (C) morose
  (D) naïve

16. The new Dress and Deportment policy states that hair shall be worn in a style and colour that does not _____ from the overall professional image of the police department.

  (A) detract
  (B) deter
  (C) distract
  (D) debase

17. If a witness corroborated another witness's version of events, this means that the story was_____.

    (A) contradicted
    (B) enhanced
    (C) refuted
    (D) substantiated

18. In order to prevent possible jury tampering during the high-profile case, the judge had the jury *sequestered*, meaning_____.

    (A) assimilated
    (B) isolated
    (C) convalesced
    (D) subpoenaed

19. The junior police constable was not cognizant of the procedures for obtaining a search warrant for medical records. *Cognizant* means_____.

    (A) compliant
    (B) familiar
    (C) ignorant
    (D) uncertain

20. The police psychologist was concerned regarding Constable Park's neurotic behaviour, meaning_____.

    (A) self-absorbed
    (B) obsessed with sex
    (C) reckless
    (D) fearful

21. In the following sentence, identify from the list below the term that has the same meaning as the underlined word.

    The Inspector informed her sergeant that his neighbourhood safety operational plan was not very <u>pragmatic</u>.

    (A) practical
    (B) cost effective
    (C) plausible
    (D) thorough

22. In the following sentence, identify from the list below the term that has the same meaning as the underlined word.

    The witness appeared to be <u>inebriated</u> when providing her written statement to Constable Nguyen.

    (A) remorseful
    (B) uneducated
    (C) incoherent
    (D) intoxicated

23. In the following sentence, identify from the list below the term that has the same meaning as the underlined word.

Before he would be able to obtain a search warrant for the marijuana grow operation, Constable Grewal would check the <u>veracity</u> of the informant's claim.

(A) context
(B) lawfulness
(C) legitimacy
(D) corruptibility

24. In the following sentence, identify from the list below the term that has the same meaning as the underlined word.

Sergeant Risebrough was angered by Constable Guy's <u>blatant</u> attempt to avoid being assigned to the sudden death call.

(A) obvious
(B) subversive
(C) insubordinate
(D) rebellious

25. In the following sentence, identify from the list below the term that has the same meaning as the underlined word.

The sense of relief in the courtroom was <u>tangible</u> when the officer was acquitted of assaulting the violent prisoner.

(A) believable
(B) honourable
(C) regrettable
(D) perceptible

26. Which underlined word in the following sentences is used in the wrong context?

(A) Constable Wood said that he would rather write speeding tickets for six hours <u>than</u> conduct surveillance and hide in a bush for half a night waiting to see if a suspect leaves his house.
(B) Although the drug squad searched the entire <u>premise</u> for the alleged cache of cocaine, they found nothing.
(C) Although he had been in a serious collision, the driver appeared <u>lucid</u> and spoke clearly when talking to the ambulance attendants.
(D) The corrupt official's <u>malfeasance</u> finally caught up with him when he was finally convicted of fraud.

27. Which underlined word in the following sentences is used in the wrong context?

(A) Constable Trump needs to do something, he's been complaining of <u>acute</u> back pain for years.
(B) It appeared that the defence lawyer's incessant questioning was designed to <u>obfuscate</u> Constable Danroth.
(C) Constable Buchanan complained about the uneventful and <u>banal</u> shifts over the past three nights.
(D) Constable MacDonald left the handcuffs fitting too <u>loose</u>, which allowed the prisoner to slip out of them and escape.

28. Which underlined word in the following sentences is used in the wrong context?

    (A) Given the current economic <u>milieu</u>, it did not look very encouraging that the members would be getting a significant raise in this contract.

    (B) Corporal Schick said he had to leave work early, <u>ostensibly</u> due to a family emergency.

    (C) Sergeant Walden never came right out and said it, but I think he was trying to <u>infer</u> that constable Dawson would be leaving the squad very soon.

    (D) Some people believe that the city's current drug policy has only <u>exacerbated</u> its drug addiction problems, leading to more and more open drug use.

29. Which underlined word in the following sentences is used in the wrong context?

    (A) Although he did not sustain any broken bones or laceration from falling off his motorcycle, Constable Clifford did have a large <u>contusion</u> on his left elbow.

    (B) The chief was clear in his remarks that racist comments and other <u>pejorative</u> references to co-workers were grounds for disciplinary action.

    (C) There are always those individuals that <u>perpetrate</u> the myth that traffic cops are more likely to stop red cars for speeding than any other colour.

    (D) Few people enjoyed working for Sergeant Callaway; he was known to be <u>officious</u> and overbearing.

30. Which underlined word in the following sentences is used in the wrong context?

    (A) The drug squad was surprised to find the large grow op located in the aeroplane <u>hangar</u>.

    (B) Sergeant Grossman did not look well. He said, "I think I need to <u>lie</u> down for a minute."

    (C) Constable Crane was advised that he had reached his <u>tenure</u> in the Traffic Section, and it was time for him to return to Patrol.

    (D) The suspect was found at the construction site, hiding behind a wooden <u>palate</u>.

31. In the following sentence, identify from the list below the term that has the same meaning as the underlined word.

    As a result of a restructuring of the Special Investigation Section, managers are required to <u>pare</u> the number of resources assigned to Vice.

    (A) change
    (B) cut back
    (C) align
    (D) support

32. In the following sentence, identify from the list below the term that has the same meaning as the underlined word.

    The new computer system, which produced daily crime statistics for each officer, made the weekly crime meetings <u>redundant</u>.

    (A) exceeding what is necessary
    (B) useless
    (C) unbearable
    (D) impracticable

33. In the following sentence, identify from the list below the term that has the same meaning as the underlined word.

Constable Mark's work ethic represents the <u>epitome</u> of what is expected from each member of the Emergency Response Team.

(A) tenacity

(B) criterion

(C) idyllic response

(D) typical example

34. In the following sentence, identify from the list below the term that has the same meaning as the underlined word.

The field trainer told his recruit that he had made an <u>auspicious</u> impression in his first two weeks.

(A) impressionable

(B) promising

(C) unfortunate

(D) unsure

35. In the following sentence, identify from the list below the term that has the same meaning as the underlined word.

Sergeant Formby was always looking for new ways to enhance the squad's <u>esprit de corps</u>.

(A) productivity

(B) community spirit

(C) sociability

(D) morale

36. Which underlined word in the following sentences is used in the wrong context?

(A) The chief was <u>loath</u> to sign the revised Memorandum of Understanding without prior review by her legal advisor.

(B) Although the junior officer needed next Friday off, he was leery of <u>broaching</u> the subject with his new supervisor considering that he had just started working with the team.

(C) The sergeant always advised his team at the start of each shift, "Please <u>insure</u> you conduct a pistol function test before heading out of the office."

(D) The sergeant could not believe the <u>audacity</u> of the junior officer, who started with the team just two weeks earlier, to ask for next Friday off.

37. Which underlined word in the following sentences is used in the wrong context?

(A) The thief was able to <u>allude</u> captivity for more than a week.

(B) Constable Mann could tell there was something bothering her partner and it was time to have a <u>candid</u> conversation with him.

(C) Detective Jane's investigative tenacity earned her the <u>epithet</u> "Honey Badger."

(D) Even in the face of racial abuse from the protestors, Constable Gill remained <u>stoic</u> and impassive against their taunts.

38. Which of the following terms is an antonym for the word *boorish*?

    (A) mordant
    (B) acerbic
    (C) malicious
    (D) well-mannered

39. Which word best completes the following sentence?

    An effective police officer is one that possesses strong interpersonal skills, which, for example, means having compassion for _____ individuals that are homeless and unemployable.

    (A) obtuse
    (B) miscreant
    (C) opulent
    (D) destitute

40. Which word best completes the following sentence?

    The Officer in Charge at the disturbance _____ the protestors by agreeing to some of their demands in order to prevent an escalation of the incident.

    (A) negated
    (B) placated
    (C) exhorted
    (D) exasperated

## PART 2: SPELLING

 **You have 30 minutes to complete the following 50 questions.**

41. Which of the following words is misspelled?

    (A) innocuous
    (B) vague
    (C) resistence
    (D) foreshadow

42. Which of the following words is misspelled?

    (A) presence
    (B) advantagous
    (C) renew
    (D) emulate

43. Which of the following words is misspelled?

    (A) continueous
    (B) provincial
    (C) centre
    (D) desperate

44. Which of the underlined words in the following sentence is spelled incorrectly?

    Officer Hamal was <u>flummoxed</u> by the complexity of the three new <u>policies</u> and <u>legislations</u> that were <u>announced</u> this week.

    (A) flummoxed
    (B) policies
    (C) legislations
    (D) announced

45. Which of the underlined words in the following sentence is spelled incorrectly?

    Constable Greer was <u>incensed</u> when he discovered <u>derogatory</u> <u>graffiti</u> spray painted on the door of his <u>convertable</u> Ford Mustang.

    (A) incensed
    (B) derogatory
    (C) graffiti
    (D) convertable

46. Which of the underlined words in the following sentence is spelled incorrectly?

The <u>concensus</u> among the <u>veteran</u> officers was that they all <u>benefitted</u> from the training <u>curriculum</u>.

(A) concensus
(B) veteran
(C) benefitted
(D) curriculum

47. Which of the underlined words in the following sentence is spelled incorrectly?

<u>Sergeant</u> Baron <u>totaled</u> the sum of items stolen in the <u>convenience</u> store <u>burglary</u>.

(A) Sergeant
(B) totaled
(C) convenience
(D) burglary

48. Which of the underlined words in the following sentence is spelled incorrectly?

Constable Lynd's <u>performance</u> was <u>certainly</u> <u>noteable</u> for arresting the suspect in the robbery <u>incident</u>.

(A) performance
(B) certainly
(C) noteable
(D) incident

49. Which of the underlined words in the following sentence is spelled incorrectly?

The men were told to <u>procede</u> to the gym for their <u>annual</u> <u>suitability</u> <u>assessment</u>.

(A) procede
(B) annual
(C) suitability
(D) assessment

50. Which of the underlined words in the following sentence is spelled incorrectly?

Following the robbery of the <u>elderly</u> victim, the police <u>canine</u> handler <u>trailled</u> the suspect's <u>odour</u> for nearly an hour.

(A) elderly
(B) canine
(C) trailled
(D) odour

51. Which of the following words is misspelled?

(A) anecdote
(B) likeible
(C) duly
(D) either

52. Which of the following words is misspelled?

   (A) intolerence
   (B) familiar
   (C) indulgence
   (D) irrelevant

53. Which of the following words is misspelled?

   (A) warrant
   (B) acknowledgement
   (C) tariff
   (D) vacilate

54. Which of the following words is misspelled?

   (A) perennial
   (B) theorys
   (C) trying
   (D) necessary

55. Which of the following words is misspelled?

   (A) practical
   (B) ceiling
   (C) foresee
   (D) complacance

56. Which of the underlined words in the following sentence is spelled incorrectly?

   The Robbery Section <u>ought</u> to have known that the <u>hiest</u> was <u>committed</u> by Jack Scourge, who always used an <u>imitation</u> sawed-off shotgun.

   (A) ought
   (B) hiest
   (C) committed
   (D) imitation

57. Which of the underlined words in the following sentence is spelled incorrectly?

   The sound the <u>collapsable</u> baton makes when extended is a great <u>motivator</u> to a <u>noncompliant</u> and <u>aggressive</u> audience.

   (A) collapsable
   (B) motivator
   (C) noncompliant
   (D) aggressive

58. Which of the underlined words in the following sentence is spelled incorrectly?

   The <u>embezzlement</u> investigation focused on <u>inconsistancies</u> in funds being redirected from the <u>organization's</u> <u>coffers</u>.

   (A) embezzlement
   (B) inconsistancies
   (C) organization's
   (D) coffers

59. Which of the underlined words in the following sentence is spelled incorrectly?

Sergeant Butler <u>sincerely</u> believes that Constable Nichol is one of the most <u>reliable</u> and <u>dependible</u> new <u>personnel</u> in this department.

(A) sincerely
(B) reliable
(C) dependible
(D) personnel

60. Which of the underlined words in the following sentence is spelled incorrectly?

<u>Ironically</u>, one of the <u>quintessential</u> benefits of being a police officer is the amount of time away from work that the <u>occupation</u> affords, so that one can enjoy various <u>liesure</u> activities.

(A) Ironically
(B) quintessential
(C) occupation
(D) liesure

61. Which, if any, of the following words is misspelled?

(A) through
(B) threshold
(C) truely
(D) *no errors*

62. Which, if any, of the following words is misspelled?

(A) perseverence
(B) continuance
(C) reference
(D) *no errors*

63. Which, if any, of the following words is misspelled?

(A) interrupted
(B) besieged
(C) dilapitated
(D) *no errors*

64. Which, if any, of the following words is misspelled?

(A) forcible
(B) digestable
(C) acceptable
(D) *no errors*

65. Which, if any, of the following words is misspelled?

(A) insistent
(B) cognizant
(C) absorbent
(D) *no errors*

66. Which, if any, of the underlined words in the following sentence is misspelled?

Constable Cook was very <u>irritible</u> when he heard that the <u>heroin</u> <u>trafficking</u> charge was dropped.

(A) irritible
(B) heroin
(C) trafficking
(D) *no errors*

67. Which, if any, of the underlined words in the following sentence is misspelled?

The Fraud Section was finally able to <u>achieve</u> the arrest of the <u>bookkeeper</u> in the multimillion dollar <u>counterfiet</u> scheme.

(A) achieve
(B) bookkeeper
(C) counterfiet
(D) *no errors*

68. Which, if any, of the underlined words in the following sentence is misspelled?

The police department's research section conducted multiple <u>analyses</u> of patrol workload during various shifts in order to <u>recommend</u> the <u>optimum</u> shifting model.

(A) analyses
(B) recommend
(C) optimum
(D) *no errors*

69. Which, if any, of the underlined words in the following sentence is misspelled?

The Canadian Intelligence <u>Centre</u> Steering Committee <u>travelled</u> to New York to visit their Real Time Crime <u>Center</u>.

(A) Centre
(B) travelled
(C) Center
(D) *no errors*

70. Which, if any, of the underlined words in the following sentence is misspelled?

On this <u>occasion</u>, the motorist <u>apparantly</u> had a heart attack prior to the <u>awful</u> collision.

(A) occasion
(B) apparantly
(C) awful
(D) *no errors*

71. Which, if any, of the following words is misspelled?

(A) exceed
(B) except
(C) excerpt
(D) *no errors*

72. Which, if any, of the following words is misspelled?

    (A) seize
    (B) receive
    (C) sliegh
    (D) *no errors*

73. Which, if any, of the following words is misspelled?

    (A) sufficeint
    (B) science
    (C) receive
    (D) *no errors*

74. Which, if any, of the following words is misspelled?

    (A) renovated
    (B) transmitted
    (C) acquitted
    (D) *no errors*

75. Which, if any, of the following words is misspelled?

    (A) convenience
    (B) consenses
    (C) condenses
    (D) *no errors*

76. Which of the underlined words in the following sentence is spelled incorrectly?

    The intoxicated man was <u>unconscious</u> and not responding to the officer's use of pressure points and other pain <u>stimuluses,</u> he was <u>eventually</u> arrested for public <u>drunkenness</u>.

    (A) unconscious
    (B) stimuluses
    (C) eventually
    (D) drunkenness

77. Which of the underlined words in the following sentence is spelled incorrectly?

    Constable Russell was <u>certainly</u> <u>embarrassed</u> to <u>concede</u> to his squad mates that he did not particularly like either his current or previous <u>mother-in-laws</u>.

    (A) certainly
    (B) embarrassed
    (C) concede
    (D) mother-in-laws

78. Which of the underlined words in the following sentence is spelled incorrectly?

    To think that police officers are not <u>susceptable</u> to <u>possible</u> <u>corruption</u> is <u>naïve</u>.

    (A) susceptable
    (B) possible
    (C) corruption
    (D) naïve

79. Which of the underlined words in the following sentence is spelled incorrectly?

The escape <u>occurred</u> when Constable Arkwright <u>transferred</u> the prisoner over to the custody of <u>Sherriff</u> Jones, and the convict <u>easily</u> slipped out of the handcuffs.

(A) occurred
(B) transferred
(C) Sherriff
(D) easily

80. Which of the underlined words in the following sentence is spelled incorrectly?

Constable Lee said she needed a <u>prescription</u> for new glasses, she thought the <u>address</u> <u>across</u> the street ended with an eight, but it was actually two <u>zeros</u>.

(A) prescription
(B) address
(C) across
(D) zeros

81. Which of the following words is misspelled?

(A) exaggerate
(B) exhilerate
(C) deteriorate
(D) commemorate

82. Which of the following words is misspelled?

(A) knives
(B) wives
(C) mischieves
(D) halves

83. Which of the following words is misspelled?

(A) flouride
(B) fluorescent
(C) flourish
(D) flounder

84. Which of the following words is misspelled?

(A) weird
(B) withold
(C) wither
(D) whether

85. Which of the following words is misspelled?

(A) moniter
(B) litre
(C) commander
(D) counsellor

86. Which, if any, of the underlined words in the following sentence is misspelled?

Constable Goldman was <u>re-known</u> for his <u>repertoire</u> of sarcastic, but very funny, comments when dealing with traffic <u>violators</u>.

(A) re-known
(B) repertoire
(C) violators
(D) *no errors*

87. Which, if any, of the underlined words in the following sentence is misspelled?

The <u>temperature</u> was <u>blisterring</u> hot, so the beat officers <u>endeavoured</u> to find shade and stay hydrated.

(A) temperature
(B) blisterring
(C) endeavoured
(D) *no errors*

88. Which, if any, of the underlined words in the following sentence is spelled incorrectly?

Constable Butterworth's <u>inexplicable</u> absence from work was an <u>anomaly</u>, considering his <u>exceptional</u> attendance record.

(A) inexplicable
(B) anomaly
(C) exceptional
(D) *no errors*

89. Which, if any, of the underlined words in the following sentence is misspelled?

An <u>independent</u> panel was <u>convened</u> to determine who would <u>supercede</u> the outgoing chief.

(A) independent
(B) convened
(C) supercede
(D) *no errors*

90. Which, if any, of the underlined words in the following sentence is misspelled?

The <u>camouflage</u> <u>apparel</u> worn by the Emergency Response Team members allowed them an <u>advantagous</u> position.

(A) camouflage
(B) apparel
(C) advantagous
(D) *no errors*

## PART 3: GRAMMAR

 **You have 40 minutes to complete the following 44 questions.**

91. Which option best completes the following sentence?

I am taking my new police-issue sunglasses with me, and I _____ them to the beach every day this summer.

(A) wore
(B) wear
(C) am wearing
(D) worn

92. Which option best completes the following sentence?

Some of the recent surveys seem to indicate that the general public is losing its faith _____ police officers.

(A) for
(B) in
(C) about
(D) on

93. Which option best completes the following sentence?

Constable Ward admitted to Constable Gilbert, "Something was lost in translation, it's been four years since I last _____ French."

(A) spoke
(B) have spoken
(C) was speaking
(D) have been speaking

94. Which option best completes the following sentence?

As Constable Damon was attempting to place the suspect in handcuffs, the offender turned and _____ at him.

(A) swang
(B) swung
(C) had swung
(D) was swinging

95. Which option best completes the following sentence?

Constable Jared was finding the physical training at the police academy to be grueling; he said that by the time he graduates from the academy he _____ more than 300 kilometres.

(A) ran
(B) will be running
(C) runs
(D) will have run

96. Which option best completes the following sentence?

With the number of female police officers hired each year _____, the long-term goal is that 50 percent of the force will be women by 2025.

(A) increasing
(B) are increasing
(C) increase
(D) increased

97. Which option best completes the following sentence?

Unless special permission is obtained, police officers in Canada are prohibited from carrying _____ issue firearms while off duty.

(A) there
(B) their
(C) they're
(D) thear

98. Which option best completes the following sentence?

In preparation for the upcoming promotional exam, Constable Davies _____ at the library.

(A) study
(B) studying
(C) studies
(D) will have study

99. Which option best completes the following sentence?

The instructor told the recruit class, "Everyone must do _____ best in order to make it through 'hell week' at the police academy."

(A) its
(B) their
(C) your
(D) his or her

100. Which option best completes the following sentence?

Each year we have to complete a survey relating to our confidence _____ senior police management.

(A) about
(B) for
(C) in
(D) to

101. Which of the following statements is the most grammatically correct?

(A) Constable Wong wanted to go out for an Italian dinner—Constable Scarpello wanted Chinese food.
(B) Constable Wong wanted to go out for an Italian dinner but, Constable Scarpello wanted Chinese food.
(C) Constable Wong wanted to go out for an Italian dinner, but Constable Scarpello wanted Chinese food.
(D) Constable Wong wanted to go out for an Italian dinner; but Constable Scarpello wanted Chinese food.

102. Which of the following statements is the most grammatically correct?

(A) The field trainer reviewed the recruit constable's inventory, before they went on the road: radio, baton, OC spray, Taser, pistol, and his handcuff.
(B) Before they went on the road, the field trainer reviewed the recruit constables inventory: radio, baton, OC spray, Taser, pistol, and handcuffs.
(C) The field trainer reviewed the recruit constable's inventory, which was his radio, baton, OC spray, Taser, pistol, and handcuffs, even before they went on the road.
(D) Before they went on the road, the field trainer reviewed the recruit constable's inventory: radio, baton, OC spray, Taser, pistol, and handcuffs.

103. Which of the following statements is the most grammatically correct?

(A) It was clear that neither Constable Dosanjh and I was going to get the Intelligence Officer position.
(B) It was clear that neither Constable Dosanjh, or me, were going to get the Intelligence Officer position.
(C) It was clear that neither Constable Dosanjh nor I were going to get the Intelligence Officer position.
(D) It was clear that neither Constable Dosanjh nor I was going to get the Intelligence Officer position.

104. Which of the following statements is the most grammatically correct?

(A) Considerable discussion has occurred regarding police training and its impact on officers decision making.
(B) There has been considerable discussion regarding police training and its impact on officers' decision making.
(C) There has been considerable discussion regarding police training and it's impact on officers' decision making.
(D) There have been considerable discussion regarding police training and its impact on officer's decision making.

105. Which of the following statements is the most grammatically correct?

    (A) Strict traffic enforcement and education is the most effective method of combating the high number of deaths associated to aggressive driving.

    (B) Strict traffic enforcement and education are the most effective motive of combating the high number of deaths associated to aggressive driving.

    (C) Strict traffic enforcement and education are the most effective manner of combating the high number of deaths associated with aggressive driving.

    (D) Strict traffic enforcement and education are the most effective means' of combating the high number of deaths associated to aggressive driving.

106. Which option best completes the following sentence?

    Despite the introduction of various police _____ and an increasingly scientific approach to criminal _____ the overall rate of solving crime _____ not increased.

    (A) technologies/investigations, /has

    (B) technology/investigation/have

    (C) technology/investigations/have

    (D) technology/investigation/has

107. Which option best completes the following sentence?

    Constable Fisher and ___ will be leaving the office shortly to go _____ an arrest. We will advise dispatch when we get _____.

    (A) me/affect/their

    (B) I/affect/there

    (C) me/effect/they're

    (D) I/effect/there

108. Which option best completes the following sentence?

    As time _____, neither Constable Grant _____ Constable Harrison _____ long-term effects from having dealt with last year's suicide incident.

    (A) passed/nor/suffered

    (B) passes/and/suffers

    (C) past/or/suffered

    (D) pass/nor/suffers

109. Which option best completes the following sentence?

    It is a well-known _____ that the salary and benefits of police ____ extremely competitive and _____ the best in similar occupations.

    (A) fact/is/among

    (B) facts /are/between

    (C) factoid/is/amongst

    (D) fact/are/among

110. Which option best completes the following sentence?

The staff ___ concerned about Constable Gale's sudden ____ of odd behavior. Perhaps he's having some _____ issues at home.

(A) are/onset/personnel
(B) is/onset/personal
(C) are/on set/personal
(D) is/onset/personnel

111. Which of the following statements is the most grammatically correct?

(A) A combination of attributes; positive interpersonal skills, good judgement, and effective decision making, make for a high-quality police officer.
(B) A combination of attributes, such as, positive interpersonal skills, good judgement, and effective decision making makes for a high-quality police officer.
(C) A combination of attributes, such as positive interpersonal skills, good judgement, and effective decision making, make for a high-quality police officer.
(D) A combination of attributes: such as positive interpersonal skills, good judgement, and effective decision making makes for a high-quality police officer.

112. Which of the following statements is the most grammatically correct?

(A) The sergeant felt that the commendation should be awarded to whoever had shown the greatest work ethic over the past year, however, even then it would be a difficult decision.
(B) The sergeant felt that the commendation should be awarded to whomever had shown the greatest work ethic over the past year; however, even then it would be a difficult decision.
(C) The sergeant felt that the commendation should be awarded to whomever had shown the greatest work ethic over the past year: however, even then it would be a difficult decision.
(D) The sergeant felt that the commendation should be awarded to whoever had shown the greatest work ethic over the past year—however, even then—it would be a difficult decision.

113. Which of the following statements is the most grammatically correct?

(A) The purpose of the conference was to inform all police agencies that gang violence incidents not only occur in large urban centres but in many regional communities as well.
(B) The purposes of the conference were to inform all police agencies that gang violence incidence not only occur in large urban centres but in many regional communities as well.
(C) The purpose of the conference where to inform all police agencies that gang violence incidence not only occur in large urban centres but in many regional communities as well.
(D) The purposes of the conference was to inform all police agencies' that gang violence incidence not only occur in large urban centres but in many regional communities as well.

114. Which of the following statements is the most grammatically correct?

    (A) The duty officer wanted to know whose been assigned to the stabbing, if there are enough resources working the case, and who are the investigators reporting to.
    (B) The duty officer wanted to know who's been assigned to the stabbing, if their enough resources working the case, and to whom are the investigators reporting.
    (C) The duty officer wanted to know who has been assigned to the stabbing, if there are enough resources working the case, and who are the investigators reporting to.
    (D) The duty officer wanted to know to whom the stabbing has been assigned, if there is enough resources working the case, and who are the investigators reporting to.

115. Which of the following statements is the most grammatically correct?

    (A) The field trainer not only advised her recruit that it was important to possess strong communication skills but also to demonstrate strong officer presence.
    (B) The field trainer advised her recruit that not only was it important to possess strong communication skills but also to demonstrate strong officer presence.
    (C) The field trainer gave her recruit advice: not only was it important to possess strong communication skills, it is also important to demonstrate strong officer presence.
    (D) The field trainer advised her recruit that it was important to not only possess strong communication skills and to demonstrate strong officer presence.

116. Which correction, if any, should be made to the following sentence?

    Specific groups, such as visible ethnic minorities, are in high demand because of pressure from senior management, politicians, and community representatives to increase their numbers.

    (A) Change *senior management* to *Senior Management*
    (B) Change *ethnic minorities* to *ethnic-minorities*
    (C) Change *their numbers* to *specific groups' numbers*
    (D) No correction necessary

117. Which correction, if any, should be made to the following sentence?

    Constable Greenhorn said, "between you and me it's their problem, not ours."

    (A) Capitalize *between*
    (B) Change *me* to *I*
    (C) Change *it's* to *its*
    (D) No correction necessary

118. Which correction, if any, should be made to the following sentence?

    The plainclothes officer saw the robber enter the restaurant. He rose from his seat, sprang into action, and took custody of the culprit before the robber had a chance to flee.

    (A) Change *rose* to a*rose*
    (B) Change *sprang* to *sprung*
    (C) Change *took* to *had taken*
    (D) No correction necessary

119. Which correction, if any, should be made to the following sentence?

It was apparent that the thief had entered the home and robbed the family while they were sleeping.

(A) Change *apparent* to *apparant*
(B) Change *thief* to *theif*
(C) Change *were sleeping* to *slept*
(D) No correction necessary

120. Which correction, if any, should be made to the following sentence?

Constable Sprak said, "If I was being cynical, I would think that Gary injured his leg at home and not at work."

(A) Change *was* to *were*
(B) Remove *would*
(C) Change *Gary injured his leg* to *Gary's leg was injured*
(D) No correction necessary

121. Which correction, if any, should be made to the following sentence?

Constable Ferdinand was almost on the job for twelve years before he encountered a deadly-force situation.

(A) Change *was* to *would have been*
(B) Move *almost* to immediately precede *twelve years*
(C) Change *deadly-force* to *deadly force*
(D) No correction necessary

122. Which correction, if any, should be made to the following sentence?

The International Police Association is an organization committed to promoting friendship and international cooperation among police members around the world.

(A) Change *is* to *are*
(B) Change *committed* to *commited*
(C) Change *cooperation* to *co-operation*
(D) No correction necessary

123. Which correction, if any, should be made to the following sentence?

The police department advised that they would have offered to pay for my tuition if I decide to return to university.

(A) Change *advised* to *advises*
(B) Change *would have* to *would've*
(C) Change *decide* to *had decided*
(D) No correction necessary

124. Which correction, if any, should be made to the following sentence?

The recruiting officer informed me that seven years is a long time to be out of school: I may struggle with police academy's academic regimen.

(A) Change *is* to *are*
(B) Change *school:* to *school;*
(C) Change *regimen* to *regime*
(D) No correction necessary

125. Which correction, if any, should be made to the following sentence?

The use-of-force instructors often impress in us that if we are failing to train, then we are training to fail.

(A) change *use-of-force* to *use of force*
(B) change *in* to *on*
(C) change *failing* to *fail*
(D) No correction necessary

126. Which correction, if any, should be made to the following sentence?

Constable Robinson felt that the best supervisors are those who lead by their knowledge, by their skill, and by setting a good example.

(A) Change *are those* to *is one*
(B) Change *lead* to *led*
(C) Change *setting a good example* to *their example*
(D) No correction necessary

127. Which correction, if any, should be made to the following sentence?

The Report on Pedestrian Fatalities concluded that the majority of fatal collisions occurred because they had disobeyed a traffic law, the motorist had disobeyed a traffic law, and they had been under the influence of alcohol or drugs while walking on a roadway.

(A) Remove the capital letters from *Report on Pedestrian Fatalities*
(B) Change the words *they* to *pedestrians*
(C) Change *had been* to *were*
(D) No correction necessary

128. Which correction, if any, should be made to the following sentence?

This past spring the Drug Squad launched Project Reveal, which targeted street-level drug dealers in the downtown area.

(A) Change *past* to *passed*
(B) Change *spring* to *Spring*
(C) Remove capital letters from *Drug Squad*
(D) No correction necessary

129. Which correction, if any, should be made to the following sentence?

Irregardless of the various enforcement initiatives undertaken by the Crime Control Team during the past six months, there has been no discernible difference in the area's rate of violent crime.

(A) Change *Irregardless* to *Regardless*
(B) Change *has* to *have*
(C) Change *discernible* to *discernable*
(D) No correction necessary

130. Which correction, if any, should be made to the following sentence?

The dreadful details of yesterday's homicide, that appeared in today's newspaper, must have been especially difficult on the immediate family members.

(A) Change *dreadful* to *dreadfull*
(B) Change *yesterday's* to *yesterdays*
(C) Change *that* to *which*
(D) No correction necessary

131. Which of the following statements is the most grammatically correct?

(A) The Director of the Police Academy had invited The Honourable Suzanne Anton, Minister of Justice and Attorney General, Jim Chu, the Vancouver Chief of Police, and Dave Jones, Chief of the New Westminster Police Department to the police recruit graduation ceremony.
(B) The Director of the Police Academy invited to the recruit graduation ceremony the Honourable Suzanne Anton, Minister of Justice and Attorney General; Jim Chu, the Vancouver Chief of Police; and Dave Jones, Chief of the New Westminster Police Department.
(C) Invited to the recruit graduation ceremony, by the Director of the Police Academy, were the Honourable Suzanne Anton, Minister of Justice and Attorney General; Jim Chu, the Vancouver Chief of Police; and Dave Jones, Chief of the New Westminster Police Department.
(D) The Honourable Suzanne Anton, Minister of Justice and Attorney General; Jim Chu, the Vancouver Chief of Police; and Dave Jones, Chief of the New Westminster Police Department were invited, by the Director of the Police Academy, to the recruit graduation ceremony.

132. Which of the following statements is the most grammatically correct?

(A) The police academy instructor's message was clear: if one studies hard and physically trains hard, you will succeed.
(B) The police academy instructor's message was clear, if one studies hard and trains physically hard, one will succeed.
(C) The police academy's instructor massage was clear—if one studies hard and physically trains hard, one will succeed.
(D) The police academy instructor's message was clear: if one studies hard and physically trains hard, one will succeed.

133. Which of the following statements is the most grammatically correct?

    (A) The sergeant said that either of the proposed agendas for the team development day are acceptable. Were shall we hold the meeting?
    (B) The sergeant said that either of the proposed agendas for the team development day is acceptable. Were shall we hold the meeting?
    (C) The sergeant said that either of the proposed agendas for the team development day is acceptable. Where shall we hold the meeting?
    (D) The sergeant said that either of the proposed agenda's for the team development day are acceptable. Wear shall we hold the meeting?

134. Which of the following statements is the most grammatically correct?

    (A) The police department accepted the coroner's jury recommendations, it would implement new policy immediately.
    (B) The police department accepted the coroner jury's recommendations, they would immediately implement new policy.
    (C) The police department accepted the coroner's jury recommendations: and would immediately implement new policy.
    (D) The police department accepted the coroner's jury recommendations; it would implement new policy immediately.

# ANSWER KEY

## PART 1: Vocabulary

| | | | |
|---|---|---|---|
| 1. A | 11. D | 21. A | 31. B |
| 2. B | 12. B | 22. D | 32. A |
| 3. C | 13. C | 23. C | 33. D |
| 4. C | 14. A | 24. A | 34. B |
| 5. B | 15. D | 25. D | 35. D |
| 6. D | 16. A | 26. B | 36. C |
| 7. C | 17. D | 27. A | 37. A |
| 8. A | 18. B | 28. C | 38. D |
| 9. C | 19. B | 29. C | 39. D |
| 10. B | 20. D | 30. D | 40. B |

## PART 2: Spelling

| | | | |
|---|---|---|---|
| 41. C | 54. B | 67. C | 80. D |
| 42. B | 55. D | 68. D | 81. B |
| 43. A | 56. B | 69. D | 82. C |
| 44. C | 57. A | 70. B | 83. A |
| 45. D | 58. B | 71. D | 84. B |
| 46. A | 59. C | 72. C | 85. A |
| 47. B | 60. D | 73. A | 86. A |
| 48. C | 61. C | 74. D | 87. B |
| 49. A | 62. A | 75. B | 88. D |
| 50. C | 63. C | 76. B | 89. C |
| 51. B | 64. B | 77. D | 90. C |
| 52. A | 65. D | 78. A | |
| 53. D | 66. A | 79. C | |

## PART 3: Grammar

| | | | | | | | |
|---|---|---|---|---|---|---|---|
| **91.** | C | **102.** | D | **113.** | A | **124.** | B |
| **92.** | B | **103.** | D | **114.** | C | **125.** | B |
| **93.** | A | **104.** | B | **115.** | B | **126.** | C |
| **94.** | B | **105.** | C | **116.** | C | **127.** | B |
| **95.** | D | **106.** | A | **117.** | A | **128.** | D |
| **96.** | A | **107.** | D | **118.** | A | **129.** | A |
| **97.** | B | **108.** | A | **119.** | C | **130.** | C |
| **98.** | C | **109.** | D | **120.** | A | **131.** | B |
| **99.** | D | **110.** | B | **121.** | B | **132.** | D |
| **100.** | C | **111.** | C | **122.** | D | **133.** | C |
| **101.** | C | **112.** | B | **123.** | C | **134.** | D |

# ANSWERS EXPLAINED

## Part 1: Vocabulary

1. **A** *Meliorate* means to help, mend or improve. *Insolent* means disrespectful, *gloomy* means depressed, and *fragile* means delicate.

2. **B** *Castigate* and *admonish* are synonymous with reprimand *Iniquitous* means immoral; *bide* means to wait; and, *aggravate* means to make worse.

3. **C** *Strident* means noisy and clamorous. The antonym or opposite is gentle and calm. *Spurious* means false; *arcane* means mysterious.

4. **C** In the first sentence the context of the word *bear* is used to mean sustain or hold the weight of. This is the same context as option C. In option A, the word *bear* means to bring forth. In option B, *bear* means suitable. In option D, *bear* means accept or assume.

5. **B** *Redacted* means sensitive information is removed, *Enacted* means something is performed or legislation is passed. *Dedacted* and *undacted* are not words.

6. **D** If the sentences are served *concurrently,* that means all sentences are being served simultaneously. *Austerely* means strictly; *pragmatically* means realistically; and, having to serve his sentences *consecutively* would mean sequentially—that his next sentence would not start until the previous sentence is served.

7. **C** The word *putative* means assumed or supposed *Pedantic* means unimaginative or boring. *Ostensible, reputed*, and *purported* are all synonymous with putative.

8. **A** *Bemused* means confused or baffled The correct word should have been *amused*. The other words were used in the correct context: *commiserate* means to empathize and sympathize; *meticulous* means fussy and attention to detail; and *recalcitrant* mean obstinate and headstrong.

9. **C** *Narcissistic* means egotistical and self-absorbed. *Eccentric* is not synonymous as it means unusual or strange.

10. **B** *Genial* means friendly and hospitable; therefore, an antonym for the word genial is inhospitable.

11. **D** Although *pedestrian* is usually used to reference people walking, especially in relation to traffic laws, it also means ordinary.

12. **B** *Affect* means to have an emotional impact on. The correct word should have been *effect*, which in this context means consequence. The other words were used in the correct context: *flout* means to disregard or disobey; *vehement* means intense; and an *enticement* means a bribe or incentive.

13. **C** An *allusion* is a suggestion or insinuation. The correct word should have been *illusion*, meaning misconception. The other words are used in the correct context: *compliment* means praise; *obstreperous* means rowdy; and a *misogynist* is a person who hates women.

14. **A** *Weary* means tired or exhausted. The correct word should have been *wary*, which means suspicious. The other words are used in the correct context: *acumen* means insight and discernment; *mitigate* means to lessen; and, *mollify* means to appease or soothe.

15. **D** *Naïve* means childlike and immature. *Knave* means a dishonest person; *neophyte* means a recruit or beginner; and *morose* means miserable or depressed.

16. **A** *Detract* means to lessen or diminish. *Deter* means to discourage; *distract* means to divert attention from something; and *debase* means to humiliate and demean.

17. **D** If a witness's story is *corroborated* by another witness, it goes towards substantiating the version of events. *Contradicted* and *refuted* are antonyms of corroborated *Enhanced* means improved.

18. **B** A *sequestered* jury means that they are kept separate and isolated. *Assimilated* mean integrated; *convalesced* means improved; and *subpoenaed* means required to appear in court as a witness.

19. **B** *Cognizant* means familiar or conscious. *Compliant* means obedient, and *ignorant* and *uncertain* are antonyms of cognizant.

20. **D** *Neurotic* behaviour is demonstrated as being fearful and anxious.

21. **A** *Pragmatic* means practical.

22. **D** *Inebriated* means intoxicated.

23. **C** *Veracity* means legitimacy.

24. **A** Although Constable Guy may have been insubordinate or subversive in avoiding the call, *blatant* means obvious.

25. **D** *Tangible* means perceptible and noticeable.

26. **B** *Premise* means proposition or inference. The correct word should have been premises. The other words are used in the correct context: *than* is used correctly, although sometimes confused with *then*; *lucid* means well-spoken and having all of one's faculties; and *malfeasance* means corrupt activity, especially by an elected official or corporation.

27. **A** *Acute* means a condition that rapidly worsens. The correct term should have been *chronic*, meaning persisting over time. The other words are used in the correct context: *obfuscate* means to confuse; *banal* means dull and commonplace; *loose* means the opposite of tight (lose means failing to win).

28. **C** *Infer* means to reach a conclusion, the correct word should have been *imply*, which means to suggest. The other words are used in the correct context: *milieu* means the environment or situation, *ostensibly* means apparently or allegedly, and *exacerbate* means to make worse.

29. **C** *Perpetrate* means to commit, as in perpetrating a crime. The correct word should have been *perpetuate*, which means to continue on. The other words are used in the correct context: a *contusion* is a bruise, *pejorative* comments are derogatory statements, and *officious* means being overbearing and judgmental.

30. **D** A *palate* is one's taste in food or the roof of the mouth. The correct word should have been *pallet*. The other words are used in the correct context: *Hangar* is a shelter (hanger is for clothes); *lie*, in this context, means to recline. It would have been incorrect to use *lay*, as it means to place something, and *tenure* means the amount of time a person holds a position.

31. **B** *Pare* means to trim or cut back.

32. **A** Despite its common misuse, *redundant* does not mean useless, it means exceeding what is necessary.

33. **D** *Epitome* means ideal example. *Idyllic* may also seem correct, but it means peaceful and relaxing.

34. **B** *Auspicious* means promising.

35. **D** *Esprit de corps* means morale.

36. **C** *Insure* means to obtain insurance or protection for something. The correct word should have been *ensure*, which means to confirm or safeguard. The other words are used in the correct context: *loath* means reluctant (*loathe* means despise); *broaching* means proposing or bringing forward; *audacity* means boldness.

37. **A** *Allude* means to make reference to something. The correct word should have been *elude*, which means to escape. The other words are used in the correct context: *candid* means honest and frank, in this context *epithet* means a nickname, and, *stoic* means tolerant.

38. **D** *Boorish* means rude and impolite; the antonym is well-mannered.

39. **D** *Destitute* means impoverished. *Obtuse* means simple-minded, a *miscreant* is a troublemaker, and *opulent* means wealthy.

40. **B** *Placated* means calmed and pacified. The other terms are not appropriate: *negated* means cancelled, *exhorted* means encouraged, and *exasperated* means infuriated.

## Part 2: Spelling

41. **C** Correct spelling: *resistance*. Learn to differentiate between words ending in *ance* and *ence*.

42. **B** Correct spelling: *advantageous*. If the root word ends in *ce* or *ge* and the consonant is "soft," then the *e* is retained.

43. **A** Correct spelling: *continuous*. When adding a suffix that begins with a vowel or *y* to a root word that ends with an "e", drop the *e* before adding the suffix. *Centre* is the correct Canadian spelling.

44. **C** Correct spelling: *legislation*. Some nouns do not change between the singular and plural: legislation, luggage, deer, and wood are but a few.

45. **D** Correct spelling: *convertible*. It is one of the top 50 common words with suffix ending in *ible*.

46. **A** Correct spelling: *consensus*. Both *benefitted* and *benefited* are accepted spellings of the word.

47. **B** Correct spelling: *totalled* The Canadian spelling of root words that end with the consonants *l* or *p* and are preceded by a vowel double the final consonant when adding a suffix that begins with a vowel.

48. **C** Correct spelling: *notable*. When the root word ends with an *e*, whether the *e* needs to be dropped or not, the ending of the word is spelled with *able*.

49. **A** Correct spelling: *proceed*. There are only three verbs that end with "ceed": exceed, proceed, and succeed.

50. **C** Correct spelling: *trailed*. If there is more than one vowel before the final consonant, do not double the last consonant.

51. **B** Correct spelling: *likeable*. If the root word ends with an *e*, whether the *e* needs to be dropped or not, the ending of the word is spelled with *able*.

52. **A** Correct spelling: *intolerance*. If the root word is from a verb that ends in *ate*, then the ending of the word is spelled with *ance*.

53. **D** Correct spelling: *vacillate*. When a word has more than one syllable, and the final syllable is stressed in speech, then the final consonant needs to be doubled. *Acknowledgement* is the correct Canadian spelling.

54. **B** Correct spelling: *theories*. If the noun ends in a *y* and is preceded by a consonant, add *ies*.

55. **D** Correct spelling: *complacence*. If the root word ends with a soft *ce* or *ge* then the ending of the word is spelled with *ence*.

56. **B** Correct spelling: *heist*. Exception to *i* before *e* rule; when the *i* and *e* combination make a long *i* sound.

57. **A** Correct spelling: *collapsible*. One of seven words that are exceptions to rule that if the root word ends with an *e*, whether the *e* needs to be dropped or not, the ending of the word is spelled with *able*.

58. **B** Correct spelling: *inconsistencies*. The root word *inconsistent* ends with *ent*.

59. **C** Correct spelling: *dependable*. If the root word is able to stand on its own as a complete word, then the ending of the word is spelled with *able*.

60. **D** Correct spelling: *leisure*. General exception to the *i* before *e* rule.

61. **C** Correct spelling: *truly*. The *e* is dropped before adding *ly*. One of the top 200 commonly misspelled words.

62. **A** Correct spelling: *perseverance*. Exception to the rule that if the root word is from a verb that ends in *ere*, then the ending of the word is spelled with *ence*.

63. **C** Correct spelling: *dilapidated*.

64. **B** Correct spelling: *digestible*. One of the few exceptions to the rule that when the root word is able to stand on its own as a complete word, then the ending of the word is spelled with *able*.

65. **D** No errors.

66. **A** Correct spelling: *irritable*. One of the top 200 commonly misspelled words.

67. **C** Correct spelling: *forfeit*. Exception to the *i* before *e* rule; when the *i* is used as an unstressed vowel.

68. **D** No errors. *Analyses* is correct. When making a singular word (*analysis*) plural, Greek root words that end in *is* change to *es*.

69. **D** No errors. *Travelled* and *Centre* are correct Canadian spellings. *Center* is the correct American spelling.

70. **B** Correct spelling: *apparently*. One of the top 200 commonly misspelled words.

71. **D** No errors. However, *exceed* is often misspelled.

72. **C** Exception to *i* before *e* rule; when the *i* and *e* combination make a long *a* sound.

73. **A** Correct spelling: *sufficient*. Exception to the *i* before *e* except after *c* rule.

74. **D** No errors.

75. **B** Correct spelling: *consensus*. One of the top 200 commonly misspelled words.

76. **B** Correct spelling: *stimuli*. Latin root words that end in *us*, change to *i*.

77. **D** Correct spelling: *mothers-in-law*. For compound nouns, the first word is made plural.

78. **A** Correct spelling: *susceptible*. One of the top 50 common words with suffix ending in *ible*.

79. **C** Correct spelling: *Sheriff*. *Sherriff* is only a family surname in the English language.

80. **D** Correct spelling: *zeroes*. When making a noun that ends with an *o* plural, add *es*.

81. **B** Correct spelling: *exhilarate*. One of the top 200 commonly misspelled words.

82. **C** Correct spelling: *mischiefs*. Exception to the rule that if the noun ends in *f* or *fe*, change to *ves*.

83. **A** Correct spelling: *fluoride*. One of the top 200 commonly misspelled words.

84. **B** Correct spelling: *withhold*. One of the top 200 commonly misspelled words.

85. **A** Correct spelling: *monitor*. *Litre* is the correct Canadian spelling.

86. **A** Correct spelling: *renowned*. *Renowned* means famous. One of the top 200 commonly misspelled words.

87. **B** Correct spelling: *blistering*. If the root word has more than one syllable and the stress does not fall on the last syllable, do not double the final consonant.

88. **D** No errors. However, *anomaly* is often misspelled.

89. **C** Correct spelling: *supersede*. This is the only *ceed*-sounding word that ends with *sede*.

90. **C** Correct spelling: *advantageous*. If the root word ends in *ce* or *ge* and the consonant is *soft*, then the *e* is retained.

## Part 3: Grammar

91. **C** Maintain parallelism—*am taking, am wearing*.

92. **B** People lose faith *in* something.

93. **A** Simple past tense.

94. **B** Past tense of *swing*.

95. **D** Future perfect tense of *run*.

96. **A** The number of women is *increasing*.

97. **B** *Their*—possessive form of *they*.

98. **C** *Studies*—the plural form of *study*.

99. **D** *Everyone* is a singular indefinite pronoun, in the role of an antecedent. That is, the third person possessive pronoun (i.e., *his* or *her*) referring to it must be singular as well.

100. **C** You have confidence *in* something.

101. **C** Use a comma when you join two clauses with a coordinating conjunction (e.g., *and, but, nor, for*). The comma appears before the coordinating conjunction, not after.

102. **D** Option A is incorrect: the clause *before they went on the road* is misplaced.

Option B is incorrect: *constables* should be *constable's*—to show possession.

Option C is incorrect: the clause *even before they went on the road* should not follow the inventory list.

103. **D** Option A is incorrect: the word *neither* should be followed in the sentence by *nor*.

Option B is incorrect: *me* should be *I*. *I* is the first person singular subject pronoun and refers to the person performing the action of a verb.

Option C is incorrect: *were* should be *was*. If two singular subjects are connected by *either, neither, or,* or *nor*, then the verb is singular.

104. **B** Option A is incorrect: *officers* needs to show possession with an apostrophe (i.e., *officers'*).

Option C is incorrect: *it's* means it is, the correct term is *its*, in order to show possession.

Option D is incorrect: *officer's* should be plural.

105. **C** Option A is incorrect: the subject is plural; therefore, the form of *to be* must also be plural—*are*.

Option B is incorrect: The word *motive* means the reason, cause, or purpose. The clause is stating the *method* of reducing fatalities.

Option D is incorrect: The word *means'* should not have the possessive apostrophe.

106. **A** Option A is the most grammatically correct because *various* precedes *technologies*, making the noun plural; *investigations* is also plural; and *crime rate* is referred to in the singular form.

107. **D** Option D is the most grammatically correct because *I* is the first person singular subject pronoun and refers to the person going to make the arrest. In this case, *effect* is a transitive verb meaning to accomplish or to put into operation.

108. **A** Option A is the most grammatically correct because parallel structure is maintained throughout. Also, when *neither* is used, it is to be followed by *nor*.

109. **D** Option D is the most grammatically correct. First, the subject is plural (*salary and benefits*); therefore, the verb must also be plural (i.e., *are*). The preposition *among* means in the company of. The preposition *between* means by the common action of, or in comparison to. Therefore, *among* is grammatically correct.

110. **B** Option B is the most grammatically correct. First, *staff* is a collective noun, which is referred to in the singular form. Second, *onset* is one word, and a *personal issue* is a private one; a *personnel issue* is a staffing and human resource issue.

111. **C** Option A is incorrect: the semicolon is not required.

    Option B is incorrect: the verb *makes* should be plural not singular.

    Option D is incorrect: the colon, if used, is in the wrong part of the sentence, and *makes* should be *make*.

112. **B** Option A is incorrect: *whoever* should have been *whomever* since it is the subject of the verb *awarded*. A semicolon is also required before the conjunctive adverb *however*.

    Option C is incorrect: the colon is not to be used to separate an independent and dependent clause.

    Option D is incorrect: the dash should only be used in a parenthetic manner, which it is not.

113. **A** Option B is incorrect: there was only one stated purpose for the conference—*purpose*, not *purposes*.

    Option C is incorrect: *was*, not *where*.

    Option D is incorrect: *agencies*, not *agencies'*.

114. **C** Option A is incorrect: the question is *who has* been assigned not *whose*.

    Option B is incorrect: *who has*, not *whose* and *there are*, not *their*.

    Option D is incorrect: faulty parallelism—should be *who has* been assigned and *who are* the detectives reporting to.

115. **B** Option A is incorrect: the connecting words *not only* should immediately precede the parallel element—*important*.

    Option C is incorrect: missing the connecting words… *but also*.

    Option D is incorrect: connecting word not preceding the parallel element and missing … *but also*.

116. **C** It is not clear who *their* is referring to; therefore, the pronoun should not be used.

117. **A** Capitalize the first word of a direct quote that is a complete sentence.

118. **A** *Arose* is the past tense of *arise*; parallel structure maintained throughout sentence.

119. **C** *Were sleeping* is changed to *slept* in order to maintain parallel structure of the sentence.

120. **A** Subjunctive mood refers to clauses where one is expressing wishes or desires or conditions that are false or unlikely. In these instances use *were* instead of *was*.

121. **B** *Almost* is a misplaced modifier; it should be placed as close to *twelve years* as possible.

122. **D** The sentence is grammatically correct. Specifically, organizations are referred to in the singular, not plural.

123. **C** Maintains parallel structure with *would have offered*.

124. **B** The colon is used to introduce a list, statement, or quotation; on the other hand, the semicolon, in this case, is used to link two independent clauses of equal grammatical rank.

125. **B** The term is to *impress on* (or upon) someone, not *in*.

126. **C** The sentence contains faulty parallelism if the final clause is not changed to *by their example*.

127. **B** The use of the third person pronoun *they* is too vague to be certain who the term is referring to.

128. **D** The sentence is grammatically correct. Specifically, seasons should not be capitalized, whereas names of teams and projects are.

129. **A** *Irregardless* is not a word Also, the *crime rate* is referred to in the singular.

130. **C** *That* introduces essential clauses, meaning that if no other words were to follow, it would be an incomplete sentence. Conversely, *which* introduces nonessential clauses, meaning the clause adds additional information but is not essential to forming the sentence.

131. **B** Option A is incorrect: a semicolon needs to be used to separate items in a series of items where commas are used for each person's title.

    Option C is incorrect in that the Director responsible for inviting the guests should not be stated parenthetically.

    Option D is incorrect: the sentence is written out of order.

132. **D** Option A is incorrect: the pronoun must not change its reference in the same sentence from *one* to *you*.

    Option B is incorrect: a colon, not a comma, is required to introduce a statement.

    Option C is incorrect: it is not the academy's message that was·clear, but the instructor's.

133. **C** Option A is incorrect: if two singular subjects are connected by *either* then the verb is singular.

    Option B is incorrect: *were* should be *where*.

    Option D is incorrect: multiple errors including *wear* should be *where*.

134. **D** Option A is incorrect: comma should be a semicolon used to connect two independent clauses of equal grammatical rank that are related in meaning.

    Option B is incorrect: organizations are referred to in the singular—the pronoun *they* should be *it*.

    Option C is incorrect: the colon is not for connecting independent clauses.

# Model Exam Two: Ontario's Police Analytical Thinking Inventory (PATI)

The Police Analytical Thinking Inventory (PATI) focuses on analytical thinking and assesses three main competencies: deductive reasoning, evaluated through syllogisms and travel time tasks; inductive reasoning, measured through classification and series completion tasks; and quantitative reasoning, assessed through general arithmetic questions and word problems.

There are 90 questions in total, and you will have 90 minutes to complete the entire exam. The exam is divided into six sections, with 15 questions in each section. The amount of time allowed per section is a reasonable approximation of the time allowed for each section during the PATI exam.

| ONTARIO PATI FORMAT | | | |
|---|---|---|---|
| **SECTION** | **COMPETENCY** | **QUESTIONS** | **TIME ALLOWED** |
| Part 1-1 | Travel Time | 15 | 15 minutes |
| Part 1-2 | Syllogisms | 15 | 15 minutes |
| Part 2-1 | Classification | 15 | 10 minutes |
| Part 2-2 | Pattern Series | 15 | 10 minutes |
| Part 3-1 | Arithmetic | 15 | 15 minutes |
| Part 3-2 | Word Problems | 15 | 25 minutes |
| | Total | **90** | **1.5 hours** |

# ANSWER SHEET
## Model Exam Two

### PART 1-1: Travel Time

1. (A) (B) (C) (D)    5. (A) (B) (C) (D)    9. (A) (B) (C) (D)    13. (A) (B) (C) (D)
2. (A) (B) (C) (D)    6. (A) (B) (C) (D)    10. (A) (B) (C) (D)   14. (A) (B) (C) (D)
3. (A) (B) (C) (D)    7. (A) (B) (C) (D)    11. (A) (B) (C) (D)   15. (A) (B) (C) (D)
4. (A) (B) (C) (D)    8. (A) (B) (C) (D)    12. (A) (B) (C) (D)

### PART 1-2: Syllogisms

16. (A) (B) (C) (D)   20. (A) (B) (C) (D)   24. (A) (B) (C) (D)   28. (A) (B) (C) (D)
17. (A) (B) (C) (D)   21. (A) (B) (C) (D)   25. (A) (B) (C) (D)   29. (A) (B) (C) (D)
18. (A) (B) (C) (D)   22. (A) (B) (C) (D)   26. (A) (B) (C) (D)   30. (A) (B) (C) (D)
19. (A) (B) (C) (D)   23. (A) (B) (C) (D)   27. (A) (B) (C) (D)

### PART 2-1: Classification

31. (A) (B) (C) (D)   35. (A) (B) (C) (D)   39. (A) (B) (C) (D)   43. (A) (B) (C) (D)
32. (A) (B) (C) (D)   36. (A) (B) (C) (D)   40. (A) (B) (C) (D)   44. (A) (B) (C) (D)
33. (A) (B) (C) (D)   37. (A) (B) (C) (D)   41. (A) (B) (C) (D)   45. (A) (B) (C) (D)
34. (A) (B) (C) (D)   38. (A) (B) (C) (D)   42. (A) (B) (C) (D)

### PART 2-2: Pattern Series

46. (A) (B) (C) (D)   50. (A) (B) (C) (D)   54. (A) (B) (C) (D)   58. (A) (B) (C) (D)
47. (A) (B) (C) (D)   51. (A) (B) (C) (D)   55. (A) (B) (C) (D)   59. (A) (B) (C) (D)
48. (A) (B) (C) (D)   52. (A) (B) (C) (D)   56. (A) (B) (C) (D)   60. (A) (B) (C) (D)
49. (A) (B) (C) (D)   53. (A) (B) (C) (D)   57. (A) (B) (C) (D)

## PART 3-1: Arithmetic

61. Ⓐ Ⓑ Ⓒ Ⓓ   65. Ⓐ Ⓑ Ⓒ Ⓓ   69. Ⓐ Ⓑ Ⓒ Ⓓ   73. Ⓐ Ⓑ Ⓒ Ⓓ
62. Ⓐ Ⓑ Ⓒ Ⓓ   66. Ⓐ Ⓑ Ⓒ Ⓓ   70. Ⓐ Ⓑ Ⓒ Ⓓ   74. Ⓐ Ⓑ Ⓒ Ⓓ
63. Ⓐ Ⓑ Ⓒ Ⓓ   67. Ⓐ Ⓑ Ⓒ Ⓓ   71. Ⓐ Ⓑ Ⓒ Ⓓ   75. Ⓐ Ⓑ Ⓒ Ⓓ
64. Ⓐ Ⓑ Ⓒ Ⓓ   68. Ⓐ Ⓑ Ⓒ Ⓓ   72. Ⓐ Ⓑ Ⓒ Ⓓ

## PART 3-2: Word Problems

76. Ⓐ Ⓑ Ⓒ Ⓓ   80. Ⓐ Ⓑ Ⓒ Ⓓ   84. Ⓐ Ⓑ Ⓒ Ⓓ   88. Ⓐ Ⓑ Ⓒ Ⓓ
77. Ⓐ Ⓑ Ⓒ Ⓓ   81. Ⓐ Ⓑ Ⓒ Ⓓ   85. Ⓐ Ⓑ Ⓒ Ⓓ   89. Ⓐ Ⓑ Ⓒ Ⓓ
78. Ⓐ Ⓑ Ⓒ Ⓓ   82. Ⓐ Ⓑ Ⓒ Ⓓ   86. Ⓐ Ⓑ Ⓒ Ⓓ   90. Ⓐ Ⓑ Ⓒ Ⓓ
79. Ⓐ Ⓑ Ⓒ Ⓓ   83. Ⓐ Ⓑ Ⓒ Ⓓ   87. Ⓐ Ⓑ Ⓒ Ⓓ

# PART 1-1: TRAVEL TIME

 **You have 15 minutes to complete the following 15 questions.**

The travel time chart below represents 25 city blocks. Each horizontal and vertical line denotes one block of a two-way road. Though you may only travel on the roadways, unless one of the questions below specifies otherwise, you may travel by car or bicycle, engage in a foot pursuit, or walk on any of these roads. You may use any combination of travel modes while en route from one point to another, except to transfer from car to bicycle and vice versa. The time required to travel an entire block varies according to mode of transportation:

- Police car: 1 minute
- Bicycle: 2 minutes
- Foot pursuit/running: 3 minutes
- Walking: 5 minutes

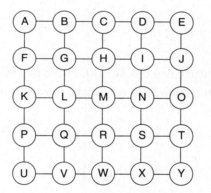

**Travel Time Chart**

1. What is the shortest amount of time it would take to travel from B to M?

    (A) 2 minutes
    (B) 3 minutes
    (C) 5 minutes
    (D) 6 minutes

2. What is the shortest amount of time it would take to travel from P to J?

    (A) 4 minutes
    (B) 6 minutes
    (C) 8 minutes
    (D) 10 minutes

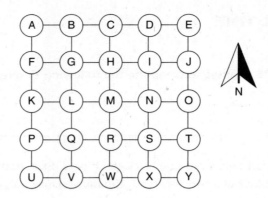

3. Using any method or combination of methods, what is the shortest amount of time it would take to travel from A to Y, without passing through intersections E or U?

(A) 6 minutes
(B) 7 minutes
(C) 8 minutes
(D) 9 minutes

4. You are at S when you receive a call of a woman in distress screaming for help at C. Unfortunately, roads are completely closed, except to pedestrians, between G and J inclusive. What is the shortest amount of time it would take to travel from S to C?

(A) 4 minutes
(B) 5 minutes
(C) 6 minutes
(D) 8 minutes

5. If you were at R and were to drive two blocks north, then two blocks east, and then walk from that intersection to T, how long will it take to walk from that point to T?

(A) 10 minutes
(B) 14 minutes
(C) 16 minutes
(D) 20 minutes

6. A car rally was held, and the teams started at E and then had to stop, in sequential order, at checkpoints A and R, and then finished at L. If a car had to stop at each checkpoint for two minutes, how long would it take to complete the race?

(A) 19 minutes
(B) 18 minutes
(C) 17 minutes
(D) 15 minutes

7. A suspect is running west from Y. A police officer is on his bicycle a K. If the suspect continues running west, the police officer, at the earliest, could intercept the suspect at intersection

(A) W
(B) V
(C) U
(D) None of the above

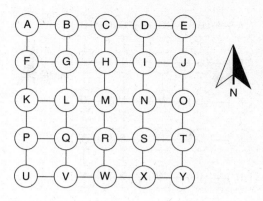

8. Officer Charles was at R when he began pursuing a purse snatch suspect north on his bicycle. After two blocks, the chain came off, and he abandoned the bike and continued east, pursuing the suspect on foot. He eventually caught the suspect at E. How long did it take to catch the purse snatcher?

   (A) 10 minutes
   (B) 13 minutes
   (C) 15 minutes
   (D) 17 minutes

9. There is a tanker gas leak and a large area has been cordoned off from C to M to O. The supervisor is in his car at U and needs to get to the command post at E; he may only get there by walking through the perimeter barricades. How long would it take to get to E?

   (A) 20 minutes
   (B) 18 minutes
   (C) 16 minutes
   (D) 14 minutes

10. The search team was checking all of the businesses in a large area for video evidence from the homicide. The members started at Q and canvassed two blocks north, then three blocks east. Each block they walked took four more minutes than usual. They were then picked up in a van and driven back to their starting point. How long was the trip in total?

    (A) 50 minutes
    (B) 55 minutes
    (C) 60 minutes
    (D) 65 minutes

11. Constable Jones was attempting to find a new jogging route. He started at M, ran one block west, two blocks south, one block west again, then one block north. If he took the quickest route from there back to M, what would be his total jogging time?

    (A) 18 minutes
    (B) 21 minutes
    (C) 24 minutes
    (D) 27 minutes

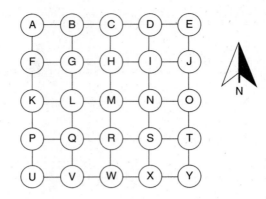

12. Constable Lee was at W and walked to F. From there he rode his bicycle to E. How long would the total trip take?

(A) 25 minutes

(B) 35 minutes

(C) 45 minutes

(D) None of the above

13. Constable Sanderson was in her car at F and was dispatched to a collision at J. Unfortunately, the roads are closed between D and S inclusive. If you must add an extra 1.5 minutes for every turn she makes, what is the minimum length of time it will take her to get to J?

(A) 17 minutes

(B) 10 minutes

(C) 14.5 minutes

(D) 13 minutes

14. Constable Bob is in his car at T; there is an emergency at E requiring several units. The road is closed between G and J inclusive. Constable Jim is at K responding by bicycle. Each turn, either by car or bicycle adds 1.5 minutes to their response time. What is quickest time that either of them could get to E?

(A) 12 minutes

(B) 13 minutes

(C) 14 minutes

(D) None of the above

15. You are required to stop and hand out leaflets for a missing child at every intersection in a square area between U–K–M–W–U. Add three minutes for every intersection that you must stop at. What is the total time if travelling by car?

(A) 45

(B) 35

(C) 32

(D) None of the above

## PART 1-2: SYLLOGISMS

 You have 15 minutes to complete the following 15 questions.

> Syllogisms are a form of deductive reasoning in which a logical conclusion is supported by two premise statements. For each question, you are provided with a major premise (first statement) and a minor premise (second statement). You must assume that each statement is true (even if you know otherwise). Only one of the four conclusion statements is valid based on the first two statements.

16. Some police officers are grey.

    All greys are human.

    (A) Therefore, some police officers are human.
    (B) Therefore, some greys are police officers.
    (C) Therefore, some greys are not human.
    (D) No valid conclusion.

17. All police reports are boring.

    All boring things are educational.

    (A) Therefore, all education things are police reports.
    (B) Therefore, not all police reports are boring.
    (C) Therefore, all police reports are educational.
    (D) No valid conclusion.

18. All police officers are brave persons.

    No brave person is made of glass.

    (A) Therefore, some things made of glass are police officers.
    (B) Therefore, no police officers are made of glass.
    (C) Therefore, not all brave persons are made of glass.
    (D) No valid conclusion.

19. Some police officers are people who stay fit.

    Some people who stay fit do not like lawyers.

    (A) Therefore, no police officers like lawyers.
    (B) Therefore, some police officers do not like lawyers.
    (C) Therefore, some lawyers stay fit.
    (D) No valid conclusion.

20. Some laws are based on moral values.

   All moral values reflect religious teachings.

   (A) Therefore, some laws reflect religious teachings.
   (B) Therefore, some moral values are not based on laws.
   (C) Therefore, some laws are not based on religious teachings.
   (D) No valid conclusion.

21. Some law abiding citizens break the law.

   No one who breaks the law is honest.

   (A) Therefore, some law abiding citizens break the law.
   (B) Therefore, some law abiding citizens are not honest.
   (C) Therefore, some dishonest citizens are not law abiding.
   (D) No valid conclusion.

22. All people who wear blue are patrol officers.

   Some people who wear blue like turtles.

   (A) Therefore, some people who wear blue like patrol officers.
   (B) Therefore, some people who like turtles are not patrol officers.
   (C) Therefore, some patrol officers like turtles.
   (D) No valid conclusion.

23. No man is perfect.

   Some men are judges.

   (A) Therefore, some judges are perfect.
   (B) Therefore, some men are not judges.
   (C) Therefore, some judges are not perfect.
   (D) No valid conclusion.

24. No firearm is safe.

   All guns are firearms.

   (A) Therefore, some guns are not safe.
   (B) Therefore, all firearms are not guns.
   (C) Therefore, all guns are not safe.
   (D) No valid conclusion.

25. No police officers are priests.

   No priests are poor.

   (A) Therefore, no police officers are poor.
   (B) Therefore, some police officers are not poor.
   (C) Therefore, no poor person is a police officer.
   (D) No valid conclusion.

26. Some police training involves firearms training.

    All firearms training requires annual qualification.

    (A) Therefore, some firearms training involves police.
    (B) Therefore, some police training does not involve firearms training.
    (C) Therefore, some police training requires annual qualification.
    (D) No valid conclusion.

27. All people who fail to pay traffic fines are referred to the traffic judge.

    All referrals to the traffic judge result in a traffic bench warrant.

    (A) Therefore, all people who fail to pay traffic fines result in a traffic bench warrant.
    (B) Therefore, all referrals to the traffic judge are for people who fail to pay traffic fines.
    (C) Therefore, some people who fail to pay traffic fines will result in a traffic bench warrant.
    (D) No valid conclusion.

28. No marijuana is a stimulant.

    Some stimulants are illegal.

    (A) Therefore, some marijuana is illegal.
    (B) Therefore, all marijuana is illegal.
    (C) Therefore, some illegal things are not marijuana.
    (D) No valid conclusion.

29. No police motorcycle is a truck.

    Some Fords are trucks.

    (A) Therefore, some police motorcycles are not Fords.
    (B) Therefore, no Ford is a police motorcycle.
    (C) Therefore, some Fords are not police motorcycles.
    (D) No valid conclusion.

30. Some police officers are not trained in handcuffing procedures.

    No training in handcuff procedures will occur this year.

    (A) Therefore, some police officers will not be trained this year.
    (B) Therefore, no police officers will be trained this year.
    (C) Therefore, some police officers will not be trained in handcuffing procedures this year.
    (D) No valid conclusion.

# PART 2-1: CLASSIFICATION

 **You have 10 minutes to complete the following 15 questions.**

In this section, you are shown four figures and shapes. Three of the images have characteristics that are consistent enough that they can be classified together and one of the images will be significantly different that it cannot be classified with the other three. Identify which image cannot be classified with the others.

31. Select the image that is not the same suspect

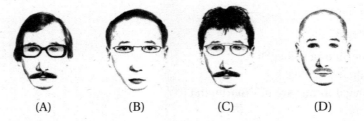

(A)      (B)      (C)      (D)

32. Select the number that does not belong.

| 28 | 13 | 26 | 50 |
|----|----|----|----|
| (A) | (B) | (C) | (D) |

33. Select the shape that does not belong.

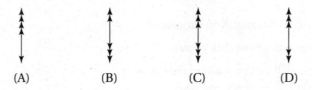

(A)      (B)      (C)      (D)

34. Select the shape that does not belong.

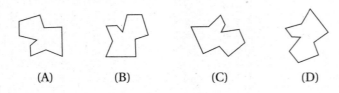

(A)      (B)      (C)      (D)

35. Select the word that does not belong.

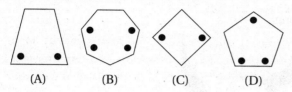

| Lemon | Mango | Orange | Lime |
|:---:|:---:|:---:|:---:|
| (A) | (B) | (C) | (D) |

36. Select the shape that does not belong.

(A)   (B)   (C)   (D)

37. Select the word that does not belong.

| Steel | Nickel | Silver | Copper |
|:---:|:---:|:---:|:---:|
| (A) | (B) | (C) | (D) |

38. Select the image that is not the same suspect.

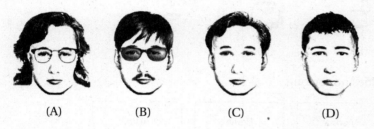

(A)   (B)   (C)   (D)

39. Select the shape that does not belong.

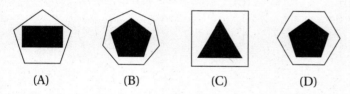

(A)   (B)   (C)   (D)

40. Select the number that does not belong.

| 0 | 3 | 5 | 7 |
|:---:|:---:|:---:|:---:|
| (A) | (B) | (C) | (D) |

41. Select the shape that does not belong.

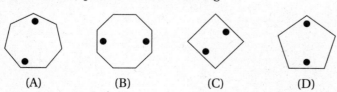

(A)   (B)   (C)   (D)

42. Select the shape that does not belong.

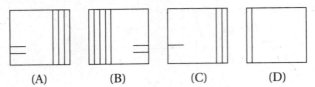

(A)        (B)        (C)        (D)

43. Select the shape that does not belong.

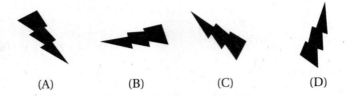

(A)        (B)        (C)        (D)

44. Select the image that is not the same suspect.

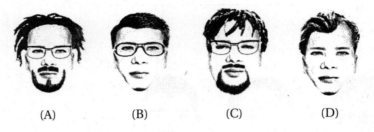

(A)        (B)        (C)        (D)

45. Select the city that does not belong.

| London | Vienna | Berlin | Milan |

(A)        (B)        (C)        (D)

# PART 2-2: PATTERN SERIES

 You have 10 minutes to complete the following 15 questions.

In this section you are required to identify common characteristics found in a series of visual shapes or numbers. From the four options, select the object or value that continues the pattern series.

46. Select the image that continues the pattern sequence.

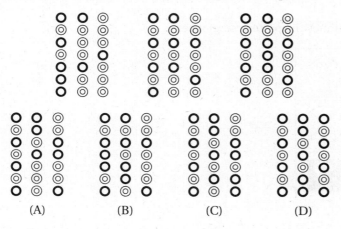

(A)     (B)     (C)     (D)

47. Select the image that continues the pattern sequence.

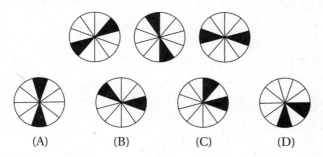

(A)     (B)     (C)     (D)

48. Select the image that continues the pattern sequence.

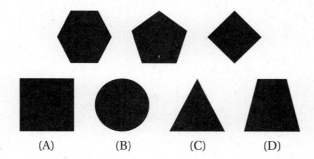

(A)     (B)     (C)     (D)

49. Select the number that continues the pattern sequence.

4, 9, 13, 22, 35,

(A) 42

(B) 57

(C) 74

(D) 81

50. Select the letter that continues the pattern sequence.

C, E, H, L, Q,

(A) S

(B) A

(C) X

(D) W

51. Select the image that continues the pattern sequence.

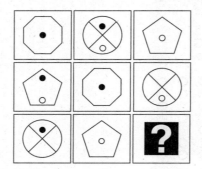

52. Select the image that continues the pattern sequence.

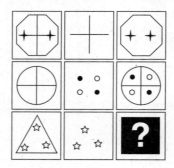

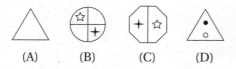

53. Select the image that continues the pattern sequence.

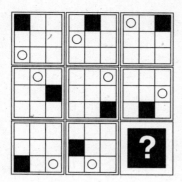

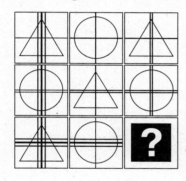

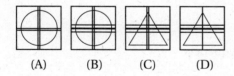

(A)        (B)        (C)        (D)

54. Select the image that continues the pattern sequence.

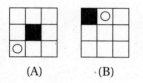

(A)        (B)        (C)        (D)

55. Select the image that continues the pattern sequence.

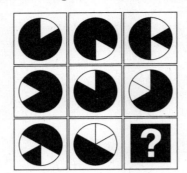

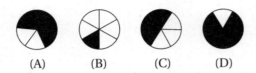

    (A)     (B)     (C)     (D)

56. Select the number that continues the pattern sequence.

2, 4, 10, 28, 82,

(A) 168
(B) 208
(C) 244
(D) 296

57. Select the letter that continues the pattern sequence.

U, S, P, L, G,

(A) A
(B) E
(C) O
(D) U

58. Select the image that continues the pattern sequence.

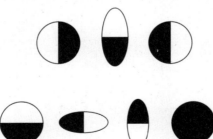

    (A)     (B)     (C)     (D)

59. Select the image that continues the pattern sequence.

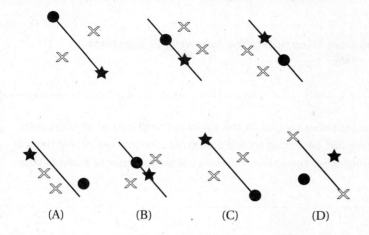

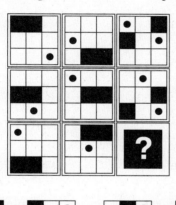

(A)       (B)       (C)       (D)

60. Select the image that continues the pattern sequence.

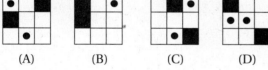

(A)       (B)       (C)       (D)

## PART 3-1: ARITHMETIC

 You have 15 minutes to complete the following 15 questions.

The first part of the quantitative section of the exam is comprised of general arithmetic questions. You are not permitted to use a calculator or any electronic device to assist you in answering these questions. You may use scrap paper to assist in your calculations.

61. What is the sum of $\frac{3}{7} + 3\frac{1}{3}$ ?

    (A) $4\frac{5}{16}$

    (B) $3\frac{8}{21}$

    (C) $4\frac{4}{21}$

    (D) $3\frac{16}{21}$

62. What is the product of $-13.34 \times 8.2$ ?

    (A) 103. 78

    (B) −109.388

    (C) 108.368

    (D) −106.28

63. Solve $37.9 + 98 \div 7 - 13.74$.

    (A) 38.16

    (B) 5.674

    (C) 20.163

    (D) 37.846

64. Find the quotient of $141.904 \div 5.6$.

    (A) 23.214

    (B) 29.624

    (C) 25.34

    (D) 24.944

65. Solve $6\frac{2}{9} - 4\frac{13}{18}$ .

   (A)  $2\frac{11}{18}$

   (B)  $1\frac{1}{2}$

   (C)  $1\frac{2}{3}$

   (D)  $1\frac{4}{9}$

66. What is $2\frac{6}{7}$ divided by $\frac{1}{8}$?

   (A)  $22\frac{6}{7}$

   (B)  $2\frac{7}{15}$

   (C)  $2\frac{55}{56}$

   (D) 4

67. What is the sum of $2(14 + (4 \times 6) - (33 \div 3))$?

   (A) 36

   (B) 27

   (C) 54

   (D) 48

68. Solve for $y$. $\frac{2}{3}y = 86$ .

   (A) 80

   (B) 96

   (C) 112

   (D) 129

69. Find the sum of $\frac{5}{8} - \frac{5}{12} + \frac{2}{3}$.

   (A)  $2\frac{3}{8}$

   (B)  $\frac{7}{8}$

   (C) 1

   (D)  $\frac{13}{16}$

70. Solve for the variable $y$. $6(y - 8) + 3 = 33$.

   (A) 13

   (B) −13

   (C) 19

   (D)  $\frac{11}{33}$

71. What is the value of $y$? $\frac{2}{11}y - 9 = 12$ .

   (A) 12
   (B) 23
   (C) 77
   (D) 69

72. What is 70 percent of 130?

   (A) 88
   (B) 89
   (C) 90
   (D) 91

73. What is the sum $4^3 + 5^3$ ?

   (A) $9^3$
   (B) $9^6$
   (C) 189
   (D) 209

74. What is the product of $5\frac{5}{7} \times 9\frac{3}{8}$ ?

   (A) $45\frac{15}{56}$
   (B) $47\frac{5}{8}$
   (C) $53\frac{4}{7}$
   (D) $48\frac{9}{52}$

75. What is the product of $-4.3 \times -8.04$?

   (A) −35.472
   (B) 3.457
   (C) 34.572
   (D) −34.572

## PART 3-2: WORD PROBLEMS

 **You have 25 minutes to complete the following 15 questions.**

In this section, you are asked word problems that require you to properly construct and solve an equation based on the information provided. You are not permitted to use a calculator or any electronic device to assist you in answering these questions. You may use scrap paper to assist in your calculations.

76. The police department bought a new car fleet of vehicles that cost $32,000 each. By the end of the first year, the vehicles had depreciated 25 percent. What was the value of each vehicle at the end of the year?

    (A) $28,000
    (B) $26,500
    (C) $25,000
    (D) $24,000

77. Constable Lawrence is paid $28 per hour. She worked her usual 12-hour shift, but then worked an additional 4 hours of overtime. Her first hour was paid at time-and-a-half, and the remaining 3 hours were paid at double time. At the end of her 16-hour shift, what was Constable Lawrence's gross pay?

    (A) $644
    (B) $546
    (C) $504
    (D) $368

78. Two years ago there were 32 homicides in the city. Last year, there were 41. What is the approximate percentage increase in homicides?

    (A) 78%
    (B) 46%
    (C) 28%
    (D) 22%

79. As a fitness incentive, the city provided interest-free loans to be used towards the purchase of bicycles. Constable Scott McKay bought a bike for $1,592, and was able to repay the loan in 12 monthly installments. What was the approximate value of each payment?

    (A) $132
    (B) $136
    (C) $142
    (D) $148

80. Over the past four years, the Searock Island Police Foundation has been raising money to purchase additional equipment for its police department. The nonprofit society raised $43,362, $37,987, and $24,092 the last three years, respectively. What is the average yearly amount of money raised?

(A) $32,988
(B) $33,464
(C) $34,589
(D) $35,147

81. Pickpocket "Fast Eddy" can sprint 200 metres in 31 seconds. What is Eddy's approximate speed in kilometres per hour?

(A) 25 km/h
(B) 21 km/h
(C) 32 km/h
(D) 24 km/h

82. Sam was convicted of drug importation and sentenced to 10 years in prison. All federally sentenced offenders are released on Mandatory Supervision after two-thirds of their sentence. Sam spent two years in jail while awaiting trial prior to his conviction and received a credit of two days for every day spent in pretrial custody. How many years before Sam would be released on Mandatory Supervision?

(A) 4 years
(B) $5\frac{1}{2}$ years
(C) 6 years
(D) 7 years

83. There are 67 constables, 7 sergeants, 2 staff sergeants, and 1 inspector working at a small detachment. What is the probability that a sergeant would be randomly selected to participate in an employee satisfaction survey.

(A) 7:67
(B) 1:11
(C) 7:11
(D) 1:7

84. Constable Fisher was conducting speed enforcement and stopped a vehicle travelling at 120 km/h. How many metres per second was the vehicle travelling at?

(A) 72 m/s
(B) 52 m/s
(C) 33 m/s
(D) 27 m/s

85. The drug squad located a storage locker in the warehouse district that was $\frac{2}{3}$ full to the ceiling with bulk marijuana. Considering that the storage space measured 2 metres wide × 4 metres deep × 3 metres high, how many cubic meters of space did the marijuana occupy?

(A) 32 m³
(B) 24 m³
(C) 16 m³
(D) 12 m³

86. Dog handler Glendale and her police service dog tracked a suspect for $1\frac{1}{2}$ hours. If she tracked at a pace of 150 metres every two minutes, what would be the total distance covered during that time?

(A) 6.7 km
(B) 4.5 km
(C) 9 km
(D) 7.5 km

87. There's definitely an arsonist on the loose. There were twice as many arsons this month compared to the previous month. Over these past two months, there have been a total of 51 arsons. How many arsons occurred this past month?

(A) 34
(B) 26
(C) 21
(D) 17

88. Freeway Patrol Officer Green drove his police vehicle at an average speed of 120 km/h for 39 minutes. How far did he drive during that time?

(A) 67 km
(B) 78 km
(C) 83 km
(D) 91 km

89. "Fast Eddy" is back to his usual thievery, this time recruit Constable Johnson is chasing him in a foot pursuit. Eddy has a 100 metre head start on Johnson. Eddy is running at 6 m/s and Johnson is running at 8 m/s. If they maintain the same speed, how far will Johnson have run before he catches Eddy?

(A) 400 metres
(B) 250 metres
(C) 200 metres
(D) 100 metres

90. If there are 90 questions on the PATI exam and if you failed to correctly answer 16 questions, approximately what percent of the questions did you answer correctly?

(A) 86%

(B) 84%

(C) 82%

(D) 80%

# ANSWER KEY

## PART 1-1: Travel Time

| | | | | | | | |
|---|---|---|---|---|---|---|---|
| **1.** B | | **5.** A | | **9.** C | | **13.** D |
| **2.** B | | **6.** D | | **10.** A | | **14.** D |
| **3.** C | | **7.** D | | **11.** C | | **15.** B |
| **4.** C | | **8.** B | | **12.** B | | |

## PART 1-2: Syllogisms

| | | | | | | | |
|---|---|---|---|---|---|---|---|
| **16.** A | | **20.** A | | **24.** C | | **28.** C |
| **17.** C | | **21.** B | | **25.** D | | **29.** D |
| **18.** B | | **22.** C | | **26.** C | | **30.** D |
| **19.** D | | **23.** C | | **27.** A | | |

## PART 2-1: Classification

| | | | | | | | |
|---|---|---|---|---|---|---|---|
| **31.** B | | **35.** B | | **39.** B | | **43.** C |
| **32.** B | | **36.** B | | **40.** A | | **44.** C |
| **33.** D | | **37.** A | | **41.** A | | **45.** D |
| **34.** C | | **38.** D | | **42.** B | | |

## PART 2-2: Figure Series

| | | | | | | | |
|---|---|---|---|---|---|---|---|
| **46.** B | | **50.** D | | **54.** C | | **58.** C |
| **47.** A | | **51.** B | | **55.** B | | **59.** C |
| **48.** C | | **52.** A | | **56.** C | | **60.** D |
| **49.** B | | **53.** D | | **57.** A | | |

## PART 3-1: Arithmetic

| | | | | | | | |
|---|---|---|---|---|---|---|---|
| **61.** | D | **65.** | B | **69.** | B | **73.** | C |
| **62.** | B | **66.** | A | **70.** | A | **74.** | C |
| **63.** | A | **67.** | C | **71.** | A | **75.** | D |
| **64.** | C | **68.** | D | **72.** | D | | |

## PART 3-2: Word Problems

| | | | | | | | |
|---|---|---|---|---|---|---|---|
| **76.** | D | **80.** | D | **84.** | C | **88.** | B |
| **77.** | B | **81.** | D | **85.** | C | **89.** | A |
| **78.** | C | **82.** | A | **86.** | A | **90.** | C |
| **79.** | A | **83.** | B | **87.** | A | | |

# ANSWERS EXPLAINED

## Part 1: Travel Time and Syllogisms

1. **B** By car: B–C–H–M (3 × 1 min) = 3 min.

2. **B** By car: P–K–F–G–H–I–J (6 × 1 min) = 6 min.

3. **C** By car: A–B–C–D–I –J–O–T–Y. Regardless of the route taken, the result will be the same (8 × 1 min) = 8 min.

4. **C** Whether by car and running (3 min + 3 min) or by driving around road closure, both equal 6 minutes.

5. **A** R two blocks north (R–M–H), then two blocks east, (H–I–J) and then walked from that intersection to T(J–O–T) = 2 × 5 min = 10 min. You are not asked to include driving time in this calculation.

6. **D** Route: E–D–C–B–A (+ 2 min)–F–K–P–Q–R (+ 2 min)–M–L = (11 × 1 min) + (2 × 2 min) = 15 min.

7. **D** Running west the suspect would have travelled from Y–X–W in six minutes. Also in six minutes, the officer on bicycle would have travelled south from K–P–U–V. Therefore, the suspect and officer would intercept mid-block between V and W.

8. **B** On bicycle in pursuit from R northbound. After two blocks the chain came off (R–M–H), he abandoned the bike and continued east, pursuing the suspect on foot. Suspect caught at E (H–I–J–E). (2 × 2 min) + (3 × 3 min) = 13 min.

9. **C** By car: U–V–W–X–Y–T–O (6 × 1 min) plus walk from O–J–E (2 × 5 min) = 16 min.

10. **A** Walking: Q–L–G–H–I–J (5 × (4 + 5 min)) plus drive back to start J–O–T–S–R–Q (5 × 1 min) = 50 min.

11. **C** Running: M–L –Q–V–W–P –Q–R–M. (8 × 3 min) = 24 min.

12. **B** Walking: W–V–U–P–K–F (5 × 5 min) plus

    Bicycle: F–A–B–C–D–E (5 × 2 min) = 35 min.

13. **D** Car: F–K–P–U (plus turn)–V–W–X–Y–(plus turn)–T–O–J (10 × 1 min) + ( 2 × 1.5 min) = 13 min.

14. **D** Bob: T–S–R–Q–P (plus turn)–K–F–A (plus turn)–B–C–D–E (11 × 1 min) + ( 2 × 1.5 min) = 14 min.

    Jim: K–F–A (plus turn)–B–C–D–E (6 × 2 min) + (1 × 1.5 min) = 13.5 min.

15. **B** By car: U–P–K–L–M–R–W–V–Q (no need to go back to U). (8 × 1 min) plus nine intersections in total to be canvassed (9 × 3 min) = 35 min.

16. **A** Rule: Some, All = Some. If either the major premise or minor premise is particular, then the conclusion must also be particular.

17. **C** Rule: All, All = All. Universal major and minor premise equals a universal conclusion.

18. **B** Rule: All, No = No. When only one premise is negative, the conclusion must also be negative.

19. **D** Rule: Some, Some = No valid conclusion. When both premises are particular (e.g., *some* and *some not*) then no logical conclusion can be derived.

20. **A** Rule: Some, All = Some. If either the major premise or minor premise is particular, then the conclusion must also be particular.

21. **B** Rule: Some, No = Some not. When only one premise is negative, the conclusion must also be negative.

22. **C** Rule: All, Some = Several possible valid conclusions; however, in this case only C is a logical conclusion.

23. **C** Rule: No, Some = Some Not and major and minor premises are reversed (i.e., "judges" become major premise). When only one premise is negative, the conclusion must also be negative.

24. **A** Rule: No, All = No and major and minor premises are reversed. "All guns are not safe." Also, when only one premise is negative, the conclusion must also be negative.

25. **D** Rule: No, No = No. When both premises are negative, then no logical conclusion can be derived.

26. **C** Rule: Some, No = Some not.

27. **A** Rule: All, All = All. When both premises are affirmative, the conclusion is also affirmative.

28. **C** Rule: No, Some = Some not and major and minor premises are reversed (i.e., "stimulants" becomes the major premise). When only one premise is negative, the conclusion must also be negative. Although the statement does not make sense, it follows correct logic for categorical syllogisms.

29. **D** Rule: The middle term (in this case "trucks") must be distributed (used as a universal or particular statement) at least once in either the major or minor premises, otherwise no conclusion can be derived.

30. **D** Some not, No = No valid conclusion. When both premises are negative, then no logical conclusion can be derived.

## Part 2: Classification and Figure Series

31. **B** This suspect has a narrow face and jaw line. His eyes are also different.

32. **B** It is the only odd number.

33. **D** All other images are rotation of the same image; choice D is rotated and mirrored.

34. **C** Other images have five arrows total, choice C has six.

35. **B** All, except the mango, are members of the citrus family.

36. **B** There are two fewer dots than sides inside each image, except B, which has seven sides but only four dots.

37. **A** All metals can be found in their native state in nature, except steel, which must be manufactured.

38. **D** The jaw line, lips, and eyes are different.

39. **B** In all the shapes, except B, the solid inside shape has just one fewer sides than the outside shape.

40. **A** The other numbers begin with an odd number and then increase by two, progressing to the right.

41. **A** In all but A, the black dots are directly opposite each other.

42. **B** In each diagram, except B, there is one less horizontal bar than vertical bar inside each square.

43. **C** All of the other images are a rotation of the same image, except C, which is rotated and mirrored.

44. **C** Face is wider, jaw line wider, and eyes are different.

45. **D** All of the cities, except Milan, are capital cities of a European country.

46. **B** The black rings increase by one from left to right 8, 9, 10. B has 11 black rings.

47. **A** Only in A are the solid pie shapes directly opposite each other.

48. **C** Number of sides reduces by one per shape: 6, 5, 4, 3.

49. **B** Add the two previous numbers together to create the next (i.e., 4 + 9 = 13; 9 + 13 = 22, etc.).

50. **D** The ascending sequence of letters starting with C. Skips one letter, then two, and so forth. (e.g., 5 letters skipped between L and Q, then 6 between Q and W).

51. **B** Octagon required to complete series on bottom row. Both black and white circles required to complete the sequence.

52. **A** In the first row, the left shape is a combination of the middle and right shapes. In the second row, the right side shape is a combination of the left and middle shapes. In the third row, the pattern returns to the left shape being a combination of the middle and right shape. Therefore, the triangle.

53. **D** The black square moves around the nine squares in a clockwise fashion, returning back to the starting point by the ninth square. The white circle follows two squares behind the black square.

54. **C** Each image in the bottom row has three horizontal bars. The images in the right column have two vertical bars. The triangle completes the pattern on the bottom row.

55. **B** The right column is a combination of the first and second column for each row.

56. **C** Multiply the previous number by 3, then subtract 2 (e.g., 4 × 3 = 12 − 2 = 10).

57. **A** Descending sequence starting with U, first skip one letter, then two, and so forth.

58. **C** Alternating mirrored image from left to right.

59. **C** The circle descends, the star ascends, and the Xs return to one on each side of the bar.

60. **D** The pattern series is by column, not row. In the first column, the black squares descend. In the second column, the black squares ascend. In the third column, the black squares descend, and the bottom square returns to the top. The circles are a random distraction and are not part of the pattern.

## Part 3: Arithmetic and Word Problems

61. **D** Use 21 as your common denominator $(7 \times 3)$, create an improper fraction, add the fractions together, and then simplify and reduce.

62. **B** A negative number multiplied by a positive results in negative product. Multiply numbers then add three decimal places to the left.

63. **A** Rule: BEDMAS. Divide $98 \div 7$, then add 37.9, and subtract 13.74.

64. **C** Use long division: $5.6\overline{)141.904}$. Move the decimal one place to the right on both numbers before dividing.

65. **B** Establish a common denominator (18). Borrow 1 $\left(\dfrac{18}{18}\right)$ from the 6 before subtracting.

66. **A** Turn $2\dfrac{6}{7}$ into an improper fraction first. When dividing fractions, you would multiply $\dfrac{1}{8}$ by its reciprocal (8).

67. **C** Rule: BEDMAS. Solve all equations inside the outside bracket first, then multiply by 2.

68. **D** Isolate $y$, by multiplying $\dfrac{2}{3}$ by its reciprocal. Do the same on the other side of the equation.

69. **B** The common denominator for $\dfrac{5}{8}$, $\dfrac{5}{12}$, and $\dfrac{2}{3}$ is 24. First add the two fractions and then subtract the third. Final result is $\dfrac{21}{24}$, which is reduced to $\dfrac{7}{8}$.

70. **A** Isolate $y$ by first subtracting 3 from both sides of the equation. Divide by 6, and then add 8 to both sides.

71. **A** Isolate $y$. First add 9 to both sides. Then, multiply $y$ by its reciprocal, and do the same to the other side of the equation.

72. **D** $0.70 \times 130 = 91$.

73. **C** When exponents are added together they must first be simplified before you can add their values.

74. **C** First, create an improper fraction $\dfrac{40}{7} \times \dfrac{75}{8}$. Second, reduce the fraction $\left(\dfrac{40}{8}\right)$. Multiply fractions: $\dfrac{345}{7}$, reduced to $53\dfrac{4}{7}$.

75. **D** A negative number multiplied by another negative number results in a positive product.

76. **D** $\$32,000 \times 0.25 = \$8,000$. Subtract $\$8,000$ from the original cost = $\$24,000$.

77. **B** Regular rate: $28 \times 12$ hr = $336. First hour $28 \times 1.5 \times 1 = $42. Subsequent hours: $28 \times 2 \times 3$ hr = $168. Combined total = $546.

78. **C** There was an increase in 9 homicides over the previous year's 32. Therefore, $\frac{9}{32} = \frac{x}{100}$. To solve, cross-multiply and divide. $900 \div 32 = 28\%$.

79. **A** Bike cost $1,592 \div 12$ monthly payments = $132.66.

80. **D** $43,362 + $37,987 + $24,092 = $105,441 \div 3 = $35,147.

81. **D** There is no need to calculate what 31 seconds means in relation to an hour of time. Instead, we know that it is approximately $\frac{1}{2}$ a minute. Therefore, $\frac{200}{0.5} = \frac{x}{60}$. To solve, cross-multiply and divide. $x = 24$ km/h.

82. **A** 10 year sentence, subtract 2 years at double time (4) for pretrial custody = 6 years remaining. Two-thirds of 6 = 4.

83. **B** There are 7 sergeants out of a total 77 employees. $\frac{7}{77}$ is reduced to $\frac{1}{11}$ or a 1:11 probability.

84. **C** 120 km needs to be converted to metres. $120 \times 1,000 = 120,000$. An hour is converted to seconds. $1 \times 60 \times 60 = 3,600$. $120,000 \div 3,600 = 33.3$ m/s.

85. **C** The locker that is 3 metres high, is only $\frac{2}{3}$ full, or 2 metres. Cubic space is calculated by multiplying length $\times$ width $\times$ height. $2 \text{ m} \times 4 \text{ m} \times 2 \text{ m} = 16 \text{ m}^3$.

86. **A** Dog handler tracks 150 m/2 min. Multiply by 30 = 4,500 m/hr. $4,500 \times 1.5 = 6,750$ m or 6.75 km.

87. **A** $x + 2x = 51$; $3x = 51$; $x = 17$. There were twice as many arsons this month = 34.

88. **B** $\frac{x}{39} = \frac{120}{60}$. Isolate $x$ by cross-multiplying and dividing. $x = 78$.

89. **A** Although this may appear like you need to create a complex formula to solve (which you can do), it can actually be calculated very easily. Johnson has a closing speed on Eddy of 2 m/s. Eddy has a 100 m head start. To close the 100 m it will take $100 \div 2 = 50$ seconds of time. Johnson runs at 8 m/s. $8 \times 50 = 400$ m.

90. **C** If 16 questions were wrong, then 74 were correct. Thus, $\frac{74}{90} = \frac{x}{100}$. Cross-multiply and divide. $x = 82\%$.

# Model Exam Three: RCMP Police Aptitude Test (RPAT)

In 2013, the RCMP transitioned its entrance exam from a paper-and-pencil format to a streamlined and more efficient online exam. The previous 114-questionnaire was divided into three booklets and took over two and one-half hours to complete. The new online test is just 50 questions long, divided into five sections, with only 10 questions per section. Though the total exam time is 75 minutes, you only have 15 minutes to complete each section, and you are not allowed to carry time over from one section to the next. One of the benefits of the new online format is that your test will be computer-scored immediately, and by the time you leave not only will you will you know your own score but also how well you scored compared to other applicants across the country.

| RCMP ONLINE FORMAT | | | |
|---|---|---|---|
| **SECTION** | **COMPETENCY** | **QUESTIONS** | **TIME ALLOWED** |
| Part 1 | English Composition | 10 | 15 minutes |
| Part 2 | Comprehension | 10 | 15 minutes |
| Part 3 | Judgment | 10 | 15 minutes |
| Part 4 | Logic | 10 | 15 minutes |
| Part 5 | Computations | 10 | 15 minutes |
| | Total | 50 | 75 |

# ANSWER SHEET
## Model Exam Three

### PART 1: English Composition

1. (A) (B) (C) (D)     4. (A) (B) (C) (D)     7. (A) (B) (C) (D)     9. (A) (B) (C) (D)
2. (A) (B) (C) (D)     5. (A) (B) (C) (D)     8. (A) (B) (C) (D)     10. (A) (B) (C) (D)
3. (A) (B) (C) (D)     6. (A) (B) (C) (D)

### PART 2: Comprehension

11. (A) (B) (C) (D)     14. (A) (B) (C) (D)     17. (A) (B) (C) (D)     19. (A) (B) (C) (D)
12. (A) (B) (C) (D)     15. (A) (B) (C) (D)     18. (A) (B) (C) (D)     20. (A) (B) (C) (D)
13. (A) (B) (C) (D)     16. (A) (B) (C) (D)

### PART 3: Judgment

21. (A) (B) (C) (D)     24. (A) (B) (C) (D)     27. (A) (B) (C) (D)     29. (A) (B) (C) (D)
22. (A) (B) (C) (D)     25. (A) (B) (C) (D)     28. (A) (B) (C) (D)     30. (A) (B) (C) (D)
23. (A) (B) (C) (D)     26. (A) (B) (C) (D)

### PART 4: Logic

31. (A) (B) (C) (D)     34. (A) (B) (C) (D)     37. (A) (B) (C) (D)     39. (A) (B) (C) (D)
32. (A) (B) (C) (D)     35. (A) (B) (C) (D)     38. (A) (B) (C) (D)     40. (A) (B) (C) (D)
33. (A) (B) (C) (D)     36. (A) (B) (C) (D)

### PART 5: Computations

41. (A) (B) (C) (D)     44. (A) (B) (C) (D)     47. (A) (B) (C) (D)     49. (A) (B) (C) (D)
42. (A) (B) (C) (D)     45. (A) (B) (C) (D)     48. (A) (B) (C) (D)     50. (A) (B) (C) (D)
43. (A) (B) (C) (D)     46. (A) (B) (C) (D)

# PART 1: ENGLISH COMPOSITION

 You have 15 minutes to complete the following 10 questions.

> This section tests your competency in spelling, vocabulary, and sentence structure.

1. Which word in the sentence below is misspelled?

   When the officer was involved in the accidental discharge of his firearm, an independant investigation was commenced to determine whether any disciplinary action was warranted.

   (A) accidental
   (B) independant
   (C) commenced
   (D) disciplinary

2. Which word in the sentence below is misspelled?

   During the trial, defence counsel tried to persuade the jury that the accused did not possess the mental capacity to commit this henious crime.

   (A) counsel
   (B) persuade
   (C) possess
   (D) henious

3. Which word in the sentence below is misspelled?

   The petty thief felt that he had been entrapped into stealing the jewellery that was left in plain view inside the bait car. The temptation was too irresistable.

   (A) thief
   (B) entrapped
   (C) jewellery
   (D) irresistable

4. Which of the following words best define **disingenuous**?

   (A) deceitful
   (B) trivial
   (C) lacking ingenuity
   (D) uncommitted

5. Which of the following words best define **renounce**?

   (A) delay
   (B) blame
   (C) give up
   (D) refuse to accept

6. Which word is best defined as "to pull away with force."

    (A) wrest
    (B) vacillate
    (C) vex
    (D) strew

7. Which word is best defined as "something that adds to or makes complete."

    (A) remnant
    (B) complement
    (C) increment
    (D) compliment

8. Which option best completes the following sentence?

    Detective Arnoldson only had a _____ number of interrogation options available if she was going to be _____ in obtaining a confession that would be admissible in court.

    (A) discrete/affective
    (B) discreet/effective
    (C) discreet/affective
    (D) discrete/effective

9. Which option best completes the following sentence?

    The transfer to Internal Affairs was going to be between Officer Chow and ___, yet this assignment was _____ neither of us wanted to go.

    (A) I/were
    (B) me/where
    (C) myself/where
    (D) I/where

10. Which option best completes the following sentence?

    Since ___ imperative not to arrest the drug dealer before the transaction takes place, the arrest team had to wait for the undercover officer's _____ before moving in on the suspect.

    (A) it's/cue
    (B) its'/clue
    (C) its/cue
    (D) it's/queue

# PART 2: COMPREHENSION

 **You have 15 minutes to complete the following 10 questions.**

This section requires that you read two separate articles and answer the five multiple-choice questions that pertain to each article. Answer each question based only on the information provided. You may refer back to the reading material while answering questions.

QUESTIONS 11–15 ARE BASED SOLELY ON THE INFORMATION CONTAINED IN THE FOLLOWING ARTICLE.

## Putting Stock in Partnerships

By Sigrid Forberg

White-collar criminals in the province of Québec have a new group of specialized investigators and analysts to contend with.

Comprised of two investigators, an analyst and a public servant from the RCMP and an investigator and analyst each from the Autorité de Marchés Financiers (AMF) and the Sûreté du Québec (SQ), the Joint Securities Intelligence Unit (JSIU) is an equal partnership between the three agencies created to combat economic crimes in Québec.

The AMF, which is responsible for overseeing the province's financial markets, found itself increasingly faced with situations of overlapping interests or the same targets as law enforcement. Reaching out to the SQ and RCMP, they voiced a need to encourage collaboration and communication among their three agencies.

The JSIU, born from that concept, is responsible for gathering intelligence to help further financial crime investigations in the province. Once all the intelligence is packaged, it then goes through the approval and consideration of the orientation committee and then the director's committee, which then assign the case to one of the three agencies for completion.

"We put on the table the names of the people who are subject to being investigated and we determine who's going to be investigating," says Philip Rousseau, the director of economic crime at the AMF and a member of the orientation committee. "If the RCMP is doing it, we can collaborate, we can help out, then we can step back and let it go."

Another aspect of the mandate is to detect and prevent fraud crimes in Québec. By collaborating, not only does the unit prevent overlapping investigations into the same crimes or offenders, it's also able to proactively collect intelligence, develop human sources, and generate leads—something regular investigators don't typically have the time for.

"We take pieces of information and we put the puzzle together and we get a clear picture of what's being done and who's doing what," says Cpl. Dominic Milotte, who has been leading the unit for the last two years. "And then, once investigators start on the case, they know where they're going and they don't waste time."

In 2012, the unit started 97 files. One third were opened intelligence files, while the remainder were the intelligence files actually shared between agencies. Rousseau likens the JSIU's work to setting the table so the investigators can dig in without having to worry about some of the potentially time-consuming prep work.

Under the Memorandum of Understanding (MOU) that officially binds the team, all three organizations share the responsibility and authority equally. The MOU also allows them to share in other ways.

Because the province's two policing agencies have access to provincial and federal criminal intelligence databases, they're able to offer one another insight into information that may otherwise be inaccessible.

"Some of the cases we get, it's not clear-cut whether it's criminal or civil. It might not even be clear-cut for the police," says Rousseau. "The best thing this unit does is they get people talking to each other to get a better view of each case from a whole variety of sources."

Milotte adds that all the RCMP members have training and experience in criminal intelligence investigations. But that's not enough on its own to handle these kinds of investigations, which Captain Michel Hamelin, the officer in charge of the SQ's organized financial crimes investigation section, says can be very different from other types of crime.

"The biggest difference is often the sheer complexity of fraud schemes," says Hamelin. "We rely on the experience of financial crime intelligence officers to gather relevant information and, more importantly, understand how the crimes are being committed."

Each member of the unit brings something to the table that is unique to their experience, education, and organization's focus. And that's the crux of why the files opened by the JSIU have been so successful so far, explains Milotte.

"We can't work in silos. It used to be like that a couple years back, everyone was protecting their intelligence but not sharing," says Milotte. "The value of putting all this together is that we're making stronger investigations, stronger intelligence probes, and in the end, because you get the whole picture, your investigations are more successful."

*The above article is reprinted courtesy of the RCMP Gazette, as published in Vol. 75, No. 3, 2013.*

11. What is the responsibility of the Autorité de Marchés Financiers?

   (A) The auditor general for the province of Québec
   (B) Investigating corporate corruption in Québec
   (C) Overseeing stock markets in Québec
   (D) Creating a criminal intelligence database

12. The Joint Securities Intelligence Unit (JSIU) is comprised of which of the following agencies?

   (A) RCMP, Canadian Security Intelligence Service, Autorité de Marchés Financiers
   (B) Sûreté du Québec, Autorité de Marchés Financiers, RCMP
   (C) Autorité de Marchés Financiers, RCMP, Criminal Intelligence Service, National Security Agency
   (D) Sûreté du Québec, RCMP, Autorité de Marchés Financiers, Canadian Security Intelligence Service

13. What does Philip Rousseau, director of economic crime at the AMF, mean by comparing his agency's work to "setting the table"?

(A) The AMF conducts significant investigational preparation work for the police agencies.

(B) The AMF brings all the other partners together around one table.

(C) The AMF does all the menial tasks for the police agencies.

(D) All the agencies bring their experiences, education, and organizational focus to the table.

14. What is the key advantage that the MOU provides?

(A) The MOU sets out the roles and responsibilities of each agency.

(B) The MOU legally binds each agency's commitment to the JSIU.

(C) The MOU allows the partner agencies to share intelligence and information among them that may have otherwise been inaccessible.

(D) The MOU provides the opportunity for the partner agencies to operate in information silos.

15. Why is it important for the three agencies to work collaboratively?

(A) It is not always clear whether cases are civil or criminal.

(B) White collar fraud schemes often involve complex and overlapping criminal investigations.

(C) Police need to make stronger investigations and stronger intelligence probes.

(D) The Sûreté du Québec does not have the capacity to investigate these complex crimes.

QUESTIONS 16–20 ARE BASED SOLELY ON THE INFORMATION CONTAINED IN THE FOLLOWING ARTICLE.

**Disturbance Requires More than Yelling at Police**
*R. v. Kukemueller, 2014 ONCA 295*
By Mike Novakowski

The fire department received a call to attend the accused's rural address for a car fire. The car, which belonged to the accused's girlfriend Wiles, had crashed into a tree. The fire department requested police assistance. At the scene there was a crowd of young people who appeared to have been drinking. As firefighters extinguished the fire, police learned the vehicle fire may have been caused by people playing "demolition derby." A police officer spoke to the accused and Wiles. They both smelled of alcohol.

When Wiles told police that she had been driving the car when it hit the tree, she was arrested for dangerous driving but struggled with the officer. The accused and some of his friends became upset and the officer used her emergency button to request backup.

The police officer and a firefighter took Wiles to the police car at the road and the crowd of young people started yelling. The accused was upset and yelling and swearing. More officers arrived and, not long afterwards, so did the accused's father driving an off-road vehicle. He was arrested for impaired driving. The accused reacted with a loud, profane, and angry tirade against the police. About 22 people, including family members, friends, firefighters, and police officers, were present. Even the accused's grandmother came out of her house and tried to calm him down. The accused was arrested and charged with causing a disturbance and later with assault. He allegedly scooped water from the toilet, threw it around and got some of it on a civilian cell monitor at the police station.

## Ontario Court of Justice

The judge concluded that the accused had caused a disturbance. She found the accused's "behaviour had an effect on the other family and friends who were present and contributed to raising the tension at the scene amongst those people as well as the police". In her view, the accused's behaviour "made things worse". A conviction of causing a disturbance in or near a public place contrary to s. 175(1)(a) of the Criminal Code was entered. As for the assault charge, the judge was not satisfied that the accused had deliberately splashed water on the cell attendant. He was acquitted of assault.

## Ontario Superior Court of Justice

The accused's appeal was unsuccessful. Since the accused's conduct "contributed to raising the tension at the scene", an appeal judge found the trial judge did not err in holding that the offence of causing a disturbance had been made out.

## Ontario Court of Appeal

A further appeal by the accused was successful. The Ontario Court of Appeal concluded that the trial judge had erred in law in determining that a disturbance occurred. Although it was not condoning yelling obscenities at the police, conduct described as obnoxious or deplorable, the Court of Appeal found it was not criminal.

Under s. 175(1)(a) it is an offence for someone who, "not being in a dwelling-house, causes a disturbance in or near a public place, (i) by fighting, screaming, shouting, swearing, singing, or using insulting or obscene language…" There are two elements to this offence:

- the commission of one of the enumerated acts.
- the commission of the acts caused a disturbance in or near a public place.

In this case there was no doubt the accused committed one of the enumerated acts. He yelled and swore at the police. As for whether those acts "cause[d] a disturbance in or near a public place," the Court of Appeal found they did not.

Here, the accused's conduct did not satisfy the second element of the offence—causing a disturbance in or near a public place. "There was no evidence and no finding that the [accused's] conduct interfered with the public's normal activities or with the ordinary and customary use by the public of the place in question," said Justice Sharpe on behalf of the Court of Appeal. "Contributing to raising the tension at the scene of an interaction between the police and the public does not amount to the kind of disturbance that is required for this offence to be made out." As for the accused's grandmother coming out of her house and trying to calm him down, she was "simply concerned about his well-being. She thought that he would listen to her. She testified that she was 'upset' but … emotional upset does not amount to a disturbance." The accused's appeal was allowed and his conviction for causing a disturbance was set aside.

*The above article is reprinted courtesy of the JIBC In Service: 10-8 Newsletter, as published in Volume 14, Issue 3–May/June 2014. Portions of the original article have been removed to reduce its length.*

16. What offence was Wiles arrested for?

(A) Impaired driving
(B) Obstruction of justice
(C) Causing a disturbance
(D) Dangerous driving

17. Why was the accused charged with assault?

(A) He assaulted a fireman.
(B) He spat on a police officer.
(C) He threw toilet water on a civilian employee.
(D) He was not charged with assault.

18. Which of the following is not one of the necessary elements of causing a disturbance?

(A) Fighting
(B) Threatening
(C) Singing
(D) Swearing

19. What was the accused's father arrested for?

(A) Impaired driving
(B) Causing a disturbance
(C) Assault
(D) He was not arrested.

20. Why was the accused not convicted for causing a disturbance by the Ontario Court of Appeal?

(A) The accused's actions were obnoxious but did not interfere with the public's normal activities.
(B) The incident did not occur in a public place.
(C) The accused did not fight with anyone.
(D) The accused's grandmother did not wish to press charges.

## PART 3: JUDGMENT

**You have 15 minutes to complete the following 10 questions.**

In this section, you are required to show sound decision-making skills and good judgment. You are not required to know police policy and procedures, the applicable law, or law enforcement tactics.

FOR QUESTIONS 21–30, SELECT THE MOST APPROPRIATE COURSE OF ACTION BASED ON THE INFORMATION PROVIDED IN EACH SCENARIO.

21. You and your partner attend a domestic dispute where neighbours are heard screaming. You see a woman has a red mark on her face. She states she fell and hit her head. Her 13-year-old son said his dad punched her in the face. The woman begs you not to arrest her husband, he is a good man, and you will make things worse by taking him away. The husband denies hitting his wife. Your next course of action is to

    (A) warn the husband that if you are called back to the home, you will arrest him.
    (B) keep the peace by having the husband find somewhere else to stay for the night.
    (C) arrest the husband and, if necessary, find a shelter for the woman to stay.
    (D) warn the husband and take a statement from the 13-year-old son in case anything happens in the future.

22. It is 31° Celsius and you are called to a report of a 15-month-old baby locked in a car parked in the sun for the past 15 minutes. The baby is in obvious distress. The panicked mother has called her husband who is about 6 minutes away with an extra set of keys. Your dispatcher advises that an ambulance will be on scene in about 4 minutes. A tow truck driver will be on scene in 5 minutes. You have a baton, but you will likely get broken window glass on the baby. Your best course of action is to

    (A) advise the mother that once the baby is safe, you will be charging her for failing to care for her child.
    (B) use your baton to break a side window furthest away from the child.
    (C) wait for the ambulance attendants to arrive, they will be able to best assess the baby's condition.
    (D) wait for the tow truck driver. He will have a "slim Jim" and be able to gain entry into the car almost immediately.

23. An AMBER Alert has been issued for an abducted child and suspect vehicle. You spot the vehicle and see the child inside. You attempt to stop the vehicle but the vehicle takes off, and you become engaged in a high-speed pursuit. You broadcast your route, speed, location, and direction of travel. After almost a minute, your supervisor broadcasts over the air that you are to stop pursuing immediately, completely disengage, and turn off your lights and siren. You are sure that if you stop pursuing, the suspect will get away. At this moment, you should

(A) turn off your lights and siren, but keep following the suspect to see where he goes.

(B) advise your supervisor that you believe the suspect will get away if you stop pursuing.

(C) advise the supervisor that protecting life is the most important mandate of the police, which supersedes policy.

(D) turn off your lights and siren and pull to the curb.

24. You are on duty driving past two men in their early 20s, as you do, one of them flips you the middle finger. You should

(A) stop and arrest the one male for abuse of a police officer.

(B) stop and obtain their names and run them on the CPIC computer system to see if they have any warrants for arrest.

(C) stop and greet the men and talk to them in a professional manner and enquire if they have any specific issue with the police. See where the conversation leads.

(D) keep driving; you should expect to be subjected to verbal insults and rude gestures.

25. You stop an off-duty police officer for speeding. He shows you his badge and states that he just left the annual police golf tournament. He has a faint odour of liquor on his breath. At this moment, you should

(A) arrest the driver for impaired driving and call for a supervisor to attend.

(B) issue the driver a ticket for speeding and send him on his way.

(C) show the expected professional courtesy and allow him to proceed.

(D) initiate an impaired driving investigation.

26. You observe a 14-year-old boy throwing rocks, and you see him damage a car. It will cost about $400 to fix the damage. You stop the boy and contact the registered owner. The owner is mostly concerned with getting the damage paid for. The boy has no prior contact with the police. You should

(A) advise the owner that insurance will cover the damage and you can make the boy pay for the insurance deductible.

(B) arrest the young offender for mischief under $5,000 and bring him to the police station for processing.

(C) contact the young person's parents and advise them of the circumstances and that the owner is looking to have the cost of repair covered and if they will agree to that.

(D) do nothing. You cannot prove the *mens rea* (criminal intent) that the young person meant to damage the car, so this is a civil problem and not a criminal matter.

27. You attend a home where a mother who was cleaning her 16-year-old son's bedroom located two marijuana cigarettes in his sock drawer. She is fed up with his reckless attitude and wants you to arrest him for possession of drugs in order to teach him a lesson. You should

    (A) seize the drugs for destruction and discuss with her son the risks of drug possession and use.
    (B) seize the drugs and arrest the son for possession of a controlled substance.
    (C) seize the drugs but advise the mother that she does not have the legal authority to search her son's property.
    (D) take no action; this is a family matter that should not involve the police.

28. You are directing traffic at a busy intersection where a serious collision has taken place and the road has been closed for hours. An angry citizen who has been in the gridlock gets out of his car in the middle of the street, approaches you and states that you are a pathetic excuse for a police officer, demands your name and regimental badge number, and wants to speak to your supervisor. You should

    (A) tell the motorist to get back into his vehicle or you will have it towed and that you will talk to him once you have been relieved of your directing traffic duties.
    (B) call for a supervisor to attend and advise the motorist that a supervisor is en route.
    (C) advise the motorist that you understand his frustration, provide your name and badge number, and advise the motorist that there is a complaint process that he can pursue; however, he must return to his vehicle.
    (D) advise the motorist that if he does not return to his vehicle you will arrest him for obstructing a police officer in the performance of his duties.

29. You are following a car, and you check the licence plate. The plate is registered to a completely different vehicle than the one it's attached to. You activate your lights and siren, and the car stops in the middle of the road. The driver and passenger get out and start running in different directions. The driver is too fast for you to catch; you could probably catch the passenger. You should

    (A) call for assistance, broadcast the description and flight direction of the driver, and chase after the passenger on foot.
    (B) Advise dispatch of suspects running and broadcast their direction of travel, stay with the insecure vehicle until a tow truck arrives as it is obstructing traffic.
    (C) call for assistance, pursue the driver on foot and try to maintain visual contact, and provide a description of the passenger and the direction of flight.
    (D) You have no evidence that the vehicle is stolen. Call for a tow truck to remove the vehicle from the roadway.

30. While you are on beach patrol, you encounter a couple in their 50s sitting in the sand and sharing a glass of wine while watching the sun set. Your supervisor has advised you that the police need to crack down on illegal consumption of liquor in public and rowdiness at the beach. You should

(A) issue the couple a warning that consuming liquor in public is unlawful. Seize their bottle of wine.

(B) issue the couple a provincial violation ticket for consumption of liquor in a public place.

(C) contact your supervisor and request clarification whether this situation would fall within the parameters of the "crackdown" on illegal consumption of liquor in public.

(D) advise the couple that consuming liquor in public is technically unlawful and that they should be a little more discreet.

## PART 4: LOGIC

 **You have 15 minutes to complete the following 10 questions.**

In this section you are required to use deductive and inductive reasoning to identify solutions and complete tasks. These tasks include placing information in sequential order, following directions on a map, and identifying and classifying patterns of information.

31. The Davidsons, Gagnons, Parmars, Chows, and the Arnolds all live in a row of townhomes. You attend the Arnold residence to investigate a break and enter. Arnold lives in one of the homes between Chow and Gagnon. Arnold states that his neighbour Parmar, who lives two homes to the west of his, was a witness to suspicious activity yesterday. You talk to Parmar and he states that his next-door neighbour to the east, Davidson, also saw a suspicious vehicle.

    Based on the information provided above, who is Arnold's next-door neighbour to the west?

    (A) Chow
    (B) Davidson
    (C) Parmar
    (D) Insufficient information provided

32. You are required to compile a police report regarding a bank robbery. Based on the information provided below, what is the best order for the information in the sentences to be compiled in?

    i. The note said, "Don't panic, I have a gun, I want all your $50s and $20s—if you alert anyone you will DIE!"

    ii. The dye-pack exploded in the suspect's hands when he was a block away from the bank.

    iii. The robber stood in line with the other customers before approaching the victim, bank teller Jeeta Sandhu.

    iv. He was captured at the nearby gas station trying to wash the dye off his hands.

    v. The bank was busy with approximately 12 customers and five staff members and had been open for approximately two hours before the robbery occurred.

    vi. The robber ran out of the bank and the west on 12th Avenue.

    (A) vi, iv, ii, iii, i, v
    (B) iii, i, vi, iv, ii, v
    (C) v, i, iii, vi, ii, iv
    (D) v, iii, i, vi, ii, iv

33. Complete the comparison

    Slice is to pie as Canada is to

    (A) democracy
    (B) France
    (C) NATO
    (D) North America

34. Complete the comparison

    Jail is to courtroom as cell is to

    (A) life
    (B) dock
    (C) prison
    (D) lawyer

35. Select the number that continues the pattern sequence.

    0, 3, 8, 14, 24, ...

    (A) 32
    (B) 35
    (C) 39
    (D) 42

36. Select the letter that continues the pattern sequence.

    V, S, O, J,

    (A) D
    (B) G
    (C) Q
    (D) Z

37. Select the shape that does not belong with the others.

    (A)            (B)            (C)            (D)

38. Select the image that continues the pattern sequence.

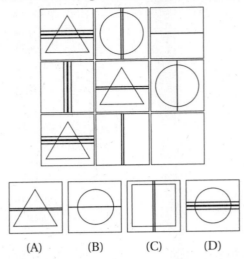

(A)      (B)      (C)      (D)

USE THE MAP BELOW TO ANSWER QUESTIONS 39 AND 40. IN THIS MAP, ALL STREETS ARE DESIGNATED FOR TWO-WAY TRAFFIC, UNLESS INDICATED AS ONE-WAY BY A ONE-DIRECTION ARROW.

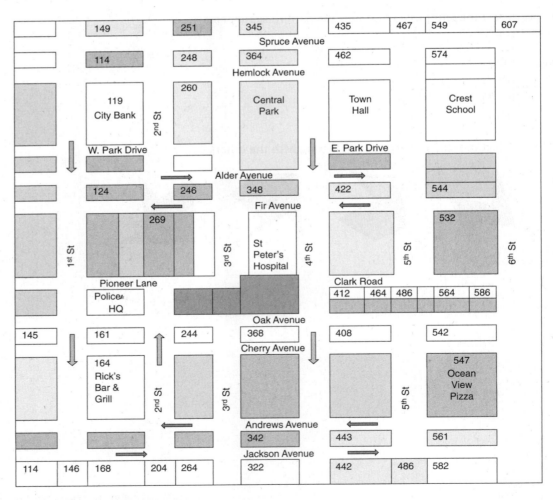

**Colder Creek City**

39. You are out front of Police HQ on Pioneer Lane when you are dispatched to a violent fight involving multiple suspects using knives and clubs outside the front of Crest School. You are authorized to use lights and siren and disobey traffic control devices (e.g., one-way streets signs). What is the most effective and accurate route to the school?

(A) West on Pioneer Lane, south on 3rd Street, east on Fir Avenue, north on 5th Street to the front of Crest School

(B) East on Pioneer Lane, north on 3rd Street, east on Fir Avenue, north on 4th Street, east on East Park Drive, north on 5th Street to the front of Crest School

(C) West on Pioneer Lane, north on 1st Street, east on Hemlock, south on 5th Street to the front of Crest School

(D) West on Pioneer Lane, south on 2nd Street, west on Oak Avenue, north on 6th Street, east on E. Park Drive, north on 5th Street to the front of Crest School

40. You are having a coffee break at Ocean View Pizza, 547 5th Street, when you are called to attend a robbery in progress at 119 1st Street. The suspect is still inside the bank. You are advised to drive routine, without your lights and siren activated so that you do not alert the robber. What is the most effective and accurate route to take to arrive at any side of the bank?

(A) North on 5th, west on Cherry, and then north on 1st to the front of the bank.

(B) North on Andrews Avenue, east on 2nd Street, south on Pioneer Lane, east on 3rd Street, north on Fir Avenue, and east on 2nd Street to the rear of the bank.

(C) North on 5th Street, east on Cherry, north on 6th Street, west on Spruce Avenue, and south on 2nd Street to the rear of the bank.

(D) North on 5th Street, west on Oak Avenue, north on 4th Street, west on Hemlock, and stop at corner of Hemlock and 1st Street.

## PART 5: COMPUTATIONS

 You have 15 minutes to complete the following 10 questions.

> The computations section requires you to conduct basic mathematical calculations in order to solve word problems. You are not permitted to use a calculator or any electronic device to assist you in answering these questions. You may use scrap paper to assist in your calculations.

41. Constable Clark is looking to buy a new home. His investment advisor told him that he should not purchase a house that is more than seven times his annual salary. Clark's annual salary is $85,000. If he listens to his advisor, what is the maximum he should pay for a home?

    (A) $498,000
    (B) $572,000
    (C) $595,000
    (D) $614,000

42. Four vehicles were involved in a collision resulting in significant damage. The Toyota's damage was $5,600, the Hyundai's damage was $3,400, the Ford's damage was $9,700, and damage to the BMW was estimated at $13,600. The damage to the BMW accounted for approximately what percent of the total damage?

    (A) 63%
    (B) 42%
    (C) 32%
    (D) 28%

43. In a recent drug warrant, police seized a sum of cash. There were ten $100 bills, seventy $20 bills, and the remaining one-third of the total value seized was made up of $10 and $5 bills. What was the total value of cash seized?

    (A) $3,600
    (B) $4,800
    (C) $5,200
    (D) Insufficient information provided

44. Constables Clary and Chapman are assigned to canvass businesses along Main Street for CCTV video evidence of yesterday's drive-by shooting. They average speaking to two store managers every 15 minutes. At this rate, how many businesses will they be able to canvass in three hours?

    (A) 12
    (B) 16
    (C) 20
    (D) 24

45. A young child had gone missing in Queen Anne Park. The search area was 900 metres long by 800 metres wide. How many square metres needed to be searched?

    (A) 3,400 m$^2$
    (B) 6,800 m$^2$
    (C) 720,000 m$^2$
    (D) 720 km$^2$

46. Highway Patrol Officer Stables was dispatched to a call of a serious collision on the Kingston overpass. He was 36 km away from the scene when dispatched and arrived in 18 minutes. What was his average speed en route to the call?

    (A) 120 km/h
    (B) 110 km/h
    (C) 100 km/h
    (D) 90 km/h

47. This year, the number of violent crimes in the city decreased by approximately 8 percent compared to last year. Last year there were 290 incidents. How many violent crimes occurred this year?

    (A) 257
    (B) 263
    (C) 273
    (D) 267

48. Constable Jane wrote a violator for speeding: $167; disobeying a red light: $192; and failing to produce his licence: $115. If the violator paid the ticket within 30 days, he will receive a 25 percent reduction. How much will he have to pay in total if he pays before 30 days?

    (A) $387.00
    (B) $355.50
    (C) $298.75
    (D) $395.00

49. Constable Grant has 32 years of police service. Constable Orland has a quarter of years of service as Constable Grant, but 60 percent more years of service than Constable Brown. How many years of service does Constable Brown have?

    (A) 13 years
    (B) 6 years
    (C) 4.8 years
    (D) 5 years

50. The RCMP was able to procure a new supplier of police officer boots that is three-quarters the unit price of the previous vendor's. The previous price was $30 more per pair of boots than the new supplier's cost. What was the cost of a pair of boots from the previous vendor?

(A) $140
(B) $120
(C) $115
(D) Insufficient information provided

# ANSWER KEY

## PART 1: English Composition

| | | | |
|---|---|---|---|
| **1.** B | **4.** A | **7.** B | **9.** B |
| **2.** D | **5.** C | **8.** D | **10.** A |
| **3.** D | **6.** A | | |

## PART 2: Comprehension

| | | | |
|---|---|---|---|
| **11.** C | **14.** C | **17.** C | **19.** A |
| **12.** B | **15.** B | **18.** B | **20.** A |
| **13.** A | **16.** D | | |

## PART 3: Judgment

| | | | |
|---|---|---|---|
| **21.** C | **24.** C | **27.** A | **29.** C |
| **22.** B | **25.** D | **28.** C | **30.** A |
| **23.** D | **26.** C | | |

## PART 4: Logic

| | | | |
|---|---|---|---|
| **31.** B | **34.** B | **37.** C | **39.** C |
| **32.** D | **35.** B | **38.** B | **40.** C |
| **33.** D | **36.** A | | |

## PART 5: Computations

| | | | |
|---|---|---|---|
| **41.** C | **44.** D | **47.** D | **49.** D |
| **42.** B | **45.** C | **48.** B | **50.** B |
| **43.** A | **46.** A | | |

# ANSWERS EXPLAINED

## Part 1: English Composition

1. **B** Correct spelling: *independent*.

2. **D** Correct spelling: *heinous*.

3. **D** Correct spelling: *irresistible*.

4. **A** *Disingenuous* means deceitful or dishonest.

5. **C** *Renounce* means to give up.

6. **A** *Wrest* means to pull away from.

7. **B** *Complement* means to add to or to complete something. *Compliment* means to praise.

8. **D** *Discrete* means distinct or a finite amount; *discreet* means prudent or tactful. *Effective* means successful; *affective* means emotional.

9. **B** If a sentence uses the preposition *between*, it must be followed by the indirect object pronoun *me*. *Were* is the past tense of the verb *to be*. *Where* is an adverb meaning to, at, or in what place or what situation.

10. **A** *It's* is a contraction for it is; *its* is an adjective meaning belonging to or shows possession. *Cue* is a noun meaning a signal or prompt, or a wooden stick used to play billiards. *Queue* is a noun meaning a waiting line or a temporary storage area for processing work.

## Part 2: Comprehension

11. **C** Paragraph 3: "AMF, which is responsible for overseeing the province's financial markets."

12. **B** Sûreté du Québec, Autorité de Marchés Financiers, RCMP.

13. **A** Paragraphs 8: "Rousseau likens the JSIU's work to setting the table so the investigators can dig in without having to worry about some of the potentially time-consuming prep work."

14. **C** The main theme of the article is that the three agencies had been working in information silos and that information in intelligence databases was not necessarily available to other agencies. The MOU allowed for information-sharing protocols to be established among the three agencies.

15. **B** The article speaks to the complexity of fraud cases involving the stock market and the need to work collaboratively among the three agencies.

16. **D** Wiles was the girlfriend of the accused. Paragraph 2, states, "she was arrested for dangerous driving but struggled with the officer."

17. **C** Paragraph 3: "He allegedly scooped water from the toilet, threw it around and got some of it on a civilian cell monitor at the police station."

18. **B** Paragraph 7: "causes a disturbance in or near a public place, (i) by fighting, screaming, shouting, swearing, singing or using insulting or obscene language." Threatening is not one of the listed activities; it is a separate criminal charge.

19. **A** Paragraph 3: "More officers arrived and, not long afterwards, so did the accused's father driving an off-road vehicle. He was arrested for impaired driving."

20. **A** Paragraph 9: "There was no evidence and no finding that the [accused's] conduct interfered with the public's normal activities or with the ordinary and customary use by the public of the place in question."

## Part 3: Judgment

21. **C** There is clear evidence that an assault has taken place: visible red mark on face and statement of son. This requires police action to break the cycle of domestic violence, even though the victim is fearful of repercussions. That can be mitigated by placing the victim in a shelter or other alternatives.

22. **B** The baby has been inside the hot car for at least 15 minutes. If you wait for the ambulance, you will still have to break the window. There is no guarantee that the husband or tow truck driver will be there soon—they could get stuck in traffic or an accident. You need to take immediate action to save the baby's life. The risk of glass hitting the baby is far less than the risk of the baby dying from hyperthermia.

23. **D** Though you may want to continue to pursue the suspect, by doing so you are endangering the life of the child. There may be other means in place to apprehend the suspect: spike belts, helicopter surveillance, intelligence on where the suspect is headed. If a supervisor tells you to disengage a pursuit, you must do so.

24. **C** You should not ignore someone flipping you the finger in these circumstances. There is nothing wrong with confronting abusive behaviour. This must be done in a professional manner, and although you do not have grounds to search the individuals or obtain their names to run on CPIC, you should talk to them and find out why they don't respect their local police.

25. **D** This assesses your professional integrity. While it may be hugely disappointing to have to enter into an impaired investigation against a fellow police officer, you are compelled to do so because of the odour of liquor on his breath. You do not have grounds to arrest at this point. You will only need to involve a supervisor if you determine that the driver's blood alcohol level warrants police action (i.e., roadside prohibition or criminal charges).

26. **C** The registered owner is interested in having the damages covered and not a criminal charge. You cannot make the boy pay for the deductible. You should involve the parents and advise that the registered owner is willing to resolve this civilly.

27. **A** Seize the drugs from the mother for destruction. There is no chance of criminal charges in this situation—you cannot even prove that the son knew the drugs were there. You should speak to the son about the risks of drug use and possession.

28. **C** Use interpersonal skills to show understanding and sympathy for the driver's frustration. If a person asks for your name and badge number while in the performance of your duties, you should provide it to them. There is no need to involve a supervisor at this point. Explain to the motorist that there is a complaint process if he is not satisfied with police action at this incident—he has your name and badge number, which is all he needs.

29. **C** This incident is suspicious enough to believe that they are involved in criminal activity—the car is probably stolen. The driver is going to be the key individual to capture. Use the police radio to call for assistance and advise of the suspects' directions of travel. Try to maintain visual contact with the driver while chasing him on foot.

30. **A** You should not be bothering your supervisor in this type of situation; you need to demonstrate that you can make good decisions on your own. While you may think the best thing to do is to resolve the matter by advising the couple to be more discreet, you have to be cognizant of the perceptions of others, especially if you move down the beach and write all the young persons drinking in public a ticket and seize their alcohol. Therefore, you must take some action, even if it's just a warning and seizing their liquor.

## Part 4: Logic

31. **B** This logic question is best solved by drawing out the individual homes and then putting a letter of the surname above each home. You know that Arnold lives somewhere between the homes of Chow and Gagnon, but you do not know which side they are on, so leave it for now. Parmar lives two homes to the west. That would be two spaces to the left of Arnold's. Parmar states that Davidson is his next-door neighbour to the east. That would then be the house between Parmar and Arnold. The question is who is Arnold's next-door neighbour to the west? The house to the west of Arnold must be Davidson. The house to the east could either be Gagnon or Chow, but it is irrelevant.

32. **D** The narrative should be written in chronological order. Start by setting the scene:

"The bank was busy with approximately 12 customers and five staff members and had been open for approximately two hours before the robbery occurred."

"The robber stood in line with the other customers before approaching the victim, bank teller Jeeta Sandhu."

"The note said, "Don't panic, I have a gun, I want all your $50s and $20s—if you alert anyone you will DIE!"

"The robber ran out of the bank and the west on 12th Avenue."

"The dye-pack exploded in the suspect's hands when he was a block away from the bank."

"He was captured at the nearby gas station trying to wash the dye off his hands."

33. **D** Slice is to pie as Canada is to North America. A slice is part of the whole pie, just as Canada is physically part of North America. Though Canada is a member of NATO, it is a contributing member of an organization as opposed to a physical part of the whole of the landscape of North America.

34. **B** Jail is to courtroom as cell is to dock.

In this analogy, you need to consider the association between jail and cell. Here you should realize that the "cell" refers to a jail cell and not a biological reference. In this relationship a cell is where a prisoner is kept inside a jail. In the courtroom, the dock is where the prisoner is often held when first appearing before a judge.

35. **B** Subtract one from square of each number starting at 1 (i.e., $2^2 - 1 = 3$, $3^2 - 1 = 8$, etc.).

36. **A** Descending alphabet starting with V, skip two letters, S, then skip 3 letters, O, then four letters, J, then five letters = D.

37. **C** All of the shapes, except C are irregular hexagons. Option C is an irregular heptagon.

38. **B** Each of the columns alternates between horizontal bars and vertical bars. The third column requires a single horizontal bar. Each row contains a triangle, circle, and blank square. The bottom row is missing a circle. The horizontal bar and circle complete the pattern.

39. **C** Option A is incorrect. If you started travelling "west on Pioneer Lane" you could not go "south on 3rd Street" as you would end up on 1st Street. The direction of travel indicated is wrong.

Option B is incorrect. There are far too many turns to make, and even though you are authorized to disobey traffic laws, you are going against one-way traffic on Fir and 4th Street, which would impede your speed dramatically.

Option D is incorrect. The directions are wrong. For example, you would be travelling east on Oak Avenue, not west, in order to travel to 6th Street.

Option C is your best route. Although 1st Ave is one-way, it is a wide street and there are fewer turns to make in order to arrive at Crest School.

40. **C** Option A is not correct. You would have to travel north on 5th, which is a one-way for southbound traffic. Without being able to activate your lights and siren, you will create chaos on 1st Ave.

Option B is not correct. The directions are wrong. Andrews Avenue runs westbound, one way, not northbound.

Option D is incorrect. As in Option A you would end up fighting one-way traffic, on 4th Street, without being able to use your emergency lights and siren.

Option C is your best option. Though it seems counterintuitive to initially head away from the bank by driving east and heading to 6th Street, you can arrive at the bank more efficiently by following traffic laws and not being required to use the vehicle's emergency equipment.

## Part 5: Computations

41. **C** $7 \times \$85,000 = \$595,000$

42. **B** $\$5,000 + \$3,400 + \$9,700 + \$13,600 = \$32,000$ total damage. To calculate the percentage, create a basic algebraic equation. Start by dropping the zeroes in order to make the fractions more manageable. $\frac{136}{320} = \frac{x}{100}$. To isolate $x$, cross-multiply and divide. $x = 42.5\%$.

43. **A** $10 \times \$100 = \$1,000$. $70 \times \$20 = \$1,400$. Since the remaining cash represents one-third of the total, $2,400$ must represent the other two-thirds. Therefore $\$2,400 = \frac{2}{3}x$. To isolate $x$ multiply both sides by the reciprocal of $x$.

44. **D** $60 \div 15 = 4 \times 2 = 8$. They can canvass 8 premises per hour. $8 \times 3$ hours $= 24$ businesses.

45. **C** Area = length $\times$ width. $800 \times 900 = 720,000$ m$^2$.

    That is not that same as 720 km$^2$! That would be 72 km $\times$ 10 km, for example.

46. **A** 36 km $\div$ 18 minutes $= x$ km $\div$ 60 minutes. Isolate $x$ by cross-multiplying and dividing. $60 \times 36 = 2,160 \div 18 = 120$.

47. **D** $290 \times 0.08 = 23.2$. Subtract $290 - 23 = 267$.

48. **B** $\$167 + \$192 + \$115 = \$474 \times 0.25 = \$118.50$. $\$474 - \$118.50 = \$355.50$.

49. **D** $\frac{1}{4} \times 32 = 8$ years of service for Constable Orland, but 60% more years of service than Constable Brown. In this case you cannot simply multiply 8 times 0.60 because the statement is that Orland has 60 percent more than Brown, and not that Brown has 60 percent as much service as Orland. Therefore, the equation is that $1.6x$ ($x$ = Brown plus 60 percent) = 8 (Orland). Isolate $x$ by dividing 1.6 by its reciprocal. Do the same to the other side of the equation: $8 \div 1.6 = 5$.

50. **B** In the equation, allow $x$ to equal the cost of the previous vendor (higher cost). Since the new boots are $\frac{3}{4}$ the cost of the original, and $30 less than the original, you can construct the equation as follows:

    **STEP 1** Construct equation: $\frac{3}{4}x = x - 30$.

    **STEP 2** Remove the negative number by adding 30 to each side: $\frac{3}{4}x + 30 = x$.

    **STEP 3** Subtract $\frac{3}{4}x$ from both sides. $x - \frac{3}{4}x$ is the same as $\frac{4}{4}x - \frac{3}{4}x = \frac{1}{4}x$.

    **STEP 4** Isolate $x$. Multiply $\frac{1}{4}$ by its reciprocal on both sides: $30 \times 4 = x$.

    **STEP 5** $x = 120$.

# Model Exam Four:
# Saskatchewan SIGMA Exam

If you are applying to any municipal police department in the Province of Saskatchewan (e.g., Saskatoon, Regina, Moose Jaw) you will be required to write the Sigma Survey for Police Officers (SIGMA), created by Sigma Assessment Systems which is used by a number of police agencies throughout North America. The SIGMA police entrance exam is a 74-question multiple-choice exam that must be completed in just 35 minutes. The exam measures six competencies, with an emphasis on grammar and writing proficiencies. The table is an approximation of the amount of time, and the number of questions, that you should spend on each competency.

| SASKATCHEWAN SIGMA FORMAT | | | |
|---|---|---|---|
| **SECTION** | **COMPETENCY** | **APPROX. NUMBER OF QUESTIONS** | **APPROX. TIME** |
| Part 1 | Logic | 10 | 6 minutes |
| Part 2 | Judgment | 5 | 5 minutes |
| Part 3 | Problem Solving | 5 | 5 minutes |
| Part 4 | Spatial Identification | 4 | 3 minutes |
| Part 5 | Vocabulary | 25 | 8 minutes |
| Part 6 | Spelling & Mechanics | 25 | 8 minutes |
| | Total | 74 | 35 |

# ANSWER SHEET
## Practice Exam Four

## PART 1: Logic

1. (A) (B) (C) (D)     4. (A) (B) (C) (D)     7. (A) (B) (C) (D)     9. (A) (B) (C) (D)
2. (A) (B) (C) (D)     5. (A) (B) (C) (D)     8. (A) (B) (C) (D)     10. (A) (B) (C) (D)
3. (A) (B) (C) (D)     6. (A) (B) (C) (D)

## PART 2: Judgment

11. (A) (B) (C) (D)     13. (A) (B) (C) (D)     15. (A) (B) (C) (D)
12. (A) (B) (C) (D)     14. (A) (B) (C) (D)

## PART 3: Problem Solving

16. (A) (B) (C) (D)     18. (A) (B) (C) (D)     20. (A) (B) (C) (D)
17. (A) (B) (C) (D)     19. (A) (B) (C) (D)

## PART 4: Spatial Recognition

21. (A) (B) (C) (D)     23. (A) (B) (C) (D)
22. (A) (B) (C) (D)     24. (A) (B) (C) (D)

## PART 5: Vocabulary

25. (A) (B) (C) (D)
26. (A) (B) (C) (D)
27. (A) (B) (C) (D)
28. (A) (B) (C) (D)
29. (A) (B) (C) (D)
30. (A) (B) (C) (D)
31. (A) (B) (C) (D)

32. (A) (B) (C) (D)
33. (A) (B) (C) (D)
34. (A) (B) (C) (D)
35. (A) (B) (C) (D)
36. (A) (B) (C) (D)
37. (A) (B) (C) (D)

38. (A) (B) (C) (D)
39. (A) (B) (C) (D)
40. (A) (B) (C) (D)
41. (A) (B) (C) (D)
42. (A) (B) (C) (D)
43. (A) (B) (C) (D)

44. (A) (B) (C) (D)
45. (A) (B) (C) (D)
46. (A) (B) (C) (D)
47. (A) (B) (C) (D)
48. (A) (B) (C) (D)
49. (A) (B) (C) (D)

## PART 6: Spelling and Mechanics

50. (A) (B) (C) (D)
51. (A) (B) (C) (D)
52. (A) (B) (C) (D)
53. (A) (B) (C) (D)
54. (A) (B) (C) (D)
55. (A) (B) (C) (D)
56. (A) (B) (C) (D)

57. (A) (B) (C) (D)
58. (A) (B) (C) (D)
59. (A) (B) (C) (D)
60. (A) (B) (C) (D)
61. (A) (B) (C) (D)
62. (A) (B) (C) (D)

63. (A) (B) (C) (D)
64. (A) (B) (C) (D)
65. (A) (B) (C) (D)
66. (A) (B) (C) (D)
67. (A) (B) (C) (D)
68. (A) (B) (C) (D)

69. (A) (B) (C) (D)
70. (A) (B) (C) (D)
71. (A) (B) (C) (D)
72. (A) (B) (C) (D)
73. (A) (B) (C) (D)
74. (A) (B) (C) (D)

# PART 1: LOGIC

 **You have 6 minutes to complete the following 10 questions.**

1. Complete the comparison.

   Lake is to Huron as river is to

   (A) Beaufort
   (B) Mackenzie
   (C) Superior
   (D) British Columbia

2. If you rearrange the word OORTOTN you will have the name of a Canadian

   (A) lake
   (B) mountain
   (C) city
   (D) river

3. Select the image that continues the pattern sequence.

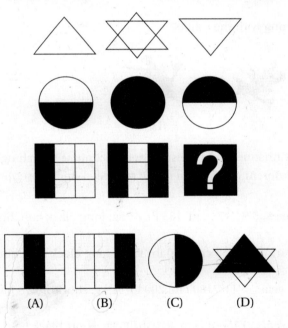

   (A)    (B)    (C)    (D)

4. Select the letters that continue the pattern sequence.

   OEP QER SET UEV

   (A) TES
   (B) WEX
   (C) VET
   (D) YEZ

5. Select the word that does not belong with the others.

   (A) Baton
   (B) Taser
   (C) Pepper spray
   (D) Handcuffs

6. What is the logical conclusion of the two statements?

   Some citizens break the law.

   No one who breaks the law is innocent.

   (A) Therefore, some law-abiding citizens break the law.
   (B) Therefore, some citizens are not law breakers.
   (C) Therefore, some citizens are not innocent.
   (D) No logical conclusion.

7. Select the number that continues the pattern sequence.

   15, 11, 17, 9, 19, ...

   (A) 21
   (B) 13
   (C) 7
   (D) 23

8. Select the shape that does not belong with the others.

   (A)            (B)            (C)            (D)

9. Four witnesses, Andrea, Barbara, Christine, and Denise, observed a purse snatching. Each witness provided a slightly different description of the suspect. Which description is probably most accurate?

   (A) Andrea: Caucasian male, 30 years, 5'9"/175 cm, 185 lb/84 kg, long black hair, black pants, black t-shirt.
   (B) Barbara: Hispanic male, 25 years, 6'1"/185 cm, 210 lb/95 kg, long black hair, blue jeans, black t-shirt.
   (C) Christine: Caucasian male, 25 years, 5'11"/180 cm, 200 lb/91 kg, short brown hair, blue jeans, blue golf shirt.
   (D) Denise: Hispanic male, 20–30 years, 6'1"/185 cm, 210 lb/95 kg, short black hair, khaki shorts, black and white striped t-shirt.

10. Complete the comparison.

    Hops is to grapes as beer is to

    (A) wine
    (B) malt
    (C) barley
    (D) liquor

# PART 2: JUDGMENT

 **You have 5 minutes to complete the following 5 questions.**

> In this section you are required to demonstrate sound decision-making skills and good judgment. You are not required to know police policy and procedures, the applicable law, or law enforcement tactics.

FOR QUESTIONS 11–15, SELECT THE MOST APPROPRIATE COURSE OF ACTION BASED ON THE INFORMATION PROVIDED IN EACH SCENARIO.

11. You are writing a motorist a ticket for excessive speeding and a car drives past you with three young men, the passenger rolls down the window and screams, "Cops suck!" and continues driving by. What should you do?

    (A) Leave the motorist and pursue after the car with the young men.
    (B) Broadcast over the air for other units to stop the car with the young men.
    (C) Continue writing the ticket to the motorist.
    (D) Write the plate number down of the car with the young men, and speak to the registered owner at a later time.

12. You and your partner attend a house party after receiving a noise complaint. There are approximately 10 youth outside the house and more inside the home. The occupants are in violation of the noise by-law and there are obvious signs of underage drinking. At this moment, you should

    (A) issue the owner of the property a noise by-law ticket.
    (B) issue all youth drinking a ticket for "Minor in Possession."
    (C) call for additional police resources.
    (D) obtain a written statement from the complainant about how the noise was disturbing the peace.

13. You have located a lost child two blocks away from the local park where the child went missing. You contacted the dispatcher who has advised the parents to come meet you at your location. Suddenly, a stolen car being driven by a known robbery suspect that you have been looking for drives past you. At that moment you should

    (A) stay with the child and radio dispatch and to other units the description, location, time delay, and direction of travel of the stolen car.
    (B) drive the child to the park and reunite her with the parents and then chase after the stolen car.
    (C) ask a citizen to stay with the child and wait for the parents to arrive while you pursue the stolen vehicle.
    (D) seatbelt the child in the front seat of your police car and pursue the stolen vehicle.

14. You stop a vehicle for speeding and you realize the passenger is a personal friend of yours. The passenger asks to speak to you privately and tells you that the driver is a business associate and they are working on closing a major business deal. He asks you for a "solid" and to let the driver off with a warning. At that moment you should

(A) warn your friend that he is attempting to obstruct a police officer and could be arrested if he continues this line of questioning.
(B) issue the driver a speeding ticket.
(C) make a decision on whether to write the ticket based on the rate of speed over the limit, the road and weather conditions, pedestrians in the area, and driver's attitude and driving record.
(D) let the driver off with a warning.

15. You come across a serious assault in progress where a victim is unconscious lying on the ground bleeding from the head, and you see the suspect hit the victim over the head with a baseball bat. You are 15 metres away from both of them. You draw your pistol and yell, "Stop Police!" The suspect looks at you and again viciously hits the victim over the head with the bat. At this moment, you should

(A) shoot the suspect to prevent imminent grievous bodily harm or death to the victim.
(B) call for a supervisor and additional units.
(C) run up to the suspect and tackle him.
(D) run up to the suspect and hit him with your baton.

# PART 3: PROBLEM SOLVING

 **You have 5 minutes to complete the following 5 questions.**

16. Traffic Officer Jones writes an average of 13 tickets per day. If he works four shifts per week, how many weeks would it take for him to write 364 tickets?

    (A) 10
    (B) 9
    (C) 8
    (D) 7

17. The south wall in the gymnasium needs a new coat of paint. If one litre of paint covers four square metres of surface area, how many litres of paint will be needed to paint the wall that is 8 metres long by 7 metres high?

    (A) 22
    (B) 14
    (C) 9
    (D) 6

18. Constable Simpson was involved in a long foot pursuit with a suspect who was fleeing a dumped stolen car. Simpson ran for a total of 2.5 kilometres and covered the distance in just 12 minutes. What was the average speed that Constable Simpson was running at?

    (A) 9.5 km/h
    (B) 10 km/h
    (C) 12.5 km/h
    (D) 14 km/h

19. The table below shows the number of reported crimes in the city and the number of those cases where a suspect was identified or charged. Using the offence types listed, what was the total ratio of criminal incidents to suspects charged or identified?

| CRIME TYPE | OFFENCES | SUSPECTS ID/CHARGED |
|---|---|---|
| Violent crime | 380 | 196 |
| Property crime | 1,343 | 482 |
| Other crime | 677 | 122 |

    (A) 2:1
    (B) 4:1
    (C) 9:4
    (D) 3:1

20. The annual cost of the new multiagency organized crime unit will be shared between the federal government and the four participating agencies. The federal government will pay half of the cost, and each of the four participating agencies will pay $130,000 per year. What is the total annual cost of the new unit?

(A) $1,400,000
(B) $1,040,000
(C) $520,000
(D) $1,200,000

# PART 4: SPATIAL IDENTIFICATION

**You have 3 minutes to complete the following 4 questions.**

Use the map below to answer Questions 21 and 22. In this map, all streets are designated for two-way traffic, unless indicated as one-way by a one-direction arrow.

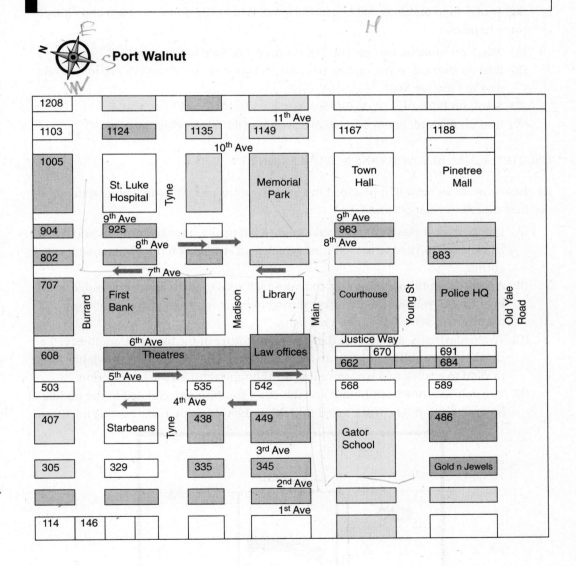

21. You are parked in front of the courthouse on Main Street when you are called to a disturbance outside the Emergency entrance of St. Luke's Hospital on Burrard Street. What is the most accurate and efficient route to take?

(A) North on Main, west on 5th Ave, north on Burrard to St. Luke's.
(B) East on Main, north on 7th Ave, east on Burrard to St. Luke's.
(C) West on Main, south on 10th Ave, east on Burrard to St. Luke's.
(D) North on Main, west on 7th Ave, north on Burrard to St. Luke's.

22. You are in front of the First Bank on Burrard Street, when you receive a report of "shots fired" on Old Yale Road, near Pinetree Mall. You are authorized to respond Code 3 (lights and siren and may disobey traffic laws). What is the most accurate and efficient route to take?

(A) North on Burrard, east on 7th Ave, north on Old Yale to Pinetree Mall.
(B) East on Burrard, south on 8th Ave, east on Young St., south on 9th Ave to Old Yale, east to Pinetree Mall.
(C) South on Burrard, east on 5th Ave, north on Old Yale to Pinetree Mall.
(D) East on Burrard, South on 11th Ave, west on Old Yale to Pinetree Mall.

USE THE FIGURE BELOW TO ANSWER QUESTION 23.

23. Based on the information provided in Figure 1, which one of the following statements best describes what occurred?

(A) Driver of a car was eastbound and made a left turn to proceed northbound when a truck failed to yield to the left turn vehicle and struck it on the front passenger side corner.
(B) A car was southbound, waiting to make a left turn to proceed westbound, the light turned yellow and the driver started to proceed, when it was struck by a northbound vehicle that ran a red light.
(C) Two pedestrians standing on the southwest corner of the intersection observed a car that was southbound start to make a left turn to proceed eastbound, but failed to yield to a truck that was travelling northbound through the intersection.
(D) Two vehicles, one northbound and the other southbound, collided in the middle of the intersection. The truck failed to yield to the vehicle that was making a left turn.

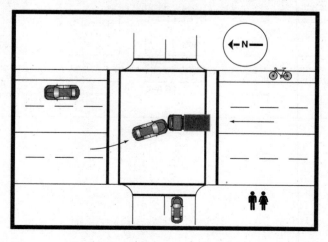

**Figure 1.** Left Turm Collision

24. Based on the information provided in Figure 2, which one of the following statements best describes what occurred?

(A) Vehicle 4, driving westbound on Canada Drive, failed to stop for a left turn vehicle 3 and struck vehicle 3 on the front passenger side corner. Vehicle 2 then hit the passenger side.

(B) Driver of Vehicle 5 was stopped at a red light and observed driver of Vehicle 3 make a left turn to proceed southbound on Buffalo Way and failed to yield to through traffic and was struck by Vehicle 2 and Vehicle 4.

(C) Vehicle 2 and Vehicle 4 were northbound on Buffalo Way when southbound Vehicle 3 made an illegal left turn in front of them to proceed on Canada Way and was struck by Vehicle 2 and Vehicle 4.

(D) Vehicle 2 and Vehicle 4 were proceeding northbound on Canada Drive. Vehicle 3 was in the southbound left turn lane and started to make a left turn to proceed eastbound on Buffalo Way and failed to yield to oncoming Vehicle 2 and Vehicle 4.

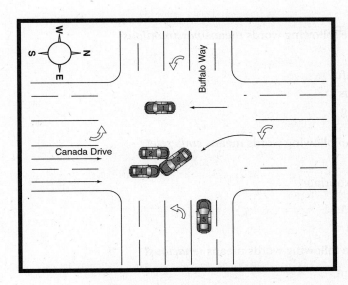

**Figure 2.** Three Car Collision

## PART 5: VOCABULARY

 **You have 8 minutes to complete the following 25 questions.**

25. Which of the following words means *admonish*?

    (A) implore
    (B) reprimand
    (C) bide
    (D) beseech

26. Which of the following words means *posthumous*?

    (A) lacks humour
    (B) after death
    (C) fierce
    (D) sparse

27. Which of the following words means *parsimonious*?

    (A) frugal
    (B) thoughtful
    (C) generous
    (D) forgiving

28. Which of the following words means *embezzle*?

    (A) extort
    (B) misappropriate
    (C) deceive
    (D) deface

29. Which of the following words means *tenacious*?

    (A) persistent
    (B) capricious
    (C) ostentatious
    (D) vivacious

30. Which of the following words means *insubordinate*?

    (A) minor
    (B) obvious
    (C) disobedient
    (D) lesser

31. Which of the following words means *placate*?

   (A) annoy
   (B) enrage
   (C) deter
   (D) pacify

32. Which of the following words means *grievance*?

   (A) serious
   (B) suffering
   (C) severe
   (D) complaint

33. Which of the following words means *salient*?

   (A) clear
   (B) salty
   (C) significant
   (D) confident

34. Which of the following words means *umbrage*?

   (A) burden
   (B) annoyance
   (C) penalty
   (D) fine

35. Which of the following words means the opposite of *domineering*?

   (A) lazy
   (B) industrious
   (C) meek
   (D) vulnerable

36. Which of the following words means the opposite of *deteriorate*?

   (A) convalesce
   (B) satiate
   (C) languish
   (D) sustain

37. Which of the following words means the opposite of *mitigate*?

   (A) castigate
   (B) alleviate
   (C) gravitate
   (D) aggravate

38. Which of the following words means the opposite of *viable*?

   (A) workable
   (B) impracticable
   (C) untrustworthy
   (D) deleterious

39. Which of the following words means the opposite of *ubiquitous*?

(A) charming
(B) lavish
(C) careful
(D) absent

40. Which option best completes the following sentence?

The prosecutor was bewildered when the witness took the stand and _____ her earlier statement that had pointed to the accused's guilt.

(A) redacted
(B) recanted
(C) refuted
(D) repleted

41. Which option best completes the following sentence?

Fortunately, Constable Cooper was able to _____ some of the personal challenges in her life and put those difficult times behind her.

(A) thwart
(B) preclude
(C) absolve
(D) surmount

42. Which option best completes the following sentence?

The defence counsel was trying to convince the jury that the circumstantial evidence presented created a very _____ link between the accused and the crime.

(A) irascible
(B) insolent
(C) tenuous
(D) ardent

43. Which option best completes the following sentence?

Constable Johns wanted to work with a new partner, but was nervous about how to _____ the topic without offending his partner.

(A) assent
(B) endeavour
(C) extol
(D) broach

44. Which option best completes the following sentence?

The police department stated that it was _____ that they were not able to capture the serial purse snatcher sooner.

(A) reluctant
(B) regrettable
(C) regretful
(D) recalcitrant

45. Which option best completes the following sentence?

The sergeant decided that the most _____ solution to the problem was to separate the two officers who were no longer getting along with each other.

(A) penchant
(B) perfunctory
(C) ostensible
(D) pragmatic

46. Which option best completes the following sentence?

You knew it was going to be a long meeting because Sergeant Williamson would never stick to the agenda, discussions would _____, and wind up completely off topic.

(A) digress
(B) assent
(C) vacillate
(D) waver

47. Which option best completes the following sentence?

Chief Robertson was a great leader, she was a(n) _____ and a captivating speaker.

(A) enigmatic
(B) charismatic
(C) inscrutable
(D) obsequious

48. Which option best completes the following sentence?

Constable Wilson was _____ by the fact that the sex offender that he spent months investigating and putting together a comprehensive case was found not guilty due to a minor Charter violation.

(A) perused
(B) prejudiced
(C) procured
(D) perturbed

49. Which option best completes the following sentence?

Annoyed at the suggestion, Sergeant Smith asked Constable Jensen, "Are you trying to _____ that I would knowingly send you into a potentially violent situation without the resources to handle it effectively?"

(A) infer
(B) imbibe
(C) imply
(D) impose

## PART 6: SPELLING AND MECHANICS

 **You have 8 minutes to complete the following 25 questions.**

50. Which one of the following words is misspelled?

    (A) often
    (B) resistance
    (C) February
    (D) tarif

51. Which one of the following words is misspelled?

    (A) immediately
    (B) irresistable
    (C) implementation
    (D) irrelevant

52. Which one of the following words is misspelled?

    (A) desperate
    (B) disobediant
    (C) suggestible
    (D) dialogue

53. Which one of the following words is misspelled?

    (A) persistant
    (B) alcohol
    (C) existence
    (D) rhyme

54. Which one of the following words is misspelled?

    (A) repertoire
    (B) fulfill
    (C) maintenence
    (D) collectable

55. Which one of the following words is misspelled?

    (A) across
    (B) accessory
    (C) accelorate
    (D) accessible

56. Which one of the underlined words in the following sentence is misspelled?

Constable Armstrong's <u>endurance</u> during the undercover investigation <u>exceeded</u> all expectations, and she has proven once again to be an <u>indispensible</u> <u>asset</u> to this organization.

(A) endurance
(B) exceeded
(C) indispensible
(D) asset

57. Which one of the underlined words in the following sentence is misspelled?

It was <u>rumoured</u> that the local grocery clerk was an <u>accessery</u> to murder, but he appeared to have a <u>plausible</u> explanation for being in the area at the time the murder was <u>committed</u>.

(A) rumoured
(B) accessery
(C) plausible
(D) committed

58. Which one of the underlined words in the following sentence is misspelled?

<u>Surveillance</u> conducted on this <u>occassion</u> demonstrated that this drug trafficking case was <u>similar</u> to other recent cases where the suspects had <u>tunnelled</u> from one side of the border to the other.

(A) surveillance
(B) occassion
(C) similar
(D) tunnelled

59. Which one of the underlined words in the following sentence is misspelled?

The <u>perpetraitor</u> entered the commercial premises, <u>revealed</u> a small <u>calibre</u> handgun, and commenced to <u>relieve</u> the convenience store of its funds.

(A) perpetraitor
(B) revealed
(C) calibre
(D) relieve

60. Which of the underlined words in the following sentence is misspelled?

When Constable Harris stopped the <u>foreign</u> diplomat, the driver alleged that he had diplomatic <u>immunity</u> from all forms of <u>prosecution</u>, including the <u>issuence</u> of violation tickets.

(A) foreign
(B) immunity
(C) prosecution
(D) issuence

61. Which option best completes the sentence?

Inspector Irwin told the new sergeants, _____ judged both by our words, _____ our actions."

(A) "we're/and

(B) "We are/and because of

(C) "We're/and by

(D) "Were/and

62. Which option best completes the sentence?

Sergeant Darwin said that he would rather hand over the project to _____, rather _____ someone less qualified.

(A) myself/than

(B) I/then

(C) me/then

(D) me/than

63. Which option best completes the sentence?

The discussion _____ all of the new recruits in the room was that they all _____ _____ wait to find out their new postings.

(A) between/can hardly

(B) among/cannot hardly

(C) between/can't hardly

(D) among/can hardly

64. Which option best completes the following sentence?

The four robbery suspects _____ remanded in custody until _____ next court appearance.

(A) where/their

(B) was/there

(C) were/their

(D) are/they're

65. Which option best completes the following sentence?

The Forensic Interview course was offered to _____ was interested in conducting interrogations. However, the notices and bulletins appeared to have little _____, as few people signed up for the course.

(A) whomever/effect

(B) whoever/affect

(C) whosoever/affect

(D) whoever/effect

66. Read the passage and the underlined part of the sentence. Which option is the most accurate in terms of capitalization, punctuation, and sentence structure?

The Crown prosecutor told the class of police <u>recruits "the</u> purpose of the arraignment is to formally charge the accused and to determine whether the accused will be granted bail or remanded in custody."

(A) recruits: "the
(B) recruits, "the
(C) recruits – "The
(D) recruits, "The

67. Read the passage and the underlined part of the sentence. Which option is the most accurate in terms of capitalization, punctuation, and sentence structure?

The robbery suspect was described as a <u>tall slim man about</u> forty-five years of age, last seen wearing a black toque.

(A) tall and slim man about
(B) tall, slim man, about
(C) tall—slim man—about
(D) tall; slim man; about

68. Read the passage and the underlined part of the sentence. Which option is the most accurate in terms of capitalization, punctuation, and sentence structure?

The race for the next police union president is too close to <u>call they have to recount the ballots.</u>

(A) call. They have to recount the ballots.
(B) call; they have to re-count the ballots.
(C) call: they have to re-count the ballots.
(D) call and now they have to recount the ballots.

69. Read the passage and the underlined part of the sentence. Which option is the most accurate in terms of capitalization, punctuation, and sentence structure?

Constable Jefferson asked me if I knew what the suspect meant when he stated, "Good thing that you are a lousy <u>shot"</u>

(A) shot."
(B) shot?"
(C) shot"?
(D) Shot!'"

70. Read the passage and the underlined part of the sentence. Which option is the most accurate in terms of capitalization, punctuation, and sentence structure?

The Drug Squad sergeant concluded that it would be prudent to wait and obtain the search warrant <u>tomorrow in this particular instants</u> we will have more resources available to assist.

(A) tomorrow, because in this particular instance
(B) tomorrow; In this particular instants,
(C) tomorrow: in this particular instance,
(D) tomorrow. Because, in this particular instants,

71. Which one of the following statements is the most grammatically correct?

   (A) In looking at the arrest rate for impaired drivers, between this year and last year, there are marked decreases.
   (B) There is a marked decrease in the arrest rate for impaired drivers between this year and last year.
   (C) Between this year and last year, there is a marked decrease in arrest rates.
   (D) In looking at the difference between this year and last year, there are marked decreases in the arrest rate for impaired drivers.

72. Which one of the following statements is the most grammatically correct?

   (A) Sergeant Beaumont encouraged my partner and I to apply for promotion in the next corporal's completion.
   (B) In the next corporal's competition, Sergeant Beaumont encouraged my partner and I to apply for promotion.
   (C) Sergeant Beaumont encouraged my partner and me to apply for promotion in the next corporal's completion.
   (D) My partner and I were encouraged by Sergeant Beaumont to apply for promotion in the next corporal's competition.

73. Which one of the following statements is the most grammatically correct?

   (A) The accused continued denying his involvement, however, when confronted with video evidence, his head was hung, but said not a word.
   (B) The accused continued to deny his involvement; however, when he was confronted with video evidence, he hung his head and said nothing.
   (C) When the accused was confronted with video evidence, even though he had been denying his involvement, he hanged his head and said not a word.
   (D) The accused was in denial of his involvement, but when he had been confronted with video evidence, he hung his head and said nothing.

74. Which one of the following statements is the most grammatically correct?

   (A) The investigating detectives felt that not only was the sex offender's sentence far too lenient, but also the fact that he could serve his sentence in the community put the public at risk.
   (B) The investigating detectives felt that the public was put at risk because not only was the sex offenders' sentence far too lenient, he was also allowed to serve his sentence in the community.
   (C) The investigating detectives felt that not only was the sentence for the sex offender far too lenient; the fact that he could serve his sentence in the community also put the public at risk.
   (D) The investigating detectives felt the sentence for the sex offender was not only far too lenient, putting the public at risk, because he was also allowed to serve it in the community.

# ANSWER KEY

## PART 1: Logic

| | | | | | | | |
|---|---|---|---|---|---|---|---|
| **1.** | B | **4.** | B | **7.** | C | **9.** | B |
| **2.** | C | **5.** | D | **8.** | B | **10.** | A |
| **3.** | B | **6.** | C | | | | |

## PART 2: Judgment

| | | | | | |
|---|---|---|---|---|---|
| **11.** | C | **13.** | A | **15.** | A |
| **12.** | C | **14.** | C | | |

## PART 3: Problem Solving

| | | | | | |
|---|---|---|---|---|---|
| **16.** | D | **18.** | C | **20.** | B |
| **17.** | B | **19.** | D | | |

## PART 4: Spatial Identification

| | | | |
|---|---|---|---|
| **21.** | B | **23.** | C |
| **22.** | D | **24.** | D |

## PART 5: Vocabulary

| | | | | | | | |
|---|---|---|---|---|---|---|---|
| **25.** | B | **32.** | D | **38.** | B | **44.** | B |
| **26.** | B | **33.** | C | **39.** | D | **45.** | D |
| **27.** | A | **34.** | B | **40.** | B | **46.** | A |
| **28.** | B | **35.** | C | **41.** | D | **47.** | B |
| **29.** | A | **36.** | A | **42.** | C | **48.** | D |
| **30.** | C | **37.** | D | **43.** | D | **49.** | C |
| **31.** | D | | | | | | |

## PART 6: Spelling and Mechanics

| | | | | | | | | | | |
|---|---|---|---|---|---|---|---|---|---|---|
| 1 | **50.** | D | 8 | **57.** | B | 14 | **63.** | D | 20 | **69.** | A |
| 2 | **51.** | B | 9 | **58.** | B | 15 | **64.** | C | 21 | **70.** | A |
| 3 | **52.** | B | 10 | **59.** | A | 16 | **65.** | A | 22 | **71.** | B |
| 4 | **53.** | A | 11 | **60.** | D | 17 | **66.** | D | 23 | **72.** | C |
| 5 | **54.** | C | 12 | **61.** | C | 18 | **67.** | B | 24 | **73.** | B |
| 6 | **55.** | C | 13 | **62.** | D | 19 | **68.** | B | 25 | **74.** | A |
| 7 | **56.** | C | | | | | | | | |

# ANSWERS EXPLAINED

## Part 1: Logic

1. **B** Lake Huron and Mackenzie River and Canadian geographic landmarks.

2. **C** The word OORTOTN is rearranged to TORONTO, Canada's largest city.

3. **B** The image in the left column and the image in the right column combine to make the image in the centre column.

4. **B** If you remove the middle letter from each cluster the sequence is obvious: OP QR ST UV

5. **D** "Handcuffs" does not belong with the others as the other words are all weapons issued to police officers; handcuffs are restraints, not a weapon.

6. **C** Rule: Some, No = Some Not. "Therefore, some citizens are not innocent."

7. **C** Starting at 15, add 2 to every second number. Starting at 11, subtract 2 from every second number.

8. **B** Except for option B, all images are rotated on a horizontal axis; B is a mirrored image (flipped on a vertical axis).

9. **B** Barbara's description (Hispanic male, 25 years, 6'1"/185 cm, 210 lb/95 kg, long black hair, blue jeans, black t-shirt) contains the most commonly repeated descriptions of the other four witnesses.

   Note: As mentioned previously, these types of logic questions are problematic in that they may lead some people to assume this is how police officers actually determine a suspect's description—all descriptions are given equal weight. In fact, it may be the one description that is completely different than the others (that hasn't been affected by groupthink mentality) that turns out to be what a suspect actually looks like. Although these types of logic questions are not necessarily found on the current SIGMA exam, unfortunately, a number of police agencies do continue to use these types of logic questions.

10. **D** Hops make beer; grapes make wine.

## Part 2: Judgment

11. **C** Passengers yelling out "Cops suck!" as you are writing a ticket is something that you cannot do much about. While I may appear to be contradicting a statement I had made in an earlier practice exam that if you're driving and a pedestrian flips you the bird that you should stop and talk to them, there is a significant difference between the two events—who is in the car. In the former example you are; in this example the rude people are. You can stop and talk to pedestrians—as long as you do not detain them—just to chat. However, you cannot just pull over a car simply because a passenger is rude. You must either witness an offence (such as provincial traffic legislation), believe the driver or occupants are associated with a criminal act, or need to stop the driver to determine his level of sobriety. It's a stretch to state that because the passenger yelled at you, the driver may not be sober. Thus, you would not have a lawful reason to stop and talk to the driver, now or later.

12. **C** It's you and your partner at the house party. There are approximately 10 youth outside the house and more inside the home. Even though there may be offences such as underage drinking and noise violations occurring, you and your partner are vastly outnumbered in a potential volatile or hostile situation. You first need additional resources before doing anything.

13. **D** Except in emergency situations (i.e., to save someone's life), you would never transport a child in a car without the use of a proper car seat or booster seat. The liability you would incur if the child was hurt would be massive. You are stuck waiting for the parents to arrive. Broadcast the description of the suspect vehicle over the radio and hope someone finds it.

14. **C** While you could decide to either write or use your discretion and not write the driver a ticket, the decision to do so should be based on the totality of the situation—especially the speed (dangerousness of act) and driving record of the motorist, and not on your friend's request.

15. **D** Police are justified in using deadly force to prevent grievous bodily harm or death to another person. If a person is on the ground and unconscious, and you have already observed him being hit over the head with a baseball bat, and the suspect refuses your warning and is about strike the victim again, your options are limited. The victim is in serious trouble already—and may die regardless. If you attempt to run and tackle this guy, he will be able to hit the victim at least one more time before you can hit him, and he may hit you next. You must stop the immediate threat—your firearm is your only option.

## Part 3: Problem Solving

16. **D** 13 tickets per day × 4 shifts per week = 52 tickets per week. 364 tickets ÷ 52 = 7 weeks.

17. **B** 1 litre of paint = 4 m² square. Surface area is calculated by multiplying length × height = 8 × 7 = 56 m² ÷ 4 = 14 litres of paint.

18. **C** The formula is $\frac{2.5}{12} = \frac{x}{60}$ (2.5 km in 12 minutes = $x$ in 60 minutes). Isolate $x$ by cross-multiplying and dividing. $x = 12.5$.

19. **D** To determine the ratio, you need to sum total offences and then separately sum those cases where the suspect has been identified or charged. Total offences are 380 + 1,343 + 677 = 2,400. Suspects ID and chargeable are: 196 + 482 + 122 = 800. Ratio is 2,400/800 = 3:1.

20. **B** 4 agencies × $130,000 = $520,000. If the federal government is paying half, then the actual cost is double. 2 × $520,000 = 1,040,000.

## Part 4: Spacial Identification

21. **B** Ensure that you know which way north is facing. Begin by rotating the map so that north is towards the top of the page. Start by travelling east on Main, then a left turn to go north on 7th Ave (one-way street easier to pass traffic than dealing with oncoming vehicles), then a right turn to proceed east on Burrard to St. Luke's.

22. **D** Option A is incorrect. Burrard runs east/west.

Option B is not an efficient route—there are far too many turns, which will dramatically slow you down.

Option C is incorrect: Although the route itself is practical, the directions are wrong. Burrard runs east/west, etc.

Option D is correct in terms of directions and is also an efficient route.

23. **C** First, ensure that the diagram is oriented so that north faces the top of the page.

Option A is incorrect: The driver of the car involved in the collision was southbound, not eastbound.

Option B is incorrect: The driver of the car was waiting to make a turn to proceed eastbound, not westbound.

Option D does not provide an accurate description of events. It would appear that the driver of the car failed to yield to a northbound truck, and not the other way around, as the vehicle was hit as it started its turn and, for example, where it would have been completing the turn and the driver of the truck would be obligated to let it complete the turn.

Option C is the most logical description of events and is correct in terms of directional orientation and identifies the location of pedestrians involved as witnesses.

24. **D** First, ensure that the diagram is oriented so that north faces the top of the page.

Option A is incorrect: Vehicle 4 was northbound, not westbound.

Option B is incorrect: Vehicle 3 was making a left turn to proceed eastbound on Buffalo Way.

Option C is incorrect: Vehicle 2 and 4 were on Canada Drive, not Buffalo Way.

## Part 5: Vocabulary

25. **B** *Admonish* means to reprimand.

26. **B** *Posthumous* means after death.

27. **A** *Parsimonious* means frugal.

28. **B** *Embezzle* means misappropriate (usually funds).

29. **A** *Tenacious* means persistent.

30. **C** *Insubordinate* means disobedient.

31. **D** *Placate* means to pacify.

32. **D** *Grievance* means a complaint.

33. **C** *Salient* means significant.

34. **B** *Umbrage* means annoyance.

35. **C** The opposite of *domineering* is meek.

36. **A** The opposite of *deteriorate* is convalesce.

37. **D** The opposite of *mitigate* is aggravate.

38. **B** The opposite of *viable* is impracticable.

39. **D** *Ubiquitous* means omnipresent or everywhere; the antonym is absent.

40. **B** "The prosecutor was bewildered when the witness took the stand and <u>recanted</u> her earlier statement that had pointed to the accused's guilt." *Recanted* means denied or renounced. *Redacted* means removed or deleted text from a document. *Refuted* means proven to be wrong. *Repleted* is not a word.

41. **D** "Fortunately, Constable Cooper was able to <u>surmount</u> some of the personal challenges in her life and put those difficult times behind her." *Surmount* means to overcome. *Thwart* and preclude mean to prevent an occurrence. *Absolve* means to forgive.

42. **C** "The defence counsel was trying to convince the jury that the circumstantial evidence presented created a very <u>tenuous</u> link between the accused and the crime." *Tenuous* means very weak. *Irascible* means easily angered. *Insolent* means rude or lack of respect. *Ardent* means enthusiastic.

43. **D** "Constable Johns wanted to work with a new partner, but was nervous about how to <u>broach</u> the topic without offending his partner.

    *Broach* means to introduce or initiate. *Assent* means to approve. *Endeavour* means to try to attain something. *Extol* means to praise.

44. **B** "The police department stated it was <u>regrettable</u> that they were not able to capture the serial purse snatcher sooner. *Regrettable* means unfortunate. *Regretful* means full of regret.

45. **D** "The sergeant decided that the most <u>pragmatic</u> solution to the problem was to separate the two officers who were no longer getting along with each other." *Pragmatic* means practical. *Ostensible* means apparent or perceived.

46. **D** "You knew it was going to be a long meeting because Sergeant Williamson would never stick to the agenda, discussions would <u>digress</u>, and wind up completely off topic." *Digress* means to wander or depart. *Vacillate* and *waver* are synonyms, meaning to hesitate or dither.

47. **B** "Chief Robertson was a great leader, she was <u>charismatic</u> and a captivating speaker." *Charismatic* means compelling and captivating. *Enigmatic* and inscrutable are synonyms meaning mysterious and indecipherable. *Obsequious* means overly eager to obey.

48. **D** "Constable Wilson was <u>perturbed</u> by the fact that the sex offender that he spent months investigating and putting together a comprehensive case was found not guilty due to a minor Charter violation." *Perturbed* means greatly upset. *Perused* means reviewed. *Prejudiced* means biased. *Procured* means obtained.

49. **C** "Annoyed at the suggestion, Sergeant Smith asked Constable Jensen, 'Are you trying to <u>imply</u> that I would knowingly send you into a potentially violent situation without the resources to handle it effectively?'" *Imply* means to indirectly indicate something. *Infer* means to draw a conclusion. *Imbibe* means to drink. *Impose* means to enforce.

## Part 6: Spelling and Mechanics

50. **D** Correct spelling: *tariff*

51. **B** Correct spelling: *irresistible*

52. **B** Correct spelling: *disobedient*

53. **A** Correct spelling: *persistent*

54. **C** Correct spelling: *maintenance*

55. **C** Correct spelling: *accelerate*

56. **C** Correct spelling: *indispensable*

57. **B** Correct spelling: *accessory*

58. **B** Correct spelling: *occasion*

59. **A** Correct spelling: *perpetrator*

60. **D** Correct spelling: *issuance*

61. **C** Inspector Irwin told the new sergeants, "<u>We're</u> judged both by our words, <u>and by</u> our actions."

    *We're* must be capitalized because it introduces a quoted statement.

    To maintain parallel structure in the sentence, "both by" needs to be followed up with "and by".

62. **D** "Sergeant Darwin said that he would rather hand over the project to <u>me</u>, rather <u>than</u> someone less qualified." *I* is the first person singular subject pronoun and refers to the person performing the action of a verb. *Me* refers to the person that the action of a verb is being done to. Therefore, the assignment is given to "me". *Than* is a conjunction and preposition that is used to compare or indicate a difference. *Then* can be used as a noun, adjective, or adverb that is used to indicate time or order.

63. **D** "The discussion <u>among</u> all of the new recruits in the room was that they all <u>can hardly</u> wait to find out their new postings. *Among* implies more than two; *between* implies just two (can be two groups or two individuals). *Can't hardly* or *cannot hardly* is a double negative. Simply state, *can hardly*.

64. **C** "The four robbery suspects <u>were</u> remanded in custody until <u>their</u> next court appearance." *Were* is the past tense of the verb to be. *Where* is an adverb meaning to, at, or in what place, or what situation. *Their* is an adjective that means the possessive form of they. *There* is an adverb meaning a place or location. *They're* is a contraction of they are.

65. **A** "The Forensic Interview course was offered to <u>whomever</u> was interested in conducting interrogations. However, the notices and bulletins appeared to have little <u>effect</u>, as few people signed up for the course." *Whoever* is a pronoun that means "whatever person"; *whomever* is the objective form of whoever. *Affect* is used both as a verb, meaning to produce an influence, and as a noun as an aspect of an emotion. *Effect* is used both as a verb, meaning to bring about or to cause, and as a noun meaning the consequence or impact.

66. **D** The Crown prosecutor told the class of police <u>recruits, "The</u> purpose of the arraignment is to formally charge the accused and to determine whether the accused will be granted bail or remanded in custody."

Rule: Use a comma to begin a direct quote within a sentence.

Rule: Capitalize the first word of a direct quote that is a complete sentence.

67. **B** The robbery suspect was described as a <u>tall, slim man, about</u> forty-five years of age, last seen wearing a black toque.

Rule: Use a comma between multiple adjectives not joined by "and."

68. **B** The race for the next police union president is too close to <u>call; they have to re-count the ballots.</u>

Rule: Use a semicolon to link two independent clauses of equal grammatical rank that are related in meaning.

The correct word is *re-count* (meaning to count again); *recount* means to describe events.

69. **A** Constable Jefferson asked me if I knew what the suspect meant when he stated, "Good thing that you're a lousy <u>shot</u>."

The passage reads as a statement; there is no direct question being asked by Constable Jefferson nor that narrator.

70. **A** The Drug Squad sergeant concluded that it would be prudent to wait and obtain the search warrant <u>tomorrow, because in this particular instance</u> we will have more resources available to assist.

The options using a semicolon and colon are incorrect—especially when "instants" is used.

A period could have been used and a new sentence started after "tomorrow," however, the option used "instants" as opposed to "instance." *Instant* means a very short period of time. *Instance* means an example of a situation.

71. **B** Option A is incorrect: Misplaced modifiers and *decrease* should be singular, not plural.

Option C is incorrect: It is missing information about the offences that arrest rates are down for: "impaired drivers".

Option D is incorrect: *Decreases* should be singular.

72. **C** Option A is incorrect: *I* is the first person singular subject pronoun and refers to the person performing the action of a verb; *me* refers to the person that the action of a verb is being done to.

Option B is incorrect: Misplaced modifying clause.

Option D is incorrect: Awkwardly written and in a passive voice.

73. **B** Option A is incorrect: There is a lack of parallel structure among *denying, confronted,* and *was hung.*

Option C is incorrect: *Hanged* should be *hung.*

Option D is incorrect: There is a lack of parallel structure and changes in tense from past (*was*) to past perfect continuous (*had been*).

74. **A** Option B is incorrect: The correlative *not only* requires *but also* in order to maintain parallel structure in the sentence.

Option C is incorrect: misuse of the semicolon.

Rule: Use a semicolon to link two independent clauses of equal grammatical rank that are related in meaning. In this instance, the first clause is an incomplete sentence.

Option D is incorrect: *Not only* correlates to *but also,* not *because.*

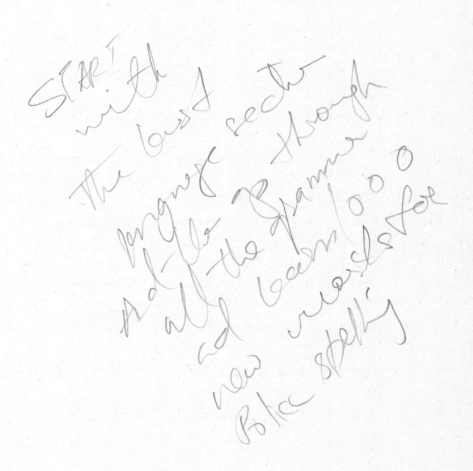

# Model Exam Five: Vancouver Police Department Intake Exam

The Vancouver Police Department's entrance exam is structured in a format that is completely different from any of the other exams you have reviewed thus far. The Vancouver Police Department (VPD) Intake Exam places a high emphasis on comprehensive writing skills, and many of the questions require that you write out your answers in full sentences and that you correct grammatical errors found in paragraphs by completely rewriting them. Therefore, there are far fewer multiple-choice questions and far more expository writing scenarios in this exam than others.

The VPD exam is three hours in duration, scored out of 105 total marks, and a score of 60 percent or higher is required in order to pass. There are four main components to the exam: observation and memorization, writing skills, reading comprehension, and synopsis writing.

| VPD INTAKE EXAM FORMAT | | | |
|---|---|---|---|
| **SECTION** | **COMPETENCY** | **MARKS** | **TIME ALLOWED** |
| Part 1 | Observation and Memorization | 20 | 30 minutes |
| Part 2 | Writing Skills | 40 | 70 minutes |
| Part 3 | Reading Comprehension | 30 | 50 minutes |
| Part 4 | Synopsis Writing | 15 | 30 minutes |
| | Total | **105** | **3 hours** |

# ANSWER SHEET
## Model Exam Five

**PART 1: Observation and Memorization**

| | | | |
|---|---|---|---|
| 1. Ⓐ Ⓑ Ⓒ Ⓓ | 6. Ⓐ Ⓑ Ⓒ Ⓓ | 11. Ⓐ Ⓑ Ⓒ Ⓓ | 16. Ⓐ Ⓑ Ⓒ Ⓓ |
| 2. Ⓐ Ⓑ Ⓒ Ⓓ | 7. Ⓐ Ⓑ Ⓒ Ⓓ | 12. Ⓐ Ⓑ Ⓒ Ⓓ | 17. Ⓐ Ⓑ Ⓒ Ⓓ |
| 3. Ⓐ Ⓑ Ⓒ Ⓓ | 8. Ⓐ Ⓑ Ⓒ Ⓓ | 13. Ⓐ Ⓑ Ⓒ Ⓓ | 18. Ⓐ Ⓑ Ⓒ Ⓓ |
| 4. Ⓐ Ⓑ Ⓒ Ⓓ | 9. Ⓐ Ⓑ Ⓒ Ⓓ | 14. Ⓐ Ⓑ Ⓒ Ⓓ | 19. Ⓐ Ⓑ Ⓒ Ⓓ |
| 5. Ⓐ Ⓑ Ⓒ Ⓓ | 10. Ⓐ Ⓑ Ⓒ Ⓓ | 15. Ⓐ Ⓑ Ⓒ Ⓓ | 20. Ⓐ Ⓑ Ⓒ Ⓓ |

**PART 2: Writing Skill**

Write your answers in the space provided in the test pages.

**PART 3: Reading Comprehension**

Write your answers in the space provided in the test pages.

**PART 4: Synopsis Writing**

Write your answers in the space provided in the test pages.

# PART 1: OBSERVATION AND MEMORIZATION

You have 30 minutes to complete the following 20 questions.

## Instructions

1. Study the photograph of the police incident below (Figure 1) for a maximum of **two minutes** and memorize as much detail about the photograph as possible.

2. You are not permitted to make any written notes or refer back to the photograph when answering subsequent questions.

3. After two minutes have passed, turn the page and read the Wanted Person Bulletin (Figure 2). You are only permitted to study the bulletin for **three minutes**.

4. You are not permitted to make any written notes or refer back to the Wanted Person Bulletin when answering subsequent questions.

5. Answer the questions in sequential order.

Start your timer and begin now.

STUDY THE PHOTOGRAPH FOR A MAXIMUM OF TWO MINUTES.

**Figure 1.** Cyclist Struck

STUDY THE BULLETIN FOR A MAXIMUM OF THREE MINUTES.

---

**WANTED PERSON BULLETIN**

| | |
|---|---|
| Caution: | Armed and Dangerous |
| | Anti-Police |
| Wanted: | Canada Wide Warrant of Arrest |
| | Robbery x 4 and Parole Violation |
| Name: | TREMBLAY, Marcus Christian |
| Alias: | La Fusée |
| Date of Birth: | 1957-11-24 |
| Description: | Caucasian male, 5'9" (175 cm), 215 lb (97 kg), brown hair, blue eyes, speaks with French Canadian accent |
| Scars/Marks: | Tattoo: Germanic symbols right forearm; fleur-de-lis on left calf; maple leaf on chest. Scars: bullet scar left shoulder; 6 cm scar on left forearm. |
| History: | Chronic offender with 29 previous convictions for attempted murder, armed robbery, drug offences, assault, assaulting a police officer, impaired driving, and fishing with a barbed hook. |
| Occupation: | general labourer, construction, roofer |
| Address: | Last known address was Knights of Kingsway Halfway House in Burnaby. Has not been seen for two weeks. |

TREMBLAY is wanted for 4 robberies that occurred across the Lower Mainland (Surrey, Vancouver, West Vancouver, and Abbotsford) between March 15, 2015 and May 02, 2015. He is on parole for attempted murder and was involved in a shootout with police 15 years ago when he was last arrested. He recently told his parole officer: "I will die in a hail of bullets before going back to prison."

Members are advised to use extreme caution if suspect located.

---

**Figure 2.** Wanted Person Bulletin

QUESTIONS 1–10 RELATE TO INFORMATION PICTURED IN FIGURE 1.

1. What was the name of the road that the collision occurred on?

   (A) 65 Ave
   (B) 85A Ave
   (C) 85 Street
   (D) 85A Street

2. What clothes were visible on the child victim?

   (A) Jeans
   (B) Track pants
   (C) Solid coloured shorts
   (D) Checkered shorts

3. What was the address on the house that was visible in the background?

    (A) 4278
    (B) 8214
    (C) 4128
    (D) 7148

4. What was the plate number on the pickup truck?

    (A) SB264
    (B) 274BA
    (C) 289TB
    (D) 547AB

5. What were the three letters visible on the rear driver's side of the pickup truck, near the tail light?

    (A) XTR
    (B) RTR
    (C) ATR
    (D) STR

6. What clothing was the woman wearing?

    (A) Jeans and dark short sleeved shirt
    (B) Capri pants and light long sleeved shirt
    (C) Knee length shorts and white shirt
    (D) Dark shorts and white short sleeved shirt

7. How many roof peaks were visible on the house that was facing the street?

    (A) Two
    (B) Three
    (C) Four
    (D) Five

8. What was the plate number on the sports car?

    (A) 569TN
    (B) 956NT
    (C) 659NT
    (D) 965TN

9. What was the woman doing with her left hand?

    (A) Talking on a cell phone
    (B) Putting her hand over her mouth
    (C) Holding the top of her head
    (D) Reaching towards the child

10. The bicycle helmet was lying beside

    (A) the pickup truck's rear tire.
    (B) the backpack.
    (C) the sports car's front tire.
    (D) the child.

QUESTIONS 11–20 RELATE TO THE INFORMATION PROVIDED IN THE WANTED PERSON
BULLETIN.

11. What was the nickname or alias used by the wanted person?

 (A) Le Fou
 (B) La Fusée
 (C) La Ferme
 (D) La Fleur

12. How many previous convictions did the wanted person have?

 (A) 27
 (B) 28
 (C) 26
 (D) 29

13. What offences were included in the warrant of arrest?

 (A) robbery and attempted murder
 (B) robbery and parole violation
 (C) robbery
 (D) robbery and assaulting a police officer

14. How tall was the wanted person?

 (A) 170 cm
 (B) 190 cm
 (C) 185 cm
 (D) 175 cm

15. What was the tattoo that the suspect had on his left calf?

 (A) Maple leaf
 (B) Fleur-de-lis
 (C) Germanic symbols
 (D) No tattoo on his left calf

16. In what jurisdictions did the suspect commit robberies for which he is now wanted?

 (A) Langley, Surrey, Vancouver, North Vancouver
 (B) Abbotsford, West Vancouver, Surrey, Langley
 (C) West Vancouver, Surrey, Abbotsford, Vancouver
 (D) Vancouver, Surrey, North Vancouver, Abbotsford

17. What did the suspect recently tell his parole officer?

 (A) "I will die in a hail of bullets before going back to prison."
 (B) "I am not going back to prison, you will have to kill me first."
 (C) "I will go into a body bag, before I go back to prison."
 (D) "Before I go back to prison, I will die in a hail of bullets."

18. What were the dates that the robberies occurred between for which the suspect is now wanted?

(A) March 02, 2015 and May 15, 2015
(B) March 21, 2015 and May 11, 2015
(C) March 15, 2015 and May 02, 2015
(D) March 11, 2015 and May 15, 2015

19. What was the colour of the suspect's eyes?

(A) Green
(B) Blue
(C) Brown
(D) Not indicated

20. What was the full name of the suspect?

(A) Christopher Marcel TREMBLAY
(B) Marcus Christian TREMBLAY
(C) Marcus Christopher TREMBLE
(D) Marcel Christian TREMBLAY

## PART 2: WRITING SKILLS

 You have 70 minutes to complete this section.

### Instructions

There are two main components to this section. The first section requires that you read four separate paragraphs and list all grammatical errors that you identify in each paragraph. You will be credited with a ½ mark for each error that you correctly list. The second section requires that you then rewrite the paragraph and correct all spelling, punctuation, and other grammatical errors. You will receive 5 marks for correctly rewriting the paragraph; however, you will be deducted ½ mark for introducing any new errors or failing to correct an original error. For example, if you failed to notice that "cheif" was misspelled in the original paragraph you would lose ½ mark. If you rewrote the paragraph and still misspelled *chief*, you would lose an additional ½ mark.

Writing your answers in the space provided.

Start your timer and begin now.

## Paragraph #1: Part 1

Read the paragraph below and in the space provided list all grammatical errors that you identify.

There is several miscellanous policies and procedures in place for all police officers. While a police officer is free to express their opinion, he or she must bare in mind that he or she is accountible to the police organisation. Its advisable to not make statements to the media while on duty unless previous authorization has been obtianed from the Sergeant or the media liason officer.

**Grammatical Errors:**

21. _____       26. _____

22. _____       27. _____

23. _____       28. _____

24. _____       29. _____

25. _____       30. _____

## Paragraph #1: Part 2

On the lines below, rewrite Paragraph #1 correcting all grammatical errors. A ½ mark will be deducted from any errors that you fail to correct, or any new errors that you introduce.

_____

_____

_____

_____

_____

_____

_____

_____

_____

## Paragraph #2: Part 1

Read the paragraph below and in the space provided list all grammatical errors that you identify.

There was no disagreement between Constable Gordon and I, rather then wait for this vicious robbery suspect to strike again, we decided to set up surveillence on his residents. A hour later the suspect appeared walking up to his apartment. As we moved in on him to make the arrest, I had seen a knife in his hand. I drew my pistol and yelled out "police, don't move. Drop your weapon." The suspect dropped the knife, and we took him into custody. It was a good feeling to finally get this desperate criminal, who had been on the loose for almost a year, back behind bars.

**Grammatical Errors:**

31. _____     36. _____

32. _____     37. _____

33. _____     38. _____

34. _____     39. _____

35. _____     40. _____

## Paragraph #2: Part 2

On the lines below, rewrite Paragraph #2 correcting all grammatical errors. A ½ mark will be deducted from any errors that you fail to correct or any new errors that you introduce.

_____

_____

_____

_____

_____

_____

_____

_____

_____

_____

## Paragraph #3: Part 1

Read the paragraph below and in the space provided list all grammatical errors that you identify.

Constable Taylor hoped to have his report regarding application for civil forfieture of the drug house completed inside of five days however that was unlikely due to other priorities. Irregardless, the arrest of the occupants of this problem premise has been a real success story. On more than eight seperate occasions, police found elicit drug activity at the home. Not only is this a success for the police, it's also one for the community. It was the neighbours persistant contact with the police that created the momentum to dedicate enough resource to shut their drug operation down.

**Grammatical Errors:**

41. _____

42. _____

43. _____

44. _____

45. _____

46. _____

47. _____

48. _____

49. _____

50. _____

## Paragraph #3: Part 2

On the lines below, rewrite Paragraph #3 correcting all grammatical errors. A ½ mark will be deducted from any errors that you fail to correct or any new errors that you introduce.

_____

_____

_____

_____

_____

_____

_____

_____

_____

_____

## Paragraph #4: Part 1

Read the paragraph below and in the space provided list all grammatical errors that you identify.

Constables Janice Smith and Cameron Brown where competing for the same position in the Drug Section. Each of them have exceptional investigative skills and are proficeint report writers. They are also considered indispensible in their current assignments. It will definitely be a difficult decision, since neither of them is a concern in terms of their professionalism. Therefore, instead of this being solely my decision, I have decided to put this to a committee, chaired by Lieutenent Green, and for me to be advised when their decision is reached. Anyway, I will be satisfied with whomever the committee chose.

**Grammatical Errors:**

51. _____

52. _____

53. _____

54. _____

55. _____

56. _____

57. _____

58. _____

59. _____

60. _____

## Paragraph #4: Part 2

On the lines below, rewrite Paragraph #4 correcting all grammatical errors. A ½ mark will be deducted from any errors that you fail to correct or any new errors that you introduce.

_____

_____

_____

_____

_____

_____

_____

_____

_____

_____

## PART 3: READING COMPREHENSION

 You have 50 minutes to complete this section.

### Instructions

There are three reading comprehension and critical thinking tasks. Each task requires that you read an article or police investigational report and answer the questions that follow. Write your answers out in complete sentences. You will receive one mark for every correct answer, and ½ mark will be deducted for each grammatical error.

Write your answers in the space provided.

## Task One: Magazine Article

Read the following *Gazette* law enforcement magazine article and answer the subsequent questions that relate to the article.

**Complex Cases, Intelligent Investigations**
**Police tackle organized crime together**
By Sigrid Forberg

Knowledge is power. Especially when it comes to complex and broad investigations, police officers have to do everything they can to build the strongest case possible.

And increasingly—particularly when it comes to organized crime investigations—that means communicating and collaborating with other police organizations and partner agencies. Everyone from liaison officers across the world and Crown counsel to the local police or another unit within the same police force bring something different to the table.

As the RCMP continues to formalize interagency relationships across the country, the successes that have come out of these joint investigations and task forces stand out as proof that the future of policing involves far fewer silos.

**Organized against crime**

Last year, the RCMP in British Columbia (B.C.) wrapped up a nearly two-year investigation in Kelowna into high-ranking members of the Hells Angels Motorcycle Club (HAMC) with the seizure of more than $4 million and the arrests of eight individuals, who were charged with conspiracy to import 500 kilograms of cocaine.

They were also able to lay charges against the club as a criminal organization and once convicted, it will be the first time in B.C. that the HAMC is identified as a criminal organization.

But part of the success for those involved was the teamwork that went on behind the scenes of the investigation. The Kelowna drug team had originally received the intelligence that a group was exporting marijuana to the United States and importing cocaine into Canada.

As they started working the file, which was called E-Predicate, it continued to grow in scope and reach, taking investigators as far as Central and South America.

"It was a large-scale investigation over two years," says Cpl. Ken Johnston, the primary investigator on the file. "There would be days where we would have 47 to 50 people at a briefing."

S/Sgt. Brian Gateley, the team commander for E-Predicate, says that level of manpower was necessary considering the targets of their investigation. One member of the gang in particular is considered one of the top three players in Western Canada.

And so as the scope of the investigation broadened, the resources and relationships with their partners needed to as well. They called in investigators from across the province, expanding their full-time team from 18 to 35. Relationships with liaison officers abroad and foreign policing agencies were pivotal in keeping the investigation on the right track and securing crucial information and evidence.

Gateley also worked very closely with the provincial associate chief prosecutor to ensure everything was done efficiently but correctly and that various techniques would not affect the trial.

"They really had to buy into it in order for us to keep moving the investigation forward," says Gateley. "It couldn't have been done without that collaboration. I just look at how many strong partnerships were built during this file both internally and externally—we've got 400 police identified that we have to get notes from."

**Mutually beneficial**

In the province of Manitoba, most organized crime activity occurs in Winnipeg. And so in 2004, the RCMP partnered with the Winnipeg Police Service (WPS) to form the Manitoba Integrated Organized Crime Task Force (MIOCTF).

Comprised of nine WPS members and nine RCMP members, the MIOCTF's mandate is to combat high-level organised crime in the province. While based in Winnipeg, their investigations sometimes take them outside of the city and even the province—often to one of their neighbouring provinces in the West. Having the two agencies working together and keeping the lines of communication constantly open have proven to be the best method for everyone.

"Instead of having two separate investigations, you combine resources and share intelligence, this allows investigations to progress more smoothly," says Insp. Len DelPino, the officer in charge of Winnipeg Drugs and Integrated Organized Crime.

The MIOCTF has led several successful investigations against the Hells Angels as well as high-level independent drug dealers in the province. Most recently was Project Deplete, a seven-month investigation that ended in February 2012 and resulted in the seizure of nearly $1 million of drugs and charges laid against 13 individuals.

While the resources and work are shared equally, S/Sgt. Marc Samson, one of the two team commanders of the MIOCTF, says that the WPS officers, who spend their entire careers in the city, have an in-depth knowledge of their municipality and connections that can be useful in the process of an investigation.

"We get very good officers that know exactly who's who in the city," says Samson. "And when we require assistance or information, we have immediate access to the front-line officers who are ready to assist on a moment's notice."

At the same time, RCMP members bring their knowledge and connections from their varied backgrounds and experiences all across the country. Samson says it's the marriage of municipal, provincial and federal backgrounds that has made their investigations so successful, with an impressive 98 percent conviction or guilty plea rate.

**Strength in numbers**

Whether in long-term partnerships or individual investigations, working collaboratively brings the best of each organization to the table. And from these partnerships, innovative techniques and best practices emerge.

Everyone from the investigators and team commander to the tech support that worked on E-Predicate have been receiving calls and questions about the techniques used. Gateley, who will be presenting at the team commander annual general meeting this summer, says a lot of intelligence came out of the clubhouse that they're now working on sharing with other police agencies across the country.

"The case was so complex and there were so many obstacles that we learned from," says Gateley. "The big thing now is to make sure we give that to other people."

No matter how police tackle the investigating of crime, criminals are continuing to evolve and perfect their techniques. With limited resources and pressure from the public to do more with less, organizations need to look at the best ways to get in front of crime and make a real dent in organized criminal activity.

While law enforcement will never be able to completely eradicate crime, more and more, the most effective solution seems to be sharing the burdens and responsibilities as well as the successes.

"Crime has changed in society. We're dealing with different generations and a different group of people, and I think it's gotten more violent over the last number of years," says DelPino. "But if we weren't together, would that still be the case? No doubt. We're doing our best and I think this is the best way for everyone to get the most bang for their buck."

*The above article is reprinted courtesy of the RCMP Gazette, as published in Vol. 75, No. 2, 2013. Portions of the original article have been removed to reduce its length.*

QUESTIONS 61–70 RELATE TO THE ARTICLE ABOVE. ANSWER THE QUESTIONS IN THE SPACE PROVIDE USING COMPLETE SENTENCES.

61. How many individuals were charged during the RCMP investigation into drug activity by members of the Hells Angels Motorcycle Club in Kelowna B.C.?

_____

_____

_____

62. What was the significance of the criminal charges that were laid against the Hells Angels Motorcycle Club in that specific investigation?

_____

_____

_____

63. Who did the RCMP collaborate with during the Kelowna investigation in order to ensure that the investigative techniques used would not affect the trial?

_____

_____

_____

64. In 2004, the RCMP and the Winnipeg police service partnered to create the MIOCTF. What does the acronym stand for?

_____

_____

_____

65. What was the outcome of Project Deplete?

_____

_____

_____

66. If the Manitoba investigation resulted in the seizure of $1 million in drugs and cash, approximately how much more was the value of money and drugs seized in the Kelowna investigation?

_____

_____

_____

67. According to the article, what was S/Sgt. Gateley planning on doing at the team commander annual general meeting?

_____

_____

_____

68. What was the outcome of Project E-Predicate?

_____

_____

_____

69. What was the quoted success rate for criminal charges in relation to the MIOCTF?

_____

_____

_____

70. In the context of this article, what does the word "silos" mean?

_____

_____

_____

## Task Two: Police Report

Review the following collision investigation report and supplemental accident scene diagram and answer the subsequent questions that relate to this incident.

### Collision Investigation 2015-1071124

On 2015-March-07, at approximately 0300 hours, Vancouver Police Constables MANN and DOSANJH attended a two-vehicle collision located at the intersection of Danforth Way and Garret Drive. It was dark, the roads were dry and the area was partially illuminated by overhead street lighting.

Upon arrival the officers discovered one vehicle (Vehicle #1) parked on Danforth Way with damage to the front end driver's side bumper and corner. The other vehicle (Vehicle #2) had gone off the road and over a small embankment approximately 75 metres to the south of the intersection. This vehicle was upside down, heavily damaged, and the driver was still in the driver's seat.

At that time Cst. DOSANJH was approached by witness Jennifer BANNERMAN. She stated that she was following behind a dark coloured Malibu on Garett Drive when the vehicle's headlights illuminated a white Honda Accord pulling out in front of it on Danforth Way directly in front of the Malibu. She stated that the driver of the Malibu braked heavily and skidded, but clipped the front end of the Accord, lost control and went over the embankment.

Cst. DOSANJH then spoke to the driver of the Accord (Vehicle #1) who identified herself as Suzanne CAMPBELL. She stated that she was on Danforth Way at the stop sign and was about to make a left turn onto Garett Drive when this vehicle came racing out of nowhere. She said she had moved forward and was about to make her turn when the vehicle hit her, but that she did not see the vehicle because it didn't have its lights on. She estimated the car must have been travelling at over 100 km/h. CAMPBELL was not injured and Cst. DOSANJH did not notice any indicia of impairment on her.

While Cst. DOSANJH dealt with the witnesses BANNERMAN and CAMPBELL, Cst. MANN dealt with the driver of Vehicle #2, who had just been removed from the vehicle by Vancouver Fire and Rescue and taken to an ambulance. While being attended to for minor scrapes to his head and a small cut on his left arm, Cst. MANN noticed an odour of liquor on his breath. Cst. MANN then went to Vehicle #2 and located 3 empty and two unopened Gross Lager beer cans inside the vehicle. Cst. MANN noticed that the headlights and taillights of the vehicle were still on.

Cst. MANN then returned to the subject in the ambulance and asked him for his driver's licence. He produced a valid and subsisting licence in the name of SPADE, Edward Anthony. While Cst. MANN was talking to SPADE, he noticed that SPADE's eyes were bloodshot and glassy, he was slurring his words, had a difficult time fumbling around for his driver's licence, and the odour of liquor on his breath was more noticeable the longer he stayed with him. Cst. MANN then formed the opinion that SPADE's driving had been affected by alcohol and Cst. MANN read him the Approved Screening Device Breath Demand. SPADE provided a breath sample, which registered "FAIL" on the instrument.

At 0321 hours, Cst. MANN read SPADE his rights under section 10 (a) and (b) of the Charter of Rights and Freedoms, advising him that he was being detained for impaired driving. When MANN asked SPADE if he understood his rights, SPADE replied, "I guess this will really be a special occasion now!"

The ambulance attendants advised that SPADE's injuries were minor, his vital signs were good, and that he did not require transport to hospital and was released at the scene. MANN then called for a police wagon to attend to transport SPADE to the police station for the purposes of conducting a breathalyser test.

At 0340 hours, SPADE was provided with the opportunity to contact a lawyer by telephone. SPADE exited the phone booth at 0345 hours and sat on a bench outside the breathalyser room. While waiting to take the test, SPADE's behaviour vacillated from boisterous and boorish one minute to remorseful and reticent the next. SPADE provided two breath samples, both reading twice the legal limit of 80 mgs of alcohol in a 100 ml of blood.

SPADE was formally charged with Impaired Driving under the Criminal Code and released on an Appearance Notice, to appear in Provincial Court on 2015-MAY-15.

Vehicle #1
2013 Honda Accord, 4 door, white
Owner: CAMPBELL, Suzanne (Date of Birth: 1980-11-07)
Driver: CAMPBELL, Suzanne (Date of Birth: 1980-11-07)
Damage: Front driver's side quarter panel and bumper.
Estimated Cost of Repair: $4,000
Estimated Value: $31,000

Vehicle #2
2010 Chevrolet Malibu, 4 door, blue
Owner: SPADE, Anthony (Date of Birth: 1956-10-13)
Driver: SPADE, Edward Anthony (Date of Birth: 1996-03-06)
Damage: Front passenger side bumper and quarter panel; large dents and intrusion along passenger side of vehicle; extensive damage to roof.
Estimated cost of Repair: $16,000
Estimated Value: $27,000

QUESTIONS 71–80 RELATE TO INFORMATION PROVIDED IN THE POLICE REPORT
AND FIGURE 3. ANSWER THE QUESTIONS IN THE SPACE PROVIDE USING COMPLETE
SENTENCES.

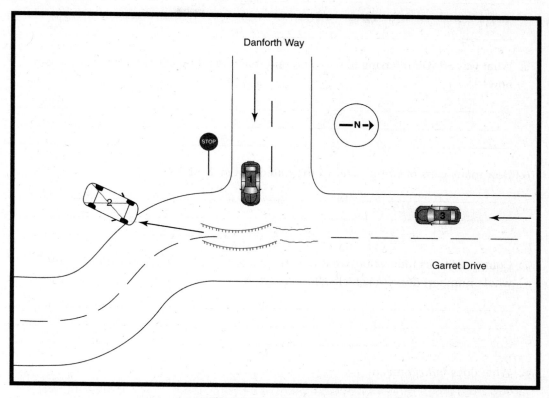

**Figure 3.** Garret Drive Collision

71. Based on the information provided, who would have been driving the vehicle identified
in the collision diagram as #3?

_____

_____

_____

72. What was the direction of travel for Vehicle #1 when it was involved in the collision?

_____

_____

_____

73. What is the most plausible relationship between the driver and the owner of
Vehicle #2?

_____

_____

_____

74. Was Suzanne CAMPBELL being truthful about the headlights of the vehicle being on or off when she pulled in front of the car? Why or why not?

_____

_____

_____

75. What was SPADE referring to when he said that it would really be a "special occasion" now?

_____

_____

_____

76. How many cans of Gross Lager were located by Cst. MANN?

_____

_____

_____

77. Compared to its total value, what was the percent of damage (rounded to nearest whole number) done to Vehicle #2?

_____

_____

_____

78. What does *indicia* mean?

_____

_____

_____

79. What does *reticent* mean?

_____

_____

_____

80. The speed in km/h of a vehicle can be roughly determined by multiplying 177.8 times the length of the skid mark in metres, and then calculating the square root of the product. If the skid mark was 40.5 metres, what would be the product that you would then need to calculate the square root of?

_____

_____

_____

## Task Three: Police Report

Read the following break and enter investigational report and answer the questions that relate to this incident.

**Break and Enter 2015-112975**

On 2015-04-21 at approximately 1855 hours, Constables WALLACE and MAXWELL attended 2156 Cottonwood Lane in regards to a report of a break and enter at that residence. Upon arrival they met with the victim Vanessa ASHCROFT who stated that she arrived home from work at approximately 1645 hours and found the back door of the house wide open. She then noticed that some of her belongings were missing from the living room and from her bedroom.

ASHCROFT stated that the following items were stolen from the living room:

- Sony HD camcorder, value: $850
- Xbox 360 Console, value: $200
- Mac Laptop, value $900
- Yamaha Stereo: $400
- Samsung DVD player: $150

ASHCROFT then advised that she also had the following jewellery stolen from her bedroom:

- Ladies solitaire diamond ring, value: $4,900
- Men's Movado watch with the words engraved: "to Aksel, forever yours" on the back, value $1,700

ASHCROFT told MAXWELL that her husband Aksel, to whom she has been married for two years, was away for a few days on a business trip and that no one else lived in the residence. She stated that she left for work at 0630 in the morning and locked the back door on her way out. Constable MAXWELL searched the residence and found a basement window was slid open and there were pry marks around the outside portion of the window frame. There were also several small wet droplets of what appeared to be blood on the window ledge. ASHCROFT was unaware of the pried window and had not seen it like that before. Constable MAXWELL then called for a member of the Forensic Identification Section (FIS) to attend the scene.

Constable WALLACE attended the rear of the neighbour's residence across the back lane and spoke to Alice SPENCER of 2167 Alderwood Lane. She states that she was home all day, and did not notice anything unusual; however, she mentioned that she did take her dog for a walk and was looking at the rear of the ASHCROFT home at around 1100 hours and noticed that the rear door was closed at that time.

At 1930 hours Constable HOWARD from FIS arrived and advised that he was able to lift a latent fingerprint from the window and also seized a sample of the apparent blood from the window ledge.

On 2015-04-22 at approximately 1300 hours, Constables WALLACE and MAXWELL attended Fast Freddy's Pawn Emporium at 312 Main Street to check the day's ledger and discovered that a person by the name of Edwin BALLANTYNE had pawned a men's Movado watch and Sony camcorder. WALLACE checked the watch and found the inscription written to "Aksel" on the back plate. WALLACE and MAXWELL advised the owner, Fred NORTHLAND, that the watch and camcorder were stolen and seized the property. A search of police records found that "Edwin BALLANTYNE" was an alias used by a local B&E suspect, James CARTIER. MAXWELL showed NORTHLAND a photo of CARTIER, and NORTHLAND confirmed he was the one who pawned the stolen items.

On 2015-04-23 at approximately 1300 hours, Constables WALLACE and MAXWELL were advised by HOWARD that a positive hit was made on the fingerprint and DNA in the blood. They both came back to Aksel ASHCROFT, who had prior convictions for theft and fraud related to illegal stock market trading from ten years ago. Upon further investigation, WALLACE discovered that Aksel ASHCROFT filed for bankruptcy last month. ASHCROFT has also filed an insurance claim for the stolen property.

On 2015-04-24 Constables WALLACE and MAXWELL interviewed Aksel ASHCROFT at his residence. He advised that he had returned from his business trip the previous day after his wife informed him of the break in. He had a bandage on his right little finger and he stated that he cut it while trying to open a hard plastic container on his business trip. MAXWELL confronted ASHCROFT regarding his prints on the window and his blood on the ledge. He stated he did that three months ago when he was trying to unjam the sliding window at that time. ASCHCROFT denies knowing BALLANTYNE or CARTIER or any knowledge of who may be responsible for the break in.

QUESTIONS 81–90 RELATE TO INFORMATION PROVIDED IN THE ABOVE BREAK AND ENTER REPORT. ANSWER THE QUESTIONS IN THE SPACE PROVIDED USING COMPLETE SENTENCES.

81. The break in most likely occurred between what hours on 2015-04-21?

_____

_____

_____

82. How much more was the value of the property stolen from the bedroom, than the value of the property stolen from the living room?

_____

_____

_____

83. What was the most likely point of entry that the suspect used to break into the home?

_____

_____

_____

84. In the context of this report, what does the term *latent* mean?

_____

_____

_____

85. Who was the owner of Fast Freddy's Pawn Emporium?

_____

_____

_____

86. What percent (rounded to nearest whole number) of the total value of property stolen was recovered at Fast Freddy's Pawn Emporium?

_____

_____

_____

87. Why is ASHCROFT's story highly unlikely that he left his blood and prints on the window three months earlier when he was trying to fix a jam?

_____

_____

_____

88. What did Askel ASHCROFT have a criminal record for?

_____

_____

_____

89. Are CARTIER and Aksel ASHCROFT the same person? Why or why not?

_____

_____

_____

90. Why is this report of a break and enter likely a staged crime?

_____

_____

_____

# PART 4: SYNOPSIS

 **You have 30 minutes to complete this section.**

---

### Instructions

Review the following statements of the police officers, victim, and witness. Summarize this information, using 125 words or fewer, to create a synopsis that captures the key elements of this incident. The synopsis must be written in a logical manner, using complete sentences. The task is worth 15 marks; however, points are deducted for failing to include all essential information and for any grammatical errors.

Write your answer in the space provided.

---

### Statement of Victim JONES

I was at home in my apartment watching the movie 21 Jump Street when I heard voices out in the hallway. They were saying, "Let's get him, I know he's in there." I heard another guy say, "I'm going to kill that goof." Then they started booting on the door. I knew the door was going to crash in because it's an old building, like built in the 60s or something. Anyways, I don't know why someone wants to kill me, I think they got the wrong address or something. I wasn't about to wait to find out. I live on the second floor, but I'm in pretty good shape man. So I dove over the balcony, landed in the bushes and just started running. Look at me, I don't even have anything more than boxers and a t-shirt on. As I was running, I could hear voices say, "Where is he?" from inside my apartment. I ran to the house three or four houses away, or something. I never looked back. I got to the house and pounded on the door and said "Hey call police!" Some old lady, nice though, she answered the door. Boy was she surprised to see me standing there in my underwear. She said she wasn't going to open the door. Who can blame her? Anyways she said she was going to call 911. I told her I lived in the apartments on the next street over and there were some bad dudes after me. She wouldn't let me inside the house but said I could hide on her back porch. So I went there and hid. She told me the cops were coming. Then about 10 minutes later she said you guys had caught these goofs. I'm not a bad guy, I don't know what this is about exactly, maybe an old friend's pissed at me about his girlfriend or something. Anyways, that's when you guys showed up to see me.

### Statement of Witness HENDERSON

My name is Irene Henderson, I'm 83 years old and I live at 2527 Lilly Drive. On today's date (May 07, 2015) just after midnight, I was in bed asleep when I heard a terrible racket and someone banging on my front door. I'm a recent widow and I was afraid to be woken up like that. I went to the front door and saw this young man standing there in his underwear and bare feet. He was white as a ghost and looked terrified. He was saying, "Help! Help! Please call the police, there's someone trying to kill me!" I wasn't going to let him in, but I told him that he could wait for the police on my back porch. I then called 911 and spoke to a lovely lady on the phone. She was so helpful and asked me some questions. I said there was a man hiding on my back porch and that he had come from the apartment building the next street over, on Mayfield Drive. A few minutes later the operator told me that the police had someone in custody, and we hung up. I spoke to the man who was hiding on my porch for a few minutes. He told me that his name was Rene and that he was in trouble because he got his former friend Josh's current girlfriend Caitlin pregnant. Such a shame. Young men and the trouble they get themselves into. A few minutes later a police officer arrived and took statements from me and the young man in trouble. I offered him some cookies for the boys (and girls) at the station—I hope that's ok? Thank you for responding so quickly and for keeping our city safe. God Bless.

Irene Henderson.

### Evidence of Constable BRETT

On 2015-05-07 PC BRETT was on duty, in full uniform, driving a marked police car. At approximately 0010 hr BRETT responded to a call of a suspicious circumstance at 2527 Lilly Drive. A complainant advised that there was a young man in his underwear hiding on her back porch and that unknown persons were looking for him and wanting to kill him. Approximately two minutes later, BRETT was in the 2700 block of Mayfield Drive, and BRETT observed two men in their 20s wearing dark clothing walking on the sidewalk. As BRETT was driving up to them BRETT noticed that one of them was carrying a baseball bat. BRETT exited the police car, told the suspects to stay where they were and called for a cover unit. PC RYAN arrived approximately 30 seconds later and we took the two men into custody. BRETT handcuffed and searched the first suspect, later identified as Josh FRESHMAN, and located zap straps and a ski mask in his pockets. FRESHMAN was the suspect who was carrying the baseball bat. BRETT then handcuffed and searched the second suspect, later identified as Cole REYNOLDS, and located a large buck knife tucked in his waistband, zap straps, and a ski mask in his jacket pocket. BRETT then advised both of them that they were under arrest for break and enter, threatening, and possession of a dangerous weapon. BRETT waited with the suspects until the police wagon arrived and then they were taken to the jail and lodged.

### Evidence of Constable RYAN

On 2015-05-07 PC RYAN was on duty, in full uniform, driving a marked police car. At approximately 0012 hr RYAN responded to a request for cover from PC BRETT in the 2700 block of Mayfield. RYAN was a short distance away and arrived on scene within less than a minute. PC BRETT had two individuals prone on the ground at gun point. RYAN maintained cover while BRETT handcuffed and searched the suspects. RYAN had no dealing with the suspects. RYAN then attended 2527 Lilly Drive and spoke to the victim JONES and the witness HENDERSON and took written statements from each of them. RYAN then attended the victim's residence at #202-2531 Mayfield Drive and observed the broken down apartment door. According to the victim, nothing else appeared to be damaged or missing. It is unknown how the suspects gained entry into the lobby of the apartment building.

**Police Synopsis**

In the space below, summarize the information above and create a maximum 125-word synopsis that captures the essential elements of this incident.

_____

_____

_____

_____

_____

_____

_____

_____

_____

_____

_____

_____

_____

_____

_____

# ANSWERS EXPLAINED

## Part 1: Observation and Memorization

1. **B** The street sign, 85A Ave, is above the stop sign.

2. **D** The child was wearing checkered shorts.

3. **C** The address on the house facing the street is 4128.

4. **B** The plate on the rear of the truck is 274BA.

5. **B** The three letters on the side of the truck near the rear driver's side were RTR.

6. **D** The woman is wearing dark coloured shorts and a white short-sleeved shirt.

7. **C** On the house that is visible (the one with 4128 on the address) there are four roof peeks.

8. **A** The plate was 569TN.

9. **C** She was holding the top of her head.

10. **B** The helmet was closest to the backpack.

11. **B** His alias was La Fusée ("The Rocket").

12. **D** 29 prior convictions

13. **B** The suspect is wanted for robbery and parole violation.

14. **D** The suspect is 175 cm tall.

15. **B** He had a fleur-de-lis tattoo on his left calf.

16. **C** West Vancouver, Surrey, Abbotsford, Vancouver

17. **A** The suspect told parole officer, "I will die in a hail of bullets before going back to prison."

18. **C** Offences occurred between March 15, 2015 and May 02, 2015.

19. **B** The suspect's eyes were blue.

20. **B** Marcus Christian TREMBLAY

## Part 2: Writing Skills

### Paragraph #1: Part 1

21. is (*are*)

22. miscellanous (*miscellaneous*)

23. their (*his or her*)

24. bare (*bear*)

25. accountible (*accountable*)

26. Its (*It's*)

27. onduty (*on duty*)

28. obtianed (*obtained*)

29. Sergeant (*sergeant*)

30. liason (*liaison*)

### Paragraph #1: Part 2

There **are** several **miscellaneous** policies and procedures in place for all police officers. While a police officer is free to express **his or her** opinion, he or she must **bear** in mind that he or she is **accountable** to the police organisation. **It's** advisable to not make statements to the media while **on duty** unless previous authorisation has been **obtained** from the **sergeant** or the media **liaison** officer.

　　Score 5 marks if all grammatical corrections were made. Deduct ½ mark for each error not corrected properly.

### Paragraph #2: Part 1

31. I (*me*)

32. then (*than*)

33. surveillence (*surveillance*)

34. residents (*residence*)

35. A (*An*)

36. later (*later,*)

37. had seen (*saw*)

38. out (*out,*)

39. "police, (*"Police,*)

40. weapon." (*weapon!"*)

### Paragraph #2: Part 2

There was no disagreement between Constable Gordon and **me,** rather **than** wait for this vicious robbery suspect to strike again, we decided to set up **surveillance** on his **residence. An** hour **later,** the suspect appeared in front of his apartment. As we moved in to make the arrest, I **saw** a knife in his hand. I drew my pistol and yelled **out, "Police**, don't more. Drop your weap**on!"** The suspect dropped the knife, and we took him into custody. It was a good feeling to finally get this desperate criminal, who had been on the loose for almost a year, back behind bars.

　　Score 5 marks if all grammatical corrections were made. Deduct ½ mark for each error not corrected properly.

### Paragraph #3: Part 1

41. forfieture (*forfeiture*)

42. inside of (*within*)

43. days however (*days; however,* or *days. However,*)

44. Irregardless, (*Regardless*)

45. premise (*premises*)

46. seperate (*separate*)

47. elicit (*illicit*)

48. it's also (*but also*—when using a correlative conjunction, both clauses have to be parallel. That is, "not only" must be followed by "but also" in order to maintain parallel structure).

49. neighbours (*neighbours'*—must show possession).

50. persistant (*persistent*)

## Paragraph #3: Part 2

Constable Taylor hoped to have his report regarding application for civil **forfeiture** of the drug house completed **within** five **days; however,** that was unlikely due to other priorities. **Regardless**, the arrest of the occupants of this problem **premises** has been a real success story. On more than eight **separate** occasions, police found **illicit** drug activity at the home. Not only is this a success for the police, **but it is also** one for the community. It was the **neighbours' persistent** contact with the police that created the momentum to dedicate enough resource to shut their drug operation down.

   Score 5 marks if all grammatical corrections were made. Deduct ½ mark for each error not corrected properly.

## Paragraph #4: Part 1

51. where (*were* or *are*)

52. have (*has*—the antecedent *each* creates a singular verb)

53. proficeint (*proficient*)

54. indispensible (*indispensable*)

55. of them (*one*—neither creates singular pronoun).

56. their (*his or her*—neither creates singular reference)

57. Lieutenent (*Lieutenant*)

58. their (*its*—committee is a collective noun referred to in the singular).

59. whomever (*whoever*—whomever is used when whatever person is the object)

60. chose (*chooses*—chose is the past tense of choose)

## Paragraph #4: Part 2

Constables Janice Smith and Cameron Brown **are** competing for the same position in the Drug Section. Each of them **has** exceptional investigative skills and are **proficient** report writers. They are also considered **indispensable** in their current assignments. It will definitely be a difficult decision, since neither **one** is a concern in terms of **his or her** professionalism. Therefore, instead of this being solely my decision, I have decided to put this to a committee, chaired by **Lieutenant** Green, and for me to be advised when **its** decision is reached. Anyway, I will be satisfied with **whoever** the committee **chooses**.

Score 5 marks if all grammatical corrections were made. Deduct ½ mark for each error not corrected properly.

## Part 3: Reading Comprehension

61. There were eight individuals charged during the RCMP investigation into drug activity by members of the Hells Angels Motorcycle Club in Kelowna B.C. (para. 4).

62. The significance of the criminal charges that were laid against the Hells Angels Motorcycle Club in the Kelowna investigation is that, if convicted, it would be the first time in B.C. that the Hells Angels have been identified by the courts as a criminal organization (para. 4).

63. The RCMP collaborated with the provincial chief prosecutor during the Kelowna investigation in order to ensure that the investigative techniques used would not affect the trial (para. 9).

64. In 2004, the RCMP and the Winnipeg police service partnered to create the MIOCTF, which is the Manitoba Integrated Organized Crime Task Force (para. 11).

65. Project Deplete culminated in the seizure of nearly $1 million in drugs and criminal charges laid against 13 individuals (para. 14).

66. The value of the money and drugs seized in the Kelowna investigation was worth three million dollars more than the value of the money and drugs seized in the Manitoba investigation (para. 4, $4 million Kelowna, and para. 14, $1 million Manitoba).

67. According to the article, S/Sgt. Gateley was planning on sharing with other police agencies at the team commander's annual general meeting intelligence that came out of the Hells Angels clubhouse and investigative techniques used during E-Predicate (para. 19).

68. Project E-Predicate was the Kelowna-based two-year-long investigation into high-ranking members of the Hells Angels that resulted in the arrest of eight individuals, the seizing of $4 million, and charges that the Hells Angels club was a criminal organization (para. 4, 5).

69. S/Sgt. Samson stated that the MIOCTF has a 98 percent conviction or guilty plea rate when charges are laid (para. 19).

70. In the context of this article, "silos" (para. 3) refer to various police investigative units and organizations that do not share intelligence and information effectively with each other.

71. Based on the information provided, Jennifer BANNERMAN would have been driving the vehicle identified in the collision diagram as #3 as she told Cst. DOSANJH that she was driving behind Vehicle #2 when the collision occurred (para. 3).

72. When Vehicle #1 was involved in the collision it was travelling eastbound (see Figure 3—ensure north is at the top of the page).

73. The most plausible relationship between the driver and the owner of Vehicle #2 is that they are father and son. The owner was born in 1956, and the driver was born in 1996. They also share the same surname and the driver shares the same middle name as the owner's first name.

74. Suzanne CAMPBELL was likely not being truthful about the headlights of the vehicle being on. Although the car was speeding and the driver was impaired, she was at fault for pulling onto the roadway in front of this vehicle. When Cst. MANN went to Vehicle #2, the headlights were on (para. 5).

75. SPADE was referring to the fact that he was celebrating his 19th birthday when he said that it would really be a "special occasion" now. (para. 1—collision occurred on 2015-03-07 at 0300 hr. Veh.#2 info—Spade's date of birth 1996-03-06).

76. Cst. MANN located five cans of Gross Lager beer (para 5—three empty and two unopened).

77. The damage done to Vehicle #2 represented 59 percent of its total value of $27,000. ($16 \div 27 \times 100 = 59.25$).

78. The word *indicia* means signs or indications of something. In this case it meant indication of alcohol consumption.

79. The word *reticent* means being withdrawn and introverted.

80. $177.8 \times 40.5 = 7{,}200.9$. For interest sake only, the $\sqrt{7{,}200.9}$ is 84.5 or 84.5 km/h.

    Note: this is a very rough estimate only, and I have probably offended collision investigators by failing to take into consideration the coefficient of friction of the roadway and a host of other factors taken into consideration when attempting to determine velocity of a vehicle based on tread skid patterns.

81. The break in most likely occurred sometime between 1100 hours, when Alice SPENCER went for her walk, and 1645 hours, when Vanessa ASHCROFT arrived home from work (para. 1, 5).

82. The value of the property stolen from the bedroom was worth $6,600, and the value of the property stolen from the living room was $2,500; therefore, the property stolen from the bedroom was worth $4,100 more than the property stolen from the living room (para. 2, 3).

83. The most likely point of entry that the suspect used to break into the home was the basement sliding glass window. The suspect pried at the window frame and cut himself while gaining entry into the premises.

84. In the context of the police report, *latent* means invisible or unseen. That is, the FIS investigator obtained an unseen fingerprint from the window.

85. The owner of Fast Freddy's Pawn Emporium was Fred NORTHLAND (para. 7).

86. The total value of the property stolen was $9,100 and just $2,550 was recovered at Fast Freddy's Pawn Emporium; therefore, approximately 28 percent of the total value of property stolen was recovered at the pawn shop (para. 2, 3, 7. $2{,}550 \div 9{,}100 = 0.2802 \times 100 = 28\%$).

87. ASHCROFT's story is highly unlikely that he left his blood and prints on the window three months earlier because when Constable MAXWELL searched the residence he found wet droplets of blood on the window ledge (para. 4).

88. Askel ASHCROFT had a criminal record for theft and fraud related to illegal trading in stocks (para. 8).

89. CARTIER and Aksel ASHCROFT are not the same person. The police officers had a photograph of CARTIER that they showed to NORTHLAND. They also separately interviewed Aksel ASHCROFT and would have known if they were dealing with the same person (para. 7, 9).

90. This report of a break and enter is likely a staged crime because Aksel ASHCROFT has come across financial hardship, evidence in his declaration of bankruptcy, he has a criminal record for fraud, and it was his fingerprints and blood on the window. He broke into his own home when his wife thought he was out of town and stole the property. He then had CARTIER, a petty thief, pawn the property for him (para. 4, 7, 8, 9).

## Part 4: Synopsis

When writing a synopsis, you should write it in chronological order so that the information flows in a cohesive way. In addition, you must capture the *who, what, where, when, why,* and *how* and disregard nonessential information (see Chapter 10 for more information on how to write a synopsis).

Synopsis:

On 2015-05-07, shortly after midnight, victim JONES was in his residence at 202-2531 Mayfield Drive when he heard people in his hallway making death threats and then begin to kick at his apartment door. Fearing for his life, he jumped over the balcony, ran to 2527 Lilly Drive and asked for police. HENDERSON saw JONES in distress and called 911. PC BRETT responded to the call and observed suspects FRESHMAN, carrying a baseball bat, and REYNOLDS walking in the 2700 block of Mayfield Drive. PC BRETT and PC RYAN detained the suspects and located weapons, zap straps, and ski masks on them. Suspects were arrested for break and enter, threatening, and possession of a dangerous weapon and lodged in jail. (121 words).

# Model Exam Six: Winnipeg Police Service Written Test

The Winnipeg Police Service written test is an 80-minute multiple-choice exam. Five competencies are assessed, and each section is timed separately. The table provides an approximation of the number of questions and the amount of time allowed for each section. A pass mark of 65 percent or higher is required in order to continue the application process.

| WINNIPEG POLICE SERVICE FORMAT | | | |
|---|---|---|---|
| **SECTION** | **COMPETENCY** | **QUESTIONS** | **TIME ALLOWED** |
| Part 1 | Vocabulary | 15 | 15 minutes |
| Part 2 | Comprehension | 15 | 15 minutes |
| Part 3 | Mechanics | 15 | 15 minutes |
| Part 4 | Grammar | 15 | 15 minutes |
| Part 5 | Mathematics | 10 | 20 minutes |
| | Total | **70** | **80** |

## PART 1: Vocabulary

| | | | |
|---|---|---|---|
| 1. (A) (B) (C) (D) | 5. (A) (B) (C) (D) | 9. (A) (B) (C) (D) | 13. (A) (B) (C) (D) |
| 2. (A) (B) (C) (D) | 6. (A) (B) (C) (D) | 10. (A) (B) (C) (D) | 14. (A) (B) (C) (D) |
| 3. (A) (B) (C) (D) | 7. (A) (B) (C) (D) | 11. (A) (B) (C) (D) | 15. (A) (B) (C) (D) |
| 4. (A) (B) (C) (D) | 8. (A) (B) (C) (D) | 12. (A) (B) (C) (D) | |

## PART 2: Comprehension

| | | | |
|---|---|---|---|
| 16. (A) (B) (C) (D) | 20. (A) (B) (C) (D) | 24. (A) (B) (C) (D) | 28. (A) (B) (C) (D) |
| 17. (A) (B) (C) (D) | 21. (A) (B) (C) (D) | 25. (A) (B) (C) (D) | 29. (A) (B) (C) (D) |
| 18. (A) (B) (C) (D) | 22. (A) (B) (C) (D) | 26. (A) (B) (C) (D) | 30. (A) (B) (C) (D) |
| 19. (A) (B) (C) (D) | 23. (A) (B) (C) (D) | 27. (A) (B) (C) (D) | |

## PART 3: Mechanics

| | | | |
|---|---|---|---|
| 31. (A) (B) (C) (D) | 35. (A) (B) (C) (D) | 39. (A) (B) (C) (D) | 43. (A) (B) (C) (D) |
| 32. (A) (B) (C) (D) | 36. (A) (B) (C) (D) | 40. (A) (B) (C) (D) | 44. (A) (B) (C) (D) |
| 33. (A) (B) (C) (D) | 37. (A) (B) (C) (D) | 41. (A) (B) (C) (D) | 45. (A) (B) (C) (D) |
| 34. (A) (B) (C) (D) | 38. (A) (B) (C) (D) | 42. (A) (B) (C) (D) | |

## PART 4: Grammar

| | | | |
|---|---|---|---|
| 46. (A) (B) (C) (D) | 50. (A) (B) (C) (D) | 54. (A) (B) (C) (D) | 58. (A) (B) (C) (D) |
| 47. (A) (B) (C) (D) | 51. (A) (B) (C) (D) | 55. (A) (B) (C) (D) | 59. (A) (B) (C) (D) |
| 48. (A) (B) (C) (D) | 52. (A) (B) (C) (D) | 56. (A) (B) (C) (D) | 60. (A) (B) (C) (D) |
| 49. (A) (B) (C) (D) | 53. (A) (B) (C) (D) | 57. (A) (B) (C) (D) | |

## PART 5: Mathematics

61. Ⓐ Ⓑ Ⓒ Ⓓ     64. Ⓐ Ⓑ Ⓒ Ⓓ     67. Ⓐ Ⓑ Ⓒ Ⓓ     69. Ⓐ Ⓑ Ⓒ Ⓓ

62. Ⓐ Ⓑ Ⓒ Ⓓ     65. Ⓐ Ⓑ Ⓒ Ⓓ     68. Ⓐ Ⓑ Ⓒ Ⓓ     70. Ⓐ Ⓑ Ⓒ Ⓓ

63. Ⓐ Ⓑ Ⓒ Ⓓ     66. Ⓐ Ⓑ Ⓒ Ⓓ

## PART 1: VOCABULARY

 You have 15 minutes to complete the following 15 questions.

1. Which word or phrase is closest in meaning to the word *eccentric*?

    (A) foreign
    (B) not regular
    (C) genuine
    (D) unusual

2. Which word or phrase is closest in meaning to the word *corroborate*?

    (A) validate
    (B) instigate
    (C) simulate
    (D) remunerate

3. Which word or phrase is closest in meaning to the word *industrious*?

    (A) hard working
    (B) mechanical
    (C) nonorganic
    (D) revolutionary

4. Read the two sentences below and choose the one word that correctly completes both sentences.

    A. The undercover officers set up surveillance on the bank in an attempt to _____ the robbery.
    B. One method to prevent suspects from deleting messages on their seized cellular phones is cover them with _____.

    (A) thwart
    (B) interception
    (C) foil
    (D) wrap

5. Which word best completes the following sentence?

    Some of the unruly protestors seemed to think that it was their _____ to damage property during the demonstration.

    (A) rite
    (B) right
    (C) write
    (D) wright

6. Which word best completes the following sentence?

   Sergeant Steen wanted to _____ the speed of the drawn out investigation by bringing in additional investigators.

   (A) elongate
   (B) accentuate
   (C) placate
   (D) hasten

7. Which word best completes the following sentence?

   The Sergeant's Association was eager to _____ new furniture for its lounge, as the old chairs were worn beyond repair.

   (A) avert
   (B) nuance
   (C) procure
   (D) sustain

8. Read the two sentences below and choose the one word that correctly completes both sentences.

   A. The suspect had an usual weapon. We believe it was the first time that a _____ was used during a robbery.
   B. The sergeant was very upset with Brad and informed him that the next time he was late for work there would be consequences. The warning was definitely a "shot across the _____."

   (A) dart
   (B) bow
   (C) cannon
   (D) hammer

9. Which option best completes the following sentence?

   Constable Gardiner first used the Taser on the suspect, but it had almost no _____. It was not until the officer pointed his firearm at the suspect before he _____ down the knife and surrendered.

   (A) effect / through
   (B) affect / threw
   (C) effect / threw
   (D) affect / through.

10. Which option best completes the following sentence?

    The Incident Commander had established the _____ for the police Command Post, but he was not prepared to _____ with attempting to contact the barricaded suspect until all the resources were properly in place.

    (A) site / proceed
    (B) sight / precede
    (C) cite / proceed
    (D) site / precede

11. Which option best completes the following sentence?

The ethics trainer advised the new recruits that it was inappropriate for them to _____ gifts from the public, and that _____ could be disciplinary consequences for ____ behaviour if they did.

(A) except / they're / their
(B) accept / their / there
(C) except / there / they're
(D) accept / there / their

12. Read the two sentences below and choose the one word that correctly completes both sentences.

A. The neighbour was certain that the tenant did not _____ there anymore.
B. The young children were excited that they were going to get to see a _____ demonstration of the police service dog in action.

(A) free
(B) reside
(C) habituate
(D) live

13. Which word best completes the following sentence?

The suspect's nervous cough and trembling hands _____ his statement that he had no knowledge of the crime.

(A) deviated
(B) belied
(C) embellished
(D) renounced

14. Which word best completes the following sentence?

A very generous person is often referred to as a(n) _____.

(A) opportunist
(B) pheneticist
(C) philanthropist
(D) paternalist

15. Which word best completes the following sentence?

If a person is very detail oriented, they are known to be _____.

(A) terse
(B) meticulous
(C) superficial
(D) poignant

## PART 2: READING COMPREHENSION

 You have 15 minutes to complete the following 15 questions.

In this section you are required to read a magazine article and a police report. There are seven multiple-choice questions relating to the first passage and eight questions relating to the second one.

## Reading Assignment One: Magazine Article

QUESTIONS 16–22 ARE BASED SOLELY ON THE INFORMATION CONTAINED IN THE FOLLOWING ARTICLE.

### Victims lend their voices to RCMP initiatives

By Sigrid Forberg

Kali and Jeremy O'Dell were 12 and nine years old when an impaired driver on the highway outside of Moncton, N.B., struck their minivan in the fall of 2006.

The impact of the crash killed their parents, Laura and Gregory, who were in the front seat. Since the accident, the O'Dell children have worked with Mothers Against Drunk Driving and the RCMP to help raise awareness about impaired driving.

Last fall, Insp. David Vautour, the officer in charge of operations for the Codiac Regional RCMP, says he decided to get the O'Dells involved in a program to acknowledge the efforts of members that go above and beyond for impaired driving enforcement.

Members that have achieved a certain number of impaired driving charges will be recognized each year and made a part of "Team O'Dell." Last December, they inducted their first dozen members into the team.

"The irony was that a couple of the members that became part of Team O'Dell had attended that call back in 2006," says Vautour. "So that was kind of sad in a way, but their efforts are now being recognized."

Vautour got the idea from an initiative in E Division, Alexa's Team. Alexa Middelaer was a four-year-old girl from Delta, B.C. On a Saturday afternoon in May 2008, she was feeding a horse on the side of the road with her aunt and grandparents, when she was struck and killed by an impaired driver.

Shortly after their daughter's death, Laura and Michael Middelaer attended a traffic safety meeting with all the traffic managers in B.C. to ask what they could do to help.

Present at that meeting, Insp. Ted Emanuels, the officer in charge of the enhanced traffic services program in E Division, was moved by the Middelaer's drive to help create change.

"They were these people who said, 'We're not prepared to be victims of this. We have the ability to do something and we want to do whatever we can to help'," says Emanuels.

In the six years since they launched the program, they've recognized 1,321 members of Alexa's Team, who've taken more than 50,000 impaired drivers off B.C.'s roads. And in the last three years, B.C. has seen a 52 percent drop in impaired driving fatalities.

"When Alexa was killed, it demonstrated those innocent parties affected by impaired driving," says Emanuels. "She wasn't coming from the bar, she wasn't a vehicle driver, she was an innocent victim and everyone in the province really connected with her."

In the Codiac Region, impaired driving charges were up 35 percent over the last six months of 2013. They even received a call about a suspected impaired driver during the press conference announcing the initiative. Because of that call, members were able to intercept and arrest a 28-year-old man driving under the influence—something Vautour says is encouraging.

"We know we don't get half the calls we could get," says Vautour. "Every time somebody calls us, we might be able to prevent an incident like what the O'Dells have gone through. The public has to understand that if they call us, we can save lives together."

*The above article is reprinted courtesy of the RCMP Gazette, as published in Vol. 76, No. 2, 2014.*

16. Since the time that Alexa Middelaer was killed by an impaired driver, how many impaired drivers have been taken off the roads in British Columbia?

    (A) 1,321
    (B) 50,000
    (C) "many thousand"
    (D) 75,000

17. In what province is the Codiac Regional police service located?

    (A) Ontario
    (B) British Columbia
    (C) Nova Scotia
    (D) New Brunswick

18. How many police officers were initially inducted onto "Team O'Dell"?

    (A) 12
    (B) 40
    (C) 60
    (D) 120

19. When Insp. Emanuals said, "We're not prepared to be victims of this," who was he referring to?

    (A) The RCMP
    (B) The Middelaers
    (C) The O'Dells
    (D) The Codiac Regional Police

20. Where was Ted Emanuels when he first met Laura and Michael Middelaer?

    (A) At the Codiac Regional Police Station
    (B) At their home in Delta
    (C) At a traffic safety meeting
    (D) At a Mothers Against Drunk Drivers meeting

21. What was the "irony" that Insp. Vautour referred to?

   (A) That some of the police officers added to "Team O'Dell" were at the fatal collision in 2006.
   (B) That some of the police officers on "Team O'Dell" are also members of "Alex's Team."
   (C) It was ironic that an impaired driver was arrested during the press conference.
   (D) It was ironic that the number of impaired charges had increased, but that the number of fatalities caused by impaired drivers had declined.

22. What did Insp. David Vautour find "encouraging"?

   (A) The number of members added to "Team O'Dell".
   (B) The success of Mothers Against Drunk Drivers.
   (C) The increase in citizens calling to report impaired drivers.
   (D) The arrest of an impaired driver during the press conference?

## Reading Assignment Two: B&E Report

QUESTIONS 23–30 ARE BASED SOLELY ON THE INFORMATION CONTAINED IN THE FOLLOWING PASSAGE.

On 2015-April-16 at approximately 0320 hours, Winnipeg police responded to a report of a break in at Debbie's Market, 920 Notre Dame Ave. Premier Alert Alarms reported a silent alarm to that address. At the same time, witness Collins called 911 from her cellular phone to report that she observed a white van that appeared to have backed up through the front doors of Debbie's Market. She said there were two men wearing dark clothing inside the market, loading boxes into the van. She maintained observation of the van and the occupants for approximately one minute from a lane across from the market. She then advised the 911 operator that the men got into the vehicle and that it left the parking lot and drove away west on Notre Dame.

At approx. 0322 hours, Cst. McClurg was responding to the silent alarm and was east-bound on Notre Dame when he observed a white van driving westbound towards him with its lights off. The vehicle suddenly made a right turn and proceeded onto Weston. McClurg activated lights and siren and initiated a pursuit of the van and its occupants. The suspect vehicle was swerving from side to side as it proceeded along Weston, at speeds up to 110 km/h. Fortunately, vehicle traffic was light and there were no pedestrians on the roadway or side-walk. The vehicle then made a right turn onto Alexander Ave. One of the suspects opened the rear door of the van and started throwing large cardboard boxes filled with cigarettes at the police car that was pursuing them. The vehicle continued its erratic driving and failed to negotiate a left turn onto Winks Street, crashing into a home on the northeast corner of Winks and Alexander. The suspects jumped out of the van and ran between the houses. McClurg radioed to other units in the area that the suspects were now on foot, running northbound.

As the pursuit was unfolding, Canine Handler Cst. O'Ryan was in the area responding to the call. When the van crashed into the home he was approximately two blocks away and quickly deployed his service dog which began to track northbound between several houses. Other officers in the area responded as well and set up perimeter containment to the north, east, and west of where the dog was tracking. Soon the dog had tracked across Logan Avenue and into McPhillips Athletic Park. As the dog honed in on a cluster of bushes in the southeast corner of the park, one of the suspects emerged from the bushes and started running across the field. O'Ryan released his dog, which quickly caught up to the suspect and apprehended him by latching onto his left arm and taking him to the ground. O'Ryan then had his dog release the suspect and O'Ryan placed him in handcuffs. The suspect was later identified as 22-year-old Gavin Fisher. While Fisher was being taken into custody, Officer McClurg heard the second suspect yelling from the bushes, saying, "Please don't send the dog in here! I give up!" McClurg called the suspect out of the bushes at gun point and had him lie prone on the ground. The suspect was later identified as 24-year-old Carl Gale. Fisher was later treated by the ambulance service for minor puncture wounds and a four centimetre laceration to his left forearm. He was bandaged by the ambulance attendants at the scene and later transported along with Gayle to police headquarters to be lodged in the jail.

Upon returning to the collision scene, the vehicle turned out to be a stolen van, reported on 2015-04-14 at 2320. The van was found with its ignition punched, extensive rear-end and front end damage, and in the cargo area were eight large boxes containing 64 cartons of cigarettes. Three more boxes filled with stolen cigarettes were also found along the route of the pursuit. The suspects had caused more than $75,000 in property damage to the store, the van itself, and the home the suspects crashed the van into. The two suspects were both charged under the Criminal Code with break and enter, theft over five thousand dollars, and initiate police pursuit. Police are recommending that both Gayle and Fisher be denied bail.

23. Who had the surname Collins?

    (A) The ambulance attendant
    (B) The dog handler
    (C) The suspect bitten by the police dog
    (D) The witness who observed the break in

24. In the context of this passage, what does the term *honed* mean?

    (A) yearned
    (B) sharpened
    (C) made more acute
    (D) focused attention

25. When the suspect vehicle was driving towards Cst. McClurg with its lights off and made a right turn onto Weston, what direction was the vehicle now travelling on Weston?

    (A) north
    (B) south
    (C) east
    (D) west

26. What did the name "McPhillips" refer to?

    (A) a street
    (B) a suspect
    (C) a police officer
    (D) a park

27. Why was it fortunate that vehicle traffic was light and there were no pedestrians on the roadway or sidewalk?

(A) It allowed the officer to pursue at higher speeds and not have to slow down for possible obstructions on the roadway.

(B) The suspect vehicle could have gotten lost in the other traffic, making it difficult to continue the pursuit.

(C) Pursuits are extremely dangerous and other vehicle traffic and pedestrians in the area would have greatly increased the risk.

(D) Citizens in other vehicles and on the street are known to interfere with police operations. It's best if they're not nearby.

28. In the context of the passage, what does *negotiate* mean?

(A) To transfer real property

(B) To find a way through

(C) To reach an agreement

(D) To settle on something of value

29. What was the minimum value of the property that was stolen?

(A) $4,000

(B) $10,000

(C) $75,000

(D) $5,000

30. How much time had passed between the van being reported stolen and being spotted by the witness at the break in?

(A) 25 hours 30 minutes

(B) 28 hours

(C) 36 hours

(D) 27 hours 40 minutes

## PART 3: LANGUAGE MECHANICS

 **You have 15 minutes to complete the following 15 questions.**

> This section tests your knowledge of language mechanics, which includes spelling, punctuation, and capitalization of words.

31. Select the correct punctuation in the underlined portion of the following formal salutation.

    Dear Chief <u>Johnston</u>

    (A) Johnston!
    (B) Johnston:
    (C) Johnston;
    (D) Johnston.

32. Select the correct punctuation in the underlined portion of the following sentence.

    "Why you were not at work on <u>time" said</u> Sergeant Copper, "is inexcusable."

    (A) time." Said
    (B) time?" said
    (C) time," said
    (D) time;" said

33. Select the correct punctuation in the underlined portion of the following sentence.

    His request to take the day off work was <u>denied besides</u> it was lousy weather.

    (A) denied, besides,
    (B) denied. Besides,
    (C) denied: besides,
    (D) denied—besides

34. Select the correct punctuation in the underlined portion of the following sentence.

    The Drug Squad was fully prepared to execute the search warrant at the <u>warehouse however they</u> decided to wait and see if the suspects were going to show up.

    (A) warehouse; however, they
    (B) warehouse—however—they
    (C) warehouse, however. They
    (D) warehouse, however, they

35. Select the correct punctuation in the underlined portion of the following sentence.

What did the suspect mean when he said, <u>"You'll be hearing from my lawyer soon"</u>

(A) "you'll be hearing from my lawyer soon?"
(B) "You'll be hearing from my lawyer soon."
(C) "You'll be hearing from my lawyer soon"?
(D) "You'll be hearing from my lawyer soon!"?

36. In the following sentence, which word is capitalized incorrectly?

"Next <u>Wednesday</u>," I suggested, "<u>We</u> should drive <u>West</u> to Brandon and watch the <u>May Day Parade</u>."

(A) Wednesday
(B) We
(C) West
(D) May Day Parade

37. In the following sentence, which word is capitalized incorrectly?

The <u>Inspector</u> was honoured to be asked to speak about restorative justice programs for <u>Aboriginal</u> youth during <u>Professor</u> Kohm's criminology class at the <u>University</u> of Winnipeg.

(A) Inspector
(B) Aboriginal
(C) Professor
(D) University

38. Which of the following words is misspelled?

(A) operate
(B) seperate
(C) collaborate
(D) commemorate

39. Which of the following words is misspelled?

(A) neither
(B) conscience
(C) deciet
(D) feisty

40. Which of the following words is misspelled?

(A) compatible
(B) perceptible
(C) digestible
(D) corruptable

41. Which of the following words is misspelled?

(A) accessory
(B) intercede
(C) forsee
(D) calendar

42. Which of the following words is misspelled?

    (A) acquit

    (B) consensus

    (C) independent

    (D) personell

43. Which one of the underlined words in the following passage is misspelled?

It was a real <u>priviledge</u> to have Mr. Watson take the time out of his busy <u>schedule</u> to come and speak to the new recruits. We gave him a small <u>memento</u> as a token of our <u>appreciation</u>.

    (A) priviledge

    (B) schedule

    (C) memento

    (D) appreciation

44. Which one of the underlined words in the following passage is misspelled?

Constable Paulson has reasonable grounds to believe that the suspect <u>possesses</u> <u>revelant</u> information regarding the unusual <u>disappearance</u> of the <u>teenaged</u> girl.

    (A) possesses

    (B) revelant

    (C) disappearance

    (D) teenaged

45. Which, if any, of the underlined words in the following sentence is misspelled?

The new impaired driving legislation will <u>supercede</u> the previous <u>cumbersome</u> law, with the goal of creating a more <u>efficient</u> mechanism for removing drunk drivers from the roadways.

    (A) supercede

    (B) cumbersome

    (C) efficient

    (D) no errors

## PART 4: GRAMMAR

 **You have 15 minutes to complete the following 15 questions.**

> This section focuses on the use of proper grammar skills and sentence structure. For the following five questions, choose the word or phrase that best completes the sentence.

46. Neither Constable Mackay ___ Constable Wood ___ interested in volunteering to stay late and work overtime tonight.

    (A) and / were
    (B) nor / is
    (C) nor / are
    (D) or / were

47. It was Constable _____ responsibility for _____ that he had properly secured and stored his firearm.

    (A) Jame's / ensuring
    (B) James / assuring
    (C) James' / insuring
    (D) James' / ensuring

48. The successful applicant for the robbery detective position was going to be between Constable Madani and ____; hopefully the job will be given to _____ is most qualified.

    (A) me / whoever
    (B) I / whomever
    (C) me / whomever
    (D) I / whosoever

49. John, the veteran officer with almost 30 years of service, lamented, "Five years ___ too long to have to wait until I retire. I wish it ___ ____ years than that."

    (A) is / were / fewer
    (B) are / was / less
    (C) is / were / less
    (D) are / was / fewer

50. The police department supports _____ members and wants us to take care of _____ both physically and mentally.

   (A) their / yourselves,
   (B) its / ourselves,
   (C) it's / ourself,
   (D) its / themselves,

51. Which of the following sentences is the least grammatically correct?

   (A) It's important for Watch Commander Evans to be properly apprised of the violent arrest that sent one of the suspects to hospital.
   (B) Constable Christian and I am not going to be held responsible for that debacle on Main Street. Because we were working out in the gym at the time.
   (C) Apparently, two drunks were fighting, and when Constable Timmons went to intervene, one of the combatants struck him in the face. It was a complete donnybrook after that.
   (D) The outcome of the street brawl: four suspects in custody, with two of them getting treated at the hospital; two officers injured by flying beer bottles and other debris; and two police cars damaged with their windows smashed out.

52. Which of the following statements is the least grammatically correct?

   (A) Sergeant Hodges didn't care if it was going to be Johnson or Hoffman, but one of them was going to be on guard duty tonight.
   (B) Surprisingly, Johnson could hardly wait to volunteer for the guard duty position.
   (C) Johnston said that the reason that he enjoyed guard duty was that it gave him an opportunity to study for the promotional exam.
   (D) Anyway, Hoffman was pleased that guard duty wasn't going to be assigned to him.

53. Which of the following statements is the most grammatically correct?

   (A) Not only did the suspect break into the house and steal jewellery, but also the computer was stolen.
   (B) The Inspector offered the new posting in the Diversity Unit to Constable Field and me.
   (C) Officer Chang was one who has previously worked with the Youth Squad and has also worked in the Robbery Squad.
   (D) Constable Sandhu was both asked to submit her application to Strike Force and to apply to the Domestic Violence Squad.

54. Which of the following statements is the most grammatically correct?

   (A) A police officer has to expect some criticism from the public when we do our job.
   (B) After listening to Constable Wong's plan to execute the search warrant and to Constable Gill's objections to the plan, I agreed with his ideas.
   (C) Officer Sikorski is a member of the Fugitive Squad, which was recently featured on the television series *To Protect and Serve*.
   (D) The senior prosecutor is going to announce tomorrow that Carson Wrington is the person who is believed to be responsible for the arson attack that killed three innocent people.

55. Indicate if there are any grammatical or spelling errors in the underlined portions of the following sentence.

The <u>superintendant</u> was eager to commence work in her new <u>position;</u> however, the <u>deluge</u> of work was more than she bargained for.

(A) superintendant
(B) position;
(C) deluge
(D) no error

56. Indicate if there are any grammatical or spelling errors in the underlined portions of the following sentence.

Sergeant O'Conner gave Constable Andrews and <u>I</u> specific instructions regarding where we <u>were</u> to meet for the briefing; <u>except</u> we forgot to write them down.

(A) I
(B) were
(C) except
(D) no error

57. Indicate if there are any grammatical or spelling errors in the underlined portions of the following sentence.

Sergeant Quinn, known for his motivational <u>speeches</u>, always challenged his team members to ask <u>themselves</u>, "Did I make a difference <u>today?"</u>

(A) speeches
(B) themselves
(C) today?"
(D) no error

58. Indicate if there are any grammatical or spelling errors in the underlined portions of the following passage.

The victim was <u>irate</u> that my partner and <u>I</u> had taken so long to arrive at the address. We were too embarrassed to mention that we had <u>past</u> the address twice!

(A) irate
(B) I
(C) past
(D) no error

59. Indicate if there are any grammatical or spelling errors in the underlined portions of the following passage.

"The most <u>apparent</u> cause," said Constable Jorge, <u>"was</u> that the victim had tripped and accidentally fallen down the <u>stairs;</u> there's no crime here."

(A) apparent
(B) "was
(C) stairs;
(D) no error

60. Indicate if there are any grammatical or spelling errors in the underlined portions of the following passage.

Constable Brown was not <u>used to</u> the firing mechanism of the pistol. He <u>should of</u> followed instructions more carefully. Brown, and another recruit, <u>is</u> now required to take remedial gun-handling instruction.

(A) used to
(B) should of
(C) is
(D) no error

## PART 5: MATHEMATICS

 **You have 20 minutes to complete the following 10 questions.**

This section tests your mathematical problem-solving skills using various math operations.

61. Which of the radicals below is equal to six?

    (A) $\sqrt{42}$
    (B) $\sqrt{36}$
    (C) $\sqrt{24.5}$
    (D) $\sqrt{12}$

62. The police training compound has a perimeter of 250 metres with a width of 45 metres. What is the length of the compound?

    (A) 90 metres
    (B) 160 metres
    (C) 205 metres
    (D) 80 metres

63. Four-sevenths of the police department's members have already completed their annual firearms qualifications. What is the ratio of the members who have not completed their qualification compared to those that have?

    (A) 7:3
    (B) 3:7
    (C) 3:4
    (D) 4:3

64. In Division 11, there are 210 constables and a total of 37 sergeants and patrol sergeants. Approximately what percentage of the members in Division 11 are constables?

    (A) 18 percent
    (B) 77 percent
    (C) 29 percent
    (D) 85 percent

65. During four successive shifts, Constable Nguyen test drove the new fuel-efficient patrol vehicle 78 km, 81 km, 124 km, and 57 km, respectively. If the vehicle averages 8 litres of fuel per 100 km, approximately how many litres of fuel in total did the vehicle use during the four shifts.

(A) 27

(B) 42

(C) 31

(D) 46

66. Constable Kostachuk was dispatched to respond code 3 to a violent domestic assault call on the outskirts of Winnipeg. She drove 6.5 kilometres in three minutes. What was her average speed?

(A) 120 km/h

(B) 115 km/h

(C) 130 km/h

(D) 125 km/h

67. A number is 30 greater than another number. If the smaller number is subtracted from three times the larger number, the difference is 120. What is the larger number?

(A) 90

(B) 45

(C) 30

(D) 60

QUESTIONS 68–70 ARE BASED ON THE INFORMATION PROVIDED IN THE TABLE BELOW, WHICH INDICATES THE VALUE OF DRUGS AND DRUG-RELATED CASH SEIZURES OVER A FOUR-YEAR PERIOD.

| DRUG AND CASH SEIZURES | | | | |
|---|---|---|---|---|
| YEAR | CASH | MARIJUANA | COCAINE | OTHER |
| 2011 | $157,300 | $275,000 | $154,000 | $35,000 |
| 2012 | $299,600 | $361,000 | $194,600 | $45,200 |
| 2013 | $454,200 | $409,000 | $134,000 | $153,000 |
| 2014 | $355,800 | $245,000 | $203,000 | $175,000 |

68. In 2013, cash seizures accounted for approximately what percentage of the total cash seizures during the four-year period?

(A) 43 percent

(B) 36 percent

(C) 29 percent

(D) 26 percent

69. In 2012, what was the approximate ratio of the value of cash seizures compared to the total value of drug and cash seizures?

(A) 2:5

(B) 3:7

(C) 1:3

(D) 299:967

70. Which year witnessed the greatest value of drugs and cash seized?

(A) 2011

(B) 2012

(C) 2013

(D) 2014

# ANSWER KEY

## PART 1: Vocabulary

| | | | | | | | |
|---|---|---|---|---|---|---|---|
| **1.** | D | **5.** | B | **9.** | C | **13.** | B |
| **2.** | A | **6.** | D | **10.** | A | **14.** | C |
| **3.** | A | **7.** | C | **11.** | D | **15.** | B |
| **4.** | C | **8.** | B | **12.** | D | | |

## PART 2: Reading Comprehension

| | | | | | | | |
|---|---|---|---|---|---|---|---|
| **16.** | B | **20.** | C | **24.** | D | **28.** | B |
| **17.** | D | **21.** | A | **25.** | A | **29.** | D |
| **18.** | A | **22.** | C | **26.** | D | **30.** | B |
| **19.** | B | **23.** | D | **27.** | C | | |

## PART 3: Language Mechanics

| | | | | | | | |
|---|---|---|---|---|---|---|---|
| **31.** | B | **35.** | C | **39.** | C | **43.** | A |
| **32.** | C | **36.** | C | **40.** | D | **44.** | B |
| **33.** | B | **37.** | A | **41.** | C | **45.** | A |
| **34.** | A | **38.** | B | **42.** | D | | |

## PART 4: Grammar

| | | | | | | | |
|---|---|---|---|---|---|---|---|
| **46.** | B | **50.** | B | **54.** | C | **58.** | C |
| **47.** | D | **51.** | B | **55.** | A | **59.** | C |
| **48.** | C | **52.** | A | **56.** | A | **60.** | B |
| **49.** | A | **53.** | B | **57.** | D | | |

## PART 5: Mathematics

| | | | |
|---|---|---|---|
| **61.** B | **64.** D | **67.** B | **69.** C |
| **62.** D | **65.** A | **68.** B | **70.** C |
| **63.** C | **66.** C | | |

## ANSWERS EXPLAINED

### Part 1: Vocabulary

1. **D** *Eccentric* means unusual.

2. **A** *Corroborate* means to validate.

3. **A** *Industrious* means hard working.

4. **C** *Foil* has at least two meanings: (1) to thwart or prevent something from happening and (2) thin sheet metal.

5. **B** In this context, *right* means morally justified.

6. **D** *Hasten* means to cause something to happen sooner.

7. **C** *Procure* mean to purchase or acquire.

8. **B** *Bow* has at least two meanings: (1) a weapon made of a flexible strip and cord and (2) the forward part of a boat. The phrase, "A shot across the bow" means a warning shot or warning. The term originates from the naval practice of firing a warning shot at an advancing or fleeing vessel to either disengage or stop so that it can be boarded.

9. **C** *Effect* means impact. *Threw* is the past tense of throw.

10. **A** Site means a specific location. *Proceed* means to continue to do something.

11. **D** *Accept* means to receive something.

    *Their* is an adjective that is the possessive form of they.

    *There* is an adverb meaning a place or location.

12. **D** *Live* has at least two meanings: (1) to dwell at a location and (2) to observe an event as it occurs.

13. **B** *Belie* means to give a false impression.

14. **C** A *philanthropist* is a very generous person.

15. **B** *Meticulous* means to be very careful or fussy.

### Part 2: Reading Comprehension

16. **B** Since the time that Alexa Middelaer was killed by an impaired driver 50,000 impaired drivers have been taken off the roads in British Columbia (para. 9).

17. **D** The Codiac Regional police service is located in the province of New Bruinswick. The article does not say this specifically; however, an inference can be made based on the information in para. 1—the parents were killed outside "Moncton, N.B" and officers from the Codiac Regional police attended the fatality back in 2006 (para. 5).

18. **A** There were initially a dozen officers inducted onto "Team O'Dell" (para. 4).

19. **B** Insp. Emanuals was referring to the Middelaers who had said, "We're not prepared to be victims of this" (para. 9).

20. **C** Ted Emanuels first met Laura and Michael Middelaer at a traffic safety meeting (para. 7, 8).

21. **A** The "irony" that Insp. Vautour was referring to was that some of the police officers added to "Team O'Dell" were at the fatal collision in 2006 (para. 5).

22. **C** Insp. Vautour was encourage by the increase in citizens calling to report impaired drivers (para. 12, 13).

23. **D** The witness who observed the break in had the surname Collins (para. 1).

24. **D** In the context of the passage, *honed* means to focus attention. In this instance, the police service dog honed in on a cluster of bushes.

25. **A** This answer requires the use of spatial orientation because the passage does not specifically indicate the suspect's direction of travel on Weston. However, it does state that the suspect vehicle was westbound on Notre Dame and then made a right turn. If you are travelling west and then turn right, you must then be travelling north.

26. **D** "McPhillips" is the name of a park that the police found the suspects hiding in (para. 3).

27. **C** It was fortunate that vehicle traffic was light and there were no pedestrians on the roadway or sidewalk because police pursuits are extremely dangerous and other vehicle traffic and pedestrians in the area would have greatly increased the risk. The answer can be deduced from the facts presented: vehicle swerving, lights off, high speeds, erratic driving behaviour, and no pedestrians on the streets or sidewalks. Clearly the suspect was driving in a very dangerous manner that put the public at great risk (para. 2).

28. **B** In the context of the passage, *negotiate* means to find a way through, in this case, it means through the successful completion of a left turn at high speeds (para. 2).

29. **D** The minimum value of the property that was stolen must have been worth in excess of $5,000 as the suspects were charged under the Criminal Code with theft over five thousand dollars (para. 4).

30. **B** Reported stolen: 2015-04-14 2320

Located: 2015-04-16 0320

Step 1. Add 40 minutes to get to midnight of the 15th.

Step 2. Add 24 hours to get to midnight of the 16th.

Step 3. Add 3 hours and 20 minutes to total.

Total = 28 hours

## Part 3: Language Mechanics

31. **B** Dear Chief Johnston:

32. **C** "Why you were not at work on time," said Sergeant Collins, "is inexcusable."

Rule: Use a comma at the end of the first part of a quotation of a fragmented sentence.

33. **B** His request to take the day off work was denied. Besides, it was lousy weather.

This was originally a run-on sentence that contained an unrelated additional idea. This needed to be split into two separate sentences.

34. **A** The Drug Squad was fully prepared to execute the search warrant at the warehouse; however, they decided to wait and see if the suspects were going to show up.

Rule: Use a semicolon in front of conjunctive adverbs (e.g., "however" and "therefore").

35. **C** What did the suspect mean when he said, "You'll be hearing from my lawyer soon"? (question mark outside of the quotation).

Rule: Do not place question marks inside of the quotation if they do not make up part of the quotation.

36. **C** "Next Wednesday," I suggested, "We should drive *west* to Brandon and watch the May Day Parade."

Rule: Do not capitalize directions.

37. **A** The *inspector* was honoured to be asked to speak about restorative justice programs for Aboriginal youth during Professor Kohm's criminology class at the University of Winnipeg.

Rule: Only capitalize titles or positions if referring to a specific individual (e.g., Inspector Burke).

38. **B** Correct spelling: *separate*

39. **C** Correct spelling: *deceit*

40. **D** Correct spelling: *corruptible*

41. **C** Correct spelling: *foresee*

42. **D** Correct spelling: *personnel*

43. **A** It was a real *privilege* to have Mr. Watson take the time out of his busy schedule to come and speak to the new recruits. We gave him a small memento as a token of our appreciation.

44. **B** Constable Paulson has reasonable grounds to believe that the suspect possesses *relevant* information regarding the unusual disappearance of the teenaged girl.

45. **A** The new impaired driving legislation will *supersede* the previous cumbersome law, with the goal of creating a more efficient mechanism for removing drunk drivers from the roadways.

## Part 4: Grammar

46. **B** Neither Constable Mackay *nor* Constable Wood *is* interested in volunteering to stay late and work overtime tonight.

*Neither* and *nor* are paired correlatives.

Rule: If two singular subjects are connected by "either," "neither," "or," or "nor," then the verb is singular.

47. **D** It was Constable *James'* responsibility for *ensuring* that he had properly secured and stored his firearm.

The apostrophe is used to show possession, and for singular nouns that end with an *s*, the apostrophe is placed after the *s*. *Ensure* is a verb that means to guarantee or make certain. *Insure* is a verb that means to obtain insurance or to take appropriate precautions.

48. **C** The successful applicant for the robbery detective position was going to be between Constable Madani and *me*; hopefully the job will be given to *whomever* is most qualified.

Rule: If a sentence uses a preposition such as "between", it must be followed by an indirect object pronoun (me).

Whoever is a pronoun that means whatever person.

Whomever is the objective form of whoever. Therefore, the job is given to *whomever*.

49. **A** John, the veteran officer with almost 30 years of service, stated, "Five years *is* too long to have to wait until I retire. I wish it *were fewer* years than that."

Rule: Use a singular verb for periods of time.

Rule: Subjunctive mood refers to clauses where one is expressing wishes or desires or conditions that are false or unlikely. In these instances, use *were* instead of *was*.

Rule: Use *fewer* when referring to countable items; use *less* when referring to noncountable values.

50. **B** The police department supports *its* members and wants us to take care of *ourselves*, both physically and mentally.

Rule: Use singular verbs for companies and organizations.

Rule: *Ourselves* is used to refer to a group that includes you (*us*) and has already been mentioned.

51. **B** Option A is correct: Proper use of contraction *it's* and proper us of *apprised* instead of *appraised*.

It's important for Watch Commander Evans to be properly apprised of the violent arrest that sent one the suspects to hospital.

Option B is incorrect: Constable Christian and I *are* (instead of *am*) not going to be held responsible for that debacle on Main Street. *Because* (the use of a period and starting the sentence with *because* creates a fragmented sentence) we were working out in the gym at the time.

Option C is incorrect: Two complete sentences are provided. *Donnybrook* is not capitalized.

Apparently, two drunks were fighting, and when Constable Timmons went to intervene, one of the combatants struck him in the face. It was a complete donnybrook after that.

Option D is incorrect: Proper use of a colon to introduce a list and proper use of the semicolon to separate a series of items which contain commas within the clause.

The outcome of the street brawl: four suspects in custody, with two of them getting treated at the hospital; two officers injured by flying beer bottles and other debris; and two police cars damaged with their windows smashed out.

52. **A** Option A is correct: *If* is used for conditional sentences (where there are more than two alternatives); *whether* is used when there are just two alternatives.

Sergeant Hodges didn't care *whether* it was going to be Johnson or Hoffman, but one of them was going to be on guard duty tonight.

Option B is correct: Use *could hardly* instead of the commonly misstated *couldn't hardly*.

Surprisingly, Johnson could hardly wait to volunteer for the guard duty position.

Option C is correct: Parallel structure of the sentence.

Johnston said *that* the reason *that* he enjoyed guard duty was *that* it gave him an opportunity to study for the promotional exam.

Option D is correct: Use *anyway* instead of the commonly misstated *anyways*.

Anyway, Hoffman was pleased that guard duty wasn't going to be assigned to him.

53. **B** Option A has an error: There is a lack of parallel structure (active verb, followed by passive verb).

The suspect broke into the house and stole not only jewellery but also the computer.

Option B is correct: *Me* refers to the person that the action of a verb is being done to; *I* is the first person singular subject pronoun and refers to the person performing the action of a verb.

The Inspector offered the new posting in the Diversity Unit to Constable Field and me.

Option C has an error: It lacks parallel structure, *who* should be followed by *and who*.

Officer Chang was one who has previously worked with the Youth Squad and *who* has also worked in the Robbery Squad.

Option D has an error: It lacks parallel structure. Correlatives (such as both) connect parallel structures and the correlative must be used immediately before the parallel element.

Constable Sandhu was asked *both* to submit (parallel element to *to apply*) her application to Strike Force and to apply to the Domestic Violence Squad.

54. **C** Option A has an error: There is a lack of subject-antecedent agreement.

A police officer has to expect some criticism from the public when *he* (or *she*) *does his* (or *her*) job.

Option B has an error: There is an ambiguous pronoun reference.

After listening to Constable Wong's plan to execute the search warrant and to Constable Gill's objections to the plan, I agreed with *Constable Gill's* ideas.

Option C is correct: Proper use of *which* (to introduce a nonrestrictive clause) instead of *that*.

Officer Sikorski is a member of the Fugitive Squad, which was recently featured on the television series *To Protect and Serve*.

Option D has an error: *Whom* should be used instead of *who* because it is the objective form that refers to Carson Wrington.

The senior prosecutor is going to announce tomorrow that Carson Wrington is the person *whom* is believed to be responsible for the arson attack that killed three innocent people.

55. **A** The *superintendent* was eager to commence work in her new position; however, the deluge of work was more than she bargained for.

56. **A** Sergeant O'Conner gave Constable Andrews and *me* specific instructions regarding where we were to meet for the briefing; except we forgot to write them down.

Rule: *I* is the first person singular subject pronoun and refers to the person performing the action of a verb; *me* refers to the person that the action of a verb is being done to.

57. **D** No errors: Use *themselves*—reflexive third person plural.

Sergeant Quinn, known for his motivational speeches, always challenged his team members to ask themselves, "Did I make a difference today?"

58. **C** The victim was irate that my partner and I had taken so long to arrive at the address. We were too embarrassed to mention that we had *passed* the address twice!

In this instance, the correct word is *passed* (past tense of the verb pass. *Past*, in this example, would be incorrect because it would be used as a preposition requiring a preceding verb, such as *driven*).

59. **C** "The most apparent cause," said Constable Jorge, "was that the victim had tripped and accidentally fallen down the stairs; *therefore*, there's no crime here."

Do not use a semicolon to link an independent clause to a dependent clause. Either use a comma or a conjunctive adverb (*however*).

60. **B** Constable Brown was not used to the firing mechanism of the pistol. He should *have* followed instructions more carefully. Brown, and another recruit, is now required to take remedial gun-handling instruction.

*Should of* is not grammatically correct; use *should have*. The use of the singular verb *is* is correct in this instance because the subject is Cst. Brown.

## Part 5: Mathematics

61. **B** The square root of 36 = 6. That is $6^2 = 36$.

62. **D** The perimeter of a rectangle = 2 × length + 2 × width. Therefore, $2x + (2 \times 45) = 250$. Isolate $x$ by first subtracting 90. $2x = 160$. Then divide by 2. $x = 80$.

63. **C** If four-sevenths of the police department's members have already completed their annual firearms qualifications, that means that three-sevenths have not. However, the question is what is the ratio of the members who have not completed their qualification compared to those that have. Therefore, it is 3:4.

64. **D** 210 + 37 = 247 members. First, find the quotient of 210 ÷ 247 = 0.850. Then multiply by 100 to calculated the percentage = 85%.

65. **A** First calculate total mileage: 78 + 81 + 124 + 57 = 340. Since the vehicle uses 8 litres per 100 km, the equation is set up as: $\frac{8}{100} = \frac{x}{340}$. Isolate $x$ by cross-multiplying ($8 \times 340$ = 2,720) and dividing (by 100). $x = 27.2$.

66. **C** Constable Kostachuk drove 6.5 kilometres in 3 minutes. Set up the equation as: $\frac{6.5}{3} = \frac{x}{60}$. Isolate $x$ by cross-multiplying ($6.5 \times 60 = 390$) and dividing (by 3). $x = 130$.

67. **B** The key in this equation is to properly convert a word problem into an algebraic equation.

If a number is 30 greater than another number, then, $x = y + 30$.

If the smaller number is subtracted from three times the larger number, the difference is 120. Therefore, $3x - y = 120$.

Isolate $y$ in each equation. Equation one: $x - 30 = y$. Equation two: $3x - 120 = y$.

Since both expressions equal $y$, they must therefore equal each other: $x - 30 = 3x - 120$.

Isolate $x$ by first adding 120 to both sides:
$x + 90 = 3x$.

Subtract $x$ from each side:
$90 = 2x$.

Divide both sides by 2:
$x = 45$.

68. **B** Total cash seized = 157,300 + 299,600 + 454,200 + 355,800 = $1,266,900. The cash seizures for 2013 were $454,200. Divide 454,200 ÷ 1,266,900 = 0.358512. To calculate percent, multiply by 100 = 35.8 percent. However, rather than trying to manage these large numbers, when asked to calculate approximate percentages, drop the last three numbers and you will find that it still comes to 35.8 percent.

69. **C** The question asks for an approximate ratio, which again means that you can drop the thousands from the equation and round off. 300:900. This is further reduced to 3:9, or 1:3.

70. **C** This question asks you to determine which year had the most drugs and cash seized. Again, make your calculations simple by eliminating the thousands:

2011: 157 + 275 + 154 + 35 = 621

2012: 299 + 361 + 194 + 45 = 899

2013: 454 + 409 + 134 + 153 = 1,150

2014: 355 + 245 + 203 + 175 = 978

# Bibliography

## CHAPTER TWO/Online Sources

www.applicanttesting.com/
www.spvm.qc.ca/en/carrieres/5_0_carrieres.asp
www.hamiltonpolice.on.ca/HPS/Careers/Sworn/SwornRecruitingMainPage.htm
www.spvm.qc.ca/en/carrieres/5_0_carrieres.asp

## CHAPTER FIVE/Books & Articles

Bedard, Ashley. (2011) Web-based Tools Help Better Manage Major Events. *RCMP Gazette*, 73 (1).
Forberg, Sigrid. (2013). Breaking the Cycle. *RCMP Gazette*, 75 (2).

## CHAPTER SEVEN/Online Sources

http://copsandbloggers.ca/

## CHAPTER NINE/Books & Articles

Procunier, Mallory. (2013). "Nunavut Says No," *RCMP Gazette*, 75 (2).

## Online Sources

www.Blueline.ca
www.rcmp-grc.gc.ca/gazette

## CHAPTER THIRTEEN/Online Sources

http://bpad.com/_media/pdfs/Technical%20Report%202013.pdf
www.nij.gov/journals/259/pages/voice-stress-analysis.aspx
www.torontopolice.on.ca/careers/forms/uni_med_req.pdf
www.mcscs.jus.gov.on.ca/english/police_serv/const_select_sys/Self-Assess-Medical
  RequirementsforCandidates/Self_Assess.html
www.halifax.ca/Police/recruiting/2008/SelectionProcess.php
www.sigmatesting.com/information/sfpq.htm
www.pearsonclinical.com/education/products/100000483/16pf-fifth-edition.html#tab
  -details

## CHAPTER FOURTEEN/Books & Articles

Forberg, Sigrid. (2013). Putting Stock in Partnerships. *RCMP Gazette*, 75 (3).
Forberg, Sigrid. (2013). Complex Cases, Intelligent Investigations. *RCMP Gazette*, 75 (2).
Forberg, Sigrid. (2014). Victims lend their voices to RCMP initiatives. *RCMP Gazette*, 76 (2).
Novakowski, Mike. (2014). Disturbance Requires more than Yelling at Police. *JIBC In Service: 10-8 Newsletter*. 14 (3) May/June.

# Index

Personality assessments, 262–264
Personal/personnel, 158
Persuasion, 257, 259
Phonetic loop, 115
Photographic memory, 115
Physical abilities, 9
Physical Abilities Requirement
    Evaluation. *See* PARE
Physical Readiness Evaluation for
    Police, 10–11
Plural nouns, 131–132
Plural pronouns, 163
Police Analytical Thinking Inventory
    description of, 203
    Ontario's, 313–345
Police application fees, 16–17
Police Aptitude Test (RCMP), 347–374
Police officers
    age requirements of, 7–8
    citizenship of, 8–9
    computer skills of, 16
    CPR requirements of, 16
    criminal record check of, 16
    cultural diversity of, 18
    description of, 1
    driver's license requirements, 15
    duties of, 3
    education requirements of, 14
    ethnic diversity of, 18
    female, 18
    first aid requirements of, 16
    health of, 9
    hearing requirements of, 14
    language skills of, 17
    life skills of, 20
    physical abilities of, 9
    Physical Abilities Requirement
        Evaluation, 9–10
    Physical Readiness Evaluation for
        Police, 10–11
    Police Officers' Physical Abilities
        Test, 9–10, 17
    pre-employment training of, 14–15
    preferred qualifications of, 17–20
    qualifications of, 7–20
    sexual diversity of, 18
    Test d'Aptitudes—École Nationale
        de Police du Québec, 12–13
    vision requirements of, 13–14, 262
    volunteering by, 19–20
    work history of, 18–19
Police Officers' Physical Abilities Test,
    9–10, 17
Police Services Act, 3
Police work, 2

Police-related volunteering, 19
Policing, 1–2
Polygraph examination, 260–261
POPAT. *See* Police Officers' Physical
    Abilities Test
Postemployment training, 14–15
Practice examinations
    Alberta Communication Test,
        273–312
    Ontario's Police Analytical Thinking
        Inventory, 313–345
    overview of, 271
    RCMP Police Aptitude Test,
        347–374
    Saskatchewan SIGMA examination,
        375–405
    Vancouver Police Department
        Intake examination, 407–440
    Winnipeg Police Service Written
        Test, 441–471
Precede/proceed, 158–159
Pre-employment training, 14–15
Premise/premises, 159
Premises (logic), 203–206
PREP. *See* Physical Readiness
    Evaluation for Police
Prescribe/proscribe, 159
Principal/principle, 159
Proactive enforcement, 5
Problem solving
    algebraic equations, 243–244
    decimals, 237–238
    exercise for, 227–232, 247–249
    fractions, 238–241
    geometry, 241–242
    mathematical operations, 232–236
    order of operations, 236–237
    word problems, 244–247
Professional experience section, of
    résumé, 28
Pronoun-antecedent agreement,
    162–163
Proofreading of essay, 189
Psychometric assessments, 262–264
Punctuation
    apostrophe, 136–137
    colon, 137
    comma, 138–139
    dash, 139
    ellipsis marks, 139–140
    exclamation mark, 140
    hyphen, 140–141
    parentheses, 141
    period, 142
    question mark, 142

quotation marks, 142–143
semicolon, 143–144

**Q**
Question(s)
    essay-answer, 43–45, 183
    interview, 265–267
    multiple-choice, 40–42
    short-answer, 42–43
Question mark, 142
Questionnaires
    background, 32–34
    multiple-choice, 40–42
Quotation marks, 142–143

**R**
Ratio word problems, 244–245
RCMP Police Aptitude Test, 347–374
Reading comprehension
    critical analysis, 176–177
    description of, 169
    diagnostic examination for, 68–72,
        96
    entrance examination, 177–178
    exercise for, 170–173, 178–181
    improving of, 173–177
    note-taking and, 174–176
    reading to improve, 174
Recreational activities, 20
Reference line, of cover letter, 24
Report writing, 5
Résumé
    awards/accolades/achievements
        section of, 29
    checklist for, 30
    development of, 27–30
    headline/title of, 27
    interests/hobbies section of, 30
    objective statement of, 27
    professional experience section of,
        28
    profile, 27
    qualifications/special skills section
        of, 28
    sample, 31
    volunteer experience section of, 28
Right/rite/write, 159
Role-play exercises, 255–260
Rote learning, 114–115

**S**
Safety, traffic, 5
Salutation, of cover letter, 24
Saskatchewan SIGMA examination,
    375–405